THE JOURNAL OF INDUSTRIAL ECONOMICS

Volume XXI NOVEMBER 1972 No. 1

A. M. ALFRED
Company Pricing Policy.

G. WHITTINGTON
Changes in the Top 100 Quoted Manufacturing Companies in the United Kingdom 1948 to 1968.

WILLIAM G. SHEPHERD
Structure and Behavior in British Industries, with U.S. Comparisons.

JOSEPH V. YANCE
Nonprice Competition in Jet Aircraft Capacity.

RICHARD W. FURST and ROBERT E. MARKLAND
Some Preliminary Evidence of Imperfections in Markets.

L. G. BROOKES
More on the Output Elasticity of Energy Consumption.

BASIL BLACKWELL OXFORD ENGLAND

Price — £1.00 net or ($3.00). Annual subscription: £2.25 or ($6.75).

CONTRIBUTORS TO THIS NUMBER

A. M. ALFRED: Director of The British Printing Corporation Ltd and Chairman of BPC's publishing interests. Formerly Chief Economist at Courtaulds and a leading industrial economist.

G. WHITTINGTON: Professor of Accountancy and Finance at Edinburgh University. Formerly Senior Research Officer at the Department of Applied Economics, Cambridge.

WILLIAM G. SHEPHERD: Professor of Economics, University of Michigan at Ann Arbor.

JOSEPH V. YANCE: Adjunct Associate Professor, Department of Economics, Boston University; and Consultant.

RICHARD W. FURST: Associate Professor of Finance and Director of the Finance Area, University of South Carolina.

ROBERT E. MARKLAND: Associate Professor of Management Science, University of Missouri—St Louis.

L. G. BROOKES: A senior member of the Economics and Programming Branch of the United Kingdom Atomic Energy Authority.

COMPANY PRICING POLICY*

by A. M. Alfred

PREFACE

On rereading this paper to prepare it for publication, regrettably nearly two years after it was given to an audience of senior civil servants, I was tempted to alter it more than I finally decided, and in fact I have left it substantially unaltered. This is because

(a) the general analysis of pricing policy it contains still stands;
(b) the appeal it contains to Government quarters appears largely to have had, at least in some small part, its effect, as today the relations between Government and industry are changed. The demise of regulating bodies such as the Prices & Incomes Board, together with the general decline in company profits due to the economic stagnation we are experiencing, has led to a new realism, where the gap between the two sides though still wide may have a chance of lessening.
The rate of inflation assumed at 2½ per cent looks a little sick too today, but I have left it as it is as we are still not necessarily going to be exposed to 8–10 per cent inflation permanently.

I. INTRODUCTION

Company pricing policy is an area where the academic world has long since retreated in despair of ascribing consistency of principles or rationality of practice. Yet the millions of pricing decisions that are always being taken by businessmen do demand some analysis. As a businessman, and faced with such a wide scope, I plan to do no more than indicate:

(a) the immense variety of conditions in which prices have to be determined;
(b) the paucity of information before the event, and the difficulty of analysis after the event;

and hence

(c) the intuitive judgement which dominates most decisions.

The first will emerge from some quotations I shall give. The second and third will, I hope, emerge from some examples. Later I shall

* This paper was first given at a Civil Service Seminar at Sunningdale Park in February 1970.

digress on the long-term determinants of price, and finally, I shall suggest some implications for Government.

But first let us ponder on the words in the title 'Pricing Policy' I think contain more overtones of a planned operation than is justified by events in real life. I suspect that if 100 firms were asked *why* they were charging their current prices, the most frequent answer would be either 'it is the price set by the competition' or 'our price has developed that way for historical reasons'.

The number of firms which have explicitly examined their costs and the likely effects of changes of price on demand are, I suspect, very few. But by this, I do not necessarily imply that most firms charge the wrong prices. The 'historical development' has been one of trial and error in which the factors, additional cost, additional revenue and demand variations, have been implicitly taken into account, even if not recognized as the economists' variables of marginal cost, marginal revenue and elasticity of demand.

Having a 'pricing policy' in a meaningful sense implies, I think, consciously examining the effects of changes in prices on the attainment of the objectives of the firm, and then charging the prices which are most rewarding in relation to that objective. It follows, therefore, that pricing policy is only of direct interest to firms that can influence the price of their product. A local baker does not normally consider 'pricing policy' because he must accept as given the price at which he sells bread. (Although, if he is active in his Trade Association, pricing policy may have more relevance.)

But we now need to define the objectives of the firm.

II. OBJECTIVES OF A PRICING POLICY

This heading could just as well be the objectives of a firm (or trading body), because in the final analysis these must be the same. I start with quotations.

UK: Electric lamps

The Commission was discussing the way in which G.E.C. and A.E.I. determined the pricing policy of E.L.M.A., the then Trade Association

> '. . . Before the war price changes were, in fact, determined on the basis of "what the traffic will bear", that is to say, the prices were those which, in the judgment primarily of G.E.C. and the A.E.I. Group, would yield the highest profit, regard being had to the profitability of their lamp businesses at existing prices, to the volume and quality of independent competition and to

the estimated effect on demand of a change in the level of prices.'[1]

UK: Electronic Valves

'The fixed retail selling prices of valves and tubes are not specifically related to members' costs of production and sale. We are told that in its early history the Association's policy was to fix prices at a level which would help to develop the market, provide for replacement of plant and expansion of business, extend the level of research and development and also offer a profit.'[2]

U.S.A.: Automobiles

General Motor's pricing policy was stated, publicly, in 1924 by their Vice-President in charge of Finance. This statement was confirmed in 1955, as being principles that 'still govern'. The statement was:

> 'An acceptable theory of pricing must be to gain over a protracted period of time a margin of profit which represents the highest attainable return commensurate with capital turnover and the enjoyment of wholesome expansion, with adequate regard to the economic consequences of fluctuating volume. Thus the profit margin, translated into its salient characteristic rate of return on capital employed, is the logical yardstick by which to gauge the price of a commodity with regard to collateral circumstances affecting supply and demand.'[3]

Three years later, the President of General Motors put it with somewhat different emphasis:

> 'Pricing is like a tripod. It has three legs. In addition to cost, there are the two other legs of market demand and competition. It is no more possible to say that one or another of these factors determines price than it is to assert that one leg rather than either of the other two supports a tripod.'[4]

These three sets of quotations are interesting for their differences in emphasis. The first specifically mentions three factors to take into account in considering maximum profitability—namely existing profits, competition and demand variation with price. The only addition I would make is—cost variation with output. The second

[1] Monopolies Commission Report on *Electric Lamps*, October 1951, para 203.
[2] Monopolies Commission Report on *Electronic Valves*, December 1956, para 185.
[3] U.S. Antitrust Investigation, *Administered Prices—Automobiles*, November 1958, p. 104.
[4] National Industrial Conference Board paper, *Pricing: Policies and Practices*, p. 86.

gives a good statement of the aims of a pricing policy in a new and developing industry, where expansion and technical developments are of greater importance than *immediate* profit. The third was more forward looking and gave pride of place to 'return on capital' but when later expanded was seen to be very similar to the first.

A neater explanation of the policy followed for a new product is given by the following quote:

> 'When a completely new product is introduced a company usually has no guides as to what the price should be. This is in contrast to the situation when there are similar products available. It has been reported that the International Harvester Company "when contemplating the introduction of a product, prices it out on the basis of prices of similar pieces of equipment, competitors' prices, and the estimated performance value to the farmer. It then works toward production at a cost that fits within this price and makes provision for the target profit." '[5,6]

A company can, and of course, does, often follow different policies for different products. Thus

> 'Du Pont . . . had different pricing policies to meet the different structures of its various markets. Nylon and other innovations, over which Du Pont has great price jurisdiction, have been priced as specialties while they were sheltered competitively. Cellophane, however, has been aggressively priced for market expansion, with drastic reductions in price. And sulphuric acid, which is sold under conditions of undifferentiated oligopoly, is priced to meet all comers.'[7,8]

The Nationalized industries were given fresh guidelines in 1967[9]

'(i) revenues should normally cover accounting costs in full
(ii) prices need to be reasonably related to costs at the margin (i.e. long run marginal costs)'.

This was a welcome recognition of the function of marginal cost pricing in the allocation of resources. But the N.B.P.I.'s report on Gas Prices[10] in Feburary 1969 said that

[5] National Industrial Conference Board paper *Pricing: Policies and Practices*, p. 44.
[6] *Ibid.*, p. 59.
[7] A. D. H. Kaplan, Joel B. Dirlam, and Robert F. Lanzillotti, *Pricing in Big Business*, The Brookings Institution, 1958. However, the study observed, '. . . on the whole, the executives tended to minimize price policy as such, or to discuss it in such broad terms that interviewers initially found it difficult to apply the explanation to particular pricing situations' (pp. 3–4).
[8] Joel Dean, *Managerial Economics*, Prentice-Hall, Inc., pp. 400–1.
[9] Cmnd 3437, November 1967 *A Review of Economic and Financial Objectives.*
[10] Cmnd 3924, February 1969.

'it may be necessary to charge some customers temporarily above marginal cost . . . The objective we recommend is not that of maximising net revenue (i.e. profit) for this could entail a price inconsistent with the rapid absorption of natural gas. We think the objective requires planning an investment programme which will meet at minimum cost the demand for gas corresponding to an appropriate pricing policy. In seeking to achieve the objective, one of the factors which has to be taken into account is the interaction between investment plans and future demand.'

This statement is, to say the least, ambiguous. But it does highlight the fact that it is impossible to identify all the facts necessary for the 'right' decision, partly because of this interaction. As one managing director said to me 'the greatest factor in demand is supply'. He was talking of a growth product—and he gave me much reason for pondering on the value of historical research.

If this leaves you with a confused impression, let me say that it is because the position is confused. A review of a major work published last year collecting together about 50 important contributions on 'Pricing Strategy'[11] said

'The publication of a collection of articles on pricing strategy, which includes most of the important articles to have appeared in marketing and marketing-related journals during the last ten years or so, serves to illustrate how little we really know about pricing. Indeed, I would suggest that the pricing policies of British industry, especially of firms involved in mass market consumer goods, show how little we really care.'

This may also apply to goods that are not mass marketed. Thus the N.B.P.I. report on the Printing Industry[12] said:

'we consider that in the past customers have seldom queried increased prices, either because they did not have a repeat job or because an increase in printing costs has appeared small in relation to their total costs.'

It is perhaps also relevant to note that in the Monopolies Commission Report on Courtaulds (or strictly speaking on the supply of man-made cellulosic fibres), in its 130 pages contained no statement of Courtaulds' pricing policy. It is either too difficult to state, or too obvious. So having confused you with reality, let me offer you for your criticism and discussion my own general statement. The objectives of a pricing policy should be:

[11] *Pricing Strategy*, edited by Taylor and Wills. (Staples) Reviewed by Roderick White.
[12] Cmnd 2750, August 1965.

(i) *within the limits of existing capacity:* to maximize cash profits in both long and short term

(ii) *where further expenditure on capacity is envisaged:* to maximize expected return on new investment expected in D.C.F. (discounted cash flow) terms.

TYPES OF SITUATION

I do not expect to be able to reduce the complex situation of reality to a neat square table of situations and relevant policies, but it may help if I were to merely categorize the types of situations that may be recognized.

(a) type of product : consumer
: industrial
(or more generally, products that reach the consumer directly, or indirectly and form part of the final product)

(b) geographical market : home
: export
(or more generally markets that can be 'discriminate' or distinct).

(c) type of competition : competitive
: oligopolistic
: monopolistic, including many products or services in the public sector
(recognizing that the first and third hardly ever exist in an absolute form)

(d) age of product existing product
: new or development product

(e) nature of production : joint products
: multi (interchangeable) products
: vertically integrated products

(f) variations in capacity : utilizing existing capacity (short term
: anticipating new capacity (long-term growth).

Most of these conditions can be combined with each other, so the number of possible situations is very large, which accounts for the complex real situation already referred to, but I believe that my simple statement of objectives will give guidance in all these cases.

ILLUSTRATIONS

(i) *Operating Within Existing Capacity—Discriminatory Pricing*

If a factory is operating at say 70 per cent of capacity and selling at a price of £100 per unit, it will pay that company to produce and sell additional output at any price above prime (or marginal) costs, provided the lower price does not affect existing sales. This condition is most clearly and easily satisfied in export sales where in general terms, for reasons of tariffs or transport, the market can be regarded as distinct.

In such cases the objective is to maximize cash flow, independent of considerations of capital or depreciation. It is vital that in looking at the advantages of a 'discriminate' market, one should look at marginal and not full costs. The consequences of relating the *additional* sales to *average* expected costs is illustrated in Appendix A. Actual profits of £15/unit are shown (incorrectly) as a loss of £6/unit. So clearly here, one determinant of pricing policy is the proper accountancy techniques!

(ii) *Discriminatory Pricing Generally*

The home/export market situation is not the only case. At home, the Monopolies Commission & N.B.P.I. have identified extreme example in the home market, e.g. car batteries, tyres and electrical accessories are (or were) sold to car manufacturers at prices which in some instances were less than half the price to the replacement market.

And in the public sector, the gas and electricity industries with standing charges, bulk tariffs, and time discounts, practice discrimination to a fine degree.

(iii) *Operating Within Existing Capacity—Declining Market*

If it is recognized that existing capacity will not need replacing, the theoretical requirement is simply that the price will lie between:

(a) that giving an adequate return on working capital and *scrap* value of the plant

(b) the maximum the market will bear.

In practice, the N.B.P.I. in its report on Rayon Yarn prices[13] allowed a price increase which it judged was not more than was a 'necessary inducement to maintain production'. They also noted the contribution to balance of payments and to employment.

(iv) *Maximizing in Relation to a Scarce Resource*

Normally, we regard 'capital' as the scarce resource, and business therefore normally seeks to maximize return on capital. But there are occasions when the scarcity of some other factor dominates, e.g. fuel in 1947, cotton, sulphur and other commodities in 1950, labour

[13] Cmnd 4092, June 1969.

quite frequently. One cotton mill manager I knew kept regularly a series of cost sheets which showed the profit he needed to earn on each count of yarn to give equal profits per unit of capital (i.e. spindle), per lb of cotton, per skilled operative—and he used the relevant schedule, depending on scarcity conditions, to influence his actual prices and demand. In principle if labour becomes a bottleneck, it would then pay to switch emphasis from labour intensive to non-labour intensive products, and if it is necessary to lower prices to sell the extra output of the latter, it would pay to do so down to the point where the marginal revenue per unit of labour equals the cost of the labour.

(v) *Joint and Multi Products*

In the multi-product factory several interesting problems arise. Fortunately, although the allocation of many overheads may be debatable, the allocation of prime costs is usually straight-forward—and it is these which, once the factory is built, indicate the room for manoeuvre in pricing policy. A multi-product factory provides a good illustration of the differences between parts (i) and (ii) of my definition of objectives. If a factory is producing A and B inter-changeably under the following conditions:

	A	*B*
Capital cost/lb—total	100	50
Depreciation @ 10 per cent	10	5
Prime costs/lb	30	30
Total cost/lb	40	35
ROC @ 20 per cent	20	10
Desired selling price	60	45

then the desired selling price at the factory project stage, (or if subsequent expansion were envisaged) and if 20 per cent return were aimed at would be 60 for A, and 45 for B. But if after the factory were built, it was apparent that no further capacity would be required, then the firm's optimum position would be independent of depreciation and return on capital, but would reflect solely additional prime costs (marginal costs) and demand conditions, and could well be with A the same price as or even cheaper than B. Where A and B are not interchangeable, but are *joint* products (e.g. by-product) prices are indeterminate, and must be assessed jointly. Basically one is using 150 capital, and incurring prime costs of 60 to produce (A+B). Any price of A, together with the associated price of B, will be acceptable provided (A+B) satisfy the total requirement. Examples are gas and coke; or sulphuric acid and heat. If heat is locally in demand, and can be sold at a price, the apparent cost of acid falls. But often the heat has to be disposed of as a useless by-product.

(vi) *Vertical Integration*

This raises the question of transfer price policy between divisions or companies in the same group. The guiding principle in deciding the price which a user division should be charged for the product of another, supplying, division is that where there is freedom to buy and sell the intermediate product on the open market, the transfer should be at the open market price. Otherwise it is impossible to judge the commercial efficiency of each division. But where there is no effective open market price, perhaps because the quantity of the intermediate involved is large in relation to the total market for the intermediate product, the two divisions are, for commercial purposes, linked. The activities of the two divisions are most sensibly regarded as a single (vertically-integrated) operation.

(vii) *Development Products*

There are two approaches[14] to these products:

(a) *penetration pricing*—seeking a large market rapidly in the belief that large volume will reduce production costs and enable high entry costs (especially promotion) to be borne, and still show a profit. Products usually in this category are consumer items *replacing* an existing market, e.g. a new detergent or cosmetic, where it is also necessary to pre-empt a market position and make it more difficult for a competitor to follow.

(b) *skimming price*—where the product has a new or preferably unique quality, it is often best to seek initially a small select market at a high price. Typical examples are new man-made fibres, plastics, or even initially ball point pens, TV sets, and drugs. Over the years the prices of such products fall drastically, e.g. Cellophane from $2.65 in 1924 to 40¢/lb in 1939, penicillin from $6,000 per billion units in 1945 to $35 in 1955. Such a pricing policy allows a greater chance of early recovery of R & D expenses, and provides a method of testing acceptability as one goes.

(viii) *Consumer Products*

The only point I wish to make here is to underline how inexpert the consumer buyer often is. You may remember Mendes-France, the

[14] U.S.A. National Industrial Conference Board paper, *Pricing: Policies and Practices* pp. 44–7.

French premier, who in an effort to educate the French public carried out tests in Paris. Retailers were requested to show the same item (e.g. cheese or tomatoes) in two different places on the counter and at different prices. Observation showed that more was sold at the higher price.

More scientifically, tests were carried out by P. Cooper of Manchester University for frozen peas, chocolates, instant coffee and washing machines. There established a firm relationship between price and quality, more strong incidentally for women than men, who appear to be more cynical. This relationship is so strong, that some products are *hindered* by their low price, which the consumer feels has to be justified. Thus when Cadbury launched their 'Royal Mints' in competition with Rowntree 'After Eights', they were 3d/packet dearer. Surprisingly, the industrial buyer is also not always expert. Thus, in one case, a special oil being sold to industry on the basis of its specification and *low* price, had no buyers, until after a lapse of a year, it was re-introduced as a premium product at a much higher price—and sold well.

(ix) *New Investment*

I said on p. 6 that where new capacity is envisaged the main criterion should be return on capital. In some of the quotations I have given, return on capital has been given pride of place. But there are two difficulties—how to measure the return; and what magnitude to look for. It is clear from the early days of the Monopolies Commission that the criterion for judging whether a 'monopoly' (in the statutory sense of supplying more than one-third of the market) was in the public interest or not was whether profits were above or below average. For many years, the comparisons were done on an historical accounts basis; but in 1966 in their report on colour film they also used a replacement value basis. In general terms the difference between historical and replacement cost was 4 per cent points in the late 1950s, narrowing to 2 per cent points by 1966/7.

U.K. MANUFACTURING INDUSTRY AVERAGE

Av. of 4 years centred on	*Return on capital*	
	Historic cost per cent	*Replacement cost per cent*
1961	14.7	11.5
1965	13.4	11.0

But the weakness of the Monopolies Commission was they seldom stated their yardstick. Thus in the report on Courtaulds (March 1968) they said that profits on viscose staple at 14.9 per cent return on one basis and 10.5 per cent on another (both replacement basis) was a 'relatively high rate of profit'. Presumably they were comparing with manufacturing industry average of 11.0 per cent. But what would happen to incentives if all industry were reduced to average, I leave you to imagine.[15]

The N.B.P.I. is slightly better. It is prepared to consider price rises if the rate of return on *new* investment is inadequate. This concept is not new. Sir Robert Shone was responsible for developing this concept in relation to steel prices whilst at the Iron & Steel Federation. The concept there was that a reasonable price was that which would earn a return of 10 per cent (later I think revised to 12½ per cent) before tax on the original cost of a plant of optimum scale and using all the latest techniques.

One of the weaknesses of this approach was that it ignored tax. And at a time when the apparent impact of tax was 50 per cent or more (but the real impact was conceivably negative[16]), this was important. A second criticism was that it was arbitrary about depreciation and duration of the project. It was natural therefore that the N.B.P.I. should move towards a D.C.F. method of measurement.

Thus in the report on Portland Cement Prices[17], they said prices should be adequate to earn a return on a new investment sufficient to meet the cost of new finance. The argument may be summarized:

	real terms	*money terms* (with 2½ per cent inflation)
Loan Capital (20 per cent of total new finance)		
7½ per cent gross; less tax = 4½ per cent net		4½ per cent
Equity (80 per cent of new finance)		
Historically shareholders have earned	7 per cent	
Requiring companies to earn, after corporation tax, but before div. & capital taxes: new issues	10–12	12½–14½
retained earnings 8½ per cent	8½ per cent	11 per cent

[15] The distribution of profitabilities in U.K. manufacturing industry in 1963/4 was as follows:

Return on capital after dep. before tax	*per cent of companies*
less than 10 per cent	25
10–14.9 per cent	40
15–19.9 per cent	25
20 per cent+	10
Average 14 per cent	100

[16] See *Investment Appraisal*, N.E.D.C. 1967, page 10.

[17] Cmnd 3381, August 1967.

Assuming no *new* equity is needed, the cost of capital was put at

(20 per cent × $4\frac{1}{2}$ per cent) + (80 per cent × 11 per cent) =	9.7 per cent
(but the report called it	9 per cent)
Plus margin for uncertainty	1 per cent
Hence desired rate of return	10 per cent

The report added:

> 'We regard this relationship between the discounted return on new investment and the cost of capital as the principal criterion against which the application for this price increase should be judged.'

On this basis of 10 per cent D.C.F. on a new plant, which they said corresponded to 9 per cent return 'on a replacement cost basis and pre tax' they recommended a price increase of 2s. od a ton instead of the 5s. od a ton requested.

Suffice it to say, I agree with the method, but not with the arithmetic or the conclusions.

By May 1969, in their report on Steel Prices, the N.B.P.I. had changed course. The argument then used may be summarized:

The Steel Corporation: sought 13 per cent before interest and tax on net current assets,
and 15 per cent before interest and tax on net fixed assets,
averaging 13 per cent before interest and tax on net fixed assets.

The N.B.P.I. said

(a) Nationalized industries have to earn 8 per cent D.C.F. ignoring all tax and investment grants,

(b) this 'might well' be equivalent to 15 per cent D.C.F. 'net of investment grants'.

They regarded the proposed increases as excessive and recommended granting only three-quarters of the request.

So much for methods of precise measurement. I believe that industry, in considering investment projects, must have in mind pricing and production strategies that will maximize its D.C.F. return. But I do not believe that precise calculations are any substitute for a proper appreciation of the physical factors that will lead to success. As one M.D. put it to me, 'I worry less about making the right decision; and more about making the decision right'.

RELATIONSHIP OF INDUSTRIAL RETURN AND RETURN REQUIRED BY NATIONALIZED INDUSTRY

			per cent
Industry—sources of new capital	: equity (incl. retentions)		80
	: fixed interest		20
average investment project	: plant		60
		buildings	25
		working capital	15

Cost of capital: in a paper I wrote on June 1968[18] I showed:

Cost of capital	*real terms per cent*
Equity 80 per cent @ 10.5 per cent	8.4
Fixed interest: 20 per cent @ 6 per cent less tax	0.7
	9.1

and showed that with the average investment above, this corresponded to *11 per cent before tax* (with 20 per cent investment grant and inflation at 2 per cent p.a.) (N.B. Note, average tax burden is under 20 per cent).

Since then equity yields have fallen markedly, and even today, February 1970[19], we have:

		per cent
FT/Actuaries 500:	dividend yield	4.0
	cover	1.5
	earnings	6.1
	plus, for improved efficiency, say	0.9
	long-term yield	7.0
Fixed interest is, say, 10½ per cent less 45 per cent =		6.0

Therefore 80 per cent equity/20 per cent fixed interest = 6.8
or allowing for inflation, say 7 per cent
The corresponding gross return would be about 9 per cent

Thus the Treasury's request of 10 per cent gross is now about right, i.e. between the 9 per cent current for industry and 11 per cent of two years ago; but was markedly wrong at the original 8 per cent.

18 'The Correct Yardstick for State Investment', *District Bank Review*, June 1968.

19 Between February 1970 and February 1972, the decline has continued, with dividend yield of 3.4 per cent, and earnings yield of 5.3 per cent.

IMPLICATIONS FOR GOVERNMENT

The post-war intervention by the Monopolies Commission, Restrictive Trading Practices Board, and more recently the N.B.P.I., has brought to the forefront the influence of Government in determining prices.

Like so many 'recent' developments there is of course a long history of similar developments. Controlled prices were common during both world wars and agriculture has 'suffered' administered prices for decades but even earlier the price of bread and the level of wages was determined at a 'just' level by the Justices of the Peace in the U.K. in Mediaeval England and persisted until the end of the eighteenth century.

It is of course true that the present Government intervention is associated with much investigation and analysis. The absence of a clear measuring rod to determine a 'just' price under today's conditions is perhaps indicated by the considerable amount of academic work which has gone into analysis of the Monopolies Commission recommendations and to the findings of the N.B.P.I. in an attempt to discern a consistent policy. One of the new and refreshing aspects considered by the N.B.P.I. has been their concern for improvements in commercial efficiency.

Given the difficulty with which conclusions are reached, the absence of clear criteria, and the frequent turning down of recommendations by Government, one is tempted to wonder whether the effort is worthwhile.

May I suggest some alternatives:

(a) The Government should not seek to control the profits of individual companies. It must be a major inhibitant of growth for managements to think that at some time if their profits exceed average they may be forced to reduce prices by the Government. If the Government for political/social purposes wishes to restrict the share of profits in the Gross National Product they could do so by adjustments in the rate of corporation tax.

(b) The Government should not attempt to influence directly methods of distribution or marketing. Thus I believe that the exercise on detergents which sought to limit promotion expenditures on soap powders was unnecessary and wasteful.

(c) Control of monopolistic power is of course still necessary. I am convinced that the 2- to 4-year long agonies of the Monopolies Commission are irrelevant. The approach of the N.B.P.I. has been better but we still suffer from the arbitrary nature of the recommendations. Monopolistic influences should therefore be controlled by the stimulation of competition which in the case of U.K. means a lowering of import duty provided this is accompanied by a strengthening of anti-dumping legislation—or not so much the legislation but the rapidity and effectiveness with which it is applied.

(e) There is a special case of monopoly powers being manifested through vertical integration where a primary producer in a monopolistic position integrates forward into a competitive market and buttresses his position by, for example, low transfer prices. Here control could be exercised by:

(i) modifying the Companies Act so that disclosure of assets, turnover, and profits by different sectors of industry is given in more detail. There is no reason why it should not be shown according to the 180 categories of the S.I.T.C.

and

(ii) concentrating the energies of the investigatory board on the level of transfer prices.

Finally, wherever there is public concern at the use of economic power this is normally measured by reference to the return on capital. It is important that:

(a) we should recognize that there is a tremendous danger in levelling everyone down to the average.

(b) we must recognize that the U.K. levels of return are low in relation to the U.S.A. This is even more so if we look at cash flow including depreciation, because depreciation provisions are greater in the U.S.A. than in the U.K. In fact in recent years cash flow (after tax) per unit of capital employed in the U.K. has been only 70 per cent of that in the U.S.A. This must inhibit investment and growth.

BRITISH PRINTING CORPORATION LTD.,
LONDON, W.C.2.

Appendix A Profitability of Export Business

	Situation 1			Situation 2		
Production		7 units			10 units	
Costs	*No.*	*per unit*	*total*	*No.*	*per unit*	*total*
Fixed		30	210		21	210
Variable		60	420		60	600
Total	7	90	630	10	81	810
Revenue						
Home	7	100	700	7	100	700
Export	–		—	3	75	225
Total	7		700	10	92.5	925
Profit—full cost basis						
Home	7	10	70	7	19	133
Export	–	—	—	3	6 loss	18 loss
Total	7	10	70	10	11.5	115

Profit		*No.*	*Per Unit*	*Total*
Marginal basis:	Extra volume	3	—	—
	Extra costs	3	60	180
	Extra revenue	*3*	*75*	*225*
	Extra profit	3	15	45

Full cost accountancy shows:

Situation 1: home market: profit 10/unit
Situation 2: home market: profit 19/unit
exports: *loss* 6/unit

But *marginal cost accountancy* will show
Situation 2: exports: *profit 15*/unit.

CHANGES IN THE TOP 100 QUOTED MANUFACTURING COMPANIES IN THE UNITED KINGDOM 1948 TO 1968*

by G. WHITTINGTON

1. INTRODUCTION

FOR 1948, the National Institute of Economic and Social Research published a list of the 100 largest quoted companies in the United Kingdom.[1] A comparable list has been prepared for 1968, with the assistance of the Statistics Division of the Department of Trade and Industry, and the object of this paper is to compare the two populations of companies. The definitions used are specified below. The comparisons answer two basic questions. Firstly, what happened in the next twenty years to the top 100 companies of 1948? Secondly, what were the origins of the top 100 companies of 1968? The answers to these questions give us a picture of the degree of security enjoyed by giant companies and are clearly relevant to contemporary theories of the firm, which emphasize the importance of size, and the security which management is supposed to derive from size. They are also relevant to industrial concentration. Data on the mobility of the largest firms through time supplements the information derived from the traditional static measures of concentration, which measure concentration in terms of the size of the largest firms relative to one another, or relative to other firms.

2. THE DATA

The companies covered in this study are the largest 100 companies whose ordinary or preference shares (excluding loan stocks) were quoted on United Kingdom stock exchanges at the relevant time. Companies whose trading activities were primarily outside the United Kingdom are excluded, as are consolidated subsidiary companies of companies which are already included in the list. Companies engaged primarily in banking, finance, insurance, investment, property and shipping are also excluded. Size is measured as the balance sheet value of net assets (i.e. total assets, less current liabilities), at the end of the relevant year. Since accounting dates differ between companies, '1948' is deemed to be covered by the balance

* The author is grateful to Mr. K. D. George for his constructive criticism of an earlier draft and to Margaret Clark for research assistance. This paper is a by-product of a research project financed by the Esmée Fairbairn Charitable Trust.

[1] *Company Income and Finance*, 1949–53, The National Institute of Economic and Social Research, London, 1956. Appendix C.

sheet date falling within the 12 months ending on April 5th, 1949, and '1968' is deemed to be covered by the balance sheet date in the year ending April 5th, 1969.

The above definitions are inevitably arbitrary. Their main objective is to define a fairly homogeneous population of quoted companies, engaged primarily in manufacturing and distribution within the United Kingdom, and to select the 100 largest from this population. The criterion of size is dependent on the book valuation of assets, and this is usually on an historical basis, which tends to under-state the market value. Furthermore, insofar as some companies are more cautious than others in their valuation methods, this will affect our measurement of the *relative* size of individual companies. However, certain attractive alternative measures of size, such as Turnover, or Value Added, were not widely available in company accounts in 1948, although they have since become available under the 1967 Companies Act.

3. WHERE ARE THEY NOW?

Our first question is: what happened to the top 100 in 1948? Table I gives an important part of the answer: roughly half of them were still 'alive' in the top 100 in 1968.

TABLE I

SURVIVAL IN SIMILAR RANKINGS FROM 1948 TO 1968

Rank in 1948	*Number Surviving in Similar Rankings in* 1968	*Proportion Surviving*
1–12	6	0.50
1–25	13	0.52
1–50	25	0.50
1–100	52	0.52

Table I suggests that life at the very top is no more secure than life in the rest of the top 100: the proportion of companies maintaining their rank and status in the top 12 is remarkably similar to that in the top 25, the top 50 and the top 100. In each case, roughly half of the companies maintained their status over a twenty-year period. The fact that 48 of the top 100 had disappeared from the top 100 by 1968 may be compared with Kaplan's result for the U.S.A.,[2] for which 24 of the 1948 top 100 had disappeared by 1960, a 'death rate' of 2 companies per annum. The 'death rate' for the U.K.,

[2] A. D. H. Kaplan, *Big Enterprise in a Competitive System*. The Brookings Institution, Washington D.C., 1964, Table 7.1.

derived from Table 1, is 2.4 companies per annum over the longer period 1948 to 1968. However, 9 of these companies 'died' as a result of the nationalization of the steel industry. This might be regarded as an exceptional event (although it ocurred twice, and de-nationalization once, in the period under consideration). If all nine steel companies had survived in the top 100 from 1948 to 1968, there would have been only 39 'deaths' from the top 100, an annual rate of just under 2 companies per annum, which is almost identical with Kaplan's rate for the U.S.A. Thus, it appears that the security of the largest U.K. firms is similar to that of their counterparts in the U.S.A.[3]

'Security' was defined in the previous paragraph as the probability of survival in a high rank. However, it may be that the maintenance of rank is less important than absolute survival. Table II shows how

TABLE II

ABSOLUTE SURVIVAL IN 1968 OF THE TOP 100 COMPANIES IN 1948

Rank in 1948	*Number Alive in* 1968	*Proportion Surviving*	*Marginal Proportion* Surviving*
1–12	10	0.83	0.83
1–25	18	0.72	0.62
1–50	32	0.64	0.56
1–100	64	0.64	0.64

* The marginal survival proportion indicates the incremental number of survivors as a proportion of the incremental number of companies in the group, e.g. that for the 1 to 25 category indicates that 8 companies survived of the 13 ranked from 13 to 25 inclusive.

many of the largest companies in 1948 were members of the population from which the 1968 top 100 were drawn. This includes companies which were 'alive' in 1968[4] but not in the top 100.

Table II shows that 64 of the 1948 top 100 survived until 1968, 52 of which were in the 1968 top 100 and 12 of which had fallen below the top 100 by 1968. Of the 12 companies which fell out of

[3] If anything, this comparison makes the U.K. firms appear to be more secure than they really are, for two reasons. Firstly it seems likely that, in the absence of nationalization, not all of the steel companies would have survived: there might well have been several mergers and take-overs in the industry. Secondly, the U.K. calculation is based upon the survival of the 1948 population over the next 20 years, as opposed to 12 years for the U.S.A. Clearly, if 'deaths' occur at fairly regular intervals, the longer the period, the smaller the population will tend to be towards the end of the period, so that an average annual death rate of 2 companies per year will represent a higher annual *probability* of death, i.e. the number of deaths in a year will, on average, be a higher *proportion* of the number of companies in the population at the beginning of the year. This is discussed further in Section (6).

[4] It should be noted that a company remains 'alive' if it is taken over by a company not in the population and retains its quotation. This happened to at least two of our 1948 top 100 group.

the top 100 between 1948 and 1968 but were 'alive' in 1968 the largest in 1948 (William Cory) was ranked 55th and 10 were ranked lower than 81st in 1948. Their disappearance was therefore due to their marginal starting position within the top 100, rather than to a dramatic fall in relative size. Comparison of Tables I and II shows that 4 companies ranked between 1 and 12 in 1948, 5 ranked between 1 and 25, and 7 ranked between 1 and 50 failed to maintain their rankings in 1968, although they remained 'alive'. All of these companies were ranked in the top 100 in 1968, which provides further confirmation that declines in relative size are rarely dramatic amongst the very large companies.

Another conclusion which can be derived from Table II is that the survival rate is distinctly higher amongst the top 12 companies than amongst the rest of the top 100. Thus, even within the top 100, greater size seems to mean greater security, in the sense of a greater chance of survival. One possible reason for this is that the very largest companies are relatively immune from take-overs by other firms or mergers with other firms, because their size protects them. This would be consistent with Singh's recently published results for take-overs of U.K. quoted companies in the 1950s, which suggested that their relatively large size was the main characteristic distinguishing taking-over firms from their victims and from other firms.[5]

Table III offers some evidence in support of the view that the giants were relatively immune from take-over. Three-quarters of the 'deaths' between 1948 and 1968 were due to mergers and acquisitions (27 out of 36) and the remainder were due to the nationalization of the steel industry.

TABLE III

CAUSE OF 'DEATH' OF THE 36 COMPANIES IN THE 1948 TOP 100 WHICH DID NOT SURVIVE UNTIL 1968

Rank in 1948	*Merged or Acquired*	*Nationalized*	*Total 'deaths'*
1–12	1 (0.08)	1 (0.08)	2 (0.17)
1–25	3 (0.12)	4 (0.16)	7 (0.28)
1–50	12 (0.24)	6 (0.12)	18 (0.36)
1–100	27 (0.27)	9 (0.09)	36 (0.36)

Note: The numbers in brackets express the number of deaths as a proportion of the total number in the group.

Nationalization did not bear particularly heavily on the smaller firms, but the incidence of merger and acquisition increased with

[5] A. Singh, *Take-overs: their relevance to the Stock Market and the Theory of the Firm*, Cambridge University Press, London, 1971. Singh does, however, postulate that the probability of take-over becomes fairly constant above a certain size of firm.

rank. The marginal proportions taken over, as rank increases, derived from the second column of Table III, are given below in Table IV. The top 12 are the least prone of all to being taken over, and those ranked in the first 25 are clearly less prone to take-over than the smaller companies in the top 100.

We may now summarize the answer to our first question: where are they now? Of the top 100 companies in 1948, 52 were still in the top 100 in 1968, leaving 48 vacant places. These places were created by 12 companies declining in relative size, so that their rank was greater than 100 in 1968, and by 36 companies 'dying'.[6] Of the 36 'deaths', 9 were due to steel nationalization and 27 were due to merger or take-over. Thus, mergers and take-overs were the dominant source of mobility in the composition of the top 100 companies during the period studied. The incidence of merger and take-over was highest amongst the smaller members of the group

TABLE IV

INCIDENCE OF MERGERS

Rank in 1948	*Number Merged or Acquired*	*Proportion Merged or Acquired*
1–12	1	0.08
13–25	2	0.15
26–50	9	0.36
51–100	15	0.30

and this accounts for the relatively high absolute survival rate amongst the larger companies, and particularly amongst the top 12.

4. WHERE DID THEY COME FROM?

Our second basic question is: what were the origins of the 1968 top 100 companies? We already know from Table I that 52 of these were in the 1948 top 100. Table V shows how many of the 1968 population were 'alive' in 1948 in the sense of being in the wider population from which the top 100 were drawn. This table is, therefore, the backward-looking equivalent of the forward-looking Table II. It shows that 84 of the top 100 had been alive in 1948, although we already know that only 52 of these were in the 1948 top 100. Thus, 32 of the 1968 top 100 companies achieved their position by promotion from lower size classes. This was partly inevitable: the high 'death' rate amongst the top 100 would naturally mean that the next largest companies in order of size would be promoted to the

[6] It should be noted that our definition of 'death' is rendered somewhat arbitrary by the restricted nature of the population. See section (2) above, and footnote (4).

ranks of the top 100. However, we have already seen that 12 of the 1948 top 100 were still alive in 1968 but had been de-moted from the top 100 by virtue of their relatively slow growth rates. The promotions from the ranks of the small companies were therefore due partly to the relatively high growth rates of the promoted companies: whether this was due to internal growth or to the acquisition of other companies by take-over is, unfortunately, beyond the scope of the data available for the present study, but it seems likely that take-overs played an important part.

The absolute survival rate is higher in the backward looking sense (Table V) than in the forward looking sense (Table II). In other words, the proportion of firms in the top 100 in 1968 which had been 'alive' in the wider population in 1948 (0.84) was greater than the proportion of firms in the top 100 in 1948 which were still alive in the wider population in 1968 (0.64). Thus, if history were to repeat itself over the next twenty years (i.e. if the proportions of firms surviving were to remain constant), at least twenty firms which were

TABLE V

DISTRIBUTION OF THE 1968 TOP 100 SURVIVING FROM THE 1948 POPULATION

Rank in 1968	*Number 'alive' in* 1948	*Proportion 'alive' in* 1948
1–12	9	0.75
1–25	21	0.84
1–50	43	0.86
1–100	84	0.84

in the 1968 top 100 and had been 'alive' in 1948 would not be alive in 1988. A large number of the top 100 in 1968 (0.84) were recruited from the ranks of companies existing in 1948, but their prospects of survival over the next twenty years are not particularly good in comparison with their past experience; if history repeats itself, only 64 of the 1968 top 100 will be 'alive' in the population in 1988, and only 52 will be in the top 100. In this sense, reaching the ranks of the top 100 should engender a feeling of anxiety for the future rather than complacency about the past, amongst managers who wish their company to survive as an independent entity.

An interesting analogy can be made here with Marshall's well-known 'biological' theory of the firm, in which he compares the population of firms to a forest, each firm having its own life cycle of growth and decay like an individual tree.[7] We may regard the top 100 companies as a particularly successful group of tall trees in the

[7] Alfred Marshall, *Principles of Economics*, eighth edition, Macmillan & Co., London, 1920, Chapter XIII, pp. 315–16.

forest, but the fact that they have achieved such heights also means that they have reached an advanced stage of their life cycle and that their life expectation is limited. However, it would be misleading to press such an analogy very far: we have already seen, in Section (2) above, that the tallest trees of all, the very largest companies, had a greater capacity for absolute survival than the rest. Perhaps a giant managerially controlled company has a greater capacity for survival than the family firms which Marshall had in mind.

To return to our main theme, of 'Where did they come from?', we must now explore the origins of the 16 companies in the 1968 top 100 which were not 'alive' in the 1948 population. Mergers account for exactly half of these. All of the 7 new companies in the top 50 in 1968 were formed as a result of mergers. Of the 9 new companies falling in the ranks 51 to 100 in 1968, only one was formed as a result of a merger (making 8 out of the top 100), 7 were due to an existing company becoming quoted, and one (Thomas Tilling) was due to a company changing the emphasis of its activities to fall within the industrial coverage of our population. It is notable that there were 3 new companies ranked in the top 9 in 1968 and all were products of large mergers.[8] The only other company in the top 9 in 1968 which was not in the top 9 in 1948 was General Electric, which had recently acquired two other giants, A.E.I. and English Electric, but without the acquiring company (General Electric) losing its identity. Thus the ranks of the very largest companies were only reached by companies which were involved in major acquisitions and mergers, not by companies which managed to generate high internal growth rates.

We can now summarize the answer to the question: 'Where did they come from?' Of the 48 vacancies in the ranks of the top 100 in 1968 caused by companies disappearing from the 1948 top 100, 32 (exactly two-thirds) were filled by promotions from the lower-size classes and 16 were filled by the entry of new companies to the population. Of the new companies, 8 (exactly one half) were the products of mergers, and the remainder with one exception, were due to new companies obtaining quotations.[9] Mergers were the sole source of the new companies which were ranked in the top 50 in 1968.

It is now possible to make a preliminary comparison of the answers to our two basic questions, described above and in Section (3). The subsequent disappearance of members of the 1948 top

[8] The three companies concerned are British Leyland, Bass Charrington, and Allied Breweries. The top 12 companies in 1948 and in 1968 are listed in the Appendix.

[9] These are listed in the Appendix.

100 was primarily due to take-overs, and these bore most heavily on the smaller companies. The main source of new members of the top 100 in 1968 (32 out of 48 new members) was the promotion of existing companies which were formerly in lower size groups. Insofar as the promotion of these companies to the top 100 was due to their relatively rapid growth rate, take-overs of other companies probably made an important contribution, but we have been unable to quantify this.[10] The secondary source of new members of the top 100 in 1968 was the entry of new companies to the quoted manufacturing[11] sector. The creation of new companies as a result of merger accounted for half of these new companies, and was particularly important amongst the very largest companies.

Thus, the answers to both of our basic questions draw attention to the importance of take-overs and mergers. These clearly play an important part in both the 'death' process and the 'birth' process of the top 100 companies. This suggests that the top 100 will be growing rapidly in overall size, since any merger or take-over involving a member of the top 100 must give rise to the creation of an even larger firm. Static measures may therefore be expected to show an increase in the concentration of assets both within the top 100 companies and between the top 100 companies and the rest of the company sector. This is investigated in a later section, but we must first deal with two other issues: the industrial distribution of the top 100, and the relative mobility of the top 100 in the separate halves of the period studied.

5. THE INDUSTRIAL DISTRIBUTION OF THE TOP 100

An important factor in relating the above empirical results to competition in the economy as a whole is the industrial distribution of the top 100 companies. If the top 100 were all concentrated in a limited range of industrial activities, the economy as a whole might be considered to be more competitive than if the giant firms were spread over a wider range of activities, for two reasons. Firstly, if the giant firms are concentrated over a narrow range of activities, they will compete with one another more. Secondly, the absence of giant firms from a wide range of industrial activities would imply that these activities are unlikely to be dominated by an individual firm.

[10] A cursory survey of the 32 promoted companies showed that 15 of them had made important take-overs in the period 1948 to 1960. Take-over activity was, in general greater after 1960, so it seems likely that the majority of promoted companies grew partly by take-over.

[11] 'Manufacturing' is used here as a shorthand for the more precise industrial coverage defined in Section (2).

Table VI gives the industrial distribution of our top 100 companies in 1948 and in 1968. The industrial classification used is very broad; basically it is the two-digit standard industrial classification, merging some of the smaller groups. Each company is allocated to one industrial group and this may be misleading in the case of some very diversified companies, although it is an advantage of the broad groupings used here that most companies fall clearly into a particular group.[12] The disadvantage of using broad groupings is that the activities covered by the group are very diverse and cannot be said to be sold in the same, or a similar, market, e.g. Chemicals includes both pharmaceuticals and fertilizers, or, in terms of specific companies, includes both Boots and Fisons. However, the broad groupings do include firms with similar industrial processes, and it might be argued, following Andrews, that firms with similar industrial processes are at least potential competitors.[13]

It will be observed from Table VI that the industrial coverage of the top 100 was very broad. In 1948 only one industrial group was not represented, and all were represented in 1968. The most strongly represented groups were Drink, with 13 companies, in 1948 and Retailing, with 11 companies, in 1968. The three best represented industries provided 34 of the 1948 top 100 and 29 of the 1968 top 100, and the five best represented industries provided 51 of the 1948 top 100 and 45 of the 1968 top 100. Thus, the top 100 were spread over a wide range of industrial activities, and the distribution between industries was more even than might have been expected.

It should also be noted that there was a considerable change between 1948 and 1968 in the relative strength of individual industries in the top 100. The third column of Table VI shows the net change in the representation of each industry. The industries whose representation increased gained 18 new members of the top 100: these were accommodated by the loss of 18 members in the other industries. The largest change, the loss of 8 Metal Manufacturing companies, was due to steel nationalization. The other cases of substantially decreasing representation are Drink and Textiles, both of which lost 4 representatives, mainly as a result of take-overs and mergers. Of the increases, the Construction industry and its suppliers ('Bricks, Pottery, etc.', which includes cement manufacturing) achieved 7 new representatives. The other gains were spread across a wide range of industries, so that there was a tendency for the industrial coverage of the top 100 to even out during the

[12] Evidence of the relatively low degree of overlapping of companies into other industrial groups was given in the N.I.E.S.R. publication, *Company Income and Finance*, 1949–52, *op. cit.*, p. 68.

[13] P. W. S. Andrews, *Manufacturing Business*, Macmillan, London, 1949, p. 156.

period, which is reflected in the figures for the proportionate representation of the top three and top five industries, quoted in the previous paragraph.

One possible change in the industrial structure of giant companies, which we are unable to explore here, is the possible increase in diversification which has taken place. The take-over process, which we have found to be important, may serve to increase the individual firm's range of products both within and between the broad industrial groups studied here. Such diversification might bring the giant firms into competition with one another more often than might appear from an arbitrary assignment of individual companies to single industrial categories. On the other hand, it might extend the influence of giant firms to markets which had previously escaped their attention. It is, therefore, unclear on *a priori* grounds whether diversification would tend to increase or decrease competition: the issue is essentially one of fact. However, it is clear that an increase in the degree of diversification during the period studied (1948 to

TABLE VI

INDUSTRIAL COMPOSITION OF THE TOP 100 IN 1948 AND IN 1968

*Industry**		*Number* 1948	1968	*Change*
Bricks, Pottery, etc.	(46, 10)	1	6	+5
Chemicals	(26)	8	9	+1
Metal Manufacture	(31)	11	3	−8
Non-electrical Engineering and Shipbuilding	(33, 37)	6	5	−1
Electrical Engineering	(36)	5	8	+3
Vehicles	(38)	5	5	0
Metal Goods	(39)	2	3	+1
Textiles	(41)	10	6	−4
Clothing and Footwear	(44)	2	2	0
Food	(21)	7	8	+1
Drink	(23)	13	9	−4
Tobacco	(24)	4	3	−1
Paper, Printing and Publishing	(48)	6	7	+1
Leather, Timber, and Other Manufacturing	(43, 47, 49)	1	2	+1
Construction	(50)	0	2	+2
Wholesaling	(81)	3	3	0
Retailing	(82)	9	11	+2
Transport and Miscellaneous	(70, 88)	7	8	+1

* The numbers in brackets refer to the two-digit Standard Industrial Classification headings (1958 version) covered by the relevant industrial group.

1965) could have resulted in an increase in competition which would not be apparent from Table VI.

In conclusion, it is clear that the top 100 companies cover most of the industrial activities dealt with in this study. Our very broad industrial classification, combined with possible changes in the degree of diversification of giant companies, raises problems of interpretation, but it is clear that there is a distinct possibility of the domination of many types of production by one giant firm or by a very small group of giant firms.[14]

6. THE INCIDENCE OF MOBILITY IN DIFFERENT TIME PERIODS

One important question arising out of Sections (3) and (4) is whether the mobility of the giant companies is increasing or decreasing.

TABLE VII

THE HISTORY OF THE 1948 TOP 100 COMPANIES FROM 1948 TO 1957 AND 1957 TO 1968

Year	*Population*		*Number*
1948	Top 100 companies		100
1948 to 1957	Demoted from top 100*	19	
	Died by merger or take-over	4	
	Died by nationalization	1	
	Total lost		24
1957	Survivors in the 1957 top 100		76
1958 to 1968	Promoted back to top 100	3	
	Demoted from top 100	2	
	Net demotions	−1	
	Died by merger or take-over	17	
	Died by nationalization	8	
	Total lost		24
	Survivors in the 1968 top 100		52

* Six of these companies died between 1958 and 1968, all as a result of merger or take-over.

A simple test of this is to divide the period into two halves in order to discover whether mobility was higher in the earlier period than in the later period. Unfortunately, a list of the top 100 companies is not readily available for 1958, which would divide the period into two equal parts, but the Board of Trade did publish such a

[14] More specific data on concentration, in particular industries, will be found in A. G. Armstrong and Z. A. Silberston, 'Size of plant size of enterprise and concentration in British manufacturing industry, 1935–58', *Journal of the Royal Statistical Society*, Series A, Vol. 128, Part 3, 1965.

list for 1957.[15] Table VII makes use of this list to trace the history of the 1948 top 100 through the periods 1948–57 and 1957–68.

The table shows a superficial consistency between periods in the *number* of disappearances from the 1948 top 100, there being 24 in each period. The 24 disappearances between 1948 and 1957 represent 24 per cent of the population at the start of the period, whereas the 24 disappearances between 1957 and 1968 represent approximately 31 per cent of the starting population in 1957, so that the *proportionate* rate of disappearance was higher over the second period. Since the second period was eleven years long and the first was 9 years long, this means that the annual proportionate disappearance rates were similar over the two periods. However, steel nationalization swelled the disappearance rate in the later period: if we eliminate this, the proportionate disappearance rate for 1948 to 1957 becomes 23 per cent and that for 1957 to 1968 becomes 21 per cent, so that the rate is lower for the later period even before we allow for the greater length of that period.

The *composition* of the disappearances is remarkably different between the two periods. In 1948 to 1957, demotions predominated, indicating a high degree of mobility due to the relatively high growth rates of certain firms which were thus able to overtake members of the top 100. In 1957 to 1968 mergers and take-overs predominated and demotions were of negligible importance. Of the 27 companies in the 1948 top 100 which were merged or taken over between 1948 and 1968, 23 were merged or taken over after 1957. Thus, in the language of Section (3) above, the absolute survival rate was much lower in the later period. Thus, the merger and take-over processes, which have been described earlier as the principal feature of the mobility of the top 100 companies between 1948 to 1968, achieved their importance during the latter part of the period.

7. STATIC MEASURES OF CONCENTRATION

The final broad question which can be answered from the available data is: how are static measures of concentration changing? In other words, is the relative size of the largest firms increasing?

The question of relative concentration amongst the top 100 can be dealt with by fitting a Pareto distribution to the size data. It is well known that the size distribution of large firms approximates the Pareto form.[16] This type of distribution exhibits a linear propor-

[15] *Company Assets and Income in 1957*, H.M.S.O., London, 1960.

[16] See, for example, J. Steindl, *Random Processes and the Growth of Firms*, Griffin, London, 1965.

tionate relationship between a firm's rank in the distribution and its size. It can be written:

$$\log S = a + b. \log R$$

where S is size, and R is rank, when the firms in the distribution are ranked in order of size. The coefficient b is the Pareto coefficient, which gives an indication of the relative size of the firms in the distribution: the higher is the absolute value of b, the larger is a typical firm relative to the next firm in rank, and the greater, therefore, is the relative size of the larger firms.

Table VIII gives the results of fitting a Pareto distribution by least squares to the top 100 companies in 1948 and 1968 respectively.

TABLE VIII

RESULTS OF FITTING THE PARETO DISTRIBUTION TO THE TOP 100 FIRMS

Year	*a*	*b*	r^2
1948	5.23 (±0.03)	−0.66 (±0.01)	0.98
1957	6.42 (±0.04)	−0.75 (±0.01)	0.98
1968	7.43 (±0.06)	−0.79 (±0.02)	0.97

TABLE IX

RESULTS OF FITTING THE PARETO DISTRIBUTION TO THE TOP 12 FIRMS

Year	*a*	*b*	r^2
1948	5.25 (±0.11)	−0.70 (±0.06)	0.93
1957	6.15 (±0.07)	−0.64 (±0.04)	0.96
1968	7.07 (±0.08)	−0.65 (±0.04)	0.96

All of the coefficients are highly significant when a t-test is applied and the Pareto distribution provides a very good fit to the data (r^2 is very high). The estimated values of the coefficient b suggest that concentration, measured as the relative strength of the largest firms, increased between 1948 and 1968, and particularly between 1948 and 1957. However, this result must be treated with some caution, because, despite the goodness of fit, plotting the data provides some evidence of slight non-linearity in the relationship, particularly with respect to the largest firms. Fitting the Pareto distribution across the top 12 firms suggests that the absolute value of the coefficient b did not increase between 1948 and 1968 (Table IX), and that it *declined* particularly rapidly between 1948 and 1957.

Table X confirms the relative indecisiveness of these changes in the relative size of giant firms by providing the results of fitting a Pareto distribution to the top 50 companies. These suggest that the Pareto coefficient increased slightly, but not dramatically, between 1948 and 1957 but not at all between 1957 and 1968.

Another feature of Table VIII which deserves mention is the size of the constant term *a*. This reflects the size of the largest firm[17] in the ideal Pareto distribution described by the estimated parameters. The change in the value of the constant term from 1948 to 1968 is an increase of 2.20, which, when translated back from natural logarithms to real numbers, implies that the very largest firms grew roughly 9 times in size from 1948 to 1968. In fact, the largest firm in 1948 (Unilever) had net assets of £148.1 million, and that in 1968 (I.C.I.) had net assets of £1,412 million, an increase broadly consistent with this figure. This growth of net assets by roughly 9 times compares with a growth by a factor of only 3.4 in the gross stock of reproducible fixed assets in manufacturing in the U.K.

TABLE X

RESULTS OF FITTING THE PARETO DISTRIBUTION TO THE TOP 50 FIRMS

Year	a	b	r^2
1948	5.11 ($\pm$0.04)	−0.62 ($\pm$0.01)	0.98
1957	6.24 ($\pm$0.05)	−0.68 ($\pm$0.01)	0.98
1968	14.00 ($\pm$0.03)	−0.66 ($\pm$0.01)	0.99

at current prices, over the comparable period.[18] This comparison is a very rough one: companies' assets are valued at historic cost rather than current prices, and changes in their valuation methods may give rise to the appearance of growth in money terms when no real growth has taken place. Nevertheless, the very high proportionate growth of the largest companies suggests that concentration, measured as their share of the capital stock of manufacturing assets in the U.K., increased substantially during the period.

Alternative static measures of concentration can be obtained by adding up the net assets of the companies studied. Table XI gives some of these. It is clear that, amongst the top 100, concentration increased only slightly between 1948 and 1968: the net assets of the top 4, the top 12 and the top 50 have increased by a slightly higher

[17] Strictly, it represents the size of an imaginary firm of rank one which fell exactly on the fitted line.

[18] This figure is obtained from the London and Cambridge Economic Service publication, *The British Economy, Key Statistics* 1900–1970, Times Newspapers, London. Capital stock at constant prices appears in Table I, and an index of capital goods prices is given in Table E.

proportion than those of the top 100. The really interesting comparison is that between the top 100 and the rest of the quoted sector. It is clear that the proportion of the assets of the quoted sector controlled by the top 100 is increasing rapidly: the final column of Table XI shows that over the period 1948–68 the top 100 companies increased their net assets by a factor of 6.2 whereas for the sector as a whole the increase was by a factor of only 4.5. As a consequence of this the proportion of Total Net Assets in the quoted sector controlled by the top 100 was 0.46 in 1948, 0.51 in 1957 and 0.64 in 1968. The latter figure is exaggerated by the fact that the Board of Trade's population on which the 1968 quoted sector total is based excludes small quoted companies. However, examination of the effects of eliminating the small companies suggests that this is not an important factor: the reduction in Total Net Assets, resulting from

TABLE XI

TOTAL NET ASSETS OF VARIOUS GROUPS OF COMPANIES

Group	1948 £ million	(%)	1957 £ million	(%)	1968 £ million	(%)	Proportionate growth, 1948 to 1968
Top 4	472	10.2	1,228	11.4	3,085	14.7	6.5
Top 12	828	17.8	2,225	20.6	5,506	26.2	6.6
Top 50	1,626	35.0	4,314	39.9	10,694	50.8	6.6
Top 100	2,157	46.5	5,473	50.7	13,409	63.7	6.2
All quoted companies	4,641	100.0	10,805	100.0	21,049	100.0	4.5

Note: The 'all quoted' group total for 1948 is derived from the National Institute of Economic and Social Research publication. Those for 1957 and 1968 are derived from the Board of Trade's figures published in the *Annual Abstract of Statistics*.

the removal of more than 300 small companies by the Board of Trade in 1960, was only 2 per cent.[19]

The increase in the concentration of the total net assets of quoted companies amongst the top 100 over the period 1948 to 1968 is impressively large. It is seen to be even more impressive when it is realized that most of the increase took place between 1957 and 1968. This is consistent with the results of Section (6), which showed that take-over and merger activity was much greater in the later part of the period. Clearly, takeovers and mergers are an obvious means by which the top 100 can grow much faster than the rest of the quoted company population.

CONCLUSION

The picture which has emerged of the top 100 quoted companies

[19] This is derived from data published in the *Annual Abstract of Statistics*.

is that they are a fairly mobile and dynamic group. Over the twenty-year period, only half of the top 100 retained their status in the top 100 and roughly one-third disappeared altogether, as independent quoted companies. Steel nationalization helped to increase the 'death rate', but the main cause of death was take-over or merger. This was also the main source of new entry into the very highest ranks, and it is also the most plausible explanation for the very rapid growth of the top 100 relative to the rest of the quoted population and the national stock of reproducible fixed assets in manufacturing industry.

There was no conclusive evidence that concentration has increased *within* the top 100 companies during the period: the picture is one of the top 100 as a group growing rapidly relative to the rest of the company sector. In considering the implications of this for competition in the economy as a whole, it should be remembered that the top 100 companies covered a wide range of industrial activities (Section (5)). This suggests that they are not in constant competition with one another and may be in a position individually to dominate certain markets.

The tentative conclusion to be drawn is that the very largest companies are becoming dominant in a wide area of manufacturing industry. The consequence of this for competition is likely to vary from industry to industry, depending on the number of large firms in the industry, on their degree of diversification, and on the variety of products produced by the industry. However, the life of the giant firm does not seem to be that of a 'quiet life' monopolist: the death rate amongst giant firms by take-over and acquisition produces a significant degree of insecurity. On the other hand, the consequence of take-overs and mergers is to make the giants still larger. There is thus a contradiction between the static and the dynamic aspects of concentration. The higher the 'death' rate amongst the giant firms, the larger will be the survivors. Furthermore, the very largest survivors seem to be relatively immune from take-over.

These conclusions are consistent with the recent findings of M. A. Utton,[20] concerning the effect of mergers on concentration. Utton found that concentration (which he measured as the inter-firm variance of the logarithm of Size) increased from 1954 to 1965 and that mergers made an important contribution to this process. The present study has reached similar conclusions, using a longer time period, a different methodology, and different data.

[20] M. A. Utton, 'The Effect of Mergers on Concentration: U.K. Manufacturing Industry, 1954–65'. *The Journal of Industrial Economics*, Volume XX, No. 1, November, 1971.

The obvious policy conclusion which might be drawn from this is that mergers of and take-overs by giant companies require stringent scrutiny and control if competition is to be a serious control mechanism in the economy. This must be qualified by considering a highly relevant aspect of the growth of the giant firm which has not been studied here, namely diversification. It has been suggested above that diversification seems likely to have increased as a result of mergers and take-overs. Such an increase *could* have had the effect of increasing the number of markets which are dominated by giant firms, but it could equally well have increased the number of markets in which giant firms compete with one another. However, whatever the effects of diversification, they seem unlikely to be sufficiently strong to offset the adverse effect on competition of the very large increase between 1957 and 1968 in the proportion of the assets of the quoted population controlled by the top 100 companies.

CAMBRIDGE

APPENDIX

THE TOP 12 COMPANIES IN 1948

Rank	*Name*	*Net Assets (£ million)*
1	Unilever	148.1
2	Imperial Chemical Industries	143.1
3	Imperial Tobacco Company	117.6
4	Courtaulds	62.9
5	Distillers Company	62.7
6	Vickers	56.7
7	Dunlop Rubber Company	47.6
8	Coats (J. and P.)	45.7
9	Odeon Theatres	42.1
10	Guest, Keen and Nettlefolds	38.8
11	Stewarts and Lloyds	33.9
12	Tube Investments	28.9

THE TOP 12 COMPANIES IN 1968

Rank	*Name*	*Net Assets (£ million)*
1	Imperial Chemical Industries	1,412.0
2	General Electric Co.	670.9
3	Imperial Tobacco Group	514.7
4	Unilever	487.8
5	Courtaulds	406.7
6	British Leyland Motor Corporation	309.5
7	Distillers Company	307.6
8	Bass Charrington	302.4
9	Allied Breweries	295.0
10	Guest, Keen and Nettlefolds	275.1
11	Reed Paper Group	269.7
12	Bowater Paper Corporation	254.9

COMPANIES IN THE 1968 TOP 100 WHICH WERE NOT 'ALIVE' IN 1948

Rank in 1968	*Name*	*Cause of 'birth'*
6	British Leyland Motor Corporation	Merger
8	Bass Charrington	Merger
9	Allied Breweries	Merger
22	Coats Patons	Merger
34	International Publishing Corporation	Merger
38	Courage, Barclay & Simonds	Merger
39	Unigate	Merger
59	The Dickinson Robinson Group	Merger
62	Thomas Tilling	Conversion
66	Rootes Motors	Quotation
80	Grand Metropolitan Hotels	Quotation
82	Transport Development Group	Quotation
83	Forte's (Holdings)	Quotation
91	International Distillers and Vintners	Quotation
94	Ready Mixed Concrete	Quotation
100	Carrington and Dewhurst	Quotation

Note: 'Merger' means that the new company was formed as a result of the merger of existing quoted companies.

'Conversion' implies a change of industrial activities to the range covered by our population (manufacturing, construction, distribution, transport, and miscellaneous services).

'Quotation' means that an existing company qualified for entry to the population by obtaining a quotation for its shares on a U.K. stock exchange.

STRUCTURE AND BEHAVIOR IN BRITISH INDUSTRIES, WITH U.S. COMPARISONS*

by WILLIAM G. SHEPHERD

THE basic questions about market structure concern what it is, what determines it, and what effects it has. Conceptual and econometric answers to the questions are still formative, even after three decades of research [2, 10, 18, 25, 29, 40]. Few hypotheses have acquired firm empirical support, and structure-performance relations in large areas of market activity remain conjectural.

British industry is relatively unexplored, even after several pioneering efforts. Its patterns are of concern both for domestic industrial performance and as tests of hypotheses which are of more general interest and importance.

This paper touches on both contexts. It first derives measures of British industrial market structure in recent years and uses them to indicate the extent of structural monopoly during 1958–63, in Section 1. It next uses these measures in Section 2 to test hypotheses about comparative British and U.S. concentration. Section 3 then offers partial tests of two basic hypotheses about the determinants and effects of market structure: that growth erodes concentration over time, and that the degree of structural monopoly affects price-cost behavior.

The findings conflict with several accepted conclusions and confirm several others, even though the data are imperfect and the period is brief and possibly atypical. Section 4 summarizes the findings.

1. ELEMENTS OF MARKET STRUCTURE

The first task is to indicate the extent and patterns of market power in U.K. industry. It is generally recognized that market structure is comprised of several main elements (Bain [1], Scherer [25], Shepherd [29]). One is concentration, the aggregation of the market shares of leading firms, which influences the possibility of individual monopoly behavior and of cooperative joint maximization or 'shared monopoly'. Another is barriers against entry by non-trivial new

* I am indebted to William S. Comanor, Basil Yamey, Peter E. Hart, and Lee E. Preston for their comments on an earlier draft of this paper. Sally Zack and Robert H. Smiley performed the computations.

A paper by Malcolm Sawyer paralleling part of this one came to me after this paper had been sent to the printer (*Oxford Economic Papers*, November 1971). Its conclusions diverge from some of these reached here, for reasons which are explored in my "British Industrial Concentration': A Comment," *Oxford Economic Papers*, in process.

competitors. To some observers, such barriers are the prime element of market power (see Dewey [7]); at the least, they are widely regarded as an important factor (see Bain [1], and Scherer [25]). A third possible element is buyers' monopsony power, which may be sufficient to neutralize the other elements of monopoly on the sellers' side (see Galbraith [12]). A fourth category includes the factors which facilitate coordination among the leading firms, and these include the degree of shared values and expectations, or 'social structure'.

The relative importance of these four elements is a matter of debate, although there has been a consensus that concentration is probably the most basic single determinant, on an industry basis.[1] Concentration is also generally regarded as the most adequately measured element. For the others, one must resort to incomplete information.

In the British case, perhaps the greatest single impact on both entry and the social structure has been made by foreign firms—particularly U.S. firms—in a series of the larger industries. Entry of foreign firms is a marked breach of a clear barrier—the national boundary. Such entry has been substantial in the last 25 years [9]. The presence of such foreign-held competitors tends to destabilize inter-firm cooperation, since the outsider firms apply (or are expected to apply) different objectives and strategies (Dunning [8, 9]). U.S. firms in particular may tend to be more aggressive, less observant of established codes of competitive and managerial behavior, and able to draw on at least some parent-firm resources (see also Burn [3]). Their profitability has been consistently higher than that of domestic firms (Dunning [9]).

Virtually no systematic information about monopsony power in British industry exists, but it is possible to estimate one potential source of counter-vailing power. The possibility that public agencies and public corporations can, as purchasers, exert concerted monopsony power is present in a number of industries with high seller concentration.[2] The constraint is only a potential one; the variance in the possible bilateral outcomes is wide, possibly extending well into the range of net *increased* market power under passive buyer behavior (Bain [1] and Shanks [26]). The optimist will expect a negative partial relation between the public-entity purchasers'

[1] I have recently attempted to evaluate their relative importance for large U.S. industrial firms (see [30] and the sources cited there).

For Britain one recent study [17] also affirms the probable importance of concentration. But it is based on only 15 aggregative industry-group observations, and its other results are erratic.

[2] These include primarily heavy electrical electrical equipment, communication equipment, drugs [36] and hospital supplies, and aircraft [35].

share and market power; the pessimist will posit a positive relation. In any event the shares can be estimated and their role, if any, is potentially testable.

The rest of this section discusses concentration data for the 1958–68 period, and then it outlines the overall patterns of market structure.

(a) *Concentration data*

British individual-industry concentration ratios are available for 1935, 1951, 1958, and now 1963. The 1963 Census [34, Table 5] presents 5-firm ratios for a selection of 281 products at approximately a 4-digit degree of detail, on a standardized basis for 1958 and 1963. These form the core data for the estimates and analyses which follow. The ratios are incomplete in two main respects: they cover products with only 68.2 per cent of the sales of all products in 1963, and they do not allow for the role of imports. Corrections for these omissions were made as follows.[3]

Coverage. The published 4-digit ratios are for the most clearly definable markets, so that those which are omitted are mainly residual, 'not elsewhere classified' categories.[4] This is reflected in the high level of most of the ratios, in contrast to the low ratios which are common for such residual 'industries' in the U.S., U.K., and other countries (Evely and Little [10] and Shepherd [29]). The gaps in coverage are widely spread among industry types. A method for filling the gaps is needed, in order to estimate the total distribution of concentration. On the assumption that omitted sub-sectors are residual, the missing categories are assigned the distribution of concentration values which is shown in U.S. concentration data for the 52 residual ('not elsewhere classified') industries [37].[5] The omitted 31.8 per cent of British industry sales in 1963 (and 39.9 per cent in 1958) were assigned the values of this distribution and were

[3] In addition, two lesser corrections were necessary, in order to remove specific biases or to remedy omissions.

Small firms (below 25 employees) were omitted by the Census in preparing the published 4-digit ratios, but the share of these small firms (averaging 3–4 per cent and ranging up to 12 per cent) was reported for 3-digit industry groups. Accordingly, each 4-digit ratio was recalculated on the basis of its 3-digit industry group's small-firm ratio, as an approximation.

Also, ratios were adjusted upwards for several industries (such as milk, bricks and newspapers) whose markets are primarily local in scope or contain distinct product submarkets. This improved the accuracy of the ratios in reflecting true market conditions, and it made possible the comparison with U.S. industrial concentration in Section 2.

For 56 of the 281 products, 1958 ratios were omitted by the Census. Ten of these could be estimated from other sources. Therefore the coverage is 281 products in 1963 and 235 products in 1958.

[4] The same was true of the Census ratios for 1951; 4-digit data covered industries with only 63 per cent of employment [9]. The 1963 ratios include no 4-digit residual-type categories.

[5] A list of these industries will be provided on request by the author.

then merged with the published data in calculating the total distributions of industrial activity by degree of concentration (in Table I).

Imports. These are a significant share of many British markets, as many observers have noted, enough to warrant inclusion in concentration ratios. Import data are available only by product categories, which differ in numerous cases from the Census industry lines. A degree of estimating and averaging of imports was necessary, using Customs import data [33], in order to prepare import totals to adjust the concentration ratios. The value of imports was added to the denominator of the concentration ratio. The adjustments made

TABLE I

DISTRIBUTION OF SALES BY U.K. INDUSTRIES ACCORDING TO FIVE-FIRM CONCENTRATION RATIOS, 1958–63

Range of five-firm concentration	*Adjusted ratios* 1958 *1*	1963 *2*
90–100	7.08	10.29
80–89	6.71	8.41
70–79	6.45	6.29
60–69	11.06	12.48
50–59	9.77	10.77
40–49	15.15	14.16
30–39	16.49	16.16
20–29	15.55	13.06
10–19	10.12	7.43
0–9	1.62	0.95
Above 80	13.79	18.70
Above 70	20.24	24.99
Above 60	31.30	37.47
Above 50	41.07	48.24
Weighted Average	47.91	52.13

Source: [34], Table 5, adjusted as described in the text.

here are minimum ones, since in some cases a reliable assignment of imports to an industry could not be made. To this extent, the adjusted concentration ratios remain biased upwards, though probably not by more than two or three points. Table I presents the distribution of 4-digit product sales on the basis of the adjusted ratios in 1958 and 1963, in columns 1 and 2.[6]

[6] Sources for other information about structure are as follows. Estimates of the share of foreign-firm subsidaries in U.K. markets are available for a wide range of industries, particularly in Dunning [9] as well as in Monopolies Commission reports [37] and various trade sources. Public-entity purchases were estimated from reports of the public corporations, the Monopolies Commission [37], the Select Committee on the

(b) *General patterns*

The extent and movement of concentration during 1958–63 is indicated in Table I. During 1958–63 there was a rise of weighted average of 5-firm concentration by 2.8 to 4.2. points.[7] This continues the rise during 1951–58 (see Shepherd [28]).

It does not necessarily follow that the degree of market power rose during 1958–63 (or 1951–63), however, because other elements of structural monopoly may have receded. In particular, foreign-firm shares, public-entity buyer constraints and public ownership (in the steel industry) have probably risen (see Section 2(b) below). Therefore the rise in market power is not as obvious as the rise in concentration ratios.

It is also instructive to look briefly at one other element of market structure: relative total size. The size of an industry, relative to the total size distribution, will normally affect the degree of potential competition and ease of entry (Weiss [41], Shepherd [29]). Therefore the proportion of high concentration cases that is in 'large' product groups is of interest; if all high concentration cases were in tiny industries, then each would be likely to be easily entered and therefore all would be more under competitive constraint than if the same share of high concentration were focused in a handful of giant industries. Let the average size of all industries (sales of £50 million in 1963) be the minimum criterion for 'large' size, for illustrative purposes. How much of high concentration (adjusted basis) was in such above-average industries?

Relatively little; the 28 such products had in 1963 only 15.3 per cent of total industrial sales. Two-thirds of this 15.3 per cent was focused in 3 major industry groups (automotive tobacco and oil), while public-agency purchasing or direct public ownership affected a further 5 industries (drugs, telephone equipment and steel markets). Of the remaining 14 industries only sugar, metal containers, man-made fibers, cement, tires and tubes, glass, and newspapers were significantly above the £50 million average size. These are a large share of the industries that have long been recognized as the core of the monopoly problem in British industry.

Altogether, then, the common pattern of British industry is one of

Nationalised Industries, and the Plowden [35] and Sainsbury [36] committees, and various trade sources, supplemented by discussions with officials of the public firms, the Ministries of Health, Technology and Power, and the Board of Trade.

[7] The estimated 1958–63 rise in Table I is actually slightly overstated, because the weighted average concentration for 1958 is probably biased downward by 1.4 percentage points. This is because a larger share of sales (8.1 per cent) were omitted in the 1958 concentration ratios than in the 1963 ratios, and so the use of residual-industry concentration ratios (averaging 32 per cent) tended relatively to understate 1958 average concentration. On this basis, the actual 1958–63 rise was from 49.3 to 52.1 per cent, just 2.8 points rather than 4.2 points.

moderately tight oligopoly, with a moderate rising trend. The subset of industries with very high concentration and large size is relatively small.

2. COMPARING U.K. WITH U.S. MARKET STRUCTURE

International comparisons can assist in appraising the degree of market power, its durability, its similarity among countries, and its comparative determinants (see especially Bain [2]). This section tests the following hypotheses: (a) that structural monopoly is higher in British than U.S. industries, (b) the leading cases of high structural monopoly tend to be newer, less stable, and potentially more subject to public-policy constraint in Britain than in the U.S., and (c) concentration tends to be similar in paired U.K. and U.S. industries.

(a) *Structural Comparison*

It has been commonly, but not unanimously, thought that British industries are more concentrated than U.S. industries (see Bain [2], Florene [11], and Pashigian [20], but also Shepherd [27]). A common technological base, with identical minimum efficient scale in each case, would tend to yield lower concentration in U.S. industries, most of which are larger (Bain [2]). Alternatively, if technology differs, and if many U.S. industries are instead merely aggregates of genuine regional or local markets, then true market concentration could be higher in the U.S. than in Britain. Differences in the composition of industrial production could also affect the comparison. For example, if the U.K. had a larger share of industries with 'naturally' low concentration (such as textiles), then average U.K. concentration would be lower. External competition, especially via imports, could also affect the comparison; it is known to be more significant for U.K. than U.S. industries. Other structural elements may also differ; for example, differential degrees of foreign-firm presence and possible public-agency monopsony constraints could offset differences in concentration. One therefore begins by comparing concentration and then considers whether other elements tend to override or reinforce the differences in concentration.

The comparison of concentration in the mid-1960s in Table II is based on ratios reflecting true concentration in relevant markets.[8]

[8] In certain cases, adjustments were made to assure equivalent market definitions. The U.S. ratios are drawn from Shepherd [29], see especially pp. 104–112 and Appendix, Table 8. About half of the raw census ratios were re-estimated to reflect local or regional markets, product markets within industries, and imports. The resulting weighted average ratios are consistent with those by Weiss [40]. The British ratios are the adjusted ratios in

One can never be sure that the ratios are precisely comparable, but those used in Table II appear to be reliable and do have the merit of reducing substantial amounts of known systematic bias in certain census ratios. Table II suggests that industrial concentration is lower in Britain than in the U.S. British 5-firm concentration averages 52.1 per cent, whereas the 4-firm U.S. average is 60.3 per cent. Estimates of the size distribution of firms in industries (Worcester [42]) suggest that fifth-firm shares tend to be approximately one-fifteenth of the aggregate four-firm share. Accordingly, the actual U.K.–U.S. gap on a 4-firm basis would be just over 10 points.

TABLE II

A COMPARISON OF DISTRIBUTIONS OF U.S. AND U.K. 4-DIGIT INDUSTRIES, ACCORDING TO THE DEGREE OF CONCENTRATION, IN THE MID-1960s

Range of concentration	*U.K. five-firm ratios (total sales)*	*U.S. four-firm ratios (value-added)*
90–100	10.3	17.0
80–89	8.4	9.0
70–79	6.3	8.0
60–69	12.5	15.1
50–59	10.8	14.7
40–49	14.2	14.7
30–39	16.2	9.7
20–29	13.1	9.1
10–19	7.4	2.3
0–9	1.0	0.4
Above 70	25.0	34.0
Above 50	48.2	63.8
Weighted Average	52.1	60.3

Sources: Table I and [29, pp. 104–7].

Although the differential may have narrowed in more recent years, it is not likely to have been eliminated.

If one allows for possible foreign-firm and public-agency factors as

Table I, *supra*. The general degree of fineness of market definition is believed to be approximately the same in the two sets of ratios.

One may also compare raw census ratios for both countries, but that almost certainly injects more systematic measurement error of true market conditions than do the adjustments reported here. Further research can improve the present adjustments, but it is not likely to alter their effect substantially. Any systematic biases would need to be implausibly large to reverse the comparison in Table II.

Although in Table II the U.K. distribution is weighted by sales and the U.S. distribution is weighted by value-added, the difference is not likely to bias the comparison significantly, because the two measures tend to give closely similar patterns [18, 29].

The comparison is influenced by the assignment of residual-industry concentration values to the missing U.K. industries; but, as noted, this seems more reasonable than any other treatment.

well, the difference in degree of structural monopoly is likely to be larger and stable over time. There was (and is) little foreign-firm element in most major U.S. industries. In the utility and health-services sectors there is much less opportunity for concerted public-agency and public-firm buyer constraints (apart from military spending in the U.S., which appears to have been conducted predominantly in a passive mode; see Shepherd [29]). Yet even without these facts, the U.K.–U.S. comparison is relatively clear.

(b) *Stability of Extreme Cases*

The central monopoly problem in an economy arises both from the static extent of high structural monopoly at any point in time *and* from its resistance to erosion or outside constraints over time. Accordingly, one needs to compare the degree of permanence or stability of the prime cases of current structural monopoly in the two countries and the degree to which there are direct policy constraints on them. One first identifies the main cases of high structural monopoly in each country and screens the two sets of cases down to equal quantitative importance, such as the same share of total manufacturing activity. Even if this can be done only approximately, it may permit one to note any gross differences in the newness or instability of structure in the two sets of cases. It is generally known that certain major British industries have undergone substantial structural changes in the last two decades, some of them still in process. Therefore the hypothesis is that leading British cases of high structural monopoly are newer and less firmly established than those in the U.S.

The two sets of industries are given in Appendix Tables I and II. They reflect primarily concentration and also, in some cases, probable entry barriers and other elements of structure, drawing on the range of sources which were used in Section 1 (especially [2, 3, 10, 21, 29 and 37]). The sections are not based on mechanical criteria for combining the various elements, for no such basis exists; yet the inclusions probably embody no substantial sample bias and can be regarded as reasonable consensus choices. Both groups account for about 25 per cent of total sales in their respective manufacturing sectors.

The comparison lends support to the hypothesis. Nearly half of the British cases (accounting for three-fourths of the group's total sales) have had major changes in the 1960s. The U.S. cases are mostly of pre-1955 vintage; only 2 cases, steel and photocopying, were altered during the 1960s. The differences are most marked primarily in the largest cases, not the smallest ones; automobiles, computers, electric equipment, telephone apparatus (a legally ratified monopoly in the U.S.) and oil. In several important U.K. cases (automobiles, tobacco and cement) the shares of dominant firms have shown a repeated tendency to decline over time. The major recent cases of rising concentration in major U.K. industries have tended to be subject to potential public-agency buyer constraints and detailed intervention (e.g. electrical and telecommunications equipment, steel, and computers). And there has been in U.S. industry nothing like the incursion of U.S. and other branches into major U.K. industries (e.g. in oil, automobiles and drugs). To summarize, the British instances of high structural monopoly are newer, probably less stable, and potentially more subject to policy constraints than is the comparable U.S. set of industries. The U.S. monopoly problem does not appear to be less severe, either qualitatively or quantitatively.

(c) *Paired Cases*

Pairings of individual U.S. and U.K. industries have been tried before, both to test the similarity of concentration levels and to compare the effects of size on concentration [2, 11, 20, 27]. For 1958–63, pairings were possible for 90 product groups and industries.[9] The paired industries are similar in relative size (r = 0.70). Also the samples are reasonably representative in structural characteristics.[10]

The industry pairs display a closer similarity of concentration levels than earlier studies [2, 10, 18, 23] have indicated, with a significant simple correlation coefficient of r = 0.68. Much of this improvement of fit is probably caused by the various refinements which were made in both sets of ratios, as noted earlier. Therefore, the present comparison may be regarded as a more accurate test. Yet size differences in the pairs do not account for any significant amount of the residual differences in concentration:[11]

[9] They account for 29 per cent of U.K. sales and 15 per cent of U.S. value of shipments. Pairings were based on the two sets of census industry and product descriptions. Generally, U.S. multi-market and multi-product industries were avoided, so that the 90 U.S. cases are substantially smaller in average size than are all 4-digit industries.

[10] Thus, those in the U.K. group showed average concentration rises of 3.9 points while the U.S. rises averaged only 0.2 points. Mean adjusted concentration in the two groups (U.K. 5-firm at 63.0 per cent, U.S. 4-firm at 59.5 per cent) was about the same in 1963. Interestingly, the U.K. industries grew during 1958–63 more rapidly than those in the U.S. group (by 41.1 per cent compared to 29.5 per cent), though the difference in group means is not statistically significant. U.K. industries as a group had lower (unweighted) average price-cost margins in 1963 than did the U.S. group (20.1 per cent compared to 25.8 per cent). It is not possible to factor out the four main possible causes of this difference: (1) differing census definitions of costs, (2) differing degrees of competitive constraint, (3) differing degrees of efficiency in production, and (4) differing degrees of capital-intensity. Even so, there is interest in the paired-industry patterns of margins.

[11] Significance at the 1 per cent level is indicated by *, at the 5 per cent level by †.

$$\text{U.K. Concentration} = \underset{}{13.43} + \underset{(0.088)}{0.750^*}\ \text{U.S. Concentration}$$

$$\underset{(0.181)}{-0.107}\ \text{U.K. Size/U.S. Size} \quad R^2 = 0.46 \quad F = 37.4$$

The coefficients confirm the earlier observation that in the upper concentration ranges (above U.K. concentration of 49 per cent), U.S. industries tend to have higher ratios than U.K. industries.

Despite the similarity of paired-industry concentration, there was no observable tendency during 1958–63 for concentration in the paired industries to converge. Specifically, a regression analysis found that U.K.–U.S. differences in concentration in 1958 were not associated at all with 1958–63 changes of concentration in both U.S. and U.K. industries.

3. INTERACTIONS AMONG INDUSTRIAL STRUCTURE AND BEHAVIOR

A number of possible structure-performance relations have been hypothesized in the literature, of which few have yet been firmly supported or rejected by empirical research (see Scherer [25], Shepherd [29], and Weiss [41]). In the British case, two hypotheses are both of especial concern and potentially testable using the data which are available (including the structural data developed earlier in this paper). These two are: (a) that growth erodes concentration, and (b) that market structure influences price-cost margins.

(a) *Growth and Changes in Concentration*

The hypothesis that there is a negative and important relation between an industry's growth rate and the degree of change in its concentration over time has a tenuous and rather involved theoretical basis (see Pashigian [19] and Shepherd [29]). Yet it does have intuitive appeal, and several observers rate it as a major—perhaps the major—downward constraint on concentration (see Bain [2], Rosenbluth [24], also Shepherd [29, pp. 177–8]). Empirical support for it has been modest, based mainly on U.S. data relating to the 1947–58 period [18, 31; also 15]. Yet the estimated relationship has been weak, and it has been based on imperfect raw Census data on industry size and concentration [29]. U.K. data have not previously permitted an econometric analysis at all (see [13, 28]); instead interpretation has had to rely on impressions and judgment. With properly adjusted data, one can now prepare a more standardized test for British industry.

Size and growth are here measured in terms of absolute values of industry sales (net output being unavailable at the 4 digit level). In principle, one could attempt to incorporate a measure of 'relative' size of the industry, compared to an estimate of minimum efficient size of firm. This would cast minimum efficient scale as a possible determinant—along with size and growth—of industry concentration.[12] Yet past efforts to include this variable have had limited success, primarily because acceptable estimates only of minimum efficient *plant* size have been available, and even these have been deficient. Moreover, it is not clear in theory that minimum efficient scale will affect concentration at all except in the unusual case where it is relatively so high that it directly determines concentration, by placing a floor under it.[13] In any case, data for estimating minimum efficient firm *or plant* scale in U.K. 4-digit product groups simply are not available in the 1963 Census, and findings based on absolute size and growth can cast light on industry growth as a possibly significant determinant.

At the 4-digit product level, data are available only for size and concentration. Along with growth, the other possible measurable 'determinant' of changes in concentration is original-year concentration. A negative relation would suggest that high and low extremes of concentration are not stable and are subject to regression toward mean values. In addition, the systematic dwindling of high concentration would accord with dominant-firm models advanced by Worcester [42], although it could not specifically confirm them. The analysis was made with 160 4-digit industries, in the form:

$$\Delta CONC_{58-63} = a + b\ CONC_{58} + c\Delta SALES_{58-63}$$

where ΔSALES is the percentage increase in sales during the period.[14]

[12] For an effort in this direction, see [17].

[13] Thus in the U.S., only relatively few highly concentrated industries have equally high plant concentration [29]. These and other evidence [1, 2] indicate that concentration is not, in most industries, constrained upward by production technology. By the same token, *plant*-based estimates of minimum efficient scale, such as are used by Bain [2] and Pashigian [19], are relevant only in a subset of industries. For several case studies, see [21].

[14] For 46 4-digit industries, 1958 ratios were not reported and could not be estimated from other sources. These were omitted. A further 75 industries were excluded to provide a more accurate analysis, because they were very small, below total sales of £25 million in 1958. These small cases tended to display erratic changes, probably owing to measurement errors and coverage problems; their exclusion approximately doubled the degree of measured correlation. The remaining 160 industries cover the majority of available industries, with 78 per cent of all sales by the 281 industries with reported concentration ratios for 1963. Their mean concentration, size and growth values are not significantly different from the means for the entire group, by significance tests at the .01 level.

Some statistical bias may be imparted by the fact that concentration cannot go below zero or above 100. The bias will be substantial only if there are many cases of extremely high or low concentration *and* if their shift is actually inhibited. My impresssion is that the bias is not large.

The results for changes in concentration, as given in Table III, indicate that original-year concentration played a moderate role in 1958–63, while growth played none. This accords with conclusions by Evely and Little [10, Ch. 11] for 1935–51 and by Shepherd [28] for 1951–58 (but see also [13]). For each 10 points of 1958 concentration above the mean values centering on 50 (corrected or adjusted), there tended to be just under a one-point decline during 1958–63; and conversely for concentration below the mean value. This association was statistically highly significant, though it accounted for only 10 per cent of the changes in concentration, at most. In none of the regressions did the growth variable show any significant association, and even its sign was not consistently negative.

TABLE III

ANALYSIS OF GROWTH AND CONCENTRATION IN U.K. 4-DIGIT INDUSTRIES, 1958 AND 1963

Dependent variables	*Independent variables*	R^2	F
160 larger industries			
$\Delta Conc_{58-63}$	$6.581 - .083^{*}\ CONC_{58} - .583\%\ \Delta SALES_{58-63}$ (.020) (1.482)	.099	8.64†
235 industries			
$\Delta CONC_{58-63}$	$5.534 - .063^{*}\ CONC_{58} + 0.195\%\ \Delta SALES_{58-63}$ (.017) (0.577)	.055	6.76

Standard errors of coefficients are given in parentheses.

* Indicates that the coefficient differs from zero by a test of significance at the .99 confidence level.

† Indicates significance at the .95 level.

Some slight further confirmation is provided by regressions of the 90 U.K.–U.S. paired industries. Changes in U.K. concentration during 1958–63 show a significant association with 1958 levels of concentration, but none with industry growth:

$$\Delta\text{U.K. Concentration} = \underset{}{12.382} - \underset{(0.042)}{0.153^{*}}\ \text{Concentration 1958} + \underset{(0.018)}{0.014}\ \text{Growth 1958–63} \qquad R^2 = 0.13,\ F = 6.54$$

In the paired U.S. industries, by comparison, 1958 concentration and 1958–63 growth both play a (barely) significant role:

$$\Delta\text{U.S. Concentration} = 1.565 - \underset{(0.017)}{0.041^{*}}\ \text{Concentration 1958} + \underset{(0.018)}{0.036^{\dagger}}\ \text{Growth 1958–63} \qquad R^2 = 0.10,\ F = 4.72$$

Therefore, whatever general validity the hypothesis that concentration is related inversely to size and growth may have, it is not confirmed by U.K. industrial patterns during 1958–63. Further, analysis using lagged price-cost margins as well as these growth variables at the 3-digit level (see below) yielded equally null results. One concludes that the data available for 1958–63 period do not permit one to account for very much at all of the levels and changes in concentration in British industry. Other explanatory variables which might be used if data were available—such as size distributions of plants—tend to be too highly intercorrelated with concentration to be of much independent predictive value.

(b) *Structure and Price-cost Relationships*

The next hypothesis, that market power affects price-cost relationships, lies at the heart of the theory of market behavior. If market power operates by reducing demand elasticity, then Lerner's index prescribes a direct relation between market power and the divergence between price and cost (see Miller's discussion in [32]). This relationship may be regarded as merely reflecting the deeper relation between market power and rates of return on investment (see especially Weiss [41] and Shepherd [30]). Therefore a correction for differing capital-intensity is appropriate in testing the price-cost margin hypothesis (as is done by Collins and Preston in [6]). Market power can be represented, if imperfectly, by the structural estimates developed in Section 1.

Consistent, but statistically weak, evidence of a linear concentration-margin association has emerged from studies of U.S. industry [6, 29], but British patterns have not received such a cross-section analysis. The present data do permit an exploratory analysis on the 3-digit level, but some of the variables are of necessity imperfectly measured. Also, many industries were in disequilibrium with respect to structure or output level during 1958–63. Therefore the following tests are primarily a first approximation, with a low expected goodness of fit.

Margins may vary with capital intensity and growth as well as with market structure. Since direct measures of capital-intensity are not available, a proxy variable (capital expenditure divided by new output) was used, on the heroic assumption that industries are close enough to steady-growth states so that yearly investment flows are related to the fixed capital stock. This assumption may not hold for some industries; and it may be further falsified by fluctuations caused by macro-economic changes, though that can be partly mitigated by averaging the measure for the two years 1958 and 1963. The capital-intensity proxy is imperfect, even though it appears to be the best one available. Measuring growth in terms of total sales poses fewer conceptual problems and no serious measurement problem. Growth is included to permit the static structure-margin hypothesis to be tested independently of dynamic influences. The possible role of size is tested by including industry sales volume.

Since margin data are available for 1963 only on a 3-digit industry basis, averages of the 4-digit concentration data had to be prepared. The omitted share within each 3-digit industry group was assigned the estimated mean concentration value of all residual industries: 33.4 per cent on a 5-firm basis. This inevitably introduces error into the 3-digit concentration variable, though it minimizes that error for the available data.

The analysis was made for all industries, and then was repeated after excluding the 22 very small industries. The results in Table IV suggest (within a generally low degree of explanation) several significant interpretations. Equation 2 is probably the best single analysis. Concentration is significantly associated with margins, though the fit is not close.[15] The coefficient indicates a 1.2 point change in margin for every 10-point change in concentration; this accords with the margin coefficients found for U.S. industries [6, 29].[16] It implies that margins ranged from 14 in industries with low concentration up to 26 in industries with highest concentration. Industry growth is also significantly associated with margins; for each 10 per cent of growth during 1958–63, the 1963 margin is 0.6 points higher. These patterns do not display quite as good a statistical fit in regressions involving only larger industries.

At most only about 18 per cent of the variation in margins is explained, and several variables, including concentration changes, size and capital-intensity, do not show the expected associations.[17]

[15] The apparent insignificance of the capital-intensity variable undoubtedly reflects its imperfections as a measure of the underlying reality.

[16] Sales-assets ratios tend to average about 2 in U.K. industries. Therefore, the coefficients imply at least a 2.5 point rise in profit as a per cent of assets for each 10 per cent increase in the market share of the leading firms. This accords closely with the range of 2.2–2.6 points observed for concentration in a study of large U.S. manufacturing firms (Shepherd [30]).

[17] One would expect margins to be similar in paired industries in the U.K. and U.S., since market structure is also similar. Analysis of the 90 paired industries does indicate a degree of correlation, in 1963:

$$\text{U.S. Margin} = \underset{}{10.356} + \underset{(0.073)}{0.379^{*}}\ \text{U.K. Margin} \qquad r^2 = .24 \quad F = 27.12^{\dagger}$$

Yet this reflected mainly the significant relation of margins to concentration (though not to other possible determinants) in the U.S. industries:

$$\text{U.S. Margin} = 16.886 + \underset{(0.041)}{0.136^{*}}\ \text{Concentration} \qquad r^2 = .12 \quad F = 11.60$$

(while size, growth and the 1958–63 change in concentration showed no association). In the U.K. industries in this selection none of the possible determinants showed a significant association with margins.

TABLE IV

ANALYSIS OF CONCENTRATION, GROWTH, SIZE AND PRICE-COST MARGINS IN U.K. 3-DIGIT INDUSTRIES, 1958–63

Dependent variables		*Independent variables*					
All industries		*Average concentration 1958–63*	*Capital intensity 1958–63*	*Average sales 1958–63*	*Growth*	R^2	*F*
(1) Average margin 1958–63	14.50	0.122* (0.035)	−6.797 (13.232)	−0.005‡ (0.003)	4.788* (2.029)	.166	5.27†
All except very small industries							
(2) Average margin 1958–63	17.02	0.062‡ (0.039)	−6.298 (13.58)	0.006† (0.003)	4.275* (2.113)	.114	2.67

Standard errors of coefficients are given in parentheses.
* Indicates that the coefficient differs from zero by a test of significance at the .99 confidence level.
† Indicates significance at the .95 level.
‡ Indicates significance at the .90 level.

And yet, in view of the known imperfections of the data, the patterns are suggestive and consistent with those for U.S. industries.

4. SUMMARY

The main lessons are:

1. Moderately tight oligopoly is the common form of British industries, with extremely high concentration relatively unusual.
2. Concentration is continuing the rise observed during the 1950s, though the effect of this on market power may be offset by declines in other elements of structural monopoly.
3. The average degree of structural monopoly appears to be lower in Britain than it is in the U.S. industry.
4. Major cases of high structural monopoly appear to be newer and less firmly established than are comparable cases in the U.S.
5. Paired U.S.–U.K. industries have similar degrees of concentration.
6. Growth rates did appear to be associated with changes in concentration during 1958–63.
7. Structural monopoly and growth rates were associated postively with price-cost margins during 1958–63, suggesting that basic determinants of profitability were in operation.

Even the best available data are weak in several respects, so that the regression analyses are not able to discriminate among more complex hypotheses or include all of the potentially important determinants. As crude first approximations, the findings may lead to further refinements. One obvious need is for more complete industrial data, which will permit direct testing of structure-behavior hypotheses on a well-defined market basis (generally the 4-digit industry level). It is time to extend the official measures to more structural elements and to more complete industry coverage.

THE UNIVERSITY OF MICHIGAN

REFERENCES

[1] JOE S. BAIN, *Industrial Organization*, 2nd edition, Wiley, 1968.
[2] JOE S. BAIN, *International Differences in Industrial Structure: Eight Nations in the 1950s*, Yale University Press, 1966.
[3] DUNCAN BURN, ed., *The Structure of British Industry*, 2 vols., Cambridge University Press, 1958.
[4] RICHARD E. CAVES and ASSOCIATES, *Britain's Economic Prospects*, Brookings Institution, 1968.

[5] P. Lesley Cook, *Effects of Mergers*, Allen & Unwin, 1958.

[6] Norman R. Collins and Lee E. Preston, 'Price-Cost Margins and Industry Structure', *Review of Economics and Statistics*, August 1969, pp. 271–86.

[7] Donald J. Dewey, *The Theory of Imperfect Competition: A Radical Reconstruction*, Columbia University Press, 1970.

[8] John H. Dunning, *American Investment in British Manufacturing Industry*, *Ruskin House*, 1958.

[9] John H. Dunning (with W. Jensen), *American Investment in British Industry*, Political and Economic Planning Broadsheet 304, January 1969.

[10] Richard Evely and I. M. D. Little, *Concentration in British Industry*, Cambridge University Press, 1960.

[11] P. Sargent Florence, *The Logic of British and American Industry*, Routledge & Kegan Paul, 1953.

[12] J. K. Galbraith, *American Capitalism: The Concept of Countervailing Power*, rev. ed., Houghton Mifflin, 1956.

[13] Kenneth D. George, 'Changes in British Industrial Concentration, 1951–1958', *Journal of Industrial Economics*, July 1967.

[14] P. E. Hart, ed., *Studies in Profit, Business Saving and Investment in the United Kingdom*, 1920–62., 2 vols., Allen & Unwin, 1968.

[15] David R. Kamerschen, 'Market Growth and Industry Concentration', *Journal of the American Statistical Association*, March 1968, pp. 228–41.

[16] Caroline Miles, *Lancashire Textiles: A Case Study of Industrial Change*, Occasional Paper No. 23, National Institute of Economic and Social Research, Cambridge University Press, 1968.

[17] B. Morris, 'Multi-dimensional Aspects of Market Structure and Market Performance', No. 12, Warwick Economic Research Papers, Sept. 1970.

[18] Ralph L. Nelson, *Concentration in the Manufacturing Industries of the United States*, Yale University Press, 1965.

[19] B. Peter Pashigian, 'The Effect of Market Size on Concentration', *International Economic Review*, October 1969, pp. 291–314.

[20] B. Peter Pashigian, 'Market Concentration in the United States and Great Britain', *Journal of Law and Economics*, 1968, pp. 299–319.

[21] C. Pratten and R. M. Dean, *The Economics of Large-Scale Production in British Industry: An Introductory Study*, Cambridge University Press, 1965.

[22] Frederic L. Pryor, 'An International Comparison of Industrial Concentration', mimeographed, 1970.

[23] C. K. Rowley, 'The Monopolies Commission and Rate of Return on Capital', *Economic Journal*, 1969, pp. 42–65.

[24] Gideon Rosenbluth, *Concentration in Canadian Manufacturing Industries*, Princeton University Press, 1957.

[25] F. M. Scherer, *Industrial Market Structure and Economic Performance*, Rand McNally, 1970.

[26] MICHAEL SHANKS, ed., *The Lessons of Public Enterprise*, Jonathan Cape, 1963.

[27] WILLIAM G. SHEPHERD, 'A Comparison of Industrial Concentration in the United States and Britain', *Review of Economics and Statistics*, 1961, pp. 70–77.

[28] WILLIAM G. SHEPHERD, 'Changes in British Industrial Concentration, 1951–1958', *Oxford Economic Papers*, 1966, pp. 126–32.

[29] WILLIAM G. SHEPHERD, *Market Power and Economic Welfare: An Introduction*, Random House, 1970.

[30] WILLIAM G. SHEPHERD, 'The Elements of Market Structure', mimeographed, 1970.

[31] WILLIAM G. SHEPHERD, 'Trends of Concentration in American Manufacturing Industries, 1947–1958', *Review of Economics and Statistics*, 1964, pp. 200–12.

[32] G. J. STIGLER, ed., *Business Concentration and Price Policy*, Princeton University Press, 1955.

[33] U.K. Board of Trade, *Overseas Trade Accounts of the United Kingdom*, H.M.S.O., December edition, annual.

[34] U.K. Board of Trade, *Report on the Census of Production*, 1963, Vol. 131. H.M.S.O., 1969.

[35] U.K. Committee of Inquiry into the Aircraft Industry, 1964–1965 (Plowden Committee), *Report*, Cmnd. 2853, H.M.S.O., 1965.

[36] U.K. Committee of Inquiry into the Relationship of the Pharmaceutical Industry with the National Health Service, 1965–1967, Sainsbury Committee), *Report*, Cmnd. 3410, H.M.S.O., 1967.

[37] U.K. Monopolies Commission, Reports on *The Supply of Cigarettes and Tobacco and of Cigarette and Tobacco Machinery*, H. of C. 218, 1961; *The Supply of Household Detergents*, H. of C. 105, 1966; *The Supply of Flat Glass*, H. of C. 83, 1968; *The Supply of Man-made Cellulosic Fibres*, H. of C. 130, 1968; *The Supply and Export of Pneumatic Tyres*, H. of C. 133, 1955; *The Supply of Chemical Fertilizers*, H. of C. 267, 1959.

[38] U.S. Bureau of the Census, *Concentration Ratios in Manufacturing Industry, 1966*, M66(AS)-8, U.S. Government Printing Office, 1968.

[39] U.S. Senate Subcommittee on Antitrust and Monopoly, *Concentration Ratios in Manufacturing Industry*, 1963, Parts I and II, U.S. Government Printing Office, 1966.

[40] LEONARD W. WEISS, 'Average Concentration Ratios and Industrial Performance', *Journal of Industrial Economics*, July 1963, pp. 237–54.

[41] LEONARD W. WEISS, 'Econometric Studies of Industrial Organization', mimeographed.

[42] DEAN A. WORCESTER, Jr., *Monopoly, Big Business and Welfare in the United States*, University of Washington Press, 1967.

APPENDIX TABLE I

U.K. INDUSTRIES WITH SUBSTANTIAL MARKET POWER

S.I.C. code[a]	Name	Total sales 1963[b] (£ million)	Minimum estimate of:[c] Estimated imports as a % of all domestic sales, 1969 (%)	Minimum estimate of:[c] Foreign-firm branches' sales as a % of all domestic sales 1969 (%)	Approximate date of most recent major change in structure	Possible public-agency or public-firm constraint
311 3	Iron and steel	1840	10	0	1968	British Steel Corp. public ownership of 70%; 1961
463	Flat glass	125	0	0	1945–51	
240	Tobacco products	309	0	35	pre-1930	
395	Metal containers	85	0	0	pre-1950	
216	Sugar	198	0	0	pre-1950	Sugar board
464	Cement	84	0	0	1948–56	
271	Compressed gases	41	0	0	pre-1950	
499	Film	30	0	70	1966–68	
411	Man-made fibres	172	10	5	1956–62	
275 2	Electrical machinery	440	20	10	1968	Central Electricity Generating Board
363	Communications apparatus	154	20	20	1968	Post Office
275 2	Soaps and Detergents	77	2	45	1945–54	
272 1	Pharmaceutical products	41	20	60	pre-1960	National Health Service
369 3	Electric lamps	23	0	20	pre-1950	
262	Petroleum products	506	40	35	1960–65	
381	Motor vehicles	2081	10	50	1968	
364	Computers	32	20	37	1968	

[a] The S.I.C. code number is for the industry group in which the relevant market is located or, where available, for the specific market.
[b] Sales data refer as accurately as possible to the specific market. Data intended solely to indicate size for illustrative purposes.
[c] Estimates are for conditions in 1969 wherever possible; in several cases data are drawn from years as early as 1963. Estimates are minimum; in several cases the true value may be substantially higher.

Source: [9, 33, 34, 36, 37] plus various trade sources.

Appendix Table II

U.S. INDUSTRIES WITH SUBSTANTIAL MARKET POWER

Name[a]	Value of shipments 1966[b] ($ million)	Minimum estimate of:[c] Imports as a % of all domestic sales, 1969 (%)	Foreign-firm branch sales as a % of all domestic sales 1969 (%)	Approximate date of most recent major change in structure	Possible public-agency or public-firm constraint
Telephone equipment	10,030	0	0	pre-1930	Indirect regulation
Computers	4,833	0	0	1950–55	
Motor vehicles	45,630	11	0	pre-1950	
Heavy electrical equipment	6,500	0	0	pre-1930	Numerous public entities comprise 25% of purchasing sector
Iron and steel	24,550	19	0	1960–65	
Petroleum products	18.742	0	2	pre-1940	
Pharmaceutical products	4,432	5	3	pre-1950	Some public agencies are buyers
Soaps and detergents	2.128	0	0	pre-1950	
Electric lamps	575	0	0	pre-1930	
Photocopying equipment	1,000	0	0	1960–62	
Photographic supplies	3,286	10	0	1950–55	
Industrial chemicals	13,857	5	3	pre-1930	
Flat glass	638	0	0	pre-1935	
Copper	1,701	0	0	pre-1935	

[a] Refers in most cases to the specific industry; in some cases refers to a group of related industries most of which have substantive market power.

[b] Shipments data refer as accurately as possible to specific industries. Some are estimates. Data are intended solely to indicate approximate size for illustrative purposes.

[c] See note 3, Appendix Table 1.

[d] This is based on the rise of imports since 1960, which could be regarded more as a change of degree than of structure.

Sources: [29, 38, 39] and various other official and trade sources.

NONPRICE COMPETITION IN JET AIRCRAFT CAPACITY

by JOSEPH V. YANCE*

1. INTRODUCTION

SINCE air fares are regulated, airlines tend to compete by introducing new plane types and adding flights to provide more convenient service. A notable example of such competition, of course, is the introduction of jets, beginning in 1959. Because of their speed, and smooth flights, jets were enormously attractive to passengers. The first jets operated at load factors (ratio of passenger-miles to seat-miles) of over 90 per cent, while the average on other aircraft was 50–60 per cent. There was therefore an incentive for airlines to add jets.

Through an examination of load factor data for the period of jet introduction, this paper attempts to infer the revenue implications of jet investment by individual airlines. As jet capacity was added on an airline, the average load factor tended to decline, but allowance must be made for the fact that the load factor on an airline was also affected by the capacity changes of other airlines. The analysis indicates we can statistically distinguish the two effects.

The results illuminate the matter of capacity competition and an airline's determination of optimal capacity. My view is that the airlines, in their capacity decisions, behave like monopolistic competitors, adding capacity to the point where the additional revenue equals the cost of a flight. To put it another way, they tend to add capacity to the point where the marginal load factor is equal to a break-even level determined by fares and costs. During the process of jet introduction, the marginal load factor presumably tended to the break-even level. At the same time, the reduction in demand for propeller aircraft services led to reductions in propeller capacity to maintain their load factors at a break-even level.

The analysis is consistent with recent theoretical work [2], [4], [6] and is relevant to regulatory proceedings in which the ability of individual airlines to control load factors has been an issue.[1]

* I wish to thank James C. Miller III, U.S. Dept. of Transportation, for helpful comments.

[1] Domestic Passenger Fare Investigation, C.A.B. Docket 21866, e.g.[1]. The inability of individual airlines to control load factors is also cited by American, T.W.A., and United as the basis for their proposal to jointly control capacity in certain markets (Joint Statement by said airlines filed August 28th, 1970, C.A.B. Docket 22525). Permission has since been granted.

2. THEORY

The first jet schedules of U.S. airlines were flown in late 1958 on international routes, and service on the domestic trunk airlines began in December, 1958. Average load factor during the first two quarters of 1959 was over 92 per cent, so attractive were the jets, and for the year the average load factor was 79.9 per cent (Table I), markedly higher than that on propeller aircraft (Table VII). Since the seat-mile cost on jets was lower than that on other types of aircraft, and the ticket price somewhat higher,[2] the jets were extremely profitable. Here, we attempt to measure the revenue implications of additions to jet capacity.

TABLE I

JET OPERATIONS AND RELATION TO TOTAL
(figures in 000,000's)

	Jet				
	R.P.M.	*A.S.M.*	*(%) L.F.*	*Total A.S.M.*	*% Jet of A.S.M.*
1958	—	—	—	40,695.0	0.0
1959	3,065.8	3,839.0	79.9	45,793.2	8.4
1960	9,995.2	14,356.9	69.6	49,153.6	29.2
1961	15,595.9	26,207.1	59.5	52,525.0	50.0
1962	20,743.0	38,681.5	53.6	59,736.8	64.8
1963	25,538.9	47,264.6	54.0	69,601.3	69.9
1964	30,842.4	55,803.1	55.3	75,242.4	74.2

Note: R.P.M.—revenue passenger-miles in scheduled service; A.S.M.—available seat-miles in scheduled service; L.F.—average load factor. Compiled from [7].

It is clear that the revenue-production of jet additions cannot be estimated by the average load factor since, as jets were added, the load factor declined. A possible method of estimating the addition in jet passenger-miles resulting from additional jet service would be simply to calculate incremental magnitudes over time for each. Suppose jet traffic and capacity for an airline are as follows:

EXAMPLE 1

	1960	*1961*	*Change*
Jet passenger-miles	600,000	660,000	60,000
Jet seat-miles	1,000,000	1,200,000	200,000
Ave. Load Factor	60%	55%;	gross M.L.F. = 30%

If we can assume passenger demand did not change during this period, the ratio of increments, what we might call gross marginal

[2] As the result of a jet surcharge of $1 to $10, amounting to about 9 per cent of ticket price (*Aviation Week*, Oct. 12, 1959).

load factor (M.L.F.), suggests that additional passenger-miles resulting from 1961 investment were only 30 per cent of additional seat-miles. Further additions would presumably have been less productive.

This measure implies that all of the change in jet passenger-miles from one year to the next on a particular airline is due to changes in jet capacity on that airline. However, we would also have to take into account the (negative) effect that may have been brought about by additions of capacity on other lines.

During the period when jets were being introduced, it is quite likely that if an airline had not increased capacity in a particular year, its jet passenger-miles would have decreased because jets were being added by other airlines. In terms of the example, it could be that because of additions to capacity of other airlines, if this airline had stood still in 1961 it would have lost, say, 40,000 jet passenger-miles. The effect of the jet additions on a particular airline is the difference between what would have happened if it had made no additions, and what actually happened. Considering the loss in jet traffic if it had made no additions to capacity, the marginal traffic due to additions to its jet capacity is really 100,000 passenger-miles. The marginal load factor due only to changes in jet capacity on its own line is, then, 50 per cent:

EXAMPLE 2

		1961	*1961*	
	1960	*If no change in jet capacity*	*With added jet capacity*	*Effect of added jets*
Jet R.P.M.	600,000	560,000	660,000	+100,000
Jet A.S.M.	1,000,000	1,000,000	1,200,000	+200,000
Ave. L.F.	60%	56%	55%;	M.L.F. = 50%

It can be seen that if there is such a competitive effect, the *gross M.L.F.* underestimates the M.L.F. relevant to investment decisions. The gross M.L.F. of 30 per cent suggests that the additions were uneconomic. However, capacity has been added at a M.L.F. of 50 per cent in terms of 'own-M.L.F.'. Since an airline has practically no control over what its competitors do, what is relevant to its decisions is the effect of additions to its own capacity, not the combined effect of competitors' investment and its own.

In the analysis below, the hypothesized effects are shown using average load factor rather than marginal load factor. Holding jet capacity of other airlines and traffic demand constant, the effect of investment in jet capacity by an individual airline is represented by one of the lines in Fig. 1, say 1960.

The effect of competitive jet additions from one year to the next is to shift the function down. Thus, we postulate that the observed average load factors from one year to the next which trace out a line (through AB) do not indicate the effect of an airline's additional jet capacity. Rather, if in 1961 an airline had not added jet capacity, its average load factor would have fallen to C, and capacity additions in 1961 would be located along the line through CB. C, of course, is not directly observable; in the next section, the matter of estimation is discussed.

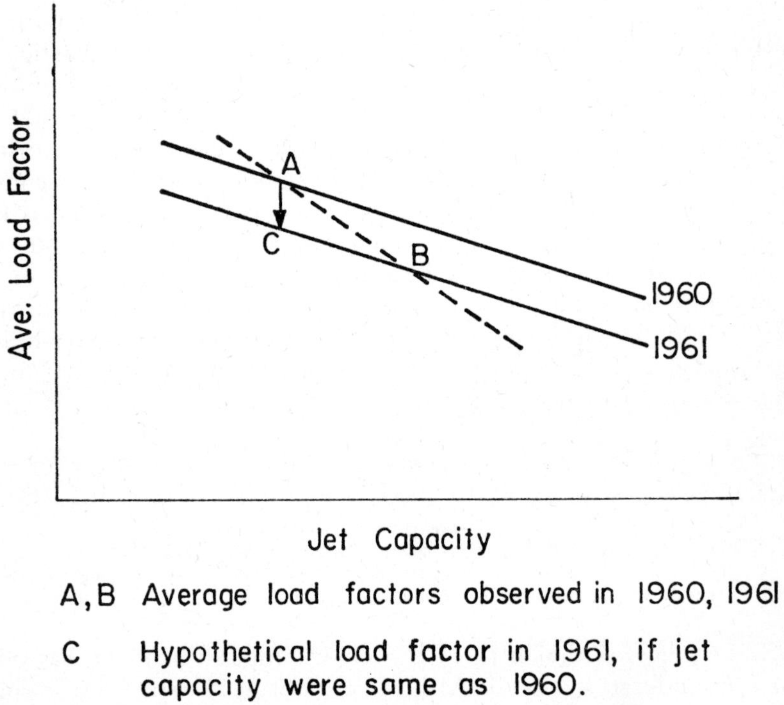

Fig. 1. Average load factor as a function of jet capacity

In the statistical analysis, the relation between ALF and jet capacity is normalized for different sized airlines by measuring jet capacity relative to the total capacity (propeller plus jet seat-miles).

If the proportion of capacity flown by jets on two individual airlines were the same and both faced the same amount of competitive jet capacity, load factors would not necessarily be equal because other factors, specific to each airline, may affect the average load factor (A.L.F.). In the regression analysis, variables which were tried include density of traffic on an airline's routes, stage length, and the number of hours planes are used daily (i.e. aircraft utilization).

TABLE II

JET AVERAGE LOAD FACTOR, BY AIRLINE*

Year	AA	BN	CO	DL	EA	NA	NE	NW	TW	UA	WA	Overall Ave. L.F.
1959	82.9	60.9	59.8	65.1	—	81.4	65.7	—	83.1	74.9	—	79.9
1960	71.6	70.0	51.9	68.1	67.1	77.0	65.3	61.8	68.6	73.2	70.1	69.6
1961	63.6	61.5	46.1	64.9	56.2	62.7	51.6	53.0	55.6	61.5	58.7	59.5
1962	56.8	53.2	43.4	63.1	50.6	52.6	54.5	53.0	49.1	54.0	55.7	53.6
1953	58.0	52.4	49.5	63.3	50.6	52.2	51.7	50.0	51.9	53.0	54.7	54.0
1964	58.9	53.1	48.1	58.7	56.4	51.0	55.1	52.5	56.1	52.3	60.0	55.3

* Respectively, American, Braniff, Continental, Delta, Eastern, National, Northeast, Northwest, Trans World, United and Western. Data sources for all tables are [7]–[9].

When the operating conditions are taken into account, the experience of each airline contributes some information about the hypothesized functional effect of jet capacity on average load factor.

3. EMPIRICAL ANALYSIS

The analysis attempts to explain variations in jet load factors for the 11 U.S. domestic trunk airlines, during the period in which jets were being introduced, 1959–63. At the same time, propeller aircraft were being withdrawn, as discussed in the next section.

TABLE III

QUARTERLY DATE FOR 1959, ARRANGED BY QUARTER

Obs.	*Airline*	*A.L.F.*	*O.I.C.*	*C*	*D(lagged)*	*S.L.*	*Seasonal index*
1	AA	94.3	.61	3.72	.6978	1,877	0
2	NA	89.0	.66	8.62	.3487	1,088	1
3	TW	93.4	1.18	.46	.5968	1,844	0
4	AA	92.5	2.48	15.47	.6978	1,877	1
5	NA	77.5	4.73	4.01	.3487	1,088	1
6	TW	95.3	3.44	12.61	.5968	1,844	1
7	CO	82.7	4.66	6.80	.0921	1,244	1
8	AA	86.6	8.32	26.46	.6978	1,877	1
9	TW	88.1	7.26	31.31	.5698	1,844	1
10	CO	63.5	9.85	40.34	.0921	1,244	1
11	DL	66.6	11.40	.70	.2495	888	0
12	UA	88.7	12.74	.36	.7587	1,662	1
13	AA	75.4	11.86	33.71	.6978	1,877	0
14	NA	76.5	16.11	11.41	.3487	1,088	0
15	TW	74.3	12.49	36.21	.5968	1,844	0
16	CO	55.1	14.76	48.32	.0921	1,244	0
17	DL	65.0	15.97	15.05	.2495	888	0
18	UA	74.3	16.97	9.30	.7587	1,662	0
19	BN	60.9	16.47	.79	.1500	1,065	0
20	NE	65.7	16.22	1.57	.1605	1,093	0

For the most part, the analysis is carried out in terms of annual data, but early in the period average load factors were changing so rapidly that quarterly data is utilized.

Table II presents *annual* jet A.L.F.'s for each of the trunk carriers. Note that entries for Braniff, Delta, Northeast and United indicate either an increase in load factor from 1959 to 1960 or a very small decrease, while other airlines experienced a substantial decrease, as one might expect. The reason for the untoward observations appears to be that jets were operated on these airlines only during the last quarters of 1959. The rapid decrease in load factors during the year, and seasonal effects, combine to give annual observations for these lines that are unusually low.

The effect of aggregating quarterly data for 1959 can be illustrated by examining United's experience. Annual A.L.F.'s for 1959 for American, T.W.A., and United are 82.9, 83.1 and 74.9 per cent respectively. This suggests that United's jets produced less revenue than those of its two major transcontinental competitors. However, consider the quarterly data presented in Table III. United's jet operations began only in the third quarter of 1959. During the third and fourth quarters, its A.L.F. was almost the same as those of its two major competitors. The figures dramatically illustrate (1) the effect of jet capacity on reducing load factor, as evidenced by the decline from 92 per cent in the first quarter, when only 1.1 per cent of industry seat-mile capacity was jet, to 72.3 per cent during the fourth quarter, by which time 15.9 per cent of the industry's seat-mile capacity was jet, and (2) the probable competitive effect of jets, in that United's jet capacity was introduced at load factors almost equal to those of its major competitors.

The quarterly analysis was carried out for 1960 as well as for 1959. However, the best overall description of jet load factors during the 1960–63 period is contained in a single equation which explains annual jet load factors.

Quarterly Analysis for 1959 and 1960

Quarterly data on average jet load factors are explained in terms of the airline's jet capacity, industry jet capacity, and other variables which denote operating conditions. While the first-mentioned variables are given by quarter, the variables denoting operating conditions are given in annual terms. Annual data may sufficiently differentiate the operating conditions under which various airlines operate.

The hypothesized effect of 'own' jet capacity and the jet capacity of other airlines has been discussed. The rationale for the other factors might be mentioned. Data for 1959 suggests that jet flights over long-stage lengths were more attractive than over medium-stage lengths. The initial transcontinental jet flights attained load factors of over 90 per cent, while those on the initial NY-Miami flights by National were lower. Hence, average jet stage length is included as a variable.

Initial load factors on some of the smaller airlines were quite low, apparently due to the low density of passengers per day on their routes, so density was included as a variable. In order that the equation could be used for purposes of forecasting, previous-year density values were adopted.

Though it turned out not to have a significant effect, daily utilization was tried as an explanatory variable. This was suggested by reports of Continental's practice of using planes many hours a day, even though load factors were carried to quite low levels.

Finally, load factors were postulated to vary with seasonal changes in traffic demand; dummy variables were used to denote peak and off-peak seasons for individual airlines.

In summary, the variables used in the analysis include:

ALF_i Average jet load factor on airline i: jet passenger-miles on a given airline/jet seat-miles on the airline, by quarter. Per cent.

C_i Own jet capacity: jet available seat-miles/total available seat-miles, by quarter. Per cent.

OIC_i Other industry jet capacity: jet seat-miles on airlines other than airline i/total available seat-miles on those other airlines, by quarter. Per cent.

SL_i Average jet stage length: jet plane-miles on a given airline/number of jet departures, annually. Miles.

D_i Density of traffic on airline i: total revenue passenger miles/route-miles, annually; previous year. In millions.

δ_i Seasonal variable. This variable, which may take the value 0 (if a quarter has below-average seasonal traffic) or 1 (above-average seasonal traffic), is derived from monthly indexes of first-class traffic and of coach and economy traffic weighted equally, and includes two high seasons for each airline.

The estimated equation, where the subscript t refers to the quarter, is given in Table IV, together with the standard error of the coefficients and the t-statistics. The equation explains 88 per cent of the variation in A.L.F.

The meaning of the equation can be seen by considering the case of T.W.A. During 1959, its average jet stage length was 1844 miles, its density (lagged) was .5968. Hence, if other industry jet capacity were zero, its load factor could be represented by:

$$A.L.F._{T.W.A.} = 94.53 - .229\, C_{T.W.A.} + 4.67\, \delta_t$$

In the first quarter, on its initial jet capacity, the average load factor would be 94.53 per cent and the average load factor would decrease by .229 for each one per cent increment in jet capacity. In a peak season, the variable δ would take the value unity, and average load factor would be expected to be 4.67 per cent greater than in an off-peak quarter.

Somewhat similar results were obtained for a quarterly analysis of

1960 (at least the critical coefficient for own-jet capacity was about the same, −.202), though this time less of the variation in A.L.F. was explained ($\bar{R}^2 = .61$). The resulting estimating equation was:

$$\text{A.L.F.}_{\cdot it} = 69.42 - .235\ \text{O.I.C.}_{\cdot it} - .202 C_{it} + 8.95\ \delta_{it} + 17.55\ D_i(\text{lagged})$$
$$n = 40 \qquad \bar{R}^2 = .61$$

During this year other industry jet capacity was larger and the curve as a whole showing the relation between A.L.F. and own jet capacity was shifted down. Stage length turns out to have a negative sign when included, so was omitted in calculating the above. The coefficients in the above are quite significant, particularly the coefficient of C_{it} which has a t-statistic of 3.99. Less emphasis is placed on the 1960 results, since the period is included in an equation for the years 1960–63.[3]

TABLE IV

REGRESSION EQUATION FOR 1959
(Quarterly Data)

Variable	*Regr. coef.*	*Std. error*	*t-stat.*	*Mean value of variable*
Constant	70.4002	6.9747		
OIC_{it}	−.9425	.2312	4.0763	9.41
C_{it}	−.2288	.0835	2.7377	15.36
δ_{it}	4.6743	2.2700	2.0591	.45
D_i (lagged)	17.8044	8.6453	2.0594	.4414
SL_i	.0070	.0062	1.1345	1,456.9

Std. deviation of A.L.F. = 12.1592.
Std. error of estimate = 4.1495.
n = 20
$\bar{R}^2 = .88$.

Analysis of Annual Data, 1960–63

After 1959, the airlines generally operated jets throughout the year, so the annual average load factors are less misleading than in 1959. However, there is so little variation in the jet A.L.F. among airlines in some of these years that it is difficult to get precise estimates of the effect of capacity. This lack of variation in load factors has an economic basis; airlines tend to add jet capacity to the point where further additions would be unprofitable, and this tends to lead to the same A.L.F. for different airlines. In any case, there is a statistical problem here, for which one solution is to obtain sharper estimates of slope coefficients by pooling the cross-section data of different years [3, Ch. 5].

[3] The observation for Northwest, fourth quarter, was omitted because of a strike affecting jet flights.

TABLE V

OBSERVATIONS FOR CROSS-SECTION EQUATIONS, 1960–63 (Bracketed observations omitted)

1960	*A.L.F.*	*C*	*D(t−1)*	*S.L.*
AA	71.6	46.2	.8002	1566
BN	70.0	17.8	.1720	764
CO	51.9	56.3	.1492	1159
DL	68.1	29.1	.2718	818
EA	67.1	8.7	.6244	766
NA	77.0	19.8	.3769	1035
NE	65.3	11.0	.2046	1068
[NW	61.8	.7	.2833	1551]
TW	68.6	43.3	.6387	1570
UA	73.2	40.7	.7208	1089
WA	70.1	8.5	.1891	590
1961	*A.L.F.*	*C*	*D(t−1)*	*S.L.*
AA	63.6	64.3	.8941	1189
BN	61.5	26.5	.1984	650
CO	46.1	63.0	.1983	952
DL	64.9	45.2	.3202	741
EA	56.2	20.9	.5315	846
NA	62.7	35.2	.3447	991
NE	51.6	48.1	.2262	804
[NW	53.0	32.0	.2767	882]
TW	55.6	68.8	.6266	1053
UA	61.5	61.4	.8315	844
WA	58.7	33.0	.2041	644
1962	*A.L.F.*	*C*	*D(t−1)*	*S.L.*
AA	56.8	73.8	.8621	1042
BN	53.2	37.5	.1991	620
CO	43.4	70.9	.2102	803
DL	63.1	61.9	.3109	688
[EA	50.6	41.8	.5012	646]
NA	52.6	50.4	.2406	933
NE	54.5	53.7	.3056	787
NW	53.0	51.6	.2098	726
TW	49.1	82.1	.6088	939
UA	54.0	72.4	.8216	741
WA	55.7	43.1	.1862	570
1963	*A.L.F.*	*C*	*D(t−1)*	*S.L.*
AA	58.0	79.2	.9407	1010
BN	52.4	46.6	.2115	606
CO	49.5	77.2	.2228	780
DL	63.3	68.2	.3250	645
EA	50.6	46.0	.4415	585
NA	52.2	63.9	.2582	797
NE	51.7	57.5	.3038	785
NW	50.0	59.0	.2958	640
TW	51.9	87.6	.6367	879
UA	53.0	76.7	.8040	752
WA	54.7	49.4	.2639	509

It is hypothesized here that the effect of own jet capacity on load factor is the same in each of the years. The level of the A.L.F. function may change, however, due to the effect of industry jet additions (pushing it down) or increases in traffic demand (moving it up). We therefore allow the intercept of the average load factor function to change from year to year (representing these effects), but obtain a single estimate of the slope coefficient. In addition, the density variable is useful in explaining variations in A.L.F. The equation estimated is:

$$A.L.F._{it} = a_0 + a_1 C_{it} + a_2 D_{it-1} + a_3 SL_{it} + a_4(1961) + a_5(1962) + a_6(1963)$$

where t now represents the year. The variables associated with a_4, a_5 and a_6 are dummy variables taking the value 1 for the year indicated, 0 otherwise. Thus, the constant for the equation in 1960 is simply a_0. In 1961, the constant is $a_0 + a_4$; in 1962, the constant is $a_0 + a_5$.

TABLE VI

REGRESSION ANALYSIS, ANNUAL DATA, 1960–63

Var.	*Regr. coef.*	*Coef. std. error*	*t-stat.*	*Partial r*
Constant	68.2668	2.1506		
C_{it}	−.1745	0.582	2.9970	−.4519
D_{it-1}	11.9001	3.5493	3.3527	−.4930
(1961)	−7.1816	2.3655	3.0359	−.4565
(1962)	−9.0038	2.8470	3.1625	−.4714
(1963)	−8.6774	2.9661	2.9255	−.4432

$\bar{R}^2 = .6471$
n = 41
Std. deviation of A.L.F. = 7.9598
Std. error of estimate = 4.7860

Of the 44 potential observations, three (Northwest in 1960 and 1961 and Eastern in 1962) were omitted because of long strikes, during which flights were suspended. The data are given in Table V and the results are shown in Table VI. Stage length did not turn out to have explanatory value (t- statistic less than one) and hence only the equation which omits stage length is presented in Table VI.

A considerable amount of the variation in A.L.F. is accounted for by the dummy variables—the shifting of the A.L.F. function from year to year—but own jet capacity and density have significant coefficients. The C_i coefficient is a negative .1745. There is a significant downward shift in the A.L.F. function in 1961 (−7.18 per cent) which presumably represents the effect of industry jet additions on the load factor of particular airlines. That is, if an airline operated the same proportion of its capacity in jets in 1961 as in 1960, the average load factor would have gone down by 7.18 per cent. There was only a slight further shift downward in 1962 (presumably because traffic began to increase rapidly), and a slight shift upward in 1963 relative to 1962 (when the rate of traffic growth increased). The dummy variables for the different years seem to represent reasonably the combined effect on load factors of industry jet capacity and traffic demand.

To illustrate the equation, putting the actual values of density (D) and jet capacity (C) for T.W.A. into the equation (from Table V), the following are the expected values of A.L.F. compared to actual:

T.W.A.

	Actual %	*Expected* %
1960	68.6	68.3
1961	55.6	56.5
1962	49.1	52.2
1963	51.9	51.9

4. CAPACITY DECISIONS

The determination of an airline's profit-maximizing capacity is examined elsewhere [2], but may be sketched here. Assume there is only one kind of capacity (e.g. jet) and that an airline faces a declining load factor function—that is, as an airline adds flights (seat-miles), the more convenient service stimulates new traffic or attracts passengers from other airlines, but the traffic increase is less than proportional to the capacity change. Assume further that an airline takes into account the effect of capacity additions only on its own traffic, and not the repercussions on, and possible reactions of, its competitors.[4]

A.L.F. multiplied by the revenue per passenger-mile gives average revenue per seat-mile. Hence, from the A.L.F. function, we obtain average revenue as a function of capacity (A.R. in Fig. 2). In making capacity decisions, an airline is interested not in average revenue, but in the marginal revenue associated with additional seat-miles offered. The M.R. function may be derived mathematically from the A.R. function and will be related to it as shown in the figure.

A profit-maximizing airline would add capacity to the point where M.R. per seat-mile equals marginal cost per seat-mile, which

[4] The assumption that airlines act as 'monopolistic competitors' in their capacity decisions is also made by De Vany in [2]. Melvin A. Brenner, of T.W.A., presents instances which can be interpreted in this way, as well as cases in which interdependence is more markedly perceived [1].

is assumed constant in Fig. 2 (M.C.). Thus, C_0 is the profit-maximizing capacity.

If other airlines add capacity, the A.L.F. function and associated revenue functions will shift. But for equilibrium among airlines, the condition M.R. = M.C. must eventually hold for each.

Suppose average cost is equal to marginal cost; then monopoly profit is represented by the area *abde*. If entry to the airline industry were free, the existence of profits would attract new firms and the A.R. function would shift to the left, reducing optimal capacity and monopoly profits. However, with entry of firms restricted, each other airline will be constrained by profit maximization to add a limited amount of capacity and hence positive profit for each airline can

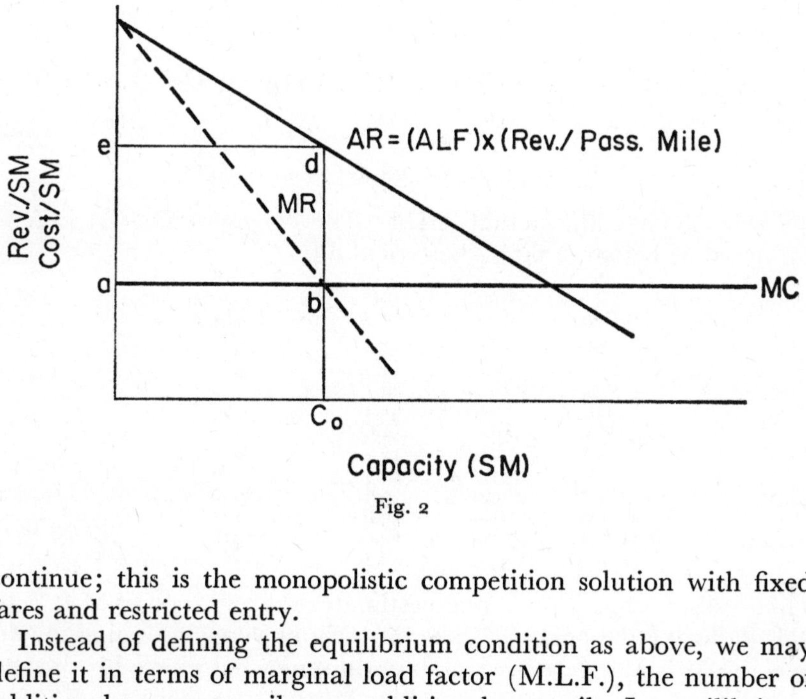

Fig. 2

continue; this is the monopolistic competition solution with fixed fares and restricted entry.

Instead of defining the equilibrium condition as above, we may define it in terms of marginal load factor (M.L.F.), the number of additional passenger-miles per additional seat-mile. In equilibrium, from the above:

$$\text{M.L.F.} \times \text{P} = \text{M.C.},$$

where P is revenue per passenger-mile; alternatively,

$$\text{M.L.F.} = \text{M.C./P}$$

The effect of increasing P is to lower the break-even M.L.F. It is worth noting that in terms of capacity decisions what is critical is the breakeven *marginal* load factor; this point is often missed in industry discussions.[5]

The marginal load factor corresponding to A.L.F. at particular levels of capacity may be obtained as follows. Suppose

$$\text{A.L.F.} = a - bC + eD$$

where C is capacity, in seat-miles, and D is density. Then total passenger-miles,

$$Q = (\text{A.L.F.}) \times C = aC - bC^2 + eDC$$

and the marginal load factor is

$$\text{M.L.F.} = dQ/dC = a - 2bC + eD.$$

For 1963, using C as defined in Section 3,

$$\text{A.L.F.} = 59.5894 - .1745\,C + 11.9001\,D_{t-1}$$

and

$$\text{M.L.F.} = 59.5894 - .3490\,C + 11.9001\,D_{t-1}$$

Table V gives the actual A.L.F. The corresponding M.L.F. is estimated as being (.1745)C less, yielding:

Airline	*Actual A.L.F.*	*Est. M.L.F.*	*M.L.F./A.L.F.*
AA	58.0	44.2	.76
BN	52.4	44.3	.85
CO	49.5	36.1	.73
DL	63.3	51.4	.83
EA	50.6	52.6	.84
NA	52.2	41.1	.80
NE	51.7	41.7	.81
NW	50.0	39.7	.79
TW	51.9	36.6	.71
UA	53.0	39.6	.75
WA	54.7	46.1	.83

These estimates provide a rough estimate of the relation of M.L.F. to A.L.F. during the period.[6] Since the airlines were continuing to add jets, the M.L.F.'s were presumably still somewhat above break-even levels.

[5] This analysis for the case of imperfect competition supplements the discussion of the competitive case by Miller [4, Appendix C, p. 4].

[6] There is a difficulty in using the estimated equation to determine the marginal load factor, in that it is uncertain how the measure of jet capacity varies with jet additions. The above procedure implies that a hypothetical unit increase in jet capacity is accompanied by a unit decrease in propeller capacity.

A further difficulty is that the marginal revenue from adding a unit of jet capacity should be offset by the passenger revenue loss on propeller flights. This cross-effect is neglected here and in the next section.

5. LOAD FACTORS ON PROPELLER FLIGHTS

The above analysis discussed only capacity changes resulting from the introduction of jet aircraft. During this same time period, however, propeller aircraft capacity was being reduced. In some cases, jet replaced propeller aircraft on a flight-for-flight basis. Often, however, the effect was more indirect: as jets were introduced, the load factor on propeller flights in the same market or related markets tended to fall and capacity was reduced. For instance, the introduction of transcontinental jet flights drew passengers from multi-stop propeller flights, resulting in a reduction of service between intermediate stations.

For the period covered here, propeller service was reduced by half (Table VII). It is clear that this contraction helped to keep the propeller A.L.F. up, but even so the A.L.F. was permitted to fall as much as 7 percentage points. There may be two reasons why a fall in load factor was permitted.

TABLE VII

PROPELLER AND TURBO-PROP SERVICE, DOMESTIC TRUNK AIRLINES

	R.P.M. (*000,000*)	*A.S.M.* (*000,000*)	*Ave. L.F.* (%)
1959	25,061.4	41,954.0	59.8
1960	19,238.0	34,796.7	55.3
1961	13,938.9	26,317.9	52.9
1962	11,084.8	21,055.3	52.8
1963	10,844.8	20,336.7	53.3
1964	10,816.0	19,439.3	55.8

Source: [7].

First, there were across-the-board fare increases in 1960 (2.5 per cent plus $1 per ticket) and 1962 (3 per cent), according to [8]. An increase in fare level would tend to reduce breakeven M.L.F. (and probably observed A.L.F.).

Second, the introduction of jets greatly reduced the opportunity cost of propeller aircraft services. During a period of propeller capacity expansion, airlines would determine optimal capacity in terms of the long-run marginal cost per seat-mile, which would include the cost of capital services per seat-mile (depreciation and interest). This is indicated in Fig. 3. The airline faced with the average and marginal revenue functions A.R., M.R., adds capacity to the point (C_0) where M.R. = short-run marginal cost (S.M.C.) = long-run marginal or fully allocated cost (L.M.C.).

However, with the introduction of jets, the cost of propeller capital services was significantly reduced (because the propeller aircraft were worth much less). Assuming the cost of propeller aircraft services (depreciation and interest) can be ignored, airlines would use propeller aircraft to the point where the marginal revenue per seat-mile is equal to variable cost. Thus, when propeller traffic drops to the extent indicated by AR′, MR′, the break-even marginal load factor drops. Judging from the data, the corresponding average load factor also falls. This is indicated in the diagram by smaller average revenue per seat-mile ($AR_1 < AR_0$).

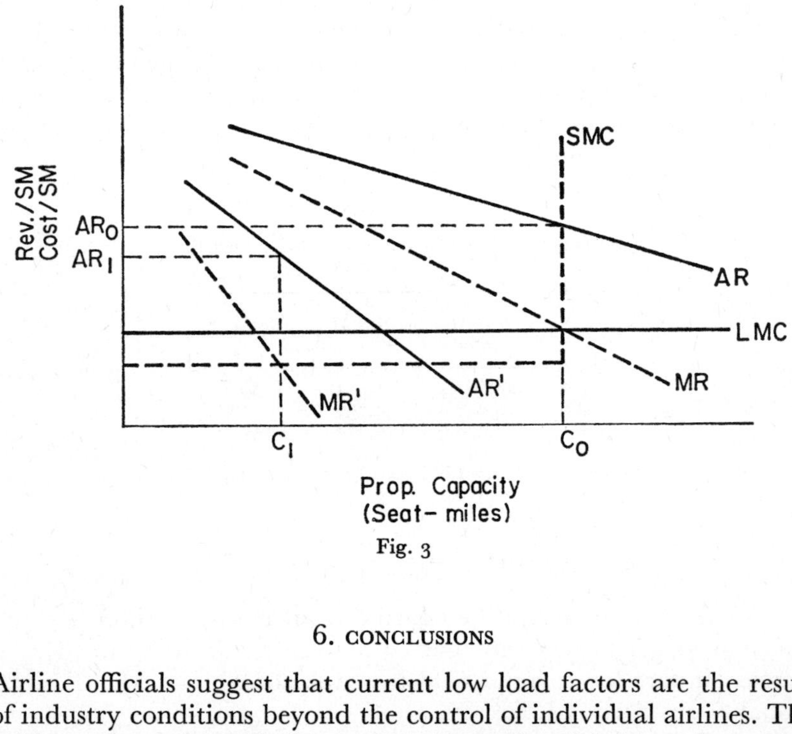

Fig. 3

6. CONCLUSIONS

Airline officials suggest that current low load factors are the result of industry conditions beyond the control of individual airlines. The evidence from the early jet period contradicts this idea, since own-jet additions are found to have a significant effect on load factor. The ability of airlines to control load factors is particularly evident for propeller aircraft, where airlines were apparently able to maintain operations at a break-even level through capacity reductions.

Analysis of a more recent period would require a different approach than that used here. At the present time, practically all the domestic trunk capacity is jet (in the last quarter of 1968, 97.8 per cent of the revenue passenger-miles were on jets). Hence, in explaining recent changes in load factors, it would not be useful to measure jet capacity in relation to total seat-miles, as is done here. In [5] Miller and I present some indication that the relative change from one year to the next in total capacity of an individual airline may be useful in explaining the change in its load factor.

BOSTON UNIVERSITY

REFERENCES

[1] MELVIN A. BRENNER, 'Discussion of Airline Load Factors and Capacity', Domestic Passenger Fare Investigation, C.A.B. Docket 21866–6, Exhibit TW 6011.

[2] ARTHUR DE VANY, 'Theory of the Airline Firm', unpublished paper, University of California at Los Angeles, 1969.

[3] EDWIN KUH, *Capital Stock Growth: A Micro-Economic Approach*, North-Holland Publishing Co., Amsterdam, 1963.

[4] JAMES C. MILLER III, *Testimony*, C.A.B. Docket 21866–6, Department of Transportation Exhibit No. DOT-T-1, Washington, D.C., July 1970.

[5] Rebuttal Testimony, C.A.B. Docket 21866–6, Department of Transportation Exhibit DOT-RT-1, Washington, D.C., July 1970.

[6] GEORGE J. STIGLER, 'Price and Nonprice Competition', *Journal of Political Economy*, Vol. LXXII, No. 1 (Feb. 1968).

Data Sources

[7] *Quarterly Comparative Statement of Air Carriers' Operating Statistics*, Domestic Trunk Airlines, Air Transport Association, Washington, D.C., various issues. (Seat-mile, passenger-mile and plane-mile data).[7]

[8] *Handbook of Airline Statistics*, Civil Aeronautics Board, Washington, D.C. 1965 edition. (Route-miles, information on strikes).

[9] *Airport Activity Statistics*, C.A.B. and Federal Aviation Administration, Washington, D.C., various years. (Departures).

[7] Copies of laboriously compiled data on jet passenger-miles and seat-miles, by airline, will be provided on request to the author.

SOME PRELIMINARY EVIDENCE OF IMPERFECTIONS IN MARKETS

by Richard W. Furst and Robert E. Markland

The analysis of security and commodity markets in industrial countries has long been a subject of interest to men who hoped to develop predictive formulae applicable to the prices in such markets. Until fairly recently, the study of such prices was primarily the domain of the speculator rather than the academician.[1] Speculators have always sought profits in excess of the average obtained in the market, inherently believing that they could profit in the market from specialized knowledge. Recently, however, economists and statisticians have become interested in the relationships of security and commodity markets as ideal, or perfect markets. In such an ideal or perfect market, speculative profits based on past price data should not exist, and stocks or commodities in such a market should always be at some intrinsic price level subject only to random fluctuations.

While there is not widespread agreement on the stochastic nature of security and commodity prices, a generalized theory of such behavior has arisen. Known as the random walk theory of security prices,[2] it is dependent upon the assumption that the current market price of a security will reflect all information available to the participants in the market at any point in time. If this is true, price changes in a security should be independent of past history concerning the security, and tomorrow's security price should have the characteristic of a random variable around some intrinsic value. This concept of security prices, as being composed of independent random increments, implies that the investor cannot use historical price movement to make buy and sell decisions that would result in greater profit than would be obtained with a simple buy and hold strategy.

Academic research concerning the random walk hypothesis has been largely empirical, and can be generally divided into two major categories. The first and largest body of research has involved statistical tests of prices over time. In general, research of this variety has tended to support the hypothesis that security price changes are

[1] The pioneering academic research in this subject was done by Louis Bachelier in a doctoral thesis presented to the Faculty of Sciences of the Academy of Paris in 1900.

[2] An excellent summary of previous research concerning the random walk hypothesis is: Paul H. Cootner, ed., *The Random Character of Stock Market Prices* (Cambridge, Massachusetts: The M.I.T. Press, 1964).

independent random variables. Studies by Fama [7], Kendall [11], Larson [12], Mandelbrot [14], Moore [15], Roberts [16] and Smidt [18] are among the more important works of this nature.

A second body of empirical research has been concerned with testing a variety of mechanical trading rules, such as those that might be employed by a market technician. If the random walk theory of security prices is valid, mechanical trading rules should not result in a profit in excess of that attainable by a simple buy and hold strategy. Results of tests made in this area vary considerably as to support or non-support of the random walk hypothesis. Research by Cootner [4], Fama and Blume [8], Seelenfreund, Parker and Van Horne [17], and Van Horne and Parker [20] tend to support the random walk hypothesis. A list of the research tending to refute the hypothesis would include papers by Alexander [1], Houthaker [10] and Levy [13].

This paper presents an extension of the previous work concerning testing of the random walk hypothesis by means of mechanical trading rules. However, the present study is unique in several aspects. First, our objective in the study was to determine if there are imperfections in the market for common stocks which can be identified through the use of a mechanical trading rule. These imperfections could be caused by a variety of factors such as unusual liquidity demands of stockholders, some unusual political or social development, or perhaps the speculative bubble described by Smidt [19] as an inappropriate response to new market information. Regardless of the cause, we defined an imperfection as a significant difference between the expected price, as predicted by the forecasting model, and the actual market price existing at a particular point in time. We considered the forecasted market price to be the intrinsic value to which actual price was compared. If actual price differed significantly from expected price (intrinsic value), an imperfection was hypothesized to exist.

Second, we sought to analyze the random walk hypothesis in terms of portfolio management. Applications of the random walk theory to portfolio management have been generally neglected. Evans [6] has shown that past market prices can be used as portfolio management device by using a 'fixed investment proportion maintenance strategy.' In order to maintain a particular security's proportion in the portfolio, Evans had to buy automatically when market price declined and sell automatically when market price advanced, regardless of the magnitude of the price change. Our study differed markedly in this respect, since a buy or sell transaction took place when actual market price differed *significantly* from the market price predicted by the mechanical trading rule. This point will be discussed in some detail in a later section of this paper.

Third, the mechanical trading rule used in this study employed a triple exponential smoothing model to 'optimally' predict market prices. We rigorously sought to obtain optimum sets of market price forecasts by using a grid search procedure to determine the value of the exponential smoothing constant which minimized the coefficient of variation of the forecasting errors.[3] Seelenfreund, Parker and Van Horne [17] used a similar forecasting model, but did not attempt to obtain sets of forecasts which minimized an error criterion.

Fourth, our study involved two empirical tests. The first test determined the rate of return earned on the average investment in common stock for each security in the sample using each of two trading rule strategies and a simple buy and hold strategy. The mean rate of return was then determined for each strategy and the differences in the means were statistically tested for significance. The second test viewed the problem from a portfolio management point of view. Herein, the compound rate of return earned for each of the three strategies was determined, assuming each strategy was given the identical portfolio to manage over a specific time period.

I. THE PREDICTIVE MODEL

The mathematical model employed to predict the expected price in a given period was the triple exponential smoothing model, described by Robert G. Brown [2], [3]. Both single and double exponential smoothing models were also tested, but the triple exponential model produced the highest degree of forecasting accuracy, and was therefore used as the predictive device. Use of this model required the fitting of a second degree polynomial to each of sixty randomly selected common stock price time series. The model was used to examine each price time series sequentially over time, with the coefficients of the model being continuously updated to minimize the error in the forecast of the next period's expected price.

The predictive process of the model can be described as follows. Assume that we are at point t in time. We use the current market price, P_t, of the stock and the estimates of the polynomial coefficients of the model derived at time $t-1$, $\hat{a}_{t-1}$, $\hat{b}_{t-1}$, and $\hat{c}_{t-1}$, to update the

[3] The coefficient of variation, defined as the ratio of the standard deviation to the mean, is a commonly used measure of relative variation. In this study, the coefficient of variation was computed as the ratio of the standard deviation of the forecasting error to the mean forecasted price. It was used a comparative statistic because of the wide variation in the mean forecasted price levels of the stocks in the sample.

estimates of the polynomial coefficients at time t. This is done using the following updating relationships:

$$\hat{a}_t = P_t + (1-\alpha)^3\ (\hat{P}_{t-1} - P_t) \qquad (1)$$
$$\hat{b}_t = {}_{t-1} + \hat{b}\hat{c}_{t-1} - 3a^2/2\ (2-\alpha)\ (\hat{P}_{t-1} - P_t) \qquad (2)$$
$$\hat{c}_t = \hat{c}_{t-1} - \alpha^3\ (\hat{P}_{t-1} - P_t) \qquad (3)$$

where α = the exponential smoothing constant, $0.0 \leqslant \alpha \leqslant 1.0$.

$\hat{a}_t$ = the mean or expected market price through time t.
$\hat{b}_t$ = the trend in market price through time t.
$\hat{c}_t$ = the change in the trend in market price through time t.
$\hat{P}_{t-1}$ = the predicted price in time period $t-1$.

The market price of the stock in period $t+T$ is then predicted by the equation:

$$\hat{P}_{t,T} = \hat{a}_t + \hat{b}_t T + \tfrac{1}{2}\hat{c}_t T^2 \qquad (4)$$

D'Esposo [5] has proven that the coefficients obtained by this adaptive exponential smoothing process will yield predictions having a minimum discounted squared forecasting error. The discounting factor in this process is $1-\alpha$, where α is the exponential smoothing constant used in updating the coefficients as shown in Equations (1), (2), and (3). Use of a small value of α will give more weight to the more distant past history of prices, while use of a large value of α will give more weight to recent past history of prices. In theory, the value of α should be selected to make the predictive model sensitive to true changes in price level without overcompensating for random fluctuations in the price level.

In our use of the model an optimum value of α was selected empirically, by searching for the value of α which produced forecasts having the minimum coefficient of variation of forecasting error. A grid of eleven values of α was employed, with these values ranging from $\alpha = 0.05$ to $\alpha = 0.45$.[4] In this respect, the present research differs from that done previously by Seelenfreund, Parker and Van Horne [17]. They reported results for three values of α, 0.01, 0.05, and 0.10, but apparently did not attempt to isolate an optimum value of α, i.e., a value of α which produced the most accurate set of price forecasts.

Filter Decision Rules

In order to utilize the predictions made by the triple exponential smoothing model in making buy-or-sell decisions, it was necessary to employ a filter decision rule. The use of a filter decision rule was

[4] The values of α were .05, .10, .15, .20, .25, .30, .33, .36, .39, .42 and .45.

based on the tentative assumption of the existence of imperfections in stock market prices, but with these imperfections being obscured by 'noise' in the market (random local fluctuations in the price level). In order to profitably utilize these imperfections, it was necessary to filter out all price movements smaller than a specified size and examine only those price movements which indicated significant over-priced or under-priced securities.

A number of researchers, including Alexander [1] and Fama and Blume [8], have suggested and tested various types of filter decision rules. In our research two filter decision rules were employed, one requiring expected price to differ from actual price by at least ± 1 standard deviation, and the second requiring a difference of ± 2 standard deviations. If the predicted price of a stock was *above* the actual price by at least one (two) standard deviation(s) of the forecast error, a *buy* signal was generated. Similarly, a *sell* signal was generated when the predicted price of a stock was *below* the actual price of the stock by at least one (two) standard deviation(s) of the forecast error.

II. EMPIRICAL TESTS OF THE TRADING RULES

The results presented in this study are based on a sample of sixty common stocks picked at random from a list of securities that had been traded on the New York Stock Exchange for the five-year period of the study (1946–68). These companies are listed in Table I. Month end market prices were recorded for each company and were adjusted to reflect any stock splits or stock dividends that occurred during the period. Actual cash dividends per share were recorded, and for computational simplicity, it was assumed that they were received in January, April, July, and October.

The first two years of market price data were used to establish the coefficients for the predictive model, using the updating equations presented previously. The value for α, the exponential smoothing constant which provided the minimum amount of forecast error for each stock appears in parenthesis after each company name in Table I. The values all are higher than those employed by Parker and Van Horne [17] since they used a daily rather than monthly price series. At the beginning of the third year, a portfolio of one hundred shares of each security, based on the adjusted per share price, was purchased for each of the three strategies. Additionally, at the beginning of the third year buy-and-sell decisions were initiated for the two mechanical trading rule strategies. A round lot of shares based on the adjusted per share price was purchased at each buy signal. No capital constraints were imposed, that is, a buy order was always executed. When a sell signal was received, *all* shares of that security were sold. In a previous study [9], the authors tested various selling strategies, using a different sample of common stocks, and found the one used here to be superior. Brokerage costs were assumed to be one per cent of the dollar amount of each transaction and transactions were recorded at the trigger price.[5]

TABLE I

RANDOM SAMPLE OF SIXTY STOCKS LISTED ON NEW YORK STOCK EXCHANGE (1964–68)

Abbott Laboratories (.30)	Johnson and Johnson (.42)
Allied Supermarkets (.36)	Kansas City Power and Light (.20)
American Bank Note Co. (.20)	Kayser Roth Corp. (.30)
Associated Dry Goods Corp. (.20)	Kellogg Company (Battle Creek) (.25)
Atlantic Richfield Co. (.20)	KLM Royal Dutch Airlines (.25)
Basic Incorporated (.30)	Macy (R. H.) & Co. (.25)
Bliss and Laughlin Industries (.20)	Madison Square Garden (.30)
Carolina Clinch. and Ohio Ry. (.30)	Minnesota Power & Light (.30)
Cleveland Cliffs Iron Co. (.36)	National Service Industries (.33)
Commercial Solvents (.36)	National Tea Company (.30)
Continental Air Lines (.33)	Niagara Mohawk Power (.25)
Cudahy Co. (.30)	Northern States Power (.25)
Dentists Supply Co. (.42)	Pacific Power & Light (.20)
Dr. Pepper Company (.39)	Perkin Elmer Corp. (.25)
Firestone Tire and Rubber Co. (.20)	Phillips—Van Husen Corp. (.42)
Florida East Coast Ry. (.30)	Plough, Inc. (.25)
Food Fair Stores, Inc. (.33)	Revlon, Inc. (.36)
Foote Mineral Co. (.20)	Ryder Systems, Inc. (.25)
Freeport Sulphur Co. (.33)	Schering Corporation (.20)
General Cable Corp. (.45)	SCM Corporation (.20)
Globe Union, Inc. (.33)	Smith Kline & French Lab. (.39)
Goodrich (B. R.) Co. (.30)	Sparton Corp. (.30)
Great Northern Ry. (.42)	Stokely—Van Camp, Inc. (.42)
Gulf States Utilities (.25)	Sun Chemical Corp. (.20)
Hammond Corp. (.33)	Twentieth Century—Fox Film (.25)
Indiana General Corp. (.42)	Union Carbide Corp. (.39)
Indianapolis Power and Light (.25)	Union Pacific R. R. (.30)
International Business Machines (.30)	Utah Power and Light (.30)
International Chemical & Nuclear Corp. (.39)	Ward Foods (.45)
International Telephone and Telegraph (.36)	Westinghouse Electrical Corp. (.39)

Rate of Return on Average Investment

The average annual rates of return, based on average investments, were computed for each of the securities in the sample using each of the two trading rule strategies. Each rate was then compared with the average annual rate of return based on average investment assuming a simple buy and hold strategy. The average annual rate

[5] There may be some objection to recording transaction prices since we perhaps could have used the next day's market price. However, any bias resulting from this simplification would be extremely minor. Most large gains occurred over relatively long periods of time and there were very few instances when buy-and-sell signals were recorded within three months of each other.

of return for each security using the buy-and-hold strategy was computed by dividing the capital gain (loss) plus dividends received by the average of the beginning (purchase) and ending (selling) prices adjusted for brokerage costs. This rate was annualized by dividing by three, the number of years used to test the model (1966–68).

The average annual rates of return for each security using the two trading rule strategies were also based on average investment and required a three-step approach. First, the rate of return for each transaction was computed by dividing the capital gain (loss) plus dividends received by the average of the purchase and selling prices (net of brokerage costs). Second, each transaction's rate of return was annualized by multiplying by the reciprocal of the fractional part of a year for which the security was held. Third, an

TABLE II

MEAN AND STANDARD DEVIATION OF THE ANNUAL RATES OF RETURN BASED ON THE AVERAGE INVESTMENT IN COMMON STOCK FOR THE THREE STRATEGIES

Strategies	*Before tax*	*After tax*
±1 Standard Deviation Filter Rule		
Mean	24.1%	13.9%
Standard Deviation	34.4%	20.8%
±2 Standard Deviation Filter Rule		
Mean	16.9%	11.3%
Standard Deviation	31.3%	20.5%
Buy and Hold		
Mean	10.7%	8.2%
Standard Deviation	12.1%	9.8%

average annual rate of return was computed by averaging the annual rates for all transactions.

The average before tax annual rate of return for the sixty stocks using a buy-and-hold strategy was 10.7 per cent. When the mechanical trading rule was employed with a ±1 standard deviation filter rule the mean before tax annual rate of return increased to 24.1 per cent. When a ±2 standard deviation filter rule was employed a mean before tax rate of return of 16.9 per cent was earned.[6] These figures are summarized in Table II.

The trading rule strategies employed forced the trader to move in and out of the market quickly. In many instances the trader had to

[6] There were 335 transactions initiated when a ±1 standard deviation filter rule was employed. This included the 60 original purchases, 275 buy signals, 298 sales within the period and 37 sales at the end of the time period covered. When the ±2 standard deviation filter was employed, there were 103 transactions, initiated the 60 original purchases, 43 buy signals, 58 sales weeks this period and 35 sales at the end of the period.

pay the regular rate of tax on his profits, whereas if he bought and held the security he would only pay taxes at one-half his normal rate (capital gains rate). To incorporate this factor into the analysis the rates of return described in the previous section were computed 'after tax', that is, short-term gains were taxed at the regular rate (assumed to be 40 per cent) and all capital gains were taxed at 20 per cent. On an after tax basis the buy-and-hold strategy yielded a rate of return of 8.2 per cent, whereas the trading rule strategy employing a ± 1 standard deviation filter rule yielded a mean rate of return of 13.9 per cent, and the trading rule strategy emplying a ± 2 standard deviation filter rule yielded a mean rate of return of 11.3 per cent. These figures are also summarized in Table II.

The differences in mean after tax rates of return earned by the two trading rules and the rate of return on buy-and-hold strategy were tested for significance using a *t*-test for paired observations. They were found to be significant at approximately the 0.01 level for the ± 1 standard deviation filter rule, and at the 0.10 significance level for the ± 2 standard deviation filter rule.[7]

III. PORTFOLIO MANAGEMENT PROBLEM

The results in the previous section imply that there are imperfections in markets and that the mechanical trading rules would allow a trader to earn a significantly greater rate of return based on his average investment than he could earn with a buy-and-hold strategy. However, for practical purposes the analysis is incomplete. The rate of return based on the average investment in common stock ignores the practical consideration of the total dollar amounts invested. The dollar amount invested is fixed with the buy-and-hold strategy (ignoring cash dividends received), but with the trading rule strategies the dollar amount varies widely. There are often time lags between the sale of one security and the purchase of another. In other words, it may be more appropriate to test the mechanical trading rules from a portfolio management point of view.

[7] In order to ascertain if the increase in the rate of return was significant a *t*-test for paired observations was employed where

$$t = \frac{\bar{d} - d_0}{s_{d/n}}$$

with $n-1$ degrees of freedom, and where
$\bar{d}$ = mean of the difference
d_0 = a specified value (in our case zero)
s_d = standard deviation of the differences
n = number of observations

For a further discussion of the text see Ronald E. Walpole, *Introduction to Statistics* (New York: The Macmillan Company, 1968), pp. 236–8.

Compound Rate of Return

One test that is often employed in testing portfolio management performance is to compare the compound annual rates of return earned by the various strategies. The compound annual rate of return for a portfolio may be computed by determining the discount rate which will equate all future cash inflows (sales of securities and dividends) with the net cash outflows (purchases of securities).

For the buy-and-hold strategy the total cash outflows for a portfolio consisting of a round lot of each of the sixty randomly selected stocks was simply the total purchase price plus brokerage fees (assumed to be 1 per cent of the purchase price). The cash inflows were the total selling price of this same portfolio, less transaction costs, plus all cash dividends received.

Each trading rule strategy was given the same beginning portfolio and buy-and-sell decisions were recorded using their respective trading rules. After recording all transactions in each period, and after adjusting for transaction costs, the cash flows for each strategy were determined. For each of the three strategies dividends were assumed to be received at the end of period and were thus not available for reinvestment. This tended to understate each of the three compound rates of return, but it should not have affected their relative rankings.

The compound rate, compounded monthly, was 11.6 per cent for the buy-and-hold strategy. The compound rates of return were higher for each of the trading rule strategies, 12.7 per cent for the ± 1 standard deviation filter rule strategy and 16.4 per cent for the ± 2 standard deviation filter rule strategy.[8]

IV. CONCLUSIONS

Both trading rule strategies earned a higher mean rate of return on the average investment in common stock and both earned higher compound rates of return than the simple buy-and-hold strategy. Thus we have some rather strong preliminary evidence that there are imperfections in markets and that it *may* be possible to develop trading rules that will allow a trader to profit from their existence. These imperfections could be caused by numerous factors including large liquidity demands of stockholders or simply inappropriate responses to some market information.

The results of the study are still inconclusive. In particular,

[8] These differences are quite large. Unfortunately, these differences cannot be tested statistically because they are not sample means, and the standard deviation for the compound rate of return is not defined.

longer periods of time must be studied and more portfolios must be chosen and tested before conclusive statistical results can be obtained. There is also the possibility that better trading rules may be constructed which would perform significantly better than the two presented in this paper. We present our preliminary evidence in hopes that others may learn from our experience and that the study of market imperfections will benefit from our results.

UNIVERSITY OF SOUTH CAROLINA
UNIVERSITY OF MISSOURI—ST. LOUIS

REFERENCES

[1] SIDNEY S. ALEXANDER, 'Price Movements in Speculative Markets: Trends or Random Walks, Parts 1 and 2', *Industrial Management Review* (1961 and 1964), reprinted in Cootner, *op. cit.*, pp. 199–218, 338–72.

[2] ROBERT G. BROWN, *Smoothing, Forecasting and Prediction of Discrete Time Series* (Englewood Cliffs, N.Y.: Prentice-Hall, Inc. 1963).

[3] ROBERT G. BROWN and RICHARD F. MEYER, 'The Fundamental Theorem of Exponential Smoothing', *Operations Research*, IX, No. 5 (September–October, 1961), pp. 673–85.

[4] PAUL H. COOTNER, 'Stock Prices: Random vs Systematic Changes', *Industrial Management Review*, III (1962), pp. 24–25.

[5] D. A. D'ESPOSO, 'A Note on Forecasting by the Exponential Smoothing Operator', *Operations Research*, IX, No. 5 (September–October, 1961), pp 686–7.

[6] JOHN L. EVANS, 'The Random Walk Hypothesis, Portfolio Analysis and the Buy and Hold Criterion', *Journal of Financial and Quantitative Analysis*, III, No. 3 (September, 1968), pp. 327–43.

[7] EUGENE F. FAMA, 'The Behavior of Stock Market Prices', *Journal of Business*, XXXVIII (January, 1965), pp. 34–105.

[8] EUGENE F. FAMA and MARSHALL E. BLUME, 'Filter Rules and Stock Market Trading', *Journal of Business*, XXXIX (January, 1966), pp. 226–41.

[9] RICHARD W. FURST and ROBERT E. MARKLAND, 'Measuring Imperfections in Markets: A Preliminary Test of a Mechanical Trading Rule', paper presented at 1970 meeting of the Appalachian Finance Association, published in *Appalachian Financial Review*, Spring, 1971.

[10] HENDRIK HOUTHAKER, 'Systematic and Random Elements in Short-Term Price Movements', *American Economic Review*, LI (1961), pp. 164–72.

[11] MAURICE G. KENDALL, 'The Analysis of Economic Time Series I', *Journal of the Royal Statistical Society* (*Ser. A*), CXVI (1953), pp. 11–25.

[12] ARNOLD B. LARSON, 'Measurement of a Random Process in Futures Prices', *Food Research Institute Studies* (November, 1960), pp. 313–24.

[13] ROBERT A. LEVY, 'Random Walks: Reality or Myth', *Financial Analysts Journal*, XXIII (November–December, 1967), pp. 69–77.

[14] BENOIT MANDLEBROT, 'Forecasts of Future Prices, Unbiased Markets, and 'Martingale' Models', *Journal of Business: Special Supplement*, XXXIX (January, 1966), pp. 242–55.

[15] ARNOLD B. MOORE, 'Some Characteristics of Changes in Common Stock Prices', in Cootner, *op. cit.*, pp. 162–88.

[16] HARRY V. ROBERTS, 'Stock Market "Patterns" and Financial Analysis: Methodological Suggestions', *Journal of Finance*, XIV (March, 1959), pp. 1–10.

[17] ALAN SEELENFRUEND, GEORGE G. C. PARKER, and JAMES C. VAN HORNE, 'Stock Price Behavior and Trading', *Journal of Financial and Quantitative Analysis*, III, No. 3 (September, 1968), pp. 263–83.

[18] SEYMOUR SMIDT, 'A Test of the Serial Independence of Price Changes in Soybean Futures', *Food Research Institute Studies*, V (1965), pp. 117–36.

[19] SEYMOUR SMIDT, 'A New Look at the Random Walk Hypothesis', *Journal of Financial and Quantitative Analysis*, III, No. 3, (September, 1968), pp. 235–61.

[20] JAMES C. VAN HORNE and GEORGE G. C. PARKER, 'The Random Walk Theory: 'An Empirical Test', *Financial Analysts Journal*, XXIII (November–December, 1967), pp. 87–92.

MORE ON THE OUTPUT ELASTICITY OF ENERGY CONSUMPTION*

by L. G. Brookes

In work published in 1968, Adams and Miovic[1] noted that the output elasticity of energy consumption (commonly called the energy coefficient) was a somewhat amorphous parameter, differing substantially between countries and changing over time. They demonstrated that if energy statistics were adjusted to take account of the different efficiencies of the different main fuels the resulting adjusted energy elasticity was much more stable. Because of substitution of more efficient for less efficient fuels the unadjusted elasticity was often less than one in developed countries. The adjusted elasticities on the other hand lay between 1.25 and 1.4 when related to GDP and between 1.04 and 1.15 when related to industrial production, the ranges in each case covering the different types of regression exercise by which the efficiency-in-use coefficients were computed.

This paper develops a simple theory governing the relationship between useful energy consumption and national output that explains why the adjusted elasticities found by Adams and Miovic turned out to be greater than one. The theory is quantified by reference to a wide range of countries covering the whole spectrum of economic development and is tested against the actual experience over 20 to 25 years of individual countries. Conformity to the theory was very close and the efficiency-in-use coefficients computed by Adams and Miovic were found to hold good for periods of 20 to 25 years.

Briefly, the hypothesis states that as a country moves through the various stages of its economic development from primitive subsistence agriculture to the ultimate state of fully energy-dependent[2] production, its useful energy elasticity steadily falls from a high value (in principle, from infinity) tending asymptotically to one. This hypothesis follows directly from the fact that if a country is moving steadily towards a higher degree of energy-intensiveness in production then the specific energy content of incremental output will be higher than the average for all output, i.e.

* Any opinions stated or implicit in this paper are those of the author and are not necessarily those of the U.K.A.E.A., whose permission to publish this paper is acknowledged.

[1] Adams, F. G. and Miovic, P, 'On Relative Fuel Efficiency and the Output Elasticity of Energy Consumption in Western Europe', *Journal of Industrial Economics* Vol. XVI, No. 1 (1968).

[2] In this context, the degree of energy-intensiveness, or energy-dependence, is equated to the number of adjusted energy units consumed per unit of economic output measured at constant prices.

$\frac{\Delta E}{\Delta G} > \frac{E}{G}$ where E is adjusted energy consumption and G is GDP.

Rearranging terms,

$$\frac{\Delta E/E}{\Delta G/G} > 1$$

$(\Delta E/E)/(\Delta G/G)$, with E measured in adjusted units, is the definition of the useful energy coefficient so it follows that as long as the energy-intensiveness of output is increasing the useful energy coefficient must be greater than 1. It is equal to 1 when $(\Delta E/AG) = (E/G)$, i.e. when energy intensiveness has stopped increasing.

It also follows that $(\Delta E/\Delta G)/(E/G)$ is an alternative definition of the energy coefficient. Moving backwards through the scale of energy-dependence of output this expression approaches infinity as the average energy content of output approaches zero. Thus as a country moves from primitive production with no energy inputs other than sunshine and muscle power to a state of maximum energy-dependence of output its energy coefficient falls from infinity tending asymptotically to one.

By itself this proposition is of little use to energy forecasters, because it simply substitutes the requirement to predict energy-intensiveness of output for the requirement to predict energy consumption. If we can satisfy ourselves that real GDP *per capita* is a good measure of energy intensiveness, however, then the relationship derived above can be used as the basis for a mathematical model linking useful energy consumption *per capita* with GDP *per capita*.

On a simple conceptual level and on a factual level it is easy to show that GDP *per capita* is a measure of energy intensiveness. Once slack has been taken up, the obvious way to increase output per man is to put more power at each man's elbow. The facts strongly suggest that this is what is done in practice. GDP *per capita* is strongly correlated with energy consumption *per capita* and energy consumption per unit of output. This implies an interesting corollary: as GDP *per capita* rises, the economic efficiency of useful energy (defined as the number of units of output produced per unit of useful energy consumed) declines. This offends those who believe that all forms of efficiency should increase with time but it simply means that higher output per man must usually be 'paid for' by raising capital and energy inputs.

Considering the problem at a slightly higher conceptual level reveals possible difficulties. Societies moving into a post-industrial phase tend to increase their consumption of services (traditionally supplied by people rather than machines) and this could lead to increments of GDP *per capita* of lower than average energy content and hence to a useful energy coefficient lower than one.

This is an extremely difficult point to answer. It can only be disproved by taking each possible example and showing that it is either insignificant or that it will in fact lead to an increase in energy consumption if there is to be an increase in real GDP *per capita* (see below). Once again the facts support the simple hypothesis. There is no evidence that countries with a high proportion of their output devoted to services are able to reduce their energy inputs per unit of output. The U.S. for example, with over half its output in the form of services has the highest useful energy consumption per unit of output in the world. And Adams and Miovic, whose studies covered all countries in Western Europe over a period of years, found that useful energy coefficients related to GDP were higher than those related to industrial output—it was the non-industrial output that was keeping the average up.

It is highly probable that the benefits claimed for a post-industrial society (greater emphasis on services, leisure and cultural activities) can only be enjoyed without reducing the flow of material goods and mundane services if capital and energy inputs are increased to release effort for the new services and provide more leisure in which to enjoy them. Anecdotal examples such as the suggestion that Britain might become the banking centre of the world and import its material needs from the recipients of its banking services are outlandish and provide insufficient incentive to abandon the simple hypothesis. Consequently it was adopted.

Before any major work was started simple tests were conducted to see whether, in the real world, energy usage appeared to follow the predicted pattern. d Log E/d Log G is yet another way of defining the energy coefficient, so the problem was to see whether a plot of the log of useful energy consumption *per capita* against the log of GDP *per capita* followed the pattern shown in Fig. 1.

If it can be assumed that difference in fuel mixes and thermal efficiencies will average out if the sample is large enough there are advantages in plotting a cross-section of countries at single points in time rather than the experiences of individual countries through time. These advantages are:

(i) the slope of the line is effectively the useful energy coefficient (because time-dependent changes are excluded) and no adjustment need be made to convert basic statistics into useful fuel equivalents;

(ii) a very large range of states of society from the most primitive to the most advanced is available without the problem of using old unreliable information and deflating GDP levels over long periods; (exchange rates cause some difficulty: all GDP data were deflated to 1958 and converted to dollars at the rates prevailing in 1958);

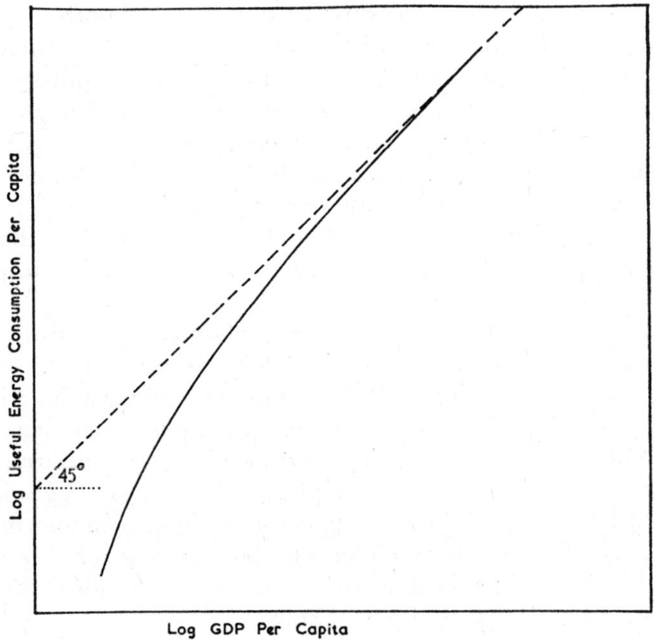

POSTULATED RELATIONSHIP BETWEEN GDP PER CAPITA AND USEFUL ENERGY CONSUMPTION PER CAPITA

The slope of the whole line at any value of GDP per capita is the useful energy coefficient at that point.
The intercept on the vertical axis made by the asymptote is the log of the asymptotic level of useful energy consumption per unit of output.

FIG. 1

(iii) a time series of cross sections of the same countries permits the experimenter to disentangle effects due to the non-linear relationship between the useful energy coefficient and GDP *per capita* from effects due to fuel substitutions and improvements in thermal efficiency that take place over time.

Twenty-two countries (listed in Appendix 1) were selected as representing all stages of development. Data for all years from 1950 to 1965 were extracted. Figures for GNP only were available so these were used as proxies for GDP. In the first instance straight lines were fitted to the logs of energy per *capita* and GNP *per capita* for each of the sixteen years 1950 to 1965[3]—first taking the whole set of 22 countries year by year and then taking, spearately, the more developed half and the less developed half, also year by year.

If the hypothesis was sound we would expect (i) the slope of the whole set to start at some value above 1 and get nearer to 1 year by

TREND OF THE CONTEMPORARY-CROSS-SECTION ENERGY COEFFICIENT

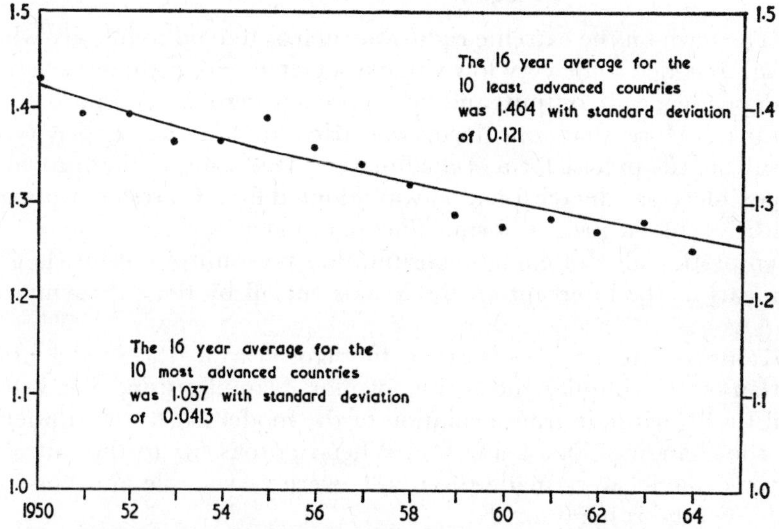

Each point represents the regression coefficient of log energy per capita on log GNP per capita for the 22 selected countries year by year. The whole line is the best fitting curve passing through the points and tending asymptotically to 1. This was a much better fit than a straight line: the standard deviation of points about the curve was only 1.2%.

FIG. 2

year as the whole set of countries moves further up the slope of industrial development; and (ii) the slope of the less developed half set always to be steeper than the corresponding slope of the more developed half set. As Fig. 2 shows the experiment produced very plausible values supporting the hypothesis.

As will also be seen from Fig. 2, a saturating curve was fitted to the

[3] To allow for the possibility of unrecorded subsistence output in near subsistence economies, $40 was added, somewhat arbitrarily, to all values of GNP *per capita*. The effect was only significant for the very low values.

time series of slopes. An unconstrained fit produced an asymptote of 1.1 but the residuals were not significantly different from those produced by fitting a curve constrained to saturate at 1.

With this encouragement fits to a number of non-linear functions were attempted. These were all of the form:

$$E = G.K.\, f(G)$$

Where f(G) is a saturating function tending to 1 as G tends to infinity. Taking logs and differentiating

$$\frac{d \operatorname{Log} E}{d \operatorname{Log} G} = 1 + \frac{d \operatorname{Log} [f(G)]}{d \operatorname{Log} G}$$

The term on the extreme right was such as to tend to infinity when G approached some very low value associated with complete energy-independence of output and to approach zero as G approached infinity. More than one form was tried to test the sensitivity of results to the precise form of the function. It was found that provided a flexible 3-parameter function was adopted for f(G) results were not sensitive to its precise form. The parameter K is, of course, the asymptotic value of energy consumption per unit of output. Log K appears as the intercept on the Y axis cut off by the 45° asymptote in Fig. 1.

It proved to be important to fit rigorously to the model itself. Attempts to simplify the fitting by, for example, using log values with a logarithmic transformation of the model led to the subtleties of the changing slope being lost. When rigorous fits to the untransformed model were made the results were very stable and bore out the hypothesis handsomely.

For data sets between 1959 and 1965 inclusive the fitted curves were virtually indistinguishable from one another; and for the earlier sets they were close to the 1959 and 1965 pattern.

The value of K, the asymptotic level of energy consumption per unit of output moved generally slightly downwards over the 16-year period. This movement would seem to reflect a slow world improvement in the efficiency of raw fuel usage. It was used as a basis for putting all results on to a common footing reflecting a world efficiency of fuel usage of about 45 per cent in 1965 but very slowly improving with time. When these adjustments were made the value of K was never very far from 1.85 kilograms of coal equivalent per \$ (1958 valuation). These adjustments do not provide for substitutions between fuels made by individual countries: substitution would only play a part if the whole of the 22 countries in general were making a substitution between fuels that contributed to the 'world' change in the efficiency of fuel use. References to useful energy in the plot shown in Fig. 3—showing a representative selection from the 22 countries—should be interpreted in that light. The slowness of the change in K is surprising until you reflect (1) that much fuel is simply purchased and consumed and (2) that fuel efficiency in production is a function of the average efficiency of plant most of which has a low rate of retirement.

In view of the wide spread of data values (two orders of magnitude), percentage least squares was adopted as the criterion of fit. The residual sums of squares were mostly in the range 15 per cent to 20 per cent. I would have regarded this as disappointingly high but

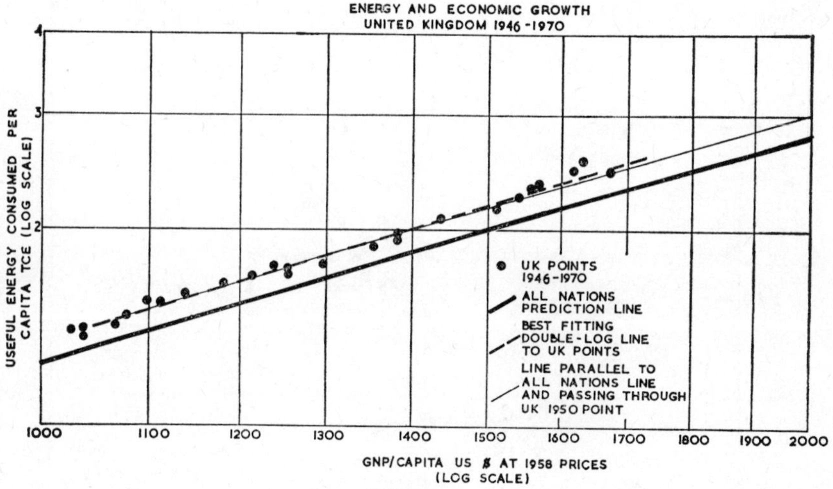

FIG. 3

for one thing: in the sequence of annual fits, countries tended to maintain their positions in relation to the line; they moved roughly parallel to it in other words. The residuals of 15 per cent to 20 per cent were, therefore, probably made up of two components: first, departures due to random combinations, peculiar to each country, of the factors affecting fuel usage at any given GDP level (climate, type of production, quirks in exchange rates); and, secondly, small random departures from each country's characteristic norm.

It follows that to predict future useful energy consumption the same position relative to the line should be maintained unless a parameter influencing that position is likely to change.

Predicting useful energy is of limited value unless there exists a ready means of converting fuel usage into and out of useful units.

Turvey and Nobay[4] have suggested that coefficients of relative usefulness of fuels should reflect their marginal rates of transformation in production and their marginal rates of substitution in consumption. In practice coefficients are calculated by regression analyses such as those conducted by Adams and Miovic for Western Europe. The usefulness of the coefficients depends upon how enduring

RELATIONSHIP BETWEEN USEFUL ENERGY CONSUMED PER CAPITA AND GNP PER CAPITA

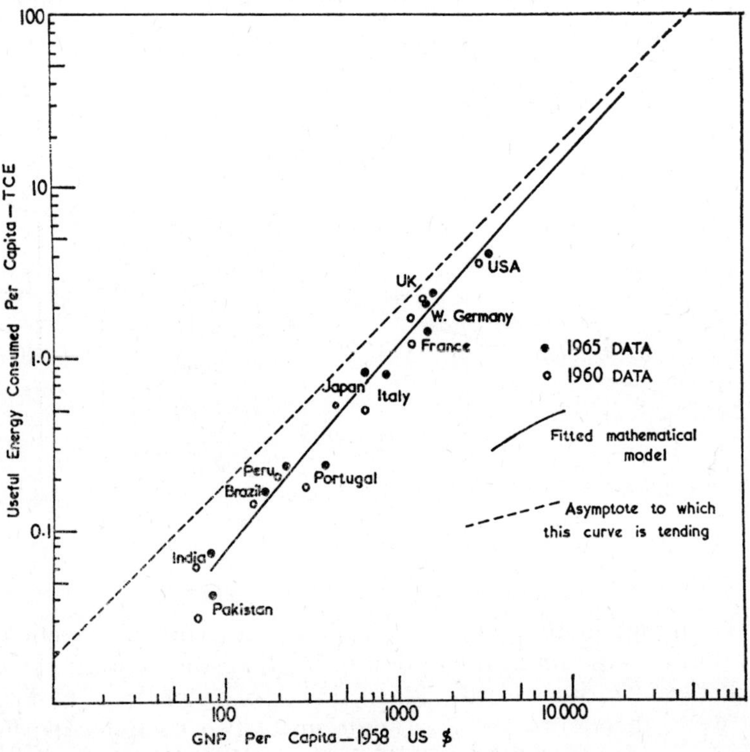

FIG. 4

they are. Using one of the sets of coefficients derived by Adams and Miovic from data for Western Europe for the period 1950 to 1960 the relationship between GNP *per capita* and useful energy consumption *per capita* was plotted for the U.K. and U.S.A. for the period 1946 to 1970. The results are shown in Figs. 4 and 5. A plot of

[4] Turvey, R. and Nobay, A. R., 'On Measuring Energy Consumption', *Economic Journal*, Vol. LXXV, No. 300 (1965).

ENERGY AND ECONOMIC GROWTH

U.S.A. 1946–1968

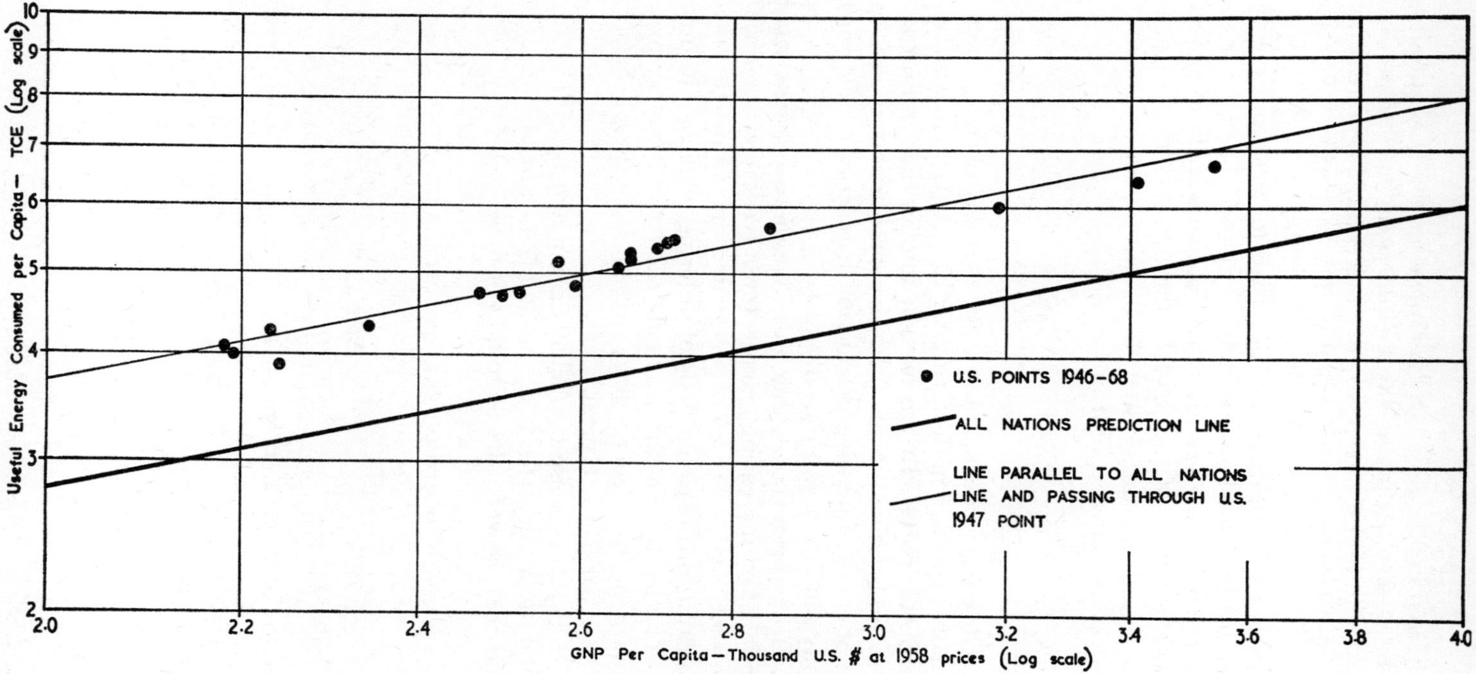

FIG. 5

unadjusted fuel against GNP *per capita* for the U.K. produces a very erratic pattern. Applying the usefulness coefficients produces a very stable result and if this experience is typical it seems that coefficients once calculated may be used for quite long periods. Figs. 4 and 5 are also remarkable for the conformity they reveal between actual useful energy consumption from 1946 to 1970 and the values predicted by the model described in this paper. These results are all the more remarkable given that the comparison data played no part in the derivation of the model—the parameters of which followed from a study of unadjusted fuel statistics for a large number of countries at a single point in time.

SUMMARY

1. The energy coefficient (output elasticity of energy consumption) normally expressed in the form $(\Delta E/E)/(\Delta G/G)$ may also be expressed as $(\Delta E/\Delta G)/(E/G)$. In this form it implies that as long as a society moves progressively from primitive production to an asymptotic state of energy-intensive production its energy coefficient falls from infinity tending asymptotically to 1.

2. It has been shown that this hypothesis is borne out by actual experience if increasing energy intensiveness is interpreted as increasing GNP *per capita*, and energy units are adjusted to take account of substitutions between fuels of differing efficiency in use.

3. The hypothesis can be made the basis of a very practical and accurate means of energy forecasting if U.K. and U.S.A. experience can be regarded as typical.

4. Efficiency-in-use coefficients computed by Adams and Miovic emerge as a very effective and stable means of correcting for the differences between the usefulness of fuels.

UNITIED KINGDOM ATOMIC ENERGY AUTHORITY

APPENDIX

LIST OF COUNTRIES USED IN THE EXPERIMENTS

Australia, Austria, Belgium, Brazil, Canada, Chile, Czechoslovakia, France, India, Israel, Italy, Japan, Pakistan, Peru, Portugal, Syria, Turkey, U.A.R., U.K., U.S.S.R., U.S.A., West Germany.

PUBLICATIONS RECEIVED

L'Agricoltura In Terra Di Bari Dal 1880 Al 1914. Published by Banca Commerciale Italiana. 1972.

From Automated Quotes to Automated Trading: Restructuring the Stock Market in the U.S., by Morris Mendelson. Published by Institute of Finance, New York University, 1972.

Business Economics, by I. R. Credland. Published by Butterworths, 1972. Price £5.00.

Business Finance: Theory and Management, second edition, by Stephen H. Archer and Charles A. D'Ambrosio. Published by Collier-Macmillan Publishers, 1972. Price £5.30.

The Case for the Par-Value System 1972, by Samuel I. Katz. Published by International Finance Section, Princeton University, 1972.

Competition, Collusion and Game Theory, by Lester G. Telser. Published by Macmillan 1972. Price £6.50.

Corporations and their Outside Auditors. A Report from the Conference Board, 1972.

The Cost of Tying Aid: A Method and some Colombian Estimates, by Thomas L. Hutcheson and R. C. Porter. Published by International Finance Section, Princeton University, 1972.

A Critique of Economic Theory, by E. Hunt and J. G. Schwartz. Published by Penguin, 1972. Price 60p.

Education in Economics for Workers and their Representatives: Supplement to the Final Report Published by O.E.C.D. in 1972, by The Regional Trade Union Seminar.

Employment Approaches to Economic Planning in Developing Countries, by Birger Moller. Published by Scandinavian Institute of Asian Studies Monograph Series, 1972.

Enterprise Manpower Planning for Change: International Management Seminar, Lisbon 13th–16th January 1970: Final Report. Published by O.E.C.D. 1972.

Excessive Taxes lead to 'Stag-Flation', by Frederick W. Tooby. Published by Economic Research Council, 1972. Price 50p.

Exchange-Risk Under Fixed and Flexible Exchange Rates, by Samuel I. Katz. Published by New York University, 1972.

The Federal Budget: Its Impact on the Economy. Published by the Conference Board, 1972. Price $2.50.

Ford Strike: The Workers' Story, by John Matthews. Published by Panther, 1972. Price 40p.

Industry and Universities, by Stephen Hargreaves and Patrick Rivett. Published by Foundation for Business Responsibilities, 1972.

International Investment, by John Dunning. Published by Penguin, 1972. Price 70p.

International Trade and Economic Development, by G. K. Helleiner. Published by Penguin, 1972. Price 60p.

Investment and Portfolio Analysis, by Haim Levy and Marshall Sarnat. Published by John Wiley and Sons Ltd., 1972. Price £5.50.

Journal of Public Economics, Vol. I, edited by A. Atkinson. Published by North Holland Publishing Company, 1972.

Land Reform and Economic Development, by Peter Dorner. Published by Penguin, 1972. Price 60p.

Marketing Logistics and Distribution Planning, by Martin Christopher and Gordon Wills. Published by George Allen and Unwin Ltd., 1972. Price £12.25. (This book is a useful treatise on physical distribution management, with chapters written by experts on transport modes, inventory control, operation control etc.)

The Measurement and Interpretation of Service Output Changes, by Anthony D. Smith. Published by National Economic Development Office, 1972.

Mergers in Swedish Industry, by Bengt Ryden. Published by the Industrial Institute for Economic and Social Research, 1972.

Monetary Integration: Essays in International Finance, by W. M. Corden. Published by International Finance Section, Princeton University, 1972.

The Motor Industry: An Economic Survey, by D. G. Rhys. Published by Butterworths, 1972. Price £6.00.

Planning of Industrial Complexes by means of Geometric Programming, by P. Nijkamp. Published by Rotterdam University Press, 1972.

The Reality of Organizations, by Rosemary Stewart. Published by Pan Management Series, 1972. Price 40p.

Regional Economics: Location theory, urban structure and regional change, by H. W. Richardson. Published by Weidenfeld and Nicolson, 1972. Price £2.50.

Technology, management and society, by P. F. Drucker. Published by Pan Management Series, 1972. Price 45p.

Socialist Economics, edited by Alec Nove and D. M. Nuti. Published by Penguin, 1972. Price 70p.

The Tax System in Sweden, by Martin Norr, Claes Sandels and Nils Hornhammar. Published by Skandinaviska Enskilda Banken, 1972.

United Kingdom International Trade 1975. Published by National Ports Council, 1972. Price £5.00.

Voluntary Dismissals Procedure and the Industrial Relations Act, by S. D. Alderman. Published by Political and Economic Planning, 1972. Price £2.00.

THE JOURNAL OF INDUSTRIAL ECONOMICS

Published first in October 1952, this Journal was founded to develop the analysis of the problems facing modern industry. It is concerned with the individual business and its relation to the economy—e.g. with outputs and prices and their behaviour in the market, and with the business decisions which affect these. It therefore aims to contribute both to economic theory and to practical public and private policies in the industrial field. The journal is naturally meant to interest business men as well as economists.

The Editors welcome contributions covering the fundamental categories in economics (such as prices, costs, investment, finance, location, wages and productivity) as well as the broader 'background' circumstances (such as the changing structure of industry, management policy and public monopoly policy). Preference is given to MSS. bearing on these subjects from the standpoint of individual firms or industries. The Journal's authors have helped to maintain the policy that articles should be found readable by those interested in its field. Theoretical discussion is welcome. Abstract theory is not barred, but authors in this case should provide an introduction and summary, so that non-specialist readers may see what the article is about. Alongside articles of more normal length the Editors are willing to publish shorter notes, especially when these give interim results of important research studies.

The Editors will be glad to receive offers of suitable articles. MSS. from the United States should be sent to Professor Menge, Department of Economics, Dartmouth College, Hanover, New Hampshire 03755, U.S.A; and from other countries to the General Editor, care of Basil Blackwell, Publishers, 49 Broad Street, Oxford, England. All other communications should be addressed to the Publisher.

The annual subscription (three numbers) is £2.25 ($6.75) post free; the price of a single issue is £1.00 ($3.00) post free. Remittances should be sent to Messrs Basil Blackwell.

The contents of Volume XX, No. 3, July 1972, were:

A Life Cycle Theory of the Firm, by Dennis C. Mueller, Associate Professor of Economics at Cornell University.

Iron Ore and Steel: a Case Study of the Economic Causes and Consequences of Vertical Integration, by Richard B. Mancke, Assistant Professor of Economics at the University of Michigan.

Heavy Commercial Vehicles: the Survival of the Small Firm, by D. G. Rhys, Lecturer in Economics at University College, Cardiff.

Vertical Qvasi-Integration, by K. J. Blois, Lecturer in the Department of Management Studies, Loughborough University of Technology.

The Fixed Coefficients Production Process under Production Uncertainty, by Gary M. Roodman, Assistant Professor of Business Administration, Amos Tuck School of Business Administration, Dartmouth College.

Raising the Capital Budgeting Hurdle, by M. J. Mumford, Senior Lecturer in Accounting at the University of Nairobi, Kenya (a post based on the University of Edinburgh).

Economies of Scale in Retailing: a Note, by K. A. Tucker, Lecturer in Economics at the University of Kent at Canterbury.

REPRINT

A photographic reprint is now available of Vols. 1–13, 1952–1965 bound in cloth or paper, single volumes in paper only.

Send orders to Blackwell's, Broad Street, Oxford, England.

STUDENT SUBSCRIPTION

Bona fide students can obtain the Journal at a greatly reduced subscription rate. Send to publisher for a form.

Printed in Great Britain by Alden & Mowbray Ltd
at the Alden Press, Oxford

THE JOURNAL OF INDUSTRIAL ECONOMICS

Volume XXI APRIL 1973 No. 2

A. R. BELL
Industrial Electricity Consumption—an Example of an Intermediate Good.
KRISHNAMURTI CHANDRASEKAR
U.S. and French Productivity in 19 Manufacturing Industries.
JAMES J. HUGHES
In Defence of the Industrial Training Act.
PAWAN K. SAWHNEY and BANSI L. SAWHNEY
Capacity-Utilization, Concentration, and Price-Cost Margins: Results on Indian Industries.
DAVID WAITE
The Economic Significance of Small Firms.
DOUGLAS W. WEBBINK
Regulation, Profits and Entry in the Television Broadcasting Industry.
FRED D. ARDITTI and RICHARD L. SANDOR
A Note on Variable Patent Life.
P. SMITH
Seasonal Fluctuations in the Motor Vehicle Industry: a Comment.
HOWARD N. ROSS
Illusions in Testing for Administered Prices.
LOUIS PHLIPS
Illusions in Testing for Administered Prices: a Reply
J. R. DAVIES
On the Sales Maximization Hypothesis—A Comment.
H. MICHAEL MANN
Concentration, Barriers to Entry, and Rates of Return Revisited: a Reply.

BASIL BLACKWELL OXFORD ENGLAND

Price — £1.00 net or ($3.00). Annual subscription: £2.25 or ($6.75).

CONTRIBUTORS TO THIS NUMBER

A. R. BELL: An economist in the Commercial Department (Economics and Forecasting Section) of the Electricity Council in London.

KRISHNAMURTI CHANDRASEKAR: Associate Professor of Economics in the Divisions of Business and Management and Social Sciences, New York Institute of Technology, New York.

JAMES J. HUGHES: Lecturer in Economics, Faculty of Social Sciences, University of Kent at Canterbury.

PAWAN K. SAWHNEY: Assistant Professor of Economics at Northeastern University.

BANSI L. SAWHNEY: Assistant Professor of Economics at the University of Baltimore.

DAVID WAITE: A recent graduate of the University of Lancaster, works at the Bank of England.

DOUGLAS W. WEBBINK: Bureau of Economics, Federal Trade Commission (this paper represents the author's own opinions and not those of the Federal Trade Commission or its staff); formerly a Brookings Economic Policy Fellow, at the Federal Communications Commission on leave from the University of North Carolina.

FRED D. ARDITTI: Associate Professor of Finance, Graduate School of Business, University of Florida.

RICHARD L. SANDOR: Assistant Professor, School of Business Administration, University of California at Berkeley, and Vice President, Chief Economist, Chicago Board of Trade.

P. SMITH: Research Assistant, Department of Political Economy, University College, London.

HOWARD N. ROSS: Visiting Professor of Economics, University of South Florida; also faculty member of Bernard M. Baruch College, The City University of New York.

LOUIS PHLIPS: Professor of Economics, Université Catholique de Louvain, and Editor of *The Journal of Industrial Economics*.

J. R. DAVIES: Lecturer in Economics at the University of Stirling.

H. MICHAEL MANN: Professor of Economics, Boston College, on leave as the Director, Bureau of Economics, Federal Trade Commission. (The views expressed in this article are not necessarily those of the Commission.)

INDUSTRIAL ELECTRICITY CONSUMPTION—AN EXAMPLE OF AN INTERMEDIATE GOOD[1]

by A. R. Bell

THE position of electricity as an intermediate good in the output of industry is illustrated in Table I. For all industry (i.e. Manufacturing, Mining and Quarrying, Construction and Gas, Electricity and Water) electricity costs as a percentage of total costs were only a little over 1 per cent in 1963. Wages and salaries, on the other hand, which are often seen as a competitor with electricity in some markets

TABLE I

ELECTRICITY COSTS RELATIVE TO INDUSTRY'S TOTAL COSTS

Industry	*Total Costs £000's*	*Electricity Costs £000's*	*Electricity Costs as % of Total Costs*
Cement	78,612	5,717	7.27
Water Supply	121,472	5,685	4.68
Metalliferous Mining	12,566	563	4.48
General Chemicals	702,053	25,772	3.67
Coal Mining	792,731	28,256	3.56
Glass	150,517	4,667	3.10
Bricks	140,115	3,841	2.74
Chalk and Clay Extraction	58,807	1,486	2.52
Pottery	69,008	1,713	2.48
Stone and Slate Quarrying	65,064	1,604	2.47
Iron and Steel (General)	1,294,592	28,504	2.20
Iron Castings	266,278	5,126	1.93
Textile Finishing	89,837	1,710	1.90
Brewing and Malting	398,299	2,241	0.56
Canvas Goods and Sacks	31,819	113	0.36
Tobacco	237,811	633	0.27
Construction	2,790,640	6,436	0.23
Locomotives	52,435	123	0.23
Jewellery	402,453	444	0.11
Household Textiles	35,101	31	0.09
Sugar	232,994	191	0.08
All Index of Production Industries	29,395,000	308,700	1.05

Source: 1963 U.K. Census of Production.

account for over 25 per cent of total costs. Nevertheless, electricity is an important component in the process of manufacture although its use across industry varies considerably. The majority of electricity consumed by industry is for power for such processes as pumping, crushing, grinding and rolling whilst there is also a sizeable load

[1] The work described in this paper has been done over several years by staff of the Electricity Council, in particular Mr. S. V. Allera (now with the Post Office Corporation).

used for heating and melting where rigorous technical standards are required. Thus, dependent on the product made and the process of manufacture, there is considerable variety in the relative importance of electricity costs to total costs. Industries such as Cement, Mining and Quarrying and Water, all of which have a large motive power demand, are the most significant in terms of their relative electricity consumption and contrast vividly with Brewing, Tobacco and Jewellery where the cost of power is small in relation to the value of the finished product.

Despite the variation in relative electricity consumption between industries the fact that electricity is an integral part of the product means that for each industry and for industry as a whole any fluctuation in the output of goods will be met by a similar fluctuation in the quantity of electricity consumed.

Appendix 1 shows the trend in electricity sales to industry and private generation by industry together with the Index of Industrial Production since 1955. The response of electricity sales to industrial output is, however, more clearly illustrated by using, for both sales and output, the quarterly percentage growth rates on the respective quarter of the previous year, this is shown in Graph 1. The increases in output lead generally to increases in the consumption of electricity, though as in late 1956/early 1957 and towards the end of 1963 there occasionally appears to be a lagged response.

The long-term association is shown more clearly by using a four quarter moving average which smooths out some of the fluctuations in both sales and output growth (Graph 2). It has been found by various statistical analyses that, approximately, a 1 per cent increase in output leads to a 2 per cent increase in electricity consumption during the period 1955–70. However, more detailed analyses suggest that this relationship is falling. Over the period 1955–61, the fluctuations in the growth of sales are considerably greater than during the period 1961–70 and whilst this is also true for the Index of Production, the relevant point is that during the 1960s the trend of the two growth rates is much closer. This can also be demonstrated by comparing average growths per annum in both variables in the two time periods. During the 1955–61 period the average growth in sales was 6.5 per cent per annum with an Index of Production growth of 2.1 per cent per annum, but between 1961 and 1970 sales growth fell to an average of 5.5 per cent per annum although the Index of Production growth rose to 3.5 per cent per annum so that the elasticity between the two dropped from 3.1:1 to 1.57:1. Hence electricity has become less demand elastic in recent years.

GRAPH 1

GROWTH RATES IN ELECTRICITY SALES AND THE INDEX OF INDUSTRIAL PRODUCTION

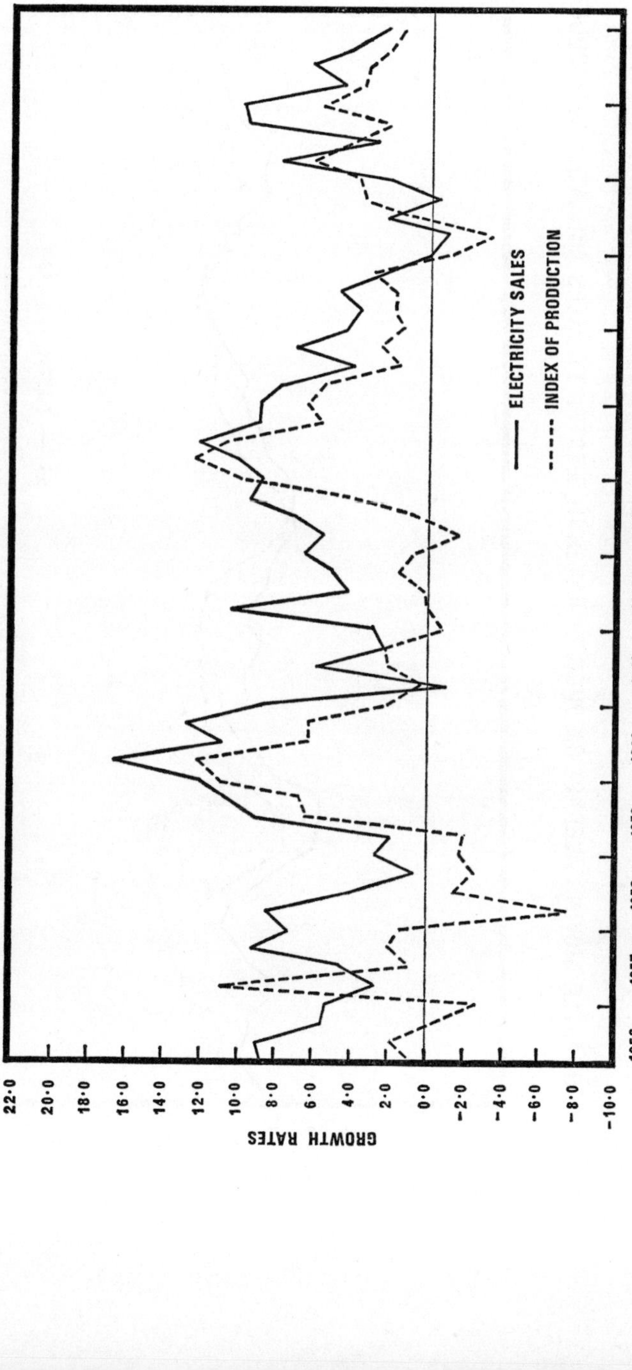

GRAPH 2

FOUR-QUARTER MOVING AVERAGE ON GROWTH RATES IN ELECTRICTY SALES AND INDEX OF PRODUCTION

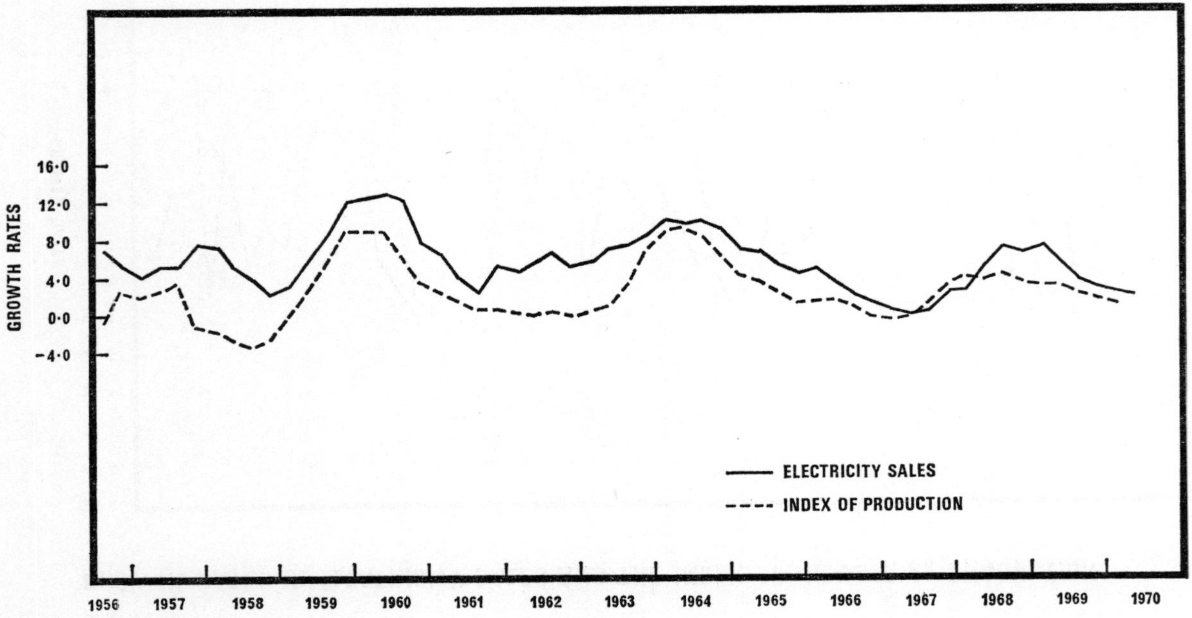

The importance of this change in the ratio of growth rates is that it can significantly affect the long-term planning and investment of the electricity supply industry. New capital equipment in the industry requires some six years for construction and quite small differences in growth rates of future demand can involve large sums of money. For example, with an assumed growth rate in the Index of Production of 3 per cent per annum over the next six years, the difference between the ratios of 2:1 and 1.5:1 would necessitate an extra investment now of some £150m if the former were used in planning. This sum is equivalent to the present total annual investment of the Construction industry in the U.K.

This shows the need to identify the change, to analyse its causes and to judge the relative importance of these in the future. There are several possible explanations to account for this decline in the ratio of sales increases to increases in output and some of these are discussed below.

1. THE LEVEL OF ECONOMIC ACTIVITY AND THE OUTPUT ELASTICITY

One possibility is that the elasticity alters with the level of economic activity. Graph 3 shows an association between the elasticity and the Index of Production growth rates. In periods of rapid economic expansion it is possible that the output elasticity might be lower as the increments in output could be associated with non-electricity intensive processes or because the full potential of modern efficient capital equipment would only be realized at the higher levels of output.

Any dissimilarity in the pattern of economic growth experienced in the two sub-periods, 1955–61 and 1961–70, could therefore lead to distortions in the output elasticities.

Various attempts were made to analyse the effect of this:

(a) In order to remove cyclical economic effects a pressure of demand variable was introduced which, initially, was taken as deviations about the trend of the Index of Production.[2] This was calculated by fitting the following equation to the Index of Production time series:

(i) $\log I_t = \log a + bt + e_t$

where I_t = Index of Production

e_t = random error (throughout paper)

t = time trend.

[2] From the method used by G. A. Renton, *National Institute Economic Review*, November, 1967.

The residual term from this equation being in log form could thus be used directly to indicate for each quarter of the time series whether industrial output was at a higher or lower level than the trend and accordingly provided a measure of cyclical economic activity. The equation results were:

$$\log I_t = 2.05354+0.00328\,t+e_t$$
$$R^2 = 0.845.$$

The pressure of demand variable was added to the normal estimating equation (a simple linear relationship relating industrial electricity sales to industrial output) for both sub periods and the overall time series and yielded significant coefficients for all time periods. The results shown in Table II are derived from the following equation:

$$\log C_t = \text{seasonal constants}+b_1 \log I_t+b_2 \log \mathcal{J}_t+e_t$$

where C_t = Electricity Sales to Industry in period t
I_t = Index of Industrial Production in period t
$\mathcal{J}_t$ = pressure of demand variable derived from (i) above.

TABLE II

THE INFLUENCE OF THE PRESSURE OF DEMAND VARIABLES ON THE OUTPUT ELASTICITIES

Time period	*Output elasticity from normal estimating equation*	*Independent variables*		R^2
		I_t	$\mathcal{J}_t$	
Early	2.21068	2.33834	−1.50728	0.995
Late	1.58988	1.76299	−0.64081	0.991
Overall	2.05118	2.08534	−0.30815	0.972

Comparison with the elasticities from the normal estimating equation shows that the difference in the elasticities between the early and late period where the $\mathcal{J}_t$ variable is included narrowed slightly, indicating that the variation in the pattern of economic growth explained only a small amount of difference in the elasticities. The negative $\mathcal{J}_t$ coefficient implying that electricity sales to industry benefit more from a recession than a boom tended to confirm the relationship shown in Graph 3.

(b) As a check on the above conclusion an alternative pressure of demand variable was introduced, in this instance a time series of manufacturing capacity utilization.[3] The form of the equation was:

[3] Pearce and Taylor, *Lloyds Bank Review*, July, 1968.

GRAPH 3

RELATIONSHIP BETWEEN THE ELASTICITY AND INDEX OF PRODUCTION

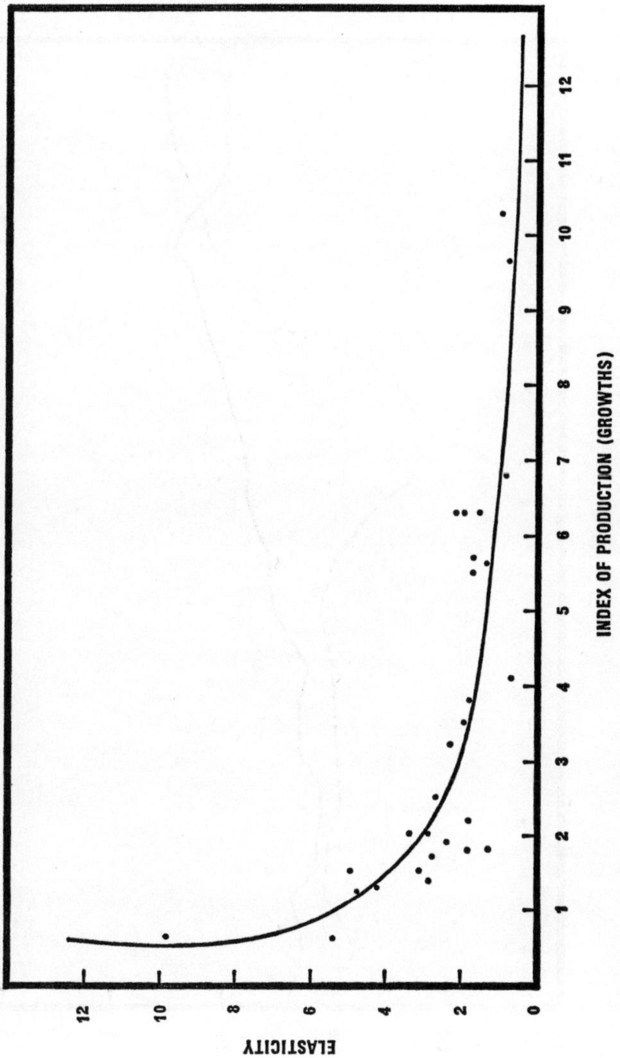

GRAPH 4

INDUSTRIAL OUTPUT ELASTICITIES (Corrected for Spare Capacity) 23 QUARTER MOVING AVERAGE

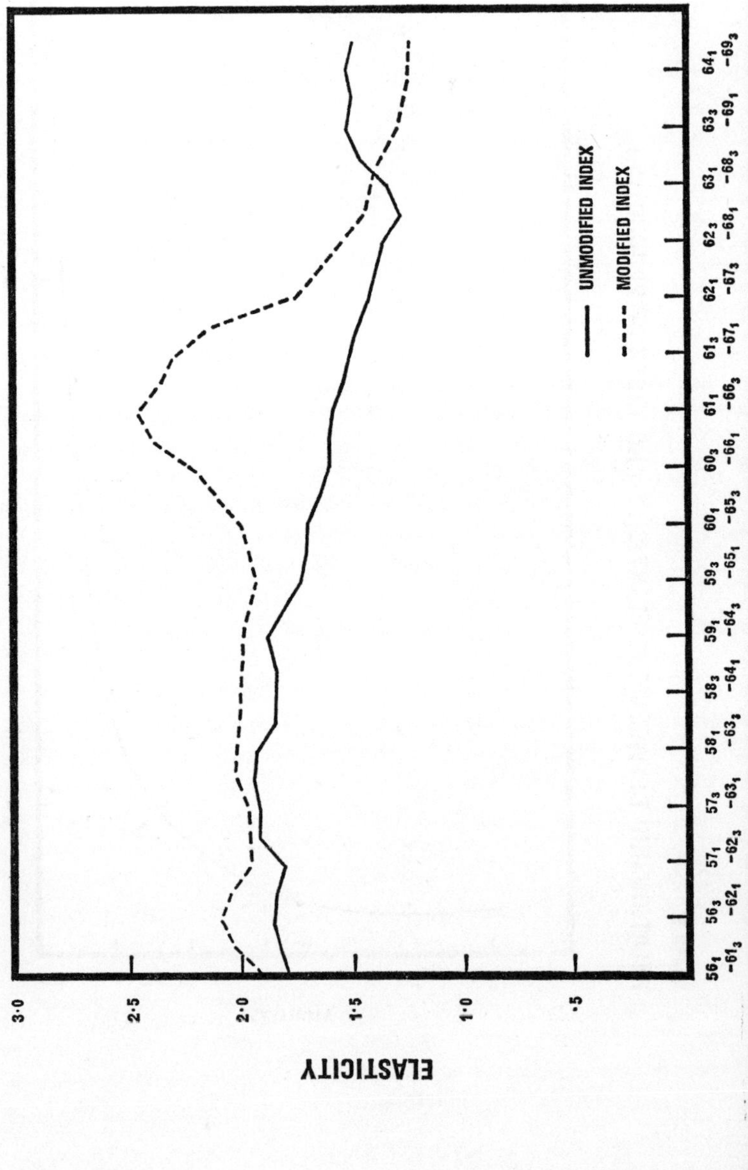

$$\log C_t = \text{seasonal constants} + b_1 \log I_t + b_2 \log U_t + e_t$$
$$\text{where } U_t = \text{Index of capacity utilization.}$$

The results are given in Table III.

TABLE III

THE INFLUENCE OF THE CAPACITY UTILIZATION VARIABLE ON THE OUTPUT ELASTICITIES

Time period	*Output elasticity from normal estimating equation*	*Independent variables* I_t	U_t	R^2
Early	2.21068	2.44401	−1.25522	0.989
Late	1.58988	2.00890	−0.96402	0.981
Overall	2.05118	2.22593	−1.24787	0.993

The results in Table III again suggest that electricity sales are negatively related to measures of the level of economic activity. The output coefficients of the two sub-periods are still significantly different although the gap between them has been narrowed.

(c) Further work on this aspect of the elasticity was prompted both by the results above which indicated some relationship between the level of economic growth and the elasticity (Graph 3) and, as previously mentioned, the need to predict the elasticity in the future. Because of the latter, an indication of the trend of the elasticity over the most recent years was necessary and a series of successive regressions were run (i.e. beginning 1956_{Q1} to 1961_{Q3} and then subtracting the earliest observation and adding a later observation until the most recent time period was reached) thus providing an up-to-date picture of the level of the elasticity which is shown on Graph 4. Because of the relationship with economic growth this same process was repeated but using an Index of Production modified by an index of capacity utilization,[4] this is shown again on Graph 4.

Even allowing for capacity utilization or pressure of demand in the economy the trend of the elasticity is still clearly downwards and as unstable as the trend of the unmodified elasticity essentially because of the 'hump' in the late fifties and early sixties which is clearly not caused by the level of economic activity.

[4] From Pearce and Taylor's index of capacity utilization (op. cit.) the quarterly deviations from the average for the period were calculated and the quarterly Indices of Production were then adjusted by the respective deviations.

2. THE EFFECT OF CHANGING INDUSTRIAL STRUCTURE

Apart from cyclical economic effects another complication arising when comparing relationships over two successive time periods is that the output variable will almost certainly be subject to changes in industrial structure. Defining the latter to be each industry's net output as a share of the total, it is apparent from the 1954, 1958 and 1963 Censuses of Production that certain industries, for example vehicles, have experienced rapid growth in production, and hence gradually form a larger proportion of the total industrial net output. This being so, it is possible that in recent years the growth in total production has occurred more in industries which have lower levels of electricity consumption, with the result that the relationship between electricity and output will inevitably change (the coefficient will decline) because the output variable does not continue to give constant emphasis to each individual industry over time.

A reasonable approximation to current industrial structure can be made by multiplying for each industry the latest known output weights by the Index of Production and expressing this as a share of the industry total. This 'industrial structure factor' for a given base year could be applied to the total index for any current year, so giving a breakdown for the total index in such a way as to imply an unchanging industrial structure. The product of the adjusted index for each industry and its appropriate consumption ratio[5] then gives the total electricity consumption had the industrial structure remained unchanged. The results of the calculations are shown in Table IV.

From the hypotheses above, if changing industrial structure is related to the changing elasticity of industrial sales then by adjusting for this the elasticity of the period 1961–70 should be unchanged from that of the earlier period. The results indicate that this is not the case. It would appear from this that adjusting for changes in industrial structure make no difference to the decline in the output elasticity. However, as a further check an industry group analysis was conducted for the same time periods as indicated above using the same equation form (see 1 (b) above:

$$\log C_t = \text{seasonal constants} + b_1 \log I_t + e_t$$

The analysis used two separate dependent variables, one of which was public supply sales (C_t) and the other was total industrial

[5] This is defined as: $\dfrac{\text{Total Electricity Consumption in period } t}{\text{Index of Industrial Production in period } t}\Big\}$ for each industry group

Over time this shows the trend in electricity consumption per unit of output, i.e. the trend in electricity intensity among industries, which provides the basis for industry group forecasts.

TABLE IV

ELECTRICITY CONSUMPTION WITH CONSTANT (1961) INDUSTRIAL STRUCTURE

	1955	1961	1970
Actual consumption (Mn Kwh)	40,751	56,597	84,639
Index of production	83.2	95.7	124.0
Adjusted consumption (Mn Kwh)	40,850	56,597	84,435
		1955–61	1961–70
Percentage change p.a.:			
Index of production		2.3	2.9
Actual consumption		5.6	4.6
Actual 'elasticity'		2.43	1.59
Adjusted consumption		5.6	4.5
Adjusted 'elasticity'		2.43	1.56

consumption of electricity, i.e. public supply sales plus privately generated electricity (C_t+P_t) as it was felt that private generation may have distorted the precise relationship between sales and output in Table IV. The results of the equations are shown in Table V below.

In the majority of the industries the output elasticities fall over time, whether or not private generation is considered. There seems

TABLE V

INDUSTRY GROUP OUTPUT ELASTICITIES

	Dependent variable					
	C_t			(C_t+P_t)		
	Early	*Late*	*Overall*	*Early*	*Late*	*Overall*
Mining & Quarrying	−1.95	−0.70*	−2.16	−1.18	−0.70	−1.39
Food, Drink & Tobacco	2.73	3.23	3.27	2.68	3.12	3.05
Chemicals & Allied Inds.	1.14	1.39	1.39	1.18†	1.10	1.18
Iron & Steel	0.92†	1.76	2.23*	0.82*	1.41	1.78*
Non-ferrous metals	1.02	0.70	1.31	0.94	0.66	1.22
Engineering	1.46	0.86	1.19	1.41	0.85	1.15
Shipbuilding	−1.20	−0.66	−1.30	−1.07	−0.66	−1.19
Vehicles & Aircraft	1.27†	1.31†	1.83	1.16†	1.21†	1.69†
Metals NES	1.32*	0.57	1.56*	1.25*	0.57	1.51*
Textiles	0.21 NS	1.31	1.72*	0.58 NS	1.17	1.54*
Leather	−3.20*	0.86*	−2.92*	−3.08*	0.92*	−2.75*
Clothing	1.52†	0.99	1.93	1.51†	0.96	1.92
Bricks, Pottery, etc.	1.18†	0.99	1.17	0.83†	0.99	0.98
Timber & Furniture	1.70*	1.01	2.41*	1.66*	1.00	2.36*
Paper & Printing	2.41	1.09	1.90	1.30	1.98	1.19
Other Manufacturing	1.31	1.08	1.55	1.41	1.04	1.57
Construction	2.85	1.87	2.58	2.85	1.87	2.58

* Equation $R^2 < 0.75$.

† Difference between coefficients not significant at 5 per cent level.

to be little likelihood therefore that changes in aggregate output elasticity over time are due either to movements in industrial structure or to differing rates of growth in private generation.

3. OTHER EFFECTS

Neither cyclical economic effects nor changes in industrial structure therefore appear to explain the changing elasticity to any significant extent. A further possibility is that a combination of a declining growth in other fuel and labour substitution and a more efficient use of electricity due to technological advance and economies of scale have exerted a downward influence on the elasticity. These factors are all embodied in the consumption ratio. If, over the whole period, thc clasticity is assumed to be unity, then any further increase in sales will be due to the consumption ratio (i.e. an increase in electricity per unit of output). Examination of Table IV shows a decrease in this factor in the later period so that there has been a decline in the growth of electricity intensity in industry during recent years.

In order to determine the influence economic factors have on electricity sales to industry a number of equations were run with industrial electricity purchases regarded as being dependent on movements in output, employment, capital investment, and price relatives of electricity with respect to all other fuels and to wage rates.[6] The results of these equations are shown in Table VI. Initially a lagged dependent variable was included, but the effect of multicollinearity led to non-significant estimates of the coefficients of other independent variables.

A crude attempt to separate direct output effects from other factors, all of which are included in the output elasticity, was made by introducing a time trend. The results set out in equation 1 show that the fall in output elasticity over time is not due to changes

[6] This approach is based on that used by R. E. Baxter and R. Rees 'Analysis of the Industrial Demand for Electricity', *Economic Journal*, Vol. LXXVIII, June, 1968.

Footnote to Table VI:

* Significant at 10 per cent level.

Where all data is seasonally unadjusted and:

C = Public Supply Sales to industry
I = Index of Industrial Production
t = Time trend
P_E = Average price of public supply sales to industry
P_W = Index of Average Wage Rates
P_T = Wholesale Price Index of Fuels, excluding electricity
N = Numbers in Employment in 'Index of Production' industries
V = Gross Fixed Capital Investment.

N.B. All variables (time trend excepted) in logs with seasonal constant dummy variables in all equations.

TABLE VI

REGRESSION RESULTS

Equation No.	*Period*	*Dependent variable*	Independent variables $(N/I)_t$	I_t	t	$(PE/PW)_t$	$(PE/PT)_t$	V_t	$(V/I)_t$	R^2
1	Early	C_t		0.83112	0.00490					·995
	Late			0.88132	0.00321					·986
	Total			0.69669	0.00472					·992
2	Early	C_t		1.42319		−0.83578*				·929
	Late			1.23236		−0.72978^{NS}				·976
	Total			1.40645		−0.96620				·978
3	Early	C_t		1.02915			−1.09605			·974
	Late			1.58814			−0.22444^{NS}			·967
	Total			1.73495			−0.70951			·984
4	Early	$(C/I)_t$					−0.59544		0.50422	·948
	Late						−0.35804^{NS}		0.63531	.616
	Total						−0.28394		1.01500	·907
5	Early	$(C/I)_t$	−1.51035							·775
	Late		−0.59440							.877
	Total		−1.15466							.881
6	Early	$(C/I)_t$							1.00041	·919
	Late								0.60557	.612
	Total								1.17737	·903
7	Early	C_t				−0.68677		0.76281		·991
	Late					−1.71453		0.46496		·946
	Total					−0.92628		0.78307		·985
								(V_t-3)		
8	Early	C_t		0.87997		−0.33025		0.58134		·993
	Late			0.94769		−0.82029		0.20304		·979
	Total			0.83065		−0.63049		0.44730		·992

Footnote on p. 106.

in the direct link between output and electricity sales, which would *a priori* tend to unity, but to the miscellaneous combination of influences subsumed in the aggregate output elasticity and shown here as the time trend coefficient.

The impact of electricity/labour substitution should be reflected by changes in the PE/PW variable which declines over time, with the output variable also present. The PE/PW variable is only significant at the 10 per cent level in the early sub-period, and not at all in the more recent sub-period, which cannot provide sufficient evidence for believing that public supply sales are benefiting less from electricity/labour substitution. Much the same occurs with equations 3 and 4 where the fuel price relative is included, the object being to see if it was the changing pattern of fuel preferences which was causing the change in the output elasticity. The results, however, are disappointing—very largely due to the inadequacy of the price measure itself.

There is some indication from equation 5 that labour productivity has been leading to a more efficient use of electricity as the N/I variable shows a considerably changed coefficient over the two periods but, as the electricity/price relative is not significant, reason for the change is uncertain. Similarly capital productivity (equation 6) appears to be part of the explanation for the falling elasticity with gains in gross fixed investment per unit of output leading to a smaller growth in electricity consumption over time but, again, whether this is due to the price of substitutes is not clear as neither of the price variables are significant at the 5 per cent level. For capital investment the results of equation 7 where V_t and PE/PW coefficients fall over time suggest that electricity is benefiting less from increased investment which is associated with electricity sales largely because movements in the electricity/labour price relative are such as to encourage labour-saving innovations. Similar results are to be found in equation 8 where the V_t variable was lagged from one to four periods but only with V_{t-3} was multicollinearity absent.

Both equations, particularly equation 8, do provide grounds for believing that the fall in the output elasticity over time is very much a reflection of the fact that innovations in electricity using investment (encouraged by labour substitution) are leading to a more efficient use of electricity which would explain the slower increase in the consumption ratio in recent years.

CONCLUSION

It seems as if the declining elasticity of electricity use to industrial production is not caused by changes in industrial structure or cyclical economic movements. A more likely explanation is that new capital investment, leading to labour substitution, is a more efficient user of electricity. Whilst a partial explanation has been obtained, the relative scarcity of data must lead to caution in the interpretation of differences between various measurements. More work is required if the errors inherent in long-term planning are to be reduced.

ELECTRICITY COUNCIL
LONDON

APPENDIX I

INDUSTRIAL ELECTRICITY CONSUMPTION (E & W) AND INDUSTRIAL OUTPUT (U.K. 1963 = 100)

	Public Supply sales to Industry (MN Kwh)	*Private Generation by Industry (MN Kwh)*	*Total Electricity Consumption (Public Supply & Private Generation) (MN Kwh)*	*Index of Industrial Production (all industries)*
1955	30,865	9,886	40,751	83.2
1956	33,053	9,831	42,884	83.6
1957	34,865	10,019	44,884	86.6
1958	36,323	10,253	46,485	84.1
1959	39,181	10,685	49,866	88.3
1960	43,935	11,416	55,351	94.5
1961	45,538	11,060	56,597	95.7
1962	47,948	10,936	58,884	96.6
1963	51,561	11,312	62,873	100.0
1964	56,681	11,721	68,402	108.5
1965	59,840	11,984	71,824	111.8
1966	61,290	12,284	73,574	113.3
1967	61,807	12,391	74,198	114.6
1968	66,258	12,879	79,137	119.7
1969	69,336	13,950	83,286	122.8
1970	70,792	13,847	84,639	124.0

U.S. AND FRENCH PRODUCTIVITY IN 19 MANUFACTURING INDUSTRIES*

by KRISHNAMURTI CHANDRASEKAR

THE study is designed to measure labor productivity in 19 manufacturing industries of the U.S.A. and of France for the census years 1958 and 1963. Labor productivity is chosen as labor costs constitute a major component of the total cost of products.

Methodology: We have attempted a comparison of productivity industry by industry. We have included mostly two-digit and three-digit industries as classified in the Standard Industrial Classification System. Each industry produces a variety of products. The personnel employed in the production of each of these different products is not available. Under these circumstances, it is not possible to compare physical output per worker. Information regarding the total number of employees, production workers, total number of hours worked and the value of shipment for each industry was obtained from the U.S. Census of Manufacture published by the U.S. Department of Commerce, and the Annuaire Statistique published by the Institut National de la Statistique et des Etudes Economique of France. The comparison of productivity is made by comparing the net value of output per worker converted into the same monetary unit. We are aware of the fact that in the comparison, numerous individual products between the two countries will vary in quality and size. As a consequence, the labor consumption in the production will also vary. Thus, comparison of physical output of products, unless they are clearly homogeneous, is fraught with inaccuracies. We believe that the value of a product would adequately reflect quality and size, and hence comparison of value of output of labor in the two countries would better reflect their relative efficiency, e.g. production of automobiles.

In Table I labor productivity in American industries has been related to labor productivity in French industries, the latter assumed to be equal to one. For nineteen industries in the years 1958 and 1963, the average U.S.–French labor productivity ratio is equal to 2.07 and 2.06 respectively.

We have used three different expressions of labor productivity. They are (1) average value of output by total employees (Table III),

* The article has been adapted from the author's doctoral dissertation at the New School, New York (1969). The author gratefully acknowledges his indebtedness to Professor Hans Neisser for his interest in the study and valuable help. Thanks are also due to Drs. A. Kahler, F. Deyrup and R. Stevens for useful comments.

(2) average value of yearly output of production workers (Table IV), and (3) average value of hourly output of production workers (Table V). We have determined productivity ratios with the aid of all the three labor inputs. We can take any one of the measurements.

TABLE I

LABOR PRODUCTIVITY COMPARISON IN 19 SELECTED MANUFACTURING INDUSTRIES

Output Per Worker	*1958*	*1963*
France	100	100
U.S.A. (unweighted)	207	206
U.S.A. (weighted with French employment)	216	234
U.S.A. (weighted with U.S. employment)	226	248
Output Per Production Worker	*1958*	*1963*
France	100	100
U.S.A. (unweighted)	224	204
Output Per Man Hour	*1958*	*1963*
France	100	100
U.S.A. (unweighted)	252	221

In the analysis that follows, we have used output per worker as the basis for comparison between the United States and France. These figures express the average contribution of each worker employed in each industry. Contribution of each worker to total product varies from industry to industry, depending upon the capital intensity of production. As France is an industrially advanced country and since the economic structure in France and the United States is similar, the average productivity ratio provides a valuable standard for comparing average achievement per economically active person in both countries.

We considered as production workers in France those whose wage rate is determined on an hourly basis. Salaried staff includes technicians, craftsmen, and white collar workers.[1] This classification in the U.S.A. gives production workers as those 'engaged in fabricating, processing, assembling, inspection, receiving, storing, handling packing, warehousing, shipping (but not delivering), maintenance, repair, janitorial, watchman service, closely associated with the production operation at the establishment covered by the report. Supervisory employees above the working foreman level are excluded from this category'.[2]

[1] *Annuaire Statistique*, Institut National de la Statistique et des Etudes Economique, Paris. Vol. 71, 1965, p. 330.

[2] *Census of Manufacture*, U.S. Department of Commerce, Vol. 1, 1963, p. 16.

American industries taken into account in the present study represent 59 per cent and 62 per cent of the total manufacturing industries for the years 1958 and 1963 respectively. French industries represent 75 per cent and 66 per cent of the total manufacturing industries for the years 1958 and 1963 respectively. In this inquiry some of the manufacturing industries like food, lumber, wood products, furniture, printing and petroleum and coal have been left out on account of incomparability of statistics.

On the measurement of productivity in the French industries alone, we have a study by André L. A. Vincent[3] who has worked out

TABLE II

AVERAGE ANNUAL RATE OF GROWTH IN SOME FRENCH MANUFACTURING INDUSTRIES

Industries	*Vincent's study for the period 1959–65*		*Present study for the period 1958–63*
	Global productivity of factors	*Net labor productivity*	*Net labor productivity*
1. Iron and steel	0.9	4.0	2.8
2. Cement }	2.9	7.0	6.1
3. Ceramics }			8.3
4. Textiles	1.5	4.2	5.3
a. Woollen			
b. Cotton			
c. Hosiery			
d. Strings and ropes			
e. Synthetic and silk fabrics			
f. Linen, hemp and jute			
5. Leather and leather products	0.8	1.8	1.6
6. Glass	2.7	4.6	6.2
7. Paper and paper products	2.1	4.9	4.1
8. Electrical machinery	1.2	3.0	4.8
9. Machinery	1.5	3.2	4.2
10. Chemicals }	1.7	4.8	9.3
11. Rubber }			3.2
12. Automobiles	0.6	3.0	6.6

Source: Vincent, A. L. A., *op. cit.*, Table 13, p. 286.

the rate of growth in productivity in 28 industry groups. Of these, 17 industries are included in the present study. Vincent has worked out the annual rate of growth of both global productivity of factors and net labor productivity between 1959 and 1965. We have reproduced the data along with the annual rate of growth in labor productivity obtained in the present study in Table II. In computing global productivity of factors, Vincent has used gross production as the numerator and labor and capital inputs as denominators.[4] In the

[3] Vincent, A. L. A., *La mesure de la productivité*, Dunod, Paris, 1968.
[4] Vincent, A. L. A., *op. cit.*, Annex A.

measurement of net labor productivity, the numerator represents the gross value of output minus the value of factors of production other than labor, i.e. fuel and power, consumable stores, services and goods drawn from other branches of industry, whereas the denominator includes labor input alone, as is the case in the present study. The rate of growth of global productivity of factors is significantly below the rate of growth of net labor productivity because of the exclusion of the value of factors other than labor from the numerator and the inclusion in the denominator of a second factor i.e., capital input. The following industries have been combined with the respective major industries in Vincent's study but have been excluded in the present study: (i) iron ore is included in the Iron and Steel industry; (ii) building products and minerals not elsewhere classified are combined with Cement and Ceramic industries; (iii) motor cycles, motorized cycles and bicycles are combined with the automobile industry. Rubber and chemical industries have been combined whereas in the present study they are computed separately.

According to Table III the ratio of American labor productivity per worker in terms of value of output ranges from 1.35 to 3.80, and from 1.01 to 3.57 for the years 1958 and 1963 respectively. In the following industries for the year 1958, the ratio of output per worker is greater than 2.07, which is the average for all industries: (i) linen and hemp, (ii) ceramics, (iii) glass, (iv) fabricated metal products, (v) automobiles, (vi) chemicals, (vii) paper, (viii) instruments and watches, (ix) machinery, and (x) electrical machinery.

For the year 1963, the industries in which U.S. labor productivity per worker in terms of value of output is more than 2.06 times (which is the average for all industries), the French productivity is as follows: (i) linen and hemp, (ii) ceramics, (iii) fabricated metal products, (iv) automobiles, (v) paper, (vi) instruments and watches, (vii) machinery, (viii) electrical machinery, and (ix) chemicals.

Table III reveals the fact that U.S. superior productivity is higher in those industries like engineering and chemical industries, where higher capital per worker is needed. The iron and steel industry, however, is the solitary exception to the general pattern. The U.S. productivity was 1.35 times that of France in 1958 and rose to 1.44 times by 1963. However, the figure for 1958 refers to value of output, whereas in 1963 it refers to physical output. In 1958 American physical output was 1.41 times that of France, which shows that physical productivity has remained at the same level.

In the less capital intensive industries, such as leather and textiles, the superiority of the U.S. industries is less marked than the average productivity ratio for all manufacturing industries. This could be

TABLE III

ESTIMATED VALUE OF OUTPUT PER WORKER IN SOME MANUFACTURING INDUSTRIES OF FRANCE AND THE U.S.A.

Index Numbers: France 1958 and 1963 = 100

No.	*Industry*	*1958*	*1963*
1.	Iron and steel	135	144
2.	Cement	139	145
3.	Woollen	161	127
4.	Cotton	162	146
5.	Hosiery	167	181
6.	Strings and ropes	174	101
7.	Leather and leather products	178	154
8.	Rubber	204	197
9.	Synthetic and silk fabrics	206	152
10.	Paper and paper products	213	237
11.	Electrical machinery	215	238
12.	Machinery	222	247
13.	Glass	222	202
14.	Chemicals	223	232
15.	Ceramics	227	195
16.	Instruments and watches	234	257
17.	Linen, hemp and jute	237	236
18.	Fabricated metal products	311	357
19.	Automobiles	380	353
	Average (unweighted)	207	206.47

TABLE IV

ESTIMATED VALUE OF OUTPUT PER PRODUCTION WORKER IN SOME MANUFACTURING INDUSTRIES OF FRANCE AND THE U.S.A.

Index Numbers: France 1958 and 1963 = 100

No.	*Industry*	*1958*	*1963*
1.	Iron and steel	146	144
2.	Cement	121	146
3.	Woollen	150	118
4.	Cotton	155	191
5.	Hosiery	160	171
6.	Strings and ropes	173	105
7.	Leather and leather products	149	175
8.	Rubber	195	186
9.	Synthetic and silk fabrics	184	138
10.	Paper and paper products	251	243
11.	Electrical machinery	218	234
12.	Machinery	239	244
13.	Glass	221	196
14.	Chemicals	292	211
15.	Ceramics	240	231
16.	Instruments and watches	259	278
17.	Linen, hemp and jute	253	237
18.	Fabricated metal products	347	377
19.	Automobiles	292	254
	Average (unweighted)	224	204

attributed to the nature of the textile industry which needs less capital and less skilled personnel than in other industries. Besides, textile technology is less sophisticated than the technology used in engineering industries. A larger percentage of the output of the textile industry of France compared to that of the U.S. is meant for export. In addition, between 1955 and 1963, there has been a difference between the rate of growth of the textile industry in both countries. On an average, France increased her output in textiles during this period by 3.75 per cent per year; the corresponding figure for the U.S.A. was 2.37 per cent.

TABLE V

ESTIMATED VALUE OF OUTPUT PER MAN HOUR IN SOME MANUFACTURING INDUSTRIES OF FRANCE AND THE U.S.A.

Index Numbers: France 1958 and 1963 = 100

No.	*Industry*	*1958*	*1963*
1.	Iron and steel	182	168
2.	Cement	189	160
3.	Woollen	163	161
4.	Cotton	157	176
5.	Hosiery	191	169
6.	Strings and ropes	199	139
7.	Leather and leather products	216	205
8.	Rubber	234	218
9.	Synthetic and silk fabrics	225	146
10.	Paper and paper products	285	269
11.	Electrical machinery	232	238
12.	Machinery	272	258
13.	Glass	239	200
14.	Chemicals	310	243
15.	Ceramics	268	265
16.	Instruments and watches	287	296
17.	Linen, hemp and jute	282	239
18.	Fabricated metal products	384	371
19.	Automobiles	310	282
	Average (unweighted)	252	221

This partially explains the narrow range of difference in productivity between the U.S. and France in the textile industry. Index of production in the textile industry for France and the U.S. is shown in Table VI.

Chemical Industry

A partial explanation of why U.S. superiority in the highly capital intensive chemical industry is not as high as in engineering industries, can be found in the phenomenal growth of the French chemical industry in the 1950s and early 1960s. The value of output in the chemical industry in France increased by 61 per cent between 1958 and 1963 whereas the total employment in the industry increased by 9 per cent only. Output and employment increased in the U.S.A. for the corresponding period by 46.5 per cent and 10.3

TABLE VI

INDEX OF PRODUCTION IN THE TEXTILE INDUSTRY

Production Index 1953 = 100

Year	*France*	*U.S.A.*
1955	102	103
1956	110	105
1957	116	101
1958	111	99
1959	108	114
1960	119	110
1961	122	112
1962	121	120
1963	132	122

Source: O.E.E.C., *Trends in Economic Sectors, The Textile Industry in Europe*; O.E.C.D., Textile Committee (1955–64).

TABLE VII

RATE OF GROWTH IN THE CHEMICAL INDUSTRY

(Percentage over previous years)

Year	*France*	*U.S.A.*
1954	15.0	—
1955	15.6	13
1956	10.1	6
1957	15.7	4
1958	14.2	0
1959	11.0	11
1960	31.0	6
1961	7.0	5
1962	9.0	10
1963	8.0	10

Source: O.E.E.C., *Trend in Economic Sectors; The Chemical Industry in O.E.E.C. Countries, 1954–58*; O.E.C.D., *Trend in Economic Sectors; The Chemical Industry in O.E.C.D. Countries, 1960–64.*

per cent respectively. A special feature of the chemical industry in France is that it has maintained a rate of growth far in excess of the general industrial growth in that country. Compared with that, the rate of growth of U.S. output was declining and in 1958 France outpaced all other European countries by achieving a very high rate of growth. However, since 1960, the U.S. rate of growth has kept pace, and has even slightly increased over that of France. The rate of growth of the American and French chemical industries for some years is given in Table VII.

Iron and Steel Industry

One of the factors that contributed to the favourable position of the French iron and steel industry was the establishment of the European Coal and Steel Community (E.C.S.C.) in 1949, which increased competition through the abolition of tariffs, equilization of tariff rates and action against subsidies, price discrimination and other forms of restrictive practices in the common market countries.

TABLE VIII

INDICES OF INVESTMENT IN THE IRON AND STEEL INDUSTRY

Base Year 1955 = 100

Year	*France*	*U.S.A.*
1955	100	100
1956	126	187
1957	147	240
1958	156	163
1959	177	161
1960	231	249
1961	341	157
1962	304	148
1963	293	170

Source: O.E.E.C. and O.E.C.D., *Trends in Economic Sectors—The Iron and Steel Industry in Europe, 1958–64.* Original figures were given in millions of dollars for both countries. Investment for France was reconverted into francs and index numbers were computed.

Competition has led to the overall growth and productivity of the European steel industry in general and that of France in particular. Between 1953 and 1961, steel production was increasing in France and levelled off by 1963. U.S. steel production, on the contrary, fell heavily in 1958, although production began to increase between 1961 and 1963; French investments in iron and steel has shown a consistent increase over every preceding year from 1955 until 1962, as seen from Table VIII. In contrast, U.S. investment has been haphazard, declining between 1958 and 1959 and again between 1961 and 1962.

It is commonly known that capital per worker is an important factor affecting labor productivity. In the absence of comparable information about the capital available per worker, we have used an indirect method of assessing capital per worker, i.e. the amount of fuel consumed per worker. More fuel is consumed if machinery increases. One of the reasons for the higher productivity of the U.S.A. is the abundant use of machinery. Different kinds of fuel are used in different industries in both countries. To arrive at a common denominator, we have reduced all inputs of fuel into a single unit of kilowatt hours of electricity to facilitate comparison. Fuel input for all French industries is not available. Therefore, our comparison has been made with regard to eight industries for which information was available (Table IX).

TABLE IX

CONSUMPTION OF KILOWATT HOURS OF ELECTRICITY PER PRODUCTION WORKER AND OUTPUT PER WORKER IN SELECTED INDUSTRIES IN THE U.S.A.
Index: France = 100

Industry	*1958*		*1963*	
	Consumption of electricity	*Output per worker*	*Consumption of electricity*	*Output per worker*
Iron and steel	94	135	87	144
Cement	175	139	193	145
Rubber	207	204	219	197
Glass	143	222	135	202
Ceramics	529	227	285	217
Paper	135	232	164	237
Chemicals	141	223	120	232

We found that consumption of fuel is higher in all the industries in the U.S.A., except in the iron and steel industry. Although output is higher in all U.S. industries, there is no correspondence between the two ratios. Since our sample of industries is small, due to non-availability of data, we cannot precisely determine the relationship between fuel consumption per worker and output per worker.

In explaining the factors that contribute to the productivity differentials, Rostas,[5] in an earlier study examined the proportion of males to females in the labor force. Table X presents data on female labor force in individual manufacturing industries (U.S. and France).

According to him, each female worker counts for 0.6 male worker. In England there are differential wages for males and females. We have applied this criterion in order to explain productivity differen-

[5] Rostas, L., *Comparative Productivity in British and American Industries*, Cambridge University Press, Cambridge, England, 1948.

tials, since in France, also, the wages of female workers are 0.6 of male workers (see Table XI). In the U.S.A. wages of female workers range between 0.62 and 0.80 of male workers[6] in manufacturing

TABLE X

PERCENTAGE OF FEMALE LABOR FORCE IN FRANCE AND U.S.A.

Industry	*1958*	*1960*	*1962*	*1963*
	France	*U.S.A.*	*France*	*U.S.A.*
Tobacco	47.4	46.2	49.38	47
Ceramics	24.4	15.0	25.0[a]	—
Leather products	36.0	49.1	43.8	53
Cement	—	5.9	—	—
Rubber	30.8	27.0	28.13[a]	29
Paper and allied products	37.98	21.3	37.39	21
Glass	24.1	25.2	17.25	—
Metal products	14.0	17.2	9.1	17
Automobiles	13.2	11.0	—	—
Machinery	10.0	13.6	15.65	13
Electrical machinery	31.4	34.2	36.78	38
Instruments and watches	28.75	48.2	—	34
Textiles	52.61	44.0	54.56	44
Chemicals	30.5	19.1	29.81	19
Iron and steel	7.2	5.1	—	—

[a] Refers to 1963 for France.
Source: Annuaire Statistique, Vol. 65 for France and Vol. 70, p. 63; *Census of Population 1960*, pp. 1–565 (U.S.A.); U.S.A. *Statistical Abstract—1963*, p. 227.

TABLE XI

RATIO OF FEMALE WAGES TO MALE WAGES IN FRANCE 1958

Metallurgy Metal products Instruments, watches and clocks	0.6
Machinery Automobiles	0.7
Glass	0.62
Leather and leather products	0.6
Paper and carbon	0.56
Chemicals and rubber	0.60

Source: 'Etudes Statistique Supplement Trimestriel du bulletin', *Mensuele d'Statistique*, Paris, 1959, p. 154.

industries. For all the manufacturing industries the percentage of the female labor force in France is 35.5 per cent[7] and 33.3 per cent[8] for the years 1958 and 1962 respectively.

[6] Bureau of Labor Statistics—*Bulletin* Nos. 103, 177, 1360, 1378, 1386 and 1486; Dept. of Commerce, U.S.A.

[7] *Annuaire Statistique*, Vol. 65.

[8] *Ibid.*, Vol. 70, p. 63.

For the United States, the figures are 26 per cent[9] and 26 per cent for the years 1960 and 1963. The dissimilarity in the years of comparison does not prejudice the analysis, since the female labor force in the manufacturing industries has remained constant in the U.S.A. at 26 per cent from 1950.[10] In those industries where the percentage of females in the total employment is significantly higher than that of the U.S.A., France stands in a much better light in terms of productivity ratio. This is especially seen in the textile industry. There are two industries (paper and chemicals) where France has both a higher percentage of female labor force and a lower productivity ratio. In industries where the percentage of females in the total employment is similar in both countries, French productivity is lower than that of the U.S.A.

One of the factors contributing to the lower wages of females in France is that they are not craft workers. In the United States the skills of the female labor force are similar to those of the males, although they do not enjoy equal wages.

If we assume that the French female workers' productivity is 0.6 of the male workers' based on the ratio of their wages, it would explain only 15 per cent of the productivity differences between the two countries.

Size of the Market

Among the factors that contribute to higher productivity, the size of the market has an important influence. Classical theory laid stress on international division of labor as a factor contributing to higher productivity, assuming, of course, that there exists a liberal system of international trade. Adam Smith wrote that 'the division of labor, however, so far as it can be introduced, occasions in every art, a proportionable increase of the productive powers of labor'.[11] Large markets give full scope for research, productivity, lower production costs and increased consumption. Mass production ensures full utilization of capacity, thereby cutting down on costs. There are also advantages in financial charges since large firms are able to borrow money on favorable terms. Modern technology, to be exploited sufficiently, requires large firms. The larger the volume of production, the greater are the economies of scale. Large production, of course, is limited by the size of the market. The size of the market is an important variable in determining the level of productivity. It can be argued that market size itself can be increased through lower

[9] *Statistical Abstract of the United States*, 1963, p. 230.
[10] *Ibid.*
[11] Smith, Adam, *The Wealth of Nations*. Everyman Library, New York, N.Y., pp. 5–9.

relative costs obtained with increased productivity. This could be more true of the domestic markets than of the foreign markets. Growth of manufacturing industries is responsive to the growth of domestic markets whereas securing foreign markets depends, in addition to cost factors, on many non-economic factors such as established trade connections and political conditions. In the case of domestic markets, one can either argue that the increase in productivity would bring about higher income levels which would increase market size, or, an increase in demand for products would result in introduction of mass production techniques, thus increasing productivity. There is a circular reasoning here. Scitovsky[12] has explained the circular reasoning with regard to the European experience. The scale of operation of European business is generally smaller than those in the United States, and European business opts for intimately known market 'than for a larger and impersonal market with small profit margin where he must ever be on the alert to keep his position and preserve his profit'.[13] In addition, European businessmen feel (although incorrectly) 'that mass production involves a sacrifice of quality, workmanship and finish. They also underestimate the price elasticity of demand'.[14]

Further we should recognize certain advantages inherent in the size of a nation. Fabricant[15] in his study of the size and efficiency of the American economy states that in larger economies, there are certain advantages of specialization available even to new firms. 'In the U.S. management, consulting and advertising firms stand ready to aid anyone in developing and launching a product. The cost curves of industries in a country as large as the U.S. are generally lower than in other countries.'[16]

We tried to verify the theory of the correspondence between large markets and higher productivity in the case of U.S.A. and France. We definitely find a correlation between high productivity and large volume of production. Our correlation coefficient between productivity ratios and the ratio of output for all industries, except sugar, for the years 1958 and 1963 are 0.51 and 0.70 respectively, significant at 5 per cent level. The size of the U.S. industries in relation to the French industries measured in terms of total output are given in Table XII.

[12] Scitovsky, T., 'International Trade and Economic Integration as a means of overcoming the disadvantages of a small nation', in *Economic Consequences of the Size of Nations*. St. Martin's Press, New York, 1963.

[13] *Ibid.*, p. 287.

[14] *Ibid.*, p. 287. Scitovsky, T., *op cit*.

[15] Fabricant, S. 'Study of the size and efficiency of the American economy' in *Economic Consequences of the Size of Nations*, *op. cit.*

[16] *Ibid.*, p. 44.

Rostas also used the hypothesis of relating market size and productivity. The results of his analysis led him to believe that

> . . . there is some inter-relationship between size of the market and productivity in the sense that greatest relative advantage in productivity in the U.S. is shown in industries where the U.S. market is relatively very big.[17]

TABLE XII

ESTIMATED VALUE OF OUTPUT IN SOME MANUFACTURING INDUSTRIES

Index Number: France = 100

No.	*Industry*	*1958*	*1963*
1.	Linen, hemp and jute	44	55
2.	Woollen	120	64
3.	Synthetic and silk fabrics	212	196
4.	Strings and ropes	316	230
5.	Ceramics	328	282
6.	Cotton	425	412
7.	Cement	458	351
8.	Hosiery	508	458
9.	Iron and steel	541	565
10.	Leather and leather products	600	518
11.	Chemicals	695	668
12.	Glass	809	687
13.	Machinery	915	850
14.	Electrical machinery	983	1150
15.	Instruments and watches	1009	1448
16.	Rubber	1026	962
17.	Automobiles	1156	1463
18.	Paper and paper products	2462	2665
19.	Fabricated metal products	2553	3307

The findings of the O.E.E.C. study by Paige and Bombach[18] covering over half the entire manufacturing sector of the U.S.A. and U.K., also corroborate the market size hypothesis. In that study the rank correlation coefficient between the output per worker indices and the volume indices for 44 industries is 0.789.[19]

In the present study the value of American output in all industries except linen and jute for the years 1958 and 1963 is higher than that of France. For the year 1963, in addition to linen and jute, the value of production in the woollen industry in the U.S.A. is below that of France.

One is impressed by the fact that American production is substantial (at least 9 times over) in the following industries in both the years under study: (i) automobiles, (ii) manufacture of metals,

[17] Rostas, *op. cit.*, p. 59.

[18] Paige, D. and Bombach, G., *A Comparison of National Output and Productivity*, O.E.E.C., Paris, 1959.

[19] *Ibid.*, p. 69.

(iii) electrical machinery, (iv) instruments and watches, (v) machinery other than electrical, (vi) paper, (vii) rubber. It is significant that in these industries American productive advantage is decisive.

In industries where the U.S. has a larger increase in the size of her industry compared with France since 1958, she also has increased her productivity advantage. The following are the industries where the above observation applies: electrical machinery, instruments and watches, paper and paper products, and iron and steel. The exception to the pattern is the automobile industry. This might suggest that beyond a certain size, economies of scale may not operate.

Where the U.S. has failed to increase the size of her industry, compared to that of France since 1958, her productivity advantage has declined. This observation applies to the following industries: Leather products, strings and ropes, woollen, cotton, artificial textiles, rubber, glass and ceramics. The exceptions are the following industries: manufacture of metals, machinery other than electric, hosiery, cement, and chemicals. In the case of the chemical industry, the decline in the size of the industry and the increased productivity advantage are negligible.

We have examined some factors, such as the degree of mechanization and composition of the labor force and the size of the industry. The role of management in contributing to the productive growth of industry cannot be overestimated. The volume of spending on creative research is a factor that contributes to the productivity in industry. There are other factors, such as technological development and raw materials used, and the attitude and willingness of the worker to make an effort, which have a bearing on the output per worker. Among them are the lack of unionization and, in some cases, fear among the unions about mechanization. It was only in the late fifties that French trade unions accepted the idea of participating in productivity improvements initiated by the employers. In the immediate post-war years, the attitude of the French worker was one of indifference. By the fifties, the French trade unions accepted the importance of increasing productivity and their resistance turned into cooperation. Since then, several organizations designed to further productivity increase were established. Among them are the French Association for higher productivity (A.F.A.P.), which is a private association, the National Productivity Board, which was set up by the French Government, and the Trade Union Center for the study of Productivity established by the trade unions.

There are yet other factors, such as internal factory conditions, layout of the plant, safety measures and hygienic conditions, etc. These factors are beyond the scope of the present study.

There is yet one more factor on which we will comment, namely the number of hours worked. Many writers have commented on the increase in productivity as a result of a drop in the number of hours worked by the worker. For instance, Fabricant, while examining the U.S. productivity during 1899–1939, commented 'as for the increased efficiency of labor itself, one third drop in hours (from 60 to 40) must have contributed to it'.[20]

The average weekly hours for manufacturing industries in France are 45.1 and 45.8 for the years 1958 and 1963 respectively, while for the U.S.A. they were 39.2 and 40.8 for the same period (see Table XIII). The index of hours per week for France is 115 and 112 for the

Table XIII

AVERAGE WEEKLY HOURS OF WORK IN FRANCE AND THE U.S.A.

No.	*Industry*	*1958*		*1963*	
		France	*U.S.A.*	*France*	*U.S.A.*
1.	Woollen	43.0	38.6	44.1	41.2
2.	Cement	46.8	40.0	47.2	41.2
3.	Linen, hemp and jute	43.0	38.6	44.1	41.3
4.	Ceramics	46.8	40.0	47.2	39.1
5.	Strings and ropes	42.0	38.6	44.1	41.3
6.	Iron and steel	47.8	38.1	47.5	40.2
7.	Leather and leather products	42.4	36.8	44.7	37.5
8.	Cotton	43.0	38.6	44.1	40.9
9.	Glass	46.8	40.0	47.2	40.0
10.	Hosiery	43.0	38.6	44.1	38.1
11.	Rubber	45.2	39.4	45.2	40.8
12.	Synthetic and silk fabrics	43.0	38.6	44.1	42.9
13.	Fabricated metal products	48.0	40.0	47.3	41.4
14.	Automobiles	47.2	39.2	47.3	42.8
15.	Chemicals	45.3	40.9	45.2	41.7
16.	Paper and paper products	45.7	41.9	46.4	42.7
17.	Instruments and watches	43.2	39.9	47.3	40.8
18.	Electrical machinery	46.4	49.6	47.3	40.3
19.	Machinery	47.2	39.6	47.3	41.8

years 1958 and 1963 respectively, with U.S.A. being equal to 100. However, in most European countries there are more holidays, longer vacations and greater time lost through sickness than in the U.S. Denison[21] has worked out an adjustment factor to reflect these conditions in France in order to make the work week comparable with that in the U.S.A. The adjustment factor is 3.1 per cent for 1960. Further, longer weekly hours do not increase output in proportion to hours worked. Output per work week is likely to be

[20] Fabricant, Solomon, *Employment in Manufacturing, 1899–1939*, National Bureau of Economic Research, 1942 (p. 25).

[21] Denison, E. F., *Why Growth Rates Differ*. The Brookings Institution, Washington, D.C. 1967, Appendix D, Table 1–4.

greater in a 48-hour week than in a 40-hour week. However, output per hour will be greater in a 40-hour week than in a 48-hour week because shorter hours result in less fatigue, greater intensity of work, fewer mistakes, better quality of output, less wastage and less absenteeism. How much reduction in weekly output will result by hours reduction has been evaluated in many European countries. The French Planning Commission assumed, for instance, a 30 per cent and 20 per cent productivity offset during the Third and Fourth Plan periods (1958–61; 1962–65) for reduction in weekly hours.[22] Using the adjustment factors mentioned above [(i) Denison, (ii) The French Planning Commission], the longer work week in France in 1958 and 1963 would mean 7.7 per cent and 6.8 per cent more effective labor input respectively per person employed than in the U.S.A.

Conclusion

The study has shown that U.S. superiority is pronounced in capital intensive industries. The exception to the above observation is the iron and steel industry. The explanation is to be sought in the special circumstances associated with the industry with the creation of the European Coal and Steel Community in 1951. Further, the study has laid stress on the size of the market as a factor in explaining the productivity differentials in manufacturing industries. We also find that the productivity gap in the 19 industries between France and the U.S. has not narrowed during the years 1958 and 1963. The usefulness of this study is that it is an important first step in evaluating competition of the two countries in world markets.

NEW YORK INSTITUTE OF TECHNOLOGY

[22] Denison, E. F., *op. cit.*, Quoted in p. 61.

IN DEFENCE OF THE INDUSTRIAL TRAINING ACT

by JAMES J. HUGHES

I. INTRODUCTION

THE purpose of this paper is to consider some of the more serious objections to the Industrial Training Act, 1964. In the view of the present writer such a review is both necessary and timely. It is necessary because certain of the criticisms are ill founded while others are exaggerated. It is timely because the government has just completed a review of training under the Act and published its recommendations for change in the form of a consultative document.[1] Although it proposes that the Industrial Training Boards remain formally constituted it also suggests that levy-grant schemes be phased out. Thus, while the boards are to be given a new lease of life they are to be largely stripped of the powers necessary to ensure that their recommendations and targets are met.

This paper is not intended as a detailed study of the effects and workings of the Act. It is intended primarily to consider those criticisms of the Act which seem to have been important in bringing about a change in government policy. However, it is impossible to discuss these criticisms except against the background leading to the Act, and against the background of how it works and what it seeks to achieve. Accordingly, Section II briefly sketches in the background to the Act while Sections III and IV describe the Act itself and the rationale behind it. Section V deals with the major criticisms of the Act and constitutes the main body of the paper.

II. BACKGROUND TO THE ACT

During the 1950s and early 1960s the volume and quality of training undertaken by British industry was insufficient to meet the skilled manpower requirements of the economy. A Ministry of Labour report published in 1962 revealed that there had been shortages of labour in most skilled occupations since the end of the war.[2] The National Plan, published in 1965, commented that 'shortages of skilled workers have long been a serious obstacle to economic growth.'[3] Some idea of the magnitude of these skill shortages can be obtained by comparing job vacancies with the number unemployed

[1] *Training for the future: a plan for discussion.* D.E., February, 1972.

[2] Report of a Working Party of the National Joint Advisory Council to the Ministry of Labour, *Ministry of Labour Gazette*, February 1962.

[3] *The National Plan*, Cmnd. 2764, H.M.S.O. 1965, p. 40, para. 18.

in skilled trades. It has been estimated[4] that in September 1956 (a year typical of the period 1950–57 in terms of labour demand) there were no more than 10,000 workers unemployed in the main skilled occupations while the number of vacancies in these trades amounted to 49,000—that is, there were about 5 vacancies for every skilled worker unemployed. The corresponding ratio for engineering and allied occupations was greater than 5 to 1, and for draughtsmen it exceeded 22 to 1. Although there was some relaxation in the tightness in the market for skilled labour after 1956 shortages still persisted well into the 1960s.[5]

During this period the failure of the training system to meet the skilled manpower requirements of the economy was attributed in large part to the prevalence of 'poaching'[6] and the inadequacy of the institutional arrangements for training.[7] Although certain changes were beginning to appear by 1964[8] it was against this background of skilled labour bottlenecks that the Industrial Training Act was passed.

III. THE 1964 ACT

The Act had three main objectives:[9]

1. To ensure an adequate supply of properly trained men and women at all levels of industry.
2. To secure an improvement in the quality and efficiency of industrial training.
3. To share the cost of training more evenly between firms.

Under the Act a Central Training Council (C.T.C.) was established and the Secretary of State empowered to set up Industrial Training Boards (I.T.B.s). To date 27 statutory boards have been established and their range of operation and influence extends over an area covering some 15 million workpeople in agriculture, services, manufacturing and public utilities. The boards are organized

[4] Sentosh Mukherjee, *Changing Manpower Needs: A Study of Industrial Training Boards* P.E.P. Broadsheet 523, November 1970, p. 10.

[5] *Ibid.*, p. 15.

[6] Poaching occurs when firms recruit skilled labour that has been trained by other firms rather than train to meet their own requirements. Obviously the scope for poaching arises because labour is mobile as between firms and industries. This necessarily implies that the type of labour that is poached possesses skills that are of general, rather than specific, use.

[7] This was especially true of the time-serving system of apprenticeship. The Carr Report *Training for Skill* 1957, drew attention to the inadequacies of this system.

[8] According to G. T. Page in *The Industrial Training Act and After*, Andre Deutsch, 1967, group training schemes were making significant developments. Also, the reduction in the period of apprenticeship in the building industry, from 5 to 4 years, can be taken as further evidence of change.

[9] These are listed on p. 5. of *Industrial Training Act General Guide*, Ministry of Labour, 1964.

vertically along industrial lines rather than horizontally according to occupational classifications.

The membership of an I.T.B. consists of an equal number of employers and employees together with independent members representing technical and further education interests. Each board is responsible for identifying the training needs within its sphere of activity and for ensuring that sufficient training is undertaken to meet these needs. In addition, each board is responsible for the establishment and enforcement of training standards. All boards, with the exception of those covering the electricity supply and man-made fibre industries, attempt to achieve these objectives, together with the wider goal of a more equitable distribution of training costs,[10] through the operation of a levy-grant system. In addition, they provide guidance on training matters, and in certain instances off-the-job training in their own centres.

Levy-grant policies differ from one board to another, each board being left free to formulate its own policy according to the training needs of its own industry. Levies are sometimes assessed on a *per capita* basis but more usually as a percentage of a firm's payroll. There are basically 3 types of grant—general, specific, and supplementary. These are usually paid, subject to approved training standards, on a *per capita* basis or on the basis of actual costs incurred. The calculation of grant can become more complicated if it is based not simply on actual training performance, but upon performance in relation to some estimated training need.

The C.T.C. has a broad based membership representing employers, trade unions, nationalized industries and the I.T.B.s themselves. The role of the Council is 'to keep under review the adequacy of training arrangements in industry and to advise the Minister on the use he should make of his powers to remedy deficiencies.'[11] It also serves to co-ordinate the work of I.T.B.s, especially with regard to training matters that relate to occupations and skills that are common to several industries.

IV. THE RATIONALE BEHIND THE ACT

The rationale behind the Act is that the free working of the market system does not result in an adequate volume and quality of training. This is explained by the existence of externalities in training which

[10] As Mukherjee, *op. cit.*, p. 28, points out, this objective is not made explicit in the Act even though it is listed as one of the three objectives in other 'official literature'. However, since the Act makes provision for the use of the levy-grant system to stimulate training, the redistribution of training cost objective is implied in the Act.

[11] *Industrial Training Act: General Guide*, *op. cit.*, p. 15.

cause social benefits to diverge from private benefits. Such an externality will arise when one firm (X) hires skilled labour that has been trained by another firm (Y). If firm X is no longer able to recruit its skilled labour from firm Y then it will have to bear the cost of training itself, or forgo the addition to output and profits which result from employing this particular type of skilled labour. Thus, while it is able to recruit labour from Y, X benefits directly from Y's investment in skill training because it does not incur costs that it otherwise would. Firm Y will determine the amount of resources to devote to training by equating the marginal return accruing to itself—resulting from the provision of the training facilities—with the marginal cost of provision. In calculating the marginal return to itself Y will take account of the likely loss of trained labour to X. That is, Y will reduce any future stream of benefits that result from the employment of skilled labour, to take account of the mobility of such labour between itself and X. The marginal return to Y will therefore understate the marginal returns accruing to X and Y jointly.

Therefore, given that there are externalities associated with private investment in training, the equilibrium volume of training resulting in the market will be sub-optimal for society because at the market determined level the marginal social return will exceed the marginal private return. Where training firms are over-cautious and make undue allowances for outward mobility of trained labour they will always underestimate the marginal private return to training—thereby increasing the divergence between marginal social return and marginal private return—and the market determined volume of training will fall further below the social optimum.

Although there will be a tendency for all firms to equate, at the margin, the private costs and returns of investment in training it does not necessarily follow that all firms will in practice provide training facilities. Neither does it follow that those firms that do train will provide only for their own skill requirements. For this reason the analysis needs modifying somewhat.

Since the skilled manpower requirements of small firms will not be great only small amounts of training will be necessary to meet their needs. However, where small amounts of training are involved the marginal cost of provision might exceed the marginal return. Under such circumstances it would be uneconomic for small firms to engage in training. On the other hand, large firms—whose training requirements will tend to be large—might have an incentive to provide training in excess of that necessary to meet their own skill requirements. If economies of scale exist in training, and if training—like production—is profitable in itself, it might pay large firms to expand training beyond their own requirements.

In a situation in which some firms train while others do not a shortfall in the supply of trained labour is not inevitable. However, such a shortfall will arise if the training firms do not train sufficient labour, in excess of their own requirements, to meet the needs of non-training firms. In practice this is likely to be the case if the private benefits derived from training 'excess' labour fall short of the benefits that accrue to society from the employment of this 'excess' supply of trainees. The private return from training excess labour will be equivalent to the direct profit derived from training excess trainees during the training period, together with any indirect reduction in the cost of providing training to meet the firm's own future skilled manpower requirements.[12]

It has been suggested by Liepmann that employers break even on apprenticeship training after about 2 years.[13] That is the total training costs incurred during the first 2 years are just matched by the addition to revenue that results from the employment of apprentices. During the third and subsequent years of training the employment of apprentices is a direct source of profit. Therefore, assuming a 5-year period of apprenticeship, the direct profit that a firm will derive from employing another trainee in excess of its own requirements will consist of the difference between the trainee's contribution to output and the wage paid to the trainee during the last 3 years of the apprenticeship. Obviously, the size of the profit will depend upon the shape and position of the trainee learning curve, which will govern the rate of increase in trainee output, relative to the rate of increase in the trainee wage during the last 3 years of apprenticeship. The direct profit resulting from the provision of apprenticeship training will therefore be greater if increases in trainee output occur earlier rather than later. Similarly, profit will be greater the longer it is possible to postpone any increase in the trainee wage.

The indirect increase in profit resulting from any reduction in unit training costs will depend upon the extent to which economies of scale exist in training. Where training takes the form of instruction on-the-job rather than simply learning from experience—and apprenticeship training would seem to fall into this category—the scope for securing economies might be limited because instructors who are also employed in production and maintenance will have a

[12] This distinction between direct and indirect profit is somewhat spurious since in practice any reduction in unit training costs will also affect direct profit.

[13] K. Liepmann, *Apprenticeship*, London 1960; cited by B. J. M. McCormick and P. S. Manley in 'The Industrial Training Act', *Westminster Bank Review*, Feb., 1967, pp. 44–56.

limited span of control.[14] Where training can be carried out efficiently off-the-job the scope for securing economies of scale is likely to be much greater.

Whether or not the training firms will compensate for the non-training firms and ensure a sufficient supply of trained labour for the economy as a whole will depend upon the relationship between marginal private return (M.P.R.) and marginal social return (M.S.R.) to training. Since the volume of training is determined by equating marginal private cost (M.P.C.) with M.P.R., a shortfall will occur if M.P.R. is less than M.S.R. Where a firm trains in excess of its own requirements M.P.R. will always fall short of M.S.R. (given externalities exist) if the firm does not make a profit on training itself. If the firm does derive a profit from training, M.P.R. will exceed M.S.R. only if the profit derived from each trainee during the training period is greater than the gains to society in the post training period when the excess supply of trainees is employed in other firms. Whether or not this condition will be fulfilled will depend upon the nature of the skill trained for, and the life expectancy of that skill. Given that the direct profit from training an extra worker can only be a fraction of trainee output over a 3-year period it is tempting to conclude that the condition will not be met if the skill trained for has a life expectancy greater than just a few years. More strictly, the condition—that M.P.R. is greater than M.S.R.—will only be met if

$$\sum_{t=3}^{5} P_t \frac{(q_t - w_t)}{(1+r)^t} > \sum_{t=6}^{n+5} \frac{(Q_t - Q'_t)}{(1+s)^t}$$

where P_t = probability that worker who enters into training will still be under training in year t.
q_t = trainee output in year t.
w_t = trainee wage in year t.
Q_t = output of trained worker in year t.
Q'_t = output of untrained worker in year t.
n = life expectancy of the skill trained for.
r = private rate of discount.
s = social rate of discount.

Thus, the higher is the trainee wage (w_t) during the last 3 years of the apprenticeship the less likely it is that the condition will be met, and the more likely is there to be a shortfall in the amount of training undertaken. Similarly, the higher the annual increment of output

[14] That is, the most efficient ratio of instructors to trainees might be low.

$(Q_t - Q'_t)$ attributable to training that accrues in the post-training period, and the greater the number of years (n) for which this accrues, the more likely is there to be a shortfall in the supply of trained labour.

Whether or not the condition is fulfilled in practice can only be adduced by observing the pattern of labour demand and supply. Evidence has already been cited concerning the inadequate supply of craftsmen in the U.K. in the 1950s and early 1960s, before the Act was passed. Furthermore, there was an actual decline of some 50,000 in the number of craftsmen during the decade 1951–61.[15] Such evidence of shortages in the supply of skilled labour would seem to imply that even though many firms might have been training in excess of their own requirements, they did not do so on a sufficiently large scale to enable the requirements of the non-training firms to be fully met. It was to meet this deficiency that the Industrial Training Act was passed. With its reliance upon the levy-grant system this should ensure that firms that train in excess of their own requirements receive a grant in excess of their levy, while firms whose training output is insufficient to meet their needs contribute more in levy than they receive in grant. Thus the external economies derived by those firms recruiting (poaching) trained labour will be reduced and the incentive for them to provide facilities for training will be increased.

V. CRITICISMS OF THE ACT

1. *Collective Intervention*

The most severe criticism of the Act is to be found in a recent article by Professor D. Lees and Mr. B. Chiplin.[16] In this article Lees and Chiplin claim that the I.T.B.s have no basis in economic logic. This criticism seems to be based in part upon a general dislike of state intervention in economic activity, and in part upon a particular dislike of the form of intervention that the 1964 Act takes. On the general level they argue that criticism of the Act 'merges with that of detailed central planning generally', which 'presumes that there is some collective wisdom and foresight that will produce a more rational and orderly outcome than the pushes and pulls of market forces'.[17]

[15] A. Brown, C. Leicester and F. Pyatt 'Output, Manpower and Industrial Skills in the U.K.' in *The Residual Factor in Economic Growth*, O.E.C.D., Paris, 1964. Cited in McCormick and Manley, *op. cit.*

[16] D. Lees and B. Chiplin, 'The Economics of Industrial Training', *Lloyds Bank Review*, April 1970, pp. 29–41.

[17] *Ibid.*, p. 40.

Obviously the architects of the Act recognized the existence of externalities in training and believed that some form of collective intervention would lead to a more optimal outcome than would the unfettered workings of the labour market. Lees and Chiplin, in their general criticism of collective intervention, offer no cogent theoretical argument as to why the Act should not result in an increase in the quantity and quality of trained labour. Indeed, they acknowledge that since the Act was passed more firms are undertaking training and that overall there has been an increase in both the quantity and quality of industrial training.[18] For this reason it is difficult to take seriously the general criticism of Lees and Chiplin concerning collective intervention in the field of industrial training.

In the main the criticism of Lees and Chiplin is directed against the type of intervention rather than intervention *per se*. Indeed, they claim that there is 'only one area of useful state intervention in the field of industrial training—the provision of finance to workers to help meet the costs of general training'.[19] The subsidization of workers rather than firms as under the Act, is also advocated by McCormick and Manley.[20]

2. *Subsidization of workers rather than Firms*[21]

This argument in favour of worker subsidization is based upon the following reasoning. The inadequate supply of trained labour results from firms taking a 'free ride' (poaching). However, employers taking a free ride will only be able to do so with respect to generally trained labour. This is because labour that is specific to one firm will be of no use to another firm. In a perfect world economic theory predicts that workers will bear the cost of investment in general training while employers will finance training that is specific to their own needs. Since this is so it is argued that employers should not be held responsible for a shortage of generally trained labour. Therefore, measures designed to increase the supply of generally trained labour should not be aimed at employers. Since the responsibility for investment in general training rests with workers themselves any measures that are introduced should be aimed at alleviating the imperfections in the market for human capital. This can be done by granting either loans or subsidies to those workers who wish to acquire general skills.

While it is true that imperfections in the market for human capital might justify loans and grants to workers undergoing general train-

[18] *Ibid.*, pp. 33–35.
[19] *Ibid.*, p. 31.
[20] McCormick and Manley, *op. cit.*, p. 56.
[21] This section has benefited from discussion with Mr. R. J. Dixon.

ing, it does not follow that this is the only worthwhile area of intervention in the field of industrial training. Indeed, to argue that it is so reveals an ignorance of what actually determines the supply of generally trained labour.

The argument in favour of worker subsidization presupposes that the supply of generally trained labour depends only upon the willingness of workers to undergo this form of training. This is not so. The supply of trained labour available in the market in any particular time period depends upon the numbers who have actually undergone training in previous time periods, less any dropouts. The volume of workers actually undergoing training in any period will depend upon the supply of training places that is available and the demand for those places. If the supply of places is absolutely fixed, no amount of increase in the demand for training places—induced by offering subsidies to trainees—will result in an increase in the actual volume of training. However, an increase in demand for training, induced by worker subsidization, would enable those who provide training to be more selective in their recruitment. Therefore the quality of workers entering into training would probably rise.

Those who advocate that worker subsidization is the only worthwhile form of intervention would seem to imply that supply side factors are unimportant in determining the volume of training that is actually undertaken. This probably stems from the mistaken belief that for any firm the supply of training places is perfectly elastic at zero price. Such a belief might arise from a misunderstanding of the full implications of Becker's[22] prediction that a firm operating in perfectly competitive product and labour markets can shift the cost of general training back onto the trainee. This is only true if the demand price for training is greater than, or at least equal to, the supply price (i.e. the cost) of training. Where the supply price exceeds the demand price then the full cost of training cannot be shifted back onto the trainee and the supply of training places will not be costless to the firm. Becker's prediction is only true for the firm that is in equilibrium and it is not dependent upon there being a perfectly elastic supply of training places at zero price. It is true even for an upward sloping supply curve.

Given that resources used in training will be subject to diminishing returns the firm's short run supply curve of training places will have a positive slope. Thus it will be possible, and perhaps even preferable, to increase training output by offering firms greater incentives to increase their supply of training places. The grants paid out by I.T.B.s are a subsidy to training and will thus cause a rightward

[22] G. S. Becker, *Human Capital*, N.B.E.R. 1964. See Chapter 2.

shift in the firms' supply curve. The levy, which is in effect a quasi-poll tax, will in theory have neither incentive nor disincentive effect upon the firms' supply of training places. However, in practice it might 'shock' firms into becoming more training-conscious. Where this happens then training efficiency might be raised and this would have the same effect as a subsidy in shifting the supply curve.

The foregoing analysis does not deny that where the supply of labour is fairly elastic poaching might best be remedied by the provision of state finance for workers. But whether this finance should take the form of subsidies rather than loans is another matter. While recognizing that considerations of equity necessitate that 'workers are treated no less fairly than students' Lees and Chiplin assert that 'strict economic logic' dictates that such finance 'should take the form of loans rather than subsidies'.[23] However, this assertion can be questioned on strictly economic grounds.

An increase in the supply of generally trained labour resulting from the provision of state finance is likely to confer benefits in excess of those accruing to individual trainees. These additional benefits will result if the increased supply of trainees alleviates bottlenecks in the market for skilled labour and thereby enables the economy to be operated at a higher pressure of aggregate demand, and thus at a higher level of employment, before the maximum tolerable rate of inflation is exceeded. Where the labour bottlenecks are in export industries an increase in the supply of trained labour might enable a higher level of employment to be consistent with any given balance of payments objective. The operation of the economy at a higher level of employment will lead to an increase in real income. Wages, profits and government tax revenue should all benefit from such an increase while the amount paid out by the government in unemployment compensation and supplementary benefits should fall. In short, workers, the owners of capital and the government will all benefit if an increase in the supply of trained labour enables a faster rate of growth of real output before the maximum tolerable rate of inflation is exceeded, or before the balance of payments position falls below some minimum acceptable level.

Therefore, given that there are external benefits associated with an increase in the supply of generally trained labour, it does not necessarily follow that government finance for general training should take the form of loans rather than grants. Indeed, economic logic would seem to indicate that the cost of providing such training ought to be shared by the various beneficiaries, with the proportionate

[23] Lees and Chiplin, *op. cit.*, p. 31.

share of the cost to be borne by each related to the share of benefits accruing to each.

3. *The Small Firm*

According to Lees and Chiplin the I.T.A. does not take account of the problems faced by small firms. They point out, quite rightly, that although small firms can 'make efficient use of skilled labour'[24] it is often uneconomic for them to provide the necessary training themselves. It is true that where economies of scale in training exist it might be uneconomic for small firms to train. But it is not a corollary of this that small firms should have access to unlimited supplies of trained labour without bearing a fair share of those training costs that have to be borne by employers. In asserting that small firms 'need wider freedom of manoeuvre than larger firms in order to survive',[25] and by specifically pointing to training costs as an area within which it should be possible to exercise this greater freedom, Lees and Chiplin would seem to be advocating that skilled labour should be made available to small firms on more favourable terms than it is to large firms. Such an argument is unacceptable on economic grounds since it confers unfair cost advantages to small firms which will, at the margin, enable inefficient units to remain in production. Indeed, such an argument is likely to be unacceptable to all except those who favour the preservation of small firms—at whatever cost.

In discussing the problems raised by the existence of small firms it should of course be stressed that the Act does not seek to enforce all firms, irrespective of size, to undertake training. The majority of boards exempt small firms from their levy-grant schemes by introducing a cut-off point at or around £5,000. That is to say, where the annual payroll does not exceed £5,000 per annum the firm is exempted. Even after this point some boards do not charge the full rate of levy until the annual wage bill exceeds a much higher figure. Thus, the introduction of flexibility into the levy-grant system, through the adoption of differential levies for different sized firms would seem to go a long way towards meeting the criticism concerning small firms.

As an example of the inequity of the levy-grant system Lees and Chiplin point to the case of the firm that is too large to be exempted from the levy payment, but too small to engage in much training. They claim that firms which pay the levy but receive little or no grant in return suffer a relative disadvantage under the system. They cite the case of the cotton industry where establishments employing

[24] Lees and Chiplin, *op. cit.*, p. 35. [25] *Ibid.*, p. 35.

less than 50 workers paid 6 per cent of the total levy in 1967/68 while receiving only 1 per cent of the total grant. However, these figures do not permit us to draw the conclusion that small cotton firms are subsidizing large cotton firms. It is impossible to say that small firms are subsidizing large firms, or vice versa, unless we know the distribution of skilled employment, training outlays (including levies) and training grants according to size of establishment. In the cotton industry example, if those firms employing less than 50 workers employ more than 6 per cent of the industry's skilled labour force, and yet only incur 1 per cent or less of the industry's total training costs, they will still be subsidized under the Act even though they pay a much higher proportion of the total levy than they receive in grant. These firms may be worse off after the Act simply because as a result of it they make a greater contribution towards the costs of training the skilled labour that they employ. But a more equitable distribution of costs such as this implies a reduction in the subsidization of small firms by large firms—not as some would infer, the subsidization of large firms by small firms.

If small firms were largely responsible for poaching before the Act was passed[26] it is only to be expected that the introduction of the levy-grant system, which implies a redistribution of training costs, would result in small firms being worse off than they were previously. This no doubt explains why small firms are more critical and more 'hostile' to the I.T.B. system than is industry generally.[27] But firms, like people, become hostile when their security is threatened and their privileges withdrawn. Such hostility does not necessarily imply that grievances are justified. As the Third Report of the C.T.C. points out, some of the complaints of small firms 'may be no more than a protest by those reluctant to face up to training'.[28]

4. *Specificity of Skills*

Becker's[29] analysis of on-the-job training reveals that firms rather than workers will bear the cost of investment in specific skills. It follows that where skills are specific to the investing firm other firms cannot benefit from the investment and thus the question of poaching does not arise. For this reason there is no general case to be made for subsidizing training in specific skills. However, the I.T.A. does not draw the distinction between general and specific skills. In

[26] Mukherjee, *op. cit.*, p. 29.

[27] Confederation of British Industry. 'Operation of the Industrial Training Act: Statement by C.B.I.' This is a supplement to C.B.I. *Education and Training Bulletin*, February, 1971.

[28] Central Training Council, *Third Report to the Secretary of State*, March 1969, p. 19.

[29] Becker, *op. cit.*, pp. 18–29.

implementing the Act the I.T.B.s have also failed to draw this distinction for the purpose of grant payments and this has led Oatey[30] to suggest that firms investing in specific skills might be subsidized by other firms in the industry. In the case of highly specialized firms this subsidy could reach 'significant amounts' because such firms will find it necessary to undertake higher than average amounts of investment in training. Furthermore, where firms with highly specialized skill requirements have poor labour relations that result in a high turnover of workers, the amount of grant received will be even higher, given that I.T.B.s operate *per capita* or cost based grant schemes. As Lees and Chiplin infer, this is tantamount to subsidizing poor labour relations.[31]

While it is true that the failure to draw the distinction between general and specific skills lays the Act open to criticism, it is also true, as Oatey[32] has observed, that in their early years of operation most boards have emphasized and tied grants to such areas as apprenticeship, secretarial, management and group training, all of which have a high general content in them. This amounts to an implicit recognition of the distinction, and as long as boards continue to promote training in these and other areas for which demand is general throughout their industry, the charge of subsidizing the investment of highly specialized firms in highly specialized skills will remain a minor one.

However, if in the future the I.T.B.s promote more energetically the 'systematic approach' to training the charge of subsidizing specialized firms could become more serious. The systematic approach to training was pioneered by the Food, Drink and Tobacco I.T.B. and has since been followed by others. Under this approach grants are related to the quality and quantity of training that is planned and achieved in individual firms. This type of training involves 4 clearly defined stages. These are:

(1) the identification of managerial and supervisory personnel responsible for the training function.
(2) an assessment of current and future training needs.
(3) the development and implementation of programmes to meet these needs.
(4) the collection and recording of data relating to all aspects of training in order to assess the effectiveness of training within the firm.

[30] Michael Oatey, 'The Economics of Training With Respect To The Firm', *B.J.I.R.* Vol. VIII, No. 1. March 1970, pp. 1–21. See especially p. 17.
[31] Lees and Chiplin, *op. cit.*, p. 34.
[32] Oatey, *op. cit.*, p. 18.

The systematic approach to training is to be welcomed inasmuch that it involves a more positive approach to manpower planning at the level of the firm, while at the same time allowing individual firms considerable flexibility in deciding what training to do, and how to do it. However, it could lead to an increase in the subsidization of firms that are dependent upon workers whose training is highly specific. But this need not arise. Under the systematic approach the *per capita* grant will tend to be replaced by a 'lump sum' grant, usually expressed as a percentage of the levy payments. So long as this 'lump sum' grant does not exceed 100 per cent of the levy the problem of subsidization does not arise. Of course the training firm might also receive specific or supplementary grants for undertaking training, in excess of its own requirements, in those areas in which the I.T.B. is particularly keen to promote training. This might mean that the firm's total grant income exceeds its levy payment, but this should not be construed as the subsidization of investment in specific skills.

5. *Negligible skill Requirements*

A related problem is that of the firm whose skill requirements are negligible or non-existent. This is a problem that might be experienced by small firms, but not all small firms fall into this category since some of them have 'complex training needs'.[33] Where training needs are neglibible firms which are sufficiently large to qualify for levy-grant schemes will still have to pay the levy but receive nothing in return. This is undoubtedly inequitable but it should not prove too difficult to identify the firms affected in this way and make special provision for them. The problem could be largely resolved if I.T.B.s made greater use of the differential levy—that is, if they varied the levy, not only according to size of payroll but also according to the needs of individual firms for skilled manpower. A firm whose skill needs are small relative to the size of its labour force would pay a much smaller levy than a firm of similar size whose skill requirements are much greater. The introduction of a levy differentiated according to skill needs would also go some way towards eliminating the subsidization of the firm whose skill needs are specific to itself.[34]

Although greater equity can be achieved through greater reliance upon differential levies this tends to make for greater complexity of the existing levy-grant machinery. However, boards should be able to classify member firms broadly according to their skill needs, and

[33] Central Training Council, Third Report, *op. cit.*, p. 19.

[34] This will be true where these firms do, as Oatey suggests they are likely to, undertake higher-than-average amounts of training.

in extreme cases exempt firms altogether from the levy charge. Any appeal against assessment of the rate of levy would not necessitate the establishment of a new disputes machinery. The machinery already exists through which firms can appeal against their assessment when they believe that they have been classified under the wrong industry grouping.

6. *Labour Mobility*

A further criticism of the levy grant system is that it does not take 'potential labour mobility' into account. This is an important defect because labour mobility does, as Oatey[35] points out, ultimately determine the specificity of investment in training. This failure to take account of potential mobility stems from an excessive emphasis on costs—to the neglect of the benefit side of the calculation.[36] Firms which suffer—through no fault of their own—from a high rate of labour turnover, will not reap the same benefits from a given amount of training investment as will firms that experience a low rate of labour turnover.

Once again the solution to this problem is relatively simple and has already been suggested by Oatey.[37] All that is required is that the training grant is adjusted to take account of potential mobility. Thus firms operating in a high mobility area, such as an industrial conurbaiton, would receive larger grants than firms operating in an isolated area.

7. *Once-for-all Improvement*

It is generally accepted that the levy-grant system is only capable of a once-for-all increase in the quantity and quality of training. This is because as more firms approach the training norms set by I.T.B.s the stimulus to train further will be diminished. As the initial impact dies away it will be necessary to raise levies[38] still further if the level of training performance is to be raised yet again.

It is true that in the early years of their life most boards have found it necessary to raise their levies but this does not mean that there will always be the need for them to do so. For each industry there will exist particular levels of levy and grant that will ensure an adequate volume and standard of training for that industry. Once this volume has been reached there will be no further need for

[35] Oatey, *op. cit.*, p. 18.
[36] *Ibid.*, p. 18.
[37] *Ibid.*, p. 20.
[38] If the amount of training increases as a result of the Act then for financial accounting reasons the size of the grants will have to be reduced unless the levy is raised. If the levy is not raised and grants are reduced the incentive to undertake further training is diminished.

increases and this has led many to conclude that the useful life of the levy-grant system is limited. Oatey quotes estimates of the useful life that vary from 5 to 25 years, with 'the levy perhaps reaching a maximum of 5 per cent, after which presumably everyone will be so training conscious that they will carry on by themselves'.[39]

However, it does not automatically follow that once the desired level of training is reached the levy-grant system should be disbanded, since in its absence the volume of training might fall below the optimum again. For this reason, those boards which are experimenting with the possibility of disengagement from the levy-grant system are not doing so without the retention of a variety of penal levies. Furthermore, even though it might be possible to attain the optimum volume of training after a few years, it is doubtful whether this is true of the quality of training. It seems likely that there will always be scope for raising training standards and the I.T.B.s can seek to achieve this, not by raising levies still further, but by subjecting the payment of grants to more stringent controls, thereby ensuring that training effort is directly relevant to the needs of industry. These needs will undoubtedly change through time but the I.T.B.s are in a unique position to stimulate and actively sponsor the development of new methods of training, not only to meet changing requirements, but also to raise the productivity of training in general. Therefore, it is not true, as Lees and Chiplin claim, that 'there is nothing built into the present system that provides dynamic encouragement to industrial training'.[40] The development of the module system of apprentice and technician training in the engineering industry, which will make it easier to adapt existing skills to new demands, testifies to this fact.

8. *Neglect of Retraining*

A 1965 P.E.P. report predicted that 'it is in the field of retraining that the deficiencies of the Act, as it is likely to be administered, appear most clearly'.[41] Writing in 1970 Mukherjee[42] confirms that the I.T.B.s have shown no inclination to engage in 'labour market oriented' retraining of adults—that is I.T.B.s have not been concerned with the wider goal of facilitating manpower shifts, either between industries or within a particular industry.

The reluctance of I.T.B.s to encourage the re-deployment of labour within their own particular sphere of activity is highlighted

[39] Oatey, *op. cit.*, pp. 20–21.
[40] Lees and Chiplin, *op. cit.*, p. 38.
[41] A P.E.P. Report by A. Gater, D. Insull, H. Lind and P. Seglow, *Attitudes in British Management*, p. 249.
[42] Mukherjee, *op. cit.*, pp. 81–83.

by the case of the Iron and Steel I.T.B. In this industry technological change and rationalization have led to a decline in operative employment but the board has discriminated against retraining for internal redeployment by placing retaining schemes associated with new technological developments 'at a lower level of priority than other forms of training.[43] While it is understandable that I.T.B.s have concentrated their efforts initially upon training young entrants for craft and operative occupations, many of them have been in business long enough to have done more for adult workers facing compulsory job change.

The reluctance of I.T.B.s to promote inter-industry redeployment of labour probably stems from their organizational structure and their method of financing. Since they are organized along industry lines and derive their income from member firms it is quite natural that boards are more responsive to the specific needs of their members than to the wider needs of the labour market.

Because of the poor record of boards in the field of adult retraining Mukherjee[44] has suggested that the I.T.B. system be replaced by a hybrid structure of horizontal and vertical groupings, directed by a new Manpower Commission that would be responsible for the co-ordination and control of all the various aspects of manpower policy.

Greater central control and direction is essential if the industrial training system is to contribute more fully to the development of manpower policy. However, the essential structure of the I.T.B. system can be preserved, although it might be desirable to upgrade to board status those C.T.C. committees which are concerned with training in occupations that are common to many industries. Contrary to what the Estimates Committee[45] asserted in 1967 the machinery does exist for achieving the effective retraining and redeployment of labour. All that is required is some change of emphasis in I.T.B. grant policy, coupled with the injection of some government finance into the system.

If the I.T.B.s are to contribute to the wider needs of the labour market they should be compelled to urge member firms to take action to prevent redundancies wherever possible. This they can do by providing financial incentives to those firms affected by technological change to adapt, through retraining, the skill structure of their labour force. To this end grant payments made by boards should

[43] Mukherjee, *op. cit.*, p. 80.
[44] *Ibid.*,pp. 112–20.
[45] The Ninth Report From The Estimates Committee Session 1966–67, on *Manpower Training for Industry*, p. xxii, para. 65, states that 'at the moment there does not seem to be the machinery for encouraging the effective retraining and redeployment of labour which is desirable'.

not discriminate against, but should actively encourage, internal retraining.

However, it has to be faced that in a dynamic economy a certain amount of redundancy—as opposed to unemployment—is not only inevitable but desirable. This need not lead to prolonged periods of unemployment if the general level of aggregate demand is kept high and government retraining grants are tied to redundancy.

Government retraining grants could be paid to employers willing to take on and retrain workers made redundant elsewhere. The grant would not simply be a subsidy to employment. It would only be payable for training approved by boards, although this could be at any level of skill and for any actual or anticipated area of labour shortage. In certain instances it might be necessary, or desirable, for I.T.B.s to provide in their own centres the training that is necessary for re-employment. Since the demand for skilled and semi-skilled labour varies from industry to industry, and from region to region, the size of the retraining grant could be differentiated to ensure that the incentive to retrain is greatest in those industries and regions where shortages of trained labour are most acute when the overall demand for labour is high. Furthermore, since the object is to induce employers to take on redundant workers and retrain for future needs it might be argued that there is a case for varying the size of the grant according to the level of labour demand within the industry or region. Thus the retraining grant would tend to be high when the incidence of redundancy and unemployment is high. Conversely the grant would be low when unemployment is low because at such times the incentives will already exist for employers to undertake on-the-job training. Indeed, when the labour market is tight generally it might be possible to recoup some of the costs of retraining by introducing a payroll tax. This could again be differentiated according to industry and region.

This would mean that for each industry and region there would be a critical level of labour demand. At this level of demand there would be neither retraining grant nor payroll levy. As labour demand rises above the critical level the payroll tax would become payable, the rate of tax increasing with the pressure of demand. As labour demand falls below the critical level the retraining grant would become payable, the size of grant increasing with the level of unemployment.

The differential system of retraining grants and payroll levies outlined above would be quite separate from the existing levy and grant payments of I.T.B.s. However the grants could be made, and the levies collected, through the existing I.T.B. machinery. This would not only avoid administrative overlap but would also ensure that the detailed knowledge and expertise acquired by boards could be used in identifying areas of training need, and in ensuring that redundant workers are retrained to meet these needs.

VI. CONCLUDING REMARKS

This paper has attempted to show that some criticisms of the Industrial Training Act are misconceived while others can be met by introducing greater flexibility into the levy-grant system. The criticism concerning I.T.B. neglect of retraining is accepted and suggestions of how this can be remedied have been put forward.

The purpose of the paper has not only been to justify the existence of the Act over the last 7–8 years but also to argue that the problem of retraining for redeployment can be tackled through the existing I.T.B. structure.

KEYNES COLLEGE,
UNIVERSITY OF KENT AT CANTERBURY

CAPACITY-UTILIZATION, CONCENTRATION, AND PRICE-COST MARGINS:

RESULTS ON INDIAN INDUSTRIES

by PAWAN K. SAWHNEY and BANSI L. SAWHNEY*

I. INTRODUCTION

THE purpose of this paper is to provide an explanation for variations in price-cost margins (or profit rates) among manufacturing industries. The most popular hypothesis advanced in this area of research is: The price-cost margins (profit rates) in oligopolistic industries with high seller concentration will tend to be significantly higher than that of other industries with moderate or low seller concentration. Several earlier studies have found this relationship but, though statistically significant, the degree of relationship obtained is low.[1] In more recent studies, the influence of other factors such as marginal concentration ratio, variables of barriers to entry, capital-output ratio, and the rate of change in output has also been examined.[2] The results of these studies indicate some improvement

* The authors are grateful to the referee for helpful suggestions on an earlier version of this paper. Thanks are also due to Professors J. J. Hughes, M. S. Baratz, I. L. Herrnstadt and S. K. Kaushik for their comments and discussions.

[1] See Joe S. Bain, 'Relation to Profit Rate to Industry Concentration: American Manufacturing, 1936–1940', *Quarterly Journal of Economics*, vol. 65 (August 1951), pp. 313, 323–4; Harold M. Levinson, 'Post War Movement of Prices and Wages in Manufacturing Industries', in U.S. Congress, Joint Economic Committee, *Study of Employment, Growth, and Price Levels.* (Study Paper No. 21) Washington: U.S. Government Printing Office, 1960, pp. 49–51; Victor R. Fuchs, 'Integration, Concentration Ratios and Profits in Manufacturing', *Quarterly Journal of Economics*, vol. 75 (May, 1961), pp. 285–88; Leonard W. Weiss, 'Average Concentration Ratios and Industry Performance', *Journal of Industrial Economics*, vol. 11 (July, 1963), pp. 248–51; and Norman R. Collins and Lee E. Preston, 'Concentration and Price-Cost Margins in Food Manufacturing Industries', *Journal of Industrial Economics*, vol. 14 (July, 1966), pp. 226–42.

[2] See Joe S. Bain, *Barriers to New Competition*, Cambridge: Harvard University Press, 1956, Chaps. 3–6, H. Michael Mann, 'Seller Concentration, Barriers to Entry, and Rates of Return in Thirty Industries, 1950–1960', *Review of Economics and Statistics*, vol. 48 (August, 1966) pp. 296–307, and William S. Comanor and Thomas A. Wilson, 'Advertising, Market Structure and Performance', *Review of Economics and Statistics*, vol. 49 (November 1967) pp. 423–40 who examined the influence of barriers to entry variables, in addition to concentration ratio. See Robert W. Kilpatrick, 'Stigler on the Relationship between Industry Profit Rates and Market Concentration', *Journal of Political Economy*, vol. 76 (May/June 1968), pp. 479–88, Fuchs, *op. cit.*, pp. 285–90, Weiss, *op. cit.*, pp. 248–51, and Comanor and Wilson, *op. cit.*, pp. 429–33 who considered the rate of growth in output as an additional explanatory variable. Norman R. Collins and Lee E. Preston, *Concentration and Price-Cost Margins in Manufacturing Industries*, Berkeley and Los Angeles: University of California Press, 1968, included capital-output ratio along with concentration as the independent variables in the explanation of price-cost margins, and Richard A. Miller, 'Market Structure and Industrial Performance: Relation of Profit Rates to Concentration, Advertising Intensity, and Diversity', *Journal of Industrial Economics*, vol. 17 (April 1969), pp. 104–18, examined the influence of marginal concentration ratio, advertising intensity and corporate diversity on profit rates in addition to concentration ratio.

in the explanation of profit rates but at the same time point out the need for more research before any sound theoretical framework on the subject can be constructed.[3] The major contribution of this paper is in putting forth an additional hypothesis, that is, the price-cost margins or profit rates among manufacturing industries depend to a considerable extent on the degree of capacity-utilization. This hypothesis as well as the linear and non-linear formulation of concentration-profit hypothesis are empirically tested for Indian manufacturing industries. In addition, the effect of capital-output ratio on price-cost margins is also examined. First, we present the theoretical framework; then, the empirical results obtained for Indian manufacturing are discussed. The data on price-cost margins are averaged over a six-year-period to avoid bias due to lag and other problems of temporary fluctuations inherent in single-year data. The sources of data and measurement of variables used are reported in the note appended to the paper.

II. THEORETICAL FRAMEWORK

The concentration-profit hypothesis which rests on the conventional price theory[4] is essentially a long-run one and recognizes that in short run actual price-cost margins may differ from normal for both oligopolistic and competitive industries for additional reasons such as changes in demand and cost, until the reallocation of resources leads the industry towards long-run equilibrium. Since we are not sure whether averaging of data for 5, 6 or 10 years[5] can depict the long-run situation, as conceived in theory,[6] the present analysis includes both short-run and long-run considerations. The dependent variable selected is the ratio of price to average variable cost (P/AVC) which refers to short-run profit maximization.[7] The test for the long-run is made by including capital-output ratio (K/O) which reflects the differences in the capital cost per unit of output along with concentration ratio as the independent variables.

[3] See, for example, Mann, *op. cit.*, p. 304.

[4] For how this hypothesis is developed from conventional price theory, see Bain, 'Relation of Profit Rate to Industry Concentration: American Manufacturing, 1936–1940', pp. 294–6.

[5] Bain has done this by averaging the data for 1936–1940 and 1947–1951. See Bain, *Barriers to New Competition*. Mann has done this by averaging the data for 1950–1960, see Mann, *op. cit.*

[6] Mann, in his concluding remarks, also points out this danger. In his wording, '. . . the period 1950–1960 may be short run for some industries in this sample . . .' see Mann, *op. cit.*, p. 304.

[7] David Schwartzman has also used P/AVC ratio in his test of short-run price theory. See David Schwartzman, 'The Effect of Monopoly on Price', *Journal of Political Economy*, August 1959, pp. 352–62.

The short-run hypothesis of P/AVC and degree of concentration (C) is tested with the help of following linear regression equation:

(1) $$P/AVC = \alpha + \beta C + \mu$$

However, it may be argued that though P/AVC ratio is expected to be higher with higher degree of seller concentration, it is also plausible that after a point there is no further rise in P/AVC with the rise in degree of concentration, because in practice it may not be possible for firms in industries with extremely high seller concentration to increase their P/AVC ratio any further due to the fear of government regulation or anti-trust laws. This suggests that a non-linear formulation of P/AVC and degree of concentration hypothesis presented below may yield better results than the linear one.

(2) $$P/AVC = \alpha + \beta C + \gamma C^2 + \mu$$

The long-run considerations require adjustment for differences in capital cost per unit of output. The higher the capital-output ratio, the higher will be the capital cost per-unit-of-output, and consequently the higher the P/AVC ratio. In the absence of K/O ratio in our expression, one might argue that computed P/AVC ratio includes the normal rate of return on capital, and therefore differences in the former may, in part, be due to the differences in the capital-output ratio. Thus if capital-output ratio is closely related with seller concentration, the relationship observed between P/AVC and concentration may be a spurious one and may, in fact, reflect the relationship between K/O ratio and concentration.[8] The problem is taken care of, on the one hand, by including K/O ratio as an independent variable along with concentration ratio, and on the other hand, by checking the intercorrelation between the K/O ratio and concentration to ensure that the results are not affected due to collinearity between the two. A positive and significant regression coefficient for K/O variable would show long-run relationship between concentration and price-cost margin, where capital cost per-unit-of-output is also important. On the other hand, an insignificant coefficient (after checking the intercorrelations) would indicate the short-run relationship between P/AVC and C, where capital cost is ignored. After including K/O ratio, our regression equation takes the following form:

[8] This is one major objection raised against the use of P/AVC as the indicator of profitability. See Maskel Benishay, 'Concentration and Price-Cost Margins: A Comment', *Journal of Industrial Economics*, November, 1967, pp. 73–74; and H. Michael Mann and James W. Meehan, Jr., 'Concentration and Profitability: An Examination of a Recent Study', *The Antitrust Bulletin*, vol. 16, Summer 1969, pp. 389–90. But as we will see below, this objection is met in our formulation of the hypothesis.

(3) $$P/AVC = \alpha + \beta C + \gamma C^2 + \delta K/O + \mu$$

The additional hypothesis advanced in this paper is that price-cost margins or profit rates among industries depend considerably on the degree-of-capacity-utilization. There are two main reasons to expect this relationship. One, better utilization of capacity reduces costs and wastage due to underutilization of existing capacity, which in turn, other things remaining the same, would result in a higher price-cost margin, and *vice-versa*. Two, lower rates of capacity-utilization generally reflect a slackening of demand and therefore would be associated with lower price-cost margins, other things being equal. The opposite will be true when higher demand results in better capacity-utilization.[9] The hypothesis is tested by incorporating the percentage-utilization-of-capacity-variable (Ut) in our regression equation as follows:

(4) $$P/AVC = \alpha + \beta C + \gamma C^2 + \delta K/O + \varepsilon Ut + \mu$$

It may be noted, however, that there are other variables which may affect price-cost margins, Notably, similar studies have also considered variables of barriers to entry in the explanation of profit rates among industries. Both Bain and Mann find significantly higher average profit rates in the very high barrier group compared to other classes.[10] However, they do not find such significant difference between the substantial and moderate-to-low barrier classes. Miller, after examining the different entry barriers, relates profit rates to advertising intensity and corporate diversity variables. His findings show that while the ratio of advertising expenditure to total revenue explains a significant variation in profit rates, the evidence on corporate diversity is not conclusive.[11] The significant contribution of advertising ratio in the explanation of profit rates is also found by Comanor and Wilson.[12] However, due to non-availability of separate data for different indicators of barriers to entry for Indian manufacturing, the present analysis is limited to the variables specified in our equation (4).[13]

[9] Earlier studies have employed relative changes in output as a measure to reflect changes in demand. See Fuchs, *op. cit.*, pp. 285–90, Kilpatrick, *op. cit.*, pp. 481–83, and Comanor and Wilson, *op. cit.*, pp. 429–33, 37.

[10] See Bain, *Barriers to New Competition*, pp. 45, 191–201 and Mann, *op. cit.*, pp. 302–4.

[11] See Miller, *op. cit.*, pp. 106–7, 110–12.

[12] See Comanor and Wilson, *op. cit.*, pp. 431–7.

[13] Vinod K. Gupta has estimated the barrier to entry due to scale economies in Indian industries. His results show that 'The height of none of these barriers to entry was found to be significantly correlated or associated either with the "accounting" rate of profit in the largest four plants, or with the actual concentration ratio.' Vinod K. Gupta, 'Cost Functions, Concentration, and Barriers to Entry in Twenty-nine Manufacturing Industries of India', *Journal of Industrial Economics*, vol. 17 (November 1968), p. 72.

III. EMPIRICAL RESULTS

The theoretical model presented in the previous section is applied to the data on twenty-five Indian manufacturing industries using the 'OLS' regression technique and step-wise regression procedure.[14] The results obtained are summarized in Table I.

TABLE I

REGRESSION RESULTS

Model: $P/AVC_1 = \alpha + \beta C + \gamma C^2 + \delta K/O + \varepsilon Ut$

eq. no.	*constant*	C	C^2	K/O	Ut	R^2	*R*
		Regression Coefficients of Independent Variables				(*N* = 25)	
1.	114.98	0.170*	—	—	—	0.21	0.46
		(2.450)	—	—	—		
2.	106.12	0.714*	−0.005*	—	—	0.35	0.59
		(2.782)	(2.188)	—	—		
3.	96.93	0.682*	−0.005*	4.093	—	0.40	0.63
		(2.692)	(2.011)	(1.853)	—		
4.	76.29	0.616*	−0.005*	3.351	0.351*	0.58	0.76
		(2.822)	(2.279)	(1.462)	(2.928)		

Note: * indicates significant at 5 per cent level or better. Figures in parentheses indicate *t* values of the regression coefficients.

P/AVC_1 = Ratio of price to average variable cost. This ratio is gross of depreciation.
C = Concentration ratio.
C^2 = the square of C.
K/O = Capital-output ratio.
Ut = Percentage utilization of capacity.
For details of measurement of the variables see the appendix.

As expected, the concentration ratio shows the positive and significant relationship with P/AVC ratio, although the degree of explanation provided by it is limited; concentration alone explains only about 21 per cent of the variations in P/AVC ratio among the industries.[15] The test of non-linear relationship between P/AVC and degree of concentration, where C^2 term is added in equation (2), gives better results than the linear relationship (equation 1). As much as 14 per cent additional variation is explained by the non-linear formulation. This result seems to contradict Kilpatrick who found the linear relationship as good as the non-linear.[16]

[14] All alternative combinations of independent variables were tried. The results obtained in each case were consistent with the findings reported in Table I; the significance or nonsignificance of each variable was the same as in equations presented here. The results not reported here are available from the authors on request.

[15] This result is consistent with the studies cited in footnotes 1 and 2.

[16] See Kilpatrick, *op. cit.*, p. 483, footnote 7. Also his 'The Choice Among Alternative Measures of Industrial Concentration', *Review of Economics and Statistics*, vol. 49 (May, 1967), pp. 259–60. Our finding also contradicts Collins and Preston who found continuous relationship to be stronger than non-continuous. See Collins and Preston, *Concentration and Price Cost Margins in Manufacturing Industries*.

But it tends to support Bain and Schwartzman, although they did not employ regression technique as in the present paper.[17]

The results of the test of the long-run hypothesis on price-cost margins and degree of concentration indicate a positive sign for 'O variable but its regression coefficient is statistically not significant. The simple correlation (r) between C and K/O was -0.17 and between C^2 and K/O was -0.20, indicating that non-significance of K/O variable in our equations is not due to its relation with concentration. One inference to be drawn is that price-cost margins averaged over a number of years (in this case, six years) do not appear to approximate long-run theoretical situation where capital cost is also important. However, to the extent it has a positive sign and its omission from the equation reduces the explanatory power by 5 percentage points, the variable is retained in our model, and the hypothesis of positive association between P/AVC averaged over a number of years and K/O ratio is not rejected.

Our additional hypothesis fits well to the data. The introduction of the capacity-utilization variable in equation 4 leads to substantial improvement in the already obtained R^2 from 0.40 to 0.58. As expected, its coefficient is positive and highly significant. Regression coefficients of C and C^2 terms continue to be significant as well as that of K/O not significant.[18]

It may be noted that our P/AVC_1 measure of price-cost margins is a gross measure which includes depreciation charges. One might object to the inclusion of depreciation in price. Therefore, an alternative measure of price-cost margins excluding depreciation, that is, P/AVC_2 was employed to see if the results obtained were different. The following equation presents these results:

$$(5)\quad P/AVC_2 = \underset{}{86.83} + \underset{(2.479)}{0.465^{*}C} \; - \underset{(1.947)}{0.003^{*}C^2} + \underset{(0.631)}{1.436K/O} + \underset{(2.436)}{0.255^{*}Ut}$$

$$R^2 = .52$$
$$R = .72$$

The results are consistent with those obtained in the case of P/AVC_1 ratio (equation 4), except the total explanation provided is 6 percentage points less than in the equation (4). This may imply two things. One, that 'accounting rates of depreciation' do not

[17] See Bain, 'Relation of Profit Rate to Industry Concentration: American Manufacturing, 1936–1940,' p. 313 and Schwartzman, *op. cit.*, pp. 360–61.

[18] Intercorrelations between Ut and C, C^2, and K/O were 0.30, 0.29 and -0.01 respectively; sufficiently lower compared to overall correlation of 0.76 in equation 4 to affect the results significantly. The simple correlations between the dependent variable, P/AVC_1 and C, C^2, K/O and Ut, were respectively 0.45, 0.35, 0.20 and 0.56. All, except the correlation between P/AVC and K/O, are significant at 5 per cent level or better according to one-tailed '*t* test'.

represent the depreciation as conceived in economics, and, therefore, deduction of depreciation data which is based on accounting concept distorts the price-cost margin picture to some extent. Two, that average of price-cost margins over a six-year-period reflects more of a short-run situation, where depreciation on capital is not an important consideration in maximizing profits, and therefore deduction of depreciation figures affects the price-cost margins structure among the industries.

Some similar studies have used profits as percentage of sales as the dependent variables as opposed to P/AVC ratio. In order to make sure that when profits as percentage of sales is employed there is no significant difference in the results, we present the results based on this measure in equation (6) and (7) below:

$$(6)\quad PR_1 = -12.87 + 0.429{*}C - 0.003{*}C^2 + 1.98K/O + 0.238{*}Ut$$
$$\qquad\qquad (2.922) \qquad (2.312) \qquad (1.143) \qquad (2.976)$$
$$R^2 = .59 \qquad R = .77$$

$$(7)\quad PR_2 = -7.98 + 0.341{*}C - 0.002{*}C^2 + 0.791K/O + 0.192{*}Ut$$
$$\qquad\qquad (2.530) \qquad (1.935) \qquad (0.494) \qquad (2.602)$$
$$R^2 = .53 \qquad R = .73$$

In both the cases when gross profit rates including depreciation (PR_1) and when net profit rates excluding depreciation (PR_2) is used, the results obtained are found to be consistent with those using P/AVC_1 and P/AVC_2.[19]

IV. CONCLUSIONS

This study shows that the degree of capacity-utilization plays an important role in the determination of price-cost margins among the industries. The concentration-profit hypothesis also gets support from data on Indian manufacturing. However, a non-linear formulation of this hypothesis gives better results than the linear one. The effect of capital-output ratio on price-cost margins averaged over the six-year period appears to be statistically insignificant, though not conclusive.

NORTHEASTERN UNIVERSITY AND BOSTON UNIVERSITY
GEORGE WASHINGTON UNIVERSITY AND UNIVERSITY OF BALTIMORE

[19] Profits as percentage of total capital or net worth was not tried as the dependent variable, for such a measure refers to long-run theoretical situation, and takes into account the differences in capital cost which are important in the long run. Thus, if in practice data on profit as percentage of capital, averaged over a number of years, do not approximate this long-run situation, use of this measure will give misleading results for both long run and short run.

APPENDIX

A NOTE ON THE SOURCES OF DATA AND MEASUREMENT OF VARIABLES

(1) *Ratio of price to average variable cost* (*P/AVC*) was computed by dividing the total sale value of output by the total direct cost (cost of raw materials and other inputs purchased from outside firms, and total labor cost, including the cost of fringe benefits). P/AVC ratios were averaged for the period 1953–58 among twenty-five Indian manufacturing industries. Data came from various issues of the *Census of Indian Manufacturers* (*CIM*), published by Central Statistical Organization, Government of India. Two P/AVC ratios were computed. One including the depreciation in the value of output (i.e. P/AVC_1) and other, excluding the depreciation (i.e. P/AVC_2). Profits as percentage of output including the depreciation (PR_1) is the corresponding alternative measure of P/AVC_1 which was obtained by deducting the value of direct cost from the value of output and expressing the residual as percentage of total value of output. Similarly, PR_2 was obtained but here, in addition to direct cost, depreciation was also deducted from the value of output to obtain the residual.

(2) *Concentration ratio* (*C*) represents the percentage share of total industrial output accounted for by the largest eight units (in terms of employment) in the industry. This was computed from the data classified according to different sizes of establishments reported in *CIM*, 1958. Vinod K. Gupta in his paper, *op. cit.*, reports concentration ratios defined as the percentage of total industrial employment accounted for by the largest four units in the industry. We, however, preferred the concentration ratios defined in terms of output than in terms of employment, although a high correlation between the two is very much expected. C^2 term is the square of concentration ratio.

(3) *Capital-output ratio* (*K/O*) is the ratio of total capital employed to value added (gross of depreciation). It represents the average of 1953 and 1963 capital-output ratios computed by dividing the output-labor ratio (O/L) into capital-labor ratio (K/L), obtained from Saroj Sawhney, 'Productivity Differentials in Indian Industries', *Asian Economic Review* (Feb./May 1970). They were originally computed from the reports of the *CIM*, 1953 and the *Annual Survey of Industries* (*ASI*), 1963, Government of India.

(4) *Rate of Capacity-Utilization* (*Ut*) represents the actual output as percentage of installed capacity. It is the average of the rates of capacity-utilization in 1953 and 1963 as reported in Saroj Sawhney's paper, *op. cit.* Original source for them was *Monthly Statistics of Production of Selected Industries of India*, vol. 13, July–Dec. 1961 and vol. 17, Jan–June 1965, C.S.O., Government of India.

It may be noted that though the total number of industries covered in the *CIM* reports is twenty-nine, our study includes only twenty-five of them. The remaining four, namely, distilleries and breweries, edible hydrogenated oils, woollen textiles, and aluminium, copper, and brass were excluded from our sample, for a preliminary exercise indicated the data on these four to be far out of proportion from rest of the industries. However, their inclusion does not affect the significance and non-significance of the variables considered in the study but adds to the unexplained variance. When $n = 29$, simple r between P/AVC and C, C^2, K/O and Ut were .42, .33, .19, and .46 respectively compared to .45, .35, .20 and .56 when $n = 25$, indicating the variables which are significant when $n = 29$ remain significant also when $n = 25$.

THE ECONOMIC SIGNIFICANCE OF SMALL FIRMS

by David Waite*

A steady growth in the concentration of industry has been a feature of most advanced countries for about half a century. Economic theory attempts to explain this process in terms of technical, managerial, marketing and financial factors affecting existing firms and industries: little is said about the emergence and growth of new firms, and official statistics tell us very little about the smaller unquoted firms in the economy. It was partly to rectify this lack of information and partly because of concern expressed about pressures operating in a discriminating fashion against small firms, that a committee was established in July 1969 to examine this sector. Under the chairmanship of John Bolton, it produced its report[1] in November 1971. Its terms of reference were:

> To consider the role of small firms in the national economy, the facilities available to them and the problems confronting them; and to make recommendations. . . . In the course of the study it will be necessary to examine in particular the profitability of small firms and the availability of finance. Regard should also be paid to the special functions of small firms, for example, as innovators and specialist suppliers.[2]

This paper is principally concerned with Part I of the Report, which is an assessment of the functions and performance of the small firm sector.

DEFINITIONS

In choosing its definition of smallness the Committee had regard not only to the form in which official statistics were presented, but also to the norms in each of their broad industry categories by which relative size could be gauged. The definitions used are reproduced in the Appendix, but in general the characteristics considered apposite to the small firm were:

1. smallness of market share (large number of similar sized firms) and hence lack of individual market power, corresponding to the theoretical concept of pure competition;

* The author is employed in the Economic Intelligence Department of the Bank of England but the views expressed herein are his own and not necessarily those of the Bank.

[1] *Report of the Committee of Inquiry on Small Firms* November 1971, Cmnd. 4811 [The Bolton Report].

[2] Bolton Report, p. xv.

2. close association of ownership and management functions, so that concern was primarily with private unquoted companies and unincorporated businesses;
3. autonomy in decision-making—this excludes subsidiaries of large organizations and individual plants belonging to the same business.

Although any definition is bound to be arbitrary, it is sensible to avoid trying to embrace all sectors in one. Manufacturing is very different from retailing, for example; a 200 employee firm in the first is quite small, while in the second it is large. Similarly, capital and turnover measures cannot be usefully applied across the board because of differing norms in each sector.

THE ROLE OF SMALL FIRMS

Economic theory has tended to sidestep issues of diversity of firm size within industries and changes in structure. Marshall's classic treatment,[3] for example, intended particularly to handle industries with falling costs, is a case in point. In dealing with the 'representative firm', the size of the individual firm is related to its age, and the behaviour of the 'forest' is dealt with by examining the average sized 'tree' in a static setting. A change in the size of the representative firm is a dynamic question affecting the relative growth rates of the constituent members of the 'forest'. There is an implicit assumption in this metaphor of a continuous growth of firms, new large firms being supplied from the ranks of smaller ones to replace those which stagnate and cease to grow. At the other end of the scale, a stream of new small firms enter to replace those leaving the small firm sector by growth or liquidation.

The emergence from the 'costs controversy' of the 'twenties of theories of imperfect competition provided models that could explain the co-existence of firms with different costs levels in terms of 'goodwill' and consumer preference. The small firm, then, could be viewed as enjoying part of the market demand curve and potentially expanding towards the optimum size in the industry.

Steindl[4] criticized the plausibility of the Marshallian view of growth within industries because of the very large range of size between the smallest and largest firms and problems of financing growth, especially the limitations on external borrowing. Against this, however, it should be mentioned that, over a timespan of several decades, substantial growth, particularly of 'high fliers', is feasible,

[3] A. Marshall, *Principles of Economics* Macmillan 8th ed., reprinted 1966.
[4] J. Steindl, *Small and Big Business* Blackwell, 1945.

and it should be remembered that only a few of the smaller firms ever grow out of the sector.

The Bolton Committee took the view that it was essential to maintain an environment that was not hostile to the formation and growth of new enterprises. It considered the prime function of a healthy small firm sector to be the provision of a 'seedbed' for new enterprise and entrepreneurial talent, a source of new lifeblood and ideas, and potential growth to maintain a spur of competition. This is, of course, a long-term view, the principal objective of the Committee.

In the manufacturing and construction sector, 23 per cent of small firms existing in 1963 went into liquidation, ceased trading, or were taken over by 1970 (excluding mortalities of firms founded between these years). The main cause of mortality was takeover, though it is not known what proportion of this activity involved acquisition by very large firms. Even so, the Committee welcomed the fact that at least some mergers were between small firms wanting to improve their market position.

In a static context, as distinct from the long-run, dynamic setting, an industry with many small firms is more likely to be competitive than a concentrated one. The Bolton Committee implicitly accepted a preference for many rather than few firms in an industry in the interest of economic efficiency, potential and actual competition, and checks on monopoly profits. This view needs considerable qualification, however, for the ability of a small firm sector to provide effective competition depends on what barriers to competition there are and the extent to which a few giant firms dominate the industry. The Committee was apparently unaware of two important considerations relating to industrial structure and performance. First, dominant firms may 'tolerate' a fringe of much smaller firms to give the lie to charges of monopoly; independence of the competitive fringe may be largely illusory if they have to follow the price leader. Secondly, concentration of itself does not necessarily breed stagnation, for in oligopoly (small number of sellers) conditions, potential competition across industry boundaries is important for checking monopoly power and maintaining efficiency; rivalry between oligopolists (as an alternative to collusion) within an industry can also serve this end.

Stepping from the implicit assumption hitherto of single product firms into a world of multi-product businesses, it becomes apparent that the greater the number of firms in an industry, the more likelihood there is of variety in output. It is arguable that smaller firms, especially those which specialize in small or luxury market segments, provide for a need that would not otherwise be met, and hence improve consumer choice. The Bolton Committee sets great store by this function in its case for the small firm. However, though it may often be that specialist items are uneconomic for the large firm to produce, it does not mean that big business never caters for such sectors: there is nothing to stop a large firm setting up a small unit to sell in these markets.

In some industries, particularly the motor and aircraft trades, small firms are important suppliers of components and sub-assemblies to large manufacturers. The latter often consider it uneconomic to produce them and there may be no need for vertical integration because the small firms are already totally dependent on them. In such a situation the independence of the small firm is, virtually, nominal.

In some industries scale economies are not so important and the optimum size of firm is quite small. From a competitive point of view the significance of this is the absence of substantial barriers to entry and the lack of advantages conferred by large size. In service industries, small firms predominate, both in terms of numbers of enterprises and numbers employed; they account for 99 per cent of all firms in that sector and 82 per cent of the employment.

In itself, the fact that the optimum size of firm is small in some industries, large in others, is not the most important consideration for the future of the small firm 'seedbed'. What is significant, for preventing stagnation, is the existence of conditions in which new businesses can be started from which the firms of the future can grow. The history of the giant firms of today has been one of growth through a combination of internal resources, external borrowing and mergers. Firms that grow to compete with the present leaders of industry need not begin life within that industry. Diversification across industry boundaries ensures a flow of ideas that helps to reduce barriers to competition.

In regard to technical progress small firms appear to make a disproportionately large contribution to invention in relation to their expenditure on research and development. This conclusion is supported by evidence of case studies, patents data, employment of qualified scientists and engineers, and shares of recorded R & D expenditure. The Bolton Committee recognized the qualifications needed in interpreting the data, but took the view that flexibility of organization coupled with personal involvement and drive contributed to a greater degree of inventiveness within small firms.

Innovation—the application of known concepts or processes in new, improved ways—is often closely allied to the idea of invention.

Innovation is difficult to quantify partly because of the problem of definition and partly the lack of empirical data which is a consequence. In this situation the Committee could only take a view that rejected two extremes, namely that only the largest firms could afford to innovate and that in large corporations the incentive was lacking. The Bolton Committee view was that small firms can and do contribute to innovation in those fields where they have the appropriate resources.[5]

The Committee laid considerable stress on the vigorous spirit of independence to be found among small businessmen. This has implications for employment opportunities especially for those people who feel lost in a large organization or who do not have formal higher educational qualifications or the desire to go through the educational mill. The less formal nature of the working environment in small firms—which appears to facilitate interpersonal communications and staff relations—is as important to the employee as to the owner (or self-employed person).

In the local community too the small businessman, with his roots there, is a valuable contributor to local government, on the bench and in local charitable and social organizations. The large firm executive, by comparison, is more mobile and less closely attached to a particular local community: a man who lives the best part of his life in one area is likely to be better acquainted with local conditions and sentiment.

WHY SMALL FIRMS SURVIVE

In considering the size distribution of firms in an industry an explanation must be found of how small firms can exist alongside the large. Realizing that an explanation of firm size solely in terms of market size and optimum scale was an over-simplification, the Committee opted for an approach suggested by Lydall.[6] Small firms are examined according to the type of market they serve, falling into three categories:

1. In an industry where production economies of scale exist, the small firm may not be able to compete directly with the large firm on costs, but it can cater for those segments of the market which are uneconomic for larger firms, e.g. luxury goods and specialist items. In a sense, however, the two are not comparable since they are supplying different markets—even if these are purely delineated by tastes. It may be that the small firm is losing out in such areas

[5] See, for example, J. Jewkes, D. Sawyers, and R. Stillerman, *The Sources of Invention* 2nd ed., Macmillan, 1969.

[6] H. F. Lydall, 'Aspects of Competition in Manufacturing Industry', *Bulletin of the Oxford University Institute of Statistics*, Vol. 20 (1958).

because of lessening dispersion of income distribution and the impact of the mass media on tastes.

2. Another role for the small firm is that of supplier to large firms of components or other individual items. Often such small firms are totally dependent on the customer and these jobbing firms[7] may be described as 'satellites'. This sort of dependence is common in the motor and aircraft industries where the large firm often finds it more economic to subcontract to smaller suppliers work that demands speed and flexibility. It is also found in retailing, where suppliers are dependent on multiple stores (such as Marks & Spencer or Woolworth). Here again, the purely nominal independence of the small firm satellite makes it differ little from a department of a fully integrated concern: it cannot be said to be fully autonomous in its decision-making.

3. A category called 'marketeers' competes directly with larger firms in the same or similar markets. Their survival may be accounted for by different production techniques (e.g. different capital/labour ratio) or the lack of scale economies in the industry. There is also the concept of imperfect competition, whereby the smaller firm has its own 'special market' protected by 'goodwill', and imperfect competition in the labour market may secure labour at lower cost, e.g. non-unionized, part-time or women workers. In oligopoly conditions, small firms may be 'tolerated' by their larger competitors. Finally, the sheer tenacity and drive of owner-managers may ensure their survival.[8]

Two surveys for the Committee suggested that the majority of small firms fall into the third category. In manufacturing industries between one-half and three-quarters of small firms seem to be in direct competition with large ones. Marketeering is more common among the larger firms of the 'small' sector, while satellites are mainly the smallest firms. Outside manufacturing the proportion of small firms competing with large ones is generally even higher, particularly in the distributive trades. The Committee did not examine in any greater detail the factors contributing to the survival of marketeers in particular. Among those not considered we may include the benefits of geographical location in relation to materials, markets, competitors and complementary firms—external economies.

PERFORMANCE

One line for comparison of small and large firms is their relative efficiency in the use of resources as measured by net output per

[7] A jobbing firm produces goods to customer specification.
[8] Steindl, Ch. VI.

person and return on capital. Both these measures are fraught with difficulties because the firms are not necessarily engaged in the same activities, selling in the same markets or using the same production processes. Apart from these conceptual problems, there are difficulties of obtaining unambiguous figures for such factor inputs as entrepreneurship and capital, more particularly from unincorporated businesses (which are not distinguished in government statistics from households).

Although net output per person is lower for small firms than for large, this does not necessarily mean a correspondingly lower level of efficiency since the production techniques and capital/labour ratios differ: there is a tendency for small firms to be more labour intensive. In the small firm there tends to be a greater proportion of less skilled operatives, the incidence of overtime and shift-working is lower, and there is a larger proportion of part-time working. When allowance is made for the generally lower level of wage rates (as distinct from average earnings), even for the same type of labour, and lower capital intensity, the level of output per unit of labour comes out at nearly 18 per cent below that in large firms.

Such information as is available from the Census of Production shows that capital intensity among small firms rises with the size of firm, and that small firms, as a group, employ less capital than large firms, but information on the rate of depreciation and the value of capital stock, etc., is not available. It is therefore not possible to relate the lower capital intensity to the lower net output per unit of labour in small firms.

The Committee turned to such information as it could gather to compare the relationship between capital employed and the return on capital (as measured by profits) in the financial accounts of businesses. The use of this measure suffers from the same defect of partiality as the labour measure in so far as it neglects differences in other factors of production (labour and management). Problems also arise in the valuation of capital, especially in the owner-managed firm where there may be an overlap between the owner's personal and business assets. Despite all the qualifications to the data, small firms seem to show a higher return on capital than larger companies, although the difference is not very great. Bolton concluded that, although the partial contribution of labour and capital to profits or net output could not be measured accurately, and there was therefore no way of comparing the relative efficiency with which firms used their resources, there appeared to be no evidence to suggest that small firms were generally any less efficient than the large.

The available evidence, then, suggests that small firms do not waste resources; evidence of a higher return on capital among small firms may simply reflect lower capital intensity; from a long-term viewpoint, the provision of opportunities for entrepreneurial talent may have no counterpart elsewhere.

PAST TRENDS IN THE SMALL FIRM SECTOR

The picture is one of continuing decline. In manufacturing, the share of small firms in employment and output has fallen almost continuously since the mid-1920s. There was also a dramatic fall in the number of small manufacturing firms up to 1948 since when the decline, though at a slower rate, has continued. In the period 1958–63 there was a net fall of 1000 enterprises per annum.

Statistical material is too inadequate in other sectors to make an accurate assessment of trends in the relative contribution of small firms to economic activity. Since 1945 there has been a substantial decline in the number of small retailers, though up to 1966 their share of retail turnover and employment fell relatively slowly. Small firms apparently increased their importance in the motor distributive trades up to the early 1960s but the number of establishments contracted sharply between 1962 and 1967, and this process has probably continued since then. Road transport is an exception in that its size of firm distribution has changed very little since the 1930s.

When comparing concentration patterns with other industrialized countries, despite the obvious pitfall of incompatible data, it appears that the process of decline is common to all, but that it has gone further in Britain than anywhere else. To examine birth and death rates of new firms it is only possible to compare the position with that in the United States where comparable figures are produced. It emerges that the birth rate of new firms is lower in Britain and the average age of surviving firms is greater: little can be said about death rates. The Committee felt that the decline in birth rate was the more important factor contributing to the decline in British small firm activity. Hence it laid great stress in its recommendations on the removal of barriers discriminating against the formation and growth of new businesses.

PROBLEMS FACING SMALL FIRMS

Part of the Bolton Committee's brief was to investigate problems peculiar to the sector, i.e. arising from the smallness of the companies. Many grievances were aired ranging from difficulties of raising capital to the burden of form-filling, and from the impact of various forms of taxation to the effect of development and planning controls. Attention here will be confined to what appear to be the two most important areas where small firms are discriminated against, namely finance and taxation.

The question of long-term finance for small and medium-sized companies was first highlighted by the Macmillan Committee on Finance and Industry as long ago as 1931[9] when the phenomenon which came to be known as the 'Macmillan Gap' was identified. This was the lack of provision for small and medium sized firms of long-term capital in amounts too small for public issue—this lower limit was reckoned at around £200,000. When the Radcliffe Committee[10] came to look at this question nearly thirty years later they concluded that this gap had been closed, and the Bolton Committee concurred; nevertheless, the latter study did identify an 'information gap' affecting small firms.

In the 'thirties, after the appearance of the Macmillan report, a number of investment companies, specializing in the finance of small business, sprang up, notably Charterhouse Industrial Development and Leadenhall Securities; also, after the war, the Industrial and Commercial Finance Corporation (I.C.F.C.) was set up by the London and Scottish Clearing Banks with support from the Bank of England. I.C.F.C. was given resources to make long-term loans, often with equity participation in the borrowing firms, of sums between £5000 and £200,000. The I.C.F.C. immediately became and remains one of the most important sources of long-term capital for small firms.

Despite the variety of institutions catering for the private company's finance, problems still arise. The small firm depends to a great extent on internal finance and bank borrowing, mainly from the Clearing Banks although the latter is essentially short term. They do so to a much greater degree than large firms. In fact the bank manager, along with the accountant and solicitor, is the most important source of advice on many matters, as well as being the first source of external finance.

The Committee received many complaints from small firms of difficulties in obtaining finance and there seem to be three main contributory factors. First, the branch manager's upper discretionary limit for unsecured loans is often quite low. When the case has to be referred to another office the potential borrower is often unable to provide adequate documentary evidence of his firm's recent

[9] *Report of the Committee on Finance and Industry*, Cmd. 3897 (1931).
[10] *Report of the Committee on the Working of the Monetary System*, Cmnd. 827 (1959).

performance by which his creditworthiness may be assessed: some degree of resentment at external influence may be involved also. Secondly, before the new form of credit control[11] was introduced in 1971, directives on bank lending which gave priority to exporting and manufacturing activities tended to discriminate against service trades—where small firms predominate—making bank borrowing difficult. The new system should remove this form of discrimination. The third factor that may make borrowing difficult is an information gap which may be the fault of the businessman, the bank manager or both. The bank manager should at least be able to advise on alternative sources of finance if his bank does not have the facilities, especially where long-term investment is required. On the other hand, the reluctance of many businessmen to seek help needs to be recognized as a trait.

The small businessman's plea is for funds at a 'fair'—not subsidized—rate of interest. Nevertheless, his idea of what is a fair charge for money seems to be conditioned by experience of (short-term) overdraft rates; the rates on longer-term capital, raised through finance houses, leasing and factoring companies, seem rather to take him aback. The only remedy for this seems to be a process of education and advice on the economics of long-term financing.

The historically high level of taxation in Britain since the war has tended to operate differentially against small private companies. Taxes on capital (especially estate duty) impose a large burden on a business with a few shareholders: this is particularly true of family concerns. Death duties are often assessed on a purely notional valuation of non-marketable assets; payment of the duty involves a severe strain on the firm's liquidity and may force the selling off or closure of the business. High taxation of profits presents greater difficulty for the private company, which relies mainly on retained earnings to finance expansion, compared with the large company that can go to the market. In addition, small firms seem to be less aware than large ones of the effect of inflation on real profits, being lulled into a false sense of security by apparently high nominal profit figures.

Close companies[12] have long been subject to special provisions aimed at preventing the controlling shareholders from using the business for the avoidance of personal taxation. Corporation tax, introduced in 1965, was aimed at encouraging the ploughback of profits by companies since distributed profits were subject additionally to income tax. To prevent owners of close companies using the lower rate on retained earnings to avoid personal tax, a 'required

[11] See 'Competition and Credit Control', *Bank of England Quarterly Bulletin*, June 1971.
[12] A close company is one controlled by five or fewer persons or by its directors.

standard' was established in the distribution of profits: for trading companies this is 60 per cent of after-tax profits plus 100 per cent of investment income. The onus is on the firm to make its case for higher retentions for expansion or current business needs, otherwise any shortfall on the required standard is subject to an assessment for income tax and surtax where appropriate. Although, as the Bolton Committee found, the Inland Revenue has not been unreasonable in making shortfall assessments, the cost of proving the need to retain more than 40 per cent of profits is said to be excessive.

Small firms suffer from taxation policy because it works against the accumulation of private capital which is the primary source of finance for new, risky enterprise. Starting a firm is, inevitably, a gamble, and institutional finance agencies could not be expected to put their money into a business with no past performance as a guide. Whatever feelings may be about the ownership of capital, the fact remains that, if new firms are to come into existence, adequate resources must be accumulated in private hands. There are fewer 'rich uncles' around these days to risk their money in new enterprises; the ones that remain seem often to prefer to invest through the means of a well-organized capital market.

CONCLUSION

The small firm sector is not static. Although the Bolton Committee could not examine the growth pattern of firms over time because of the lack of information, it did suggest that the decline of small firms as a group was due principally to a slower birth rate in a relatively hostile environment. The Committee recommended, not that small firms should be feather-bedded, but that some of the factors discriminating against them should be removed, and that freedom of entry should be maintained and encouraged. The prime importance of small firms, as a sector, is not just in remaining small (though even as small firms they have an important contribution to make) but in providing a seedbed for enterprise and ideas and as a launching pad for growth. The importance of the Bolton Committee has been to throw some light on small unquoted companies about which very little was known before: most previous studies of 'small' firms[13] have been in terms of the smaller end of the Stock Exchange List, where firms have to be a reasonable size to obtain a quotation.

The government, for its part, has accepted most of Bolton's recommendations in principle. It has set up a Small Firms Division

[13] E.g. A. Singh and G. Whittington, *Growth, Profitability and Valuation*, Cambridge University Press, 1968; T. M. Samuels and A. D. Chesher, *Growth, Survival and the Size of Companies (1960–69)* (Mimeograph).

at the D.T.I. to co-ordinate consideration of the Report and to look after the needs of small firms as a whole, and has designated a Minister with special responsibility for small firms. Already, provisions have been made to ease the tax burden on small companies and their interests are being taken into account in the arrangements for Value Added Tax and revised Corporation Tax.

LONDON

Appendix

STATISTICAL DEFINITIONS OF SMALL FIRMS ADOPTED BY THE BOLTON COMMITTEE

Industry	*Statistical definition of small firms*	*Proportion of small firms in the industry 1963*	*Proportion of industry's employment in small firms 1963*	*Average employment per small firm 1963*
		%	%	
Manufacturing	200 employees or less	94	20	25
Retailing	Turnover £50,000 p.a. or less	96	49	3
Wholesale trades	Turnover £200,000 p.a. or less	77	25	7
Construction	25 employees or less	89	33	6
Mining/quarrying	25 employees or less	77	20	11
Motor trades	Turnover £100,000 p.a. or less	87	32*	3*
Miscellaneous services	Turnover £50,000 p.a. or less	90	82	4
Road transport	5 vehicles or less	85	36*	4*
Catering	All excluding multiples and brewery-managed public houses	96*	75*	3*

* Estimated figure subject to substantial margin of error.

Source: Bolton Committee Report, Table 1.I.

REGULATION, PROFITS AND ENTRY IN THE TELEVISION BROADCASTING INDUSTRY

by Douglas W. Webbink*

The television broadcasting industry is similar to other oligopolistic industries in that in the absence of high barriers to entry, high profits among existing firms should cause new firms to enter the industry. On the other hand, it is different from oligopolistic manufacturing industries in that under current regulation by the Federal Communications Commission new firms can not enter any market without a license from the FCC and existing firms typically can not expand their quantity of output in response to rising demand. Once a television station is broadcasting the maximum number of hours per day and using a powerful transmitter to cover the largest area allowed in a particular market, it has no way to reach a larger potential audience. It can not legally build a second transmitter and simultaneously broadcast a second set of programs in the same market. On the other hand, of course, it can change the quality of its programs in order to attract a larger share of the available audience.

Suppose we wish to predict whether a new station will enter a market where several stations are already broadcasting. One condition for new entry is that the potential station be able to obtain a license from the FCC. The lack of such a license is an absolute (legal) barrier to entry in any television market. This is an important consideration because the FCC determines in advance through an allocation table the maximum number of stations which shall be allowed in any market, and there are presently markets with no unused allocations available, and therefore no possibility of new entry into the market. Such markets include most of the largest 10 cities in the U.S.

On the other hand, where barriers to entry are not too substantial, high profits should lead to new entry, particularly since existing firms can not increase the quantity of their output. A naive but still useful model of the broadcasting industry can be developed based on the assumption that each firm including any new entrant obtains an equal share of the market. Moreover, for the purpose of this model it is assumed that all firms have equal operating costs, viewing audience, revenue and profits.

This model is naive because in reality in any market with four

* I wish to thank Professors Edward Greenberg, C. A. Knox Lovell, William McFarland and an anonymous referee for helpful comments on an earlier draft. The views expressed and any errors which remain are those of the author and are not presented as those of any of the persons mentioned above.

or more stations, the three network stations capture the vast majority of audience and revenues. For example, in Los Angeles with 11 commercial stations, the three network stations obtained 79.4 per cent of the average audience in 1969.[1] However, published data on revenue, cost and profits are only available for all commercial stations combined in any single market, rather than for individual stations. For that reason, the assumption of equal shares has been used. In addition, even if this is a highly simplistic model, it is a useful place to start.

If there are n firms in a particular market and the total market revenue is R, then the average revenue per firm is R/n. Suppose we assume that a newly entering firm does not increase total market revenue but only splits it with existing firms. Then the revenue it can expect to receive is $R/(n+1)$. On the other hand, it can expect to have the same operating costs as existing firms. If combined operating costs in a market before the new firm entered were C, then the costs for this new firm will be C/n. Therefore, its net income (before income taxes) would be $y = R/(n+1) - C/n$.

TABLE I

CORRELATION COEFFICIENTS FOR VARIOUS MEASURES OF PROFITS OF ALL VHF AND ALL UHF COMMERCIAL STATIONS, 1958–68

	VHF stations		*UHF stations*	
	R/C	y	R/C	y
y/K	0.8987**	0.6406*	0.9994**	0.9447**

Source: FCC, 'TV Broadcast Financial Data', 1958–68.
* Indicates that the correlation coefficient is statistically significant at the 0.05 level.
** Indicates that the correlation coefficient is statistically significant at the 0.01 level.

If we assume that the potentially entering firm seeks to maximize the dollar amount of profits, then it should enter those markets where y has the largest value. If, on the other hand, we assume that it seeks to maximize its rate of return, then it will attempt to enter those markets where y/K is the largest (given that K is some measure of capital investment). Unfortunately, however, the FCC does not publish data on investment by individual firm or market. Indeed, the only relevant data it publishes at all is total investment in angible property for all V.H.F. and all U.H.F. television stations combined. As Table I shows, for time series data, y/K is highly

[1] Statistical Research, Inc., 'The Potential Impact of CATV on Television Stations', Appendix E of 'Comments of the National Association of Broadcasters', submitted to the FCC in Docket 18397-A, December 7th, 1970, p. A10.

correlated with y and with the revenue-cost ratio, R/C. The revenue cost ratio may be thought of as a measure of a firm's markup above expenses. However, even if y and R/C are correlated with y/K for time series data, that does not necessarily indicate that they would be correlated with cross section data across different markets.

Suppose, however, we assume that the larger is the value of y or R/C in any market, the greater is the probability of entry in that market. Similarly, if T is total number of homes with television sets in any market, since we know that market revenue is closely correlated with audience size, we can predict that the probability of entry also increases as $T/(n+1)$ increases.

TABLE II

ANALYSIS OF VARIANCE FOR ENTRY IN 103 MARKETS WITH 3 OR MORE COMMERCIAL TELEVISION STATIONS, 1966 TO 1968

		Mean Values				
Analysis	*Variable*	n = −1 (*n* = 3)	n = 0 (*n* = 76)	n = +1 (*n* = 18)	n ⩾ 2 (*n* = 6)	*F*
(1)	y	37.88 (72.61)	148.9 (470.3)	759.7 (1227.2)	1501.1 (944.4)	10.11**
(2)	$\frac{R}{n+1}$	1103 (543)	1609 (1544)	3591 (3743)	4685 (1934)	7.67**
(3)	$\frac{R}{C}$	1.244 (0.130)	1.343 (0.258)	1.465 (0.280)	1.879 (0.176)	8.94**
(4)	$\frac{T}{n+1}$	67.99 (24.91)	123.9 (82.6)	225.6 (198.7)	233.2 (79.8)	5.83**
(5)	$\frac{T}{n}$	82.65 (32.88)	160.66 (103.70)	283.14 (234.45)	302.02 (104.13)	6.08**

Source: FCC, 'TV Broadcast Financial Data'.

** Indicates that the means differ at a 0.01 level of significance. The numbers in parentheses are the standard deviations of the means. n = change in the number of commercial stations on the air from 1966 to 1968.

n = number of commercial stations on the air in 1966.
R = 1966 market revenue of commercial stations in $ thousands.
C = 1966 market expenses of commercial stations in $ thousands.
T = 1966 television homes in thousands.

$$y = \frac{R}{n+1} - \frac{C}{n}$$

Because entry is a discrete variable which only takes on a limited number of values such as +2, +1, 0, −1, we have done an analysis of variance, rather than used regressions. Television markets have been separated into different groups according to whether there was a change in the number of stations of +2, +1, 0, or −1 in the two years following the measured value of y, R/C and T. Although the two-year period might appear to be too short, analysis with a three-year period suggested that the results would not be very different.

Table II presents the results of an analysis of variance for entry and exit in 103 markets during the period 1966 to 1968.[2] The hypotheses which were tested were all of the form: given some variable (such as income per station) in 1966, one would predict that entry would take place in the next two years in markets where that variable was relatively large, and no entry or even exit from the market would occur in markets where that variable was relatively small. The 103 markets were divided into four groups: the 6 markets in which two or more new stations entered between 1966 and 1968, the 18 markets in which one new station entered in that period, the 76 markets in which there was no change in the number of stations and the 3 markets in which one station left the market in that period.

The results are quite striking. For example, in analysis (1), y (which is a measure of the expected income per new station as explained above), had a mean value of $1,501,100 in markets where two or more stations eventually entered, $759,700 in markets where one station entered, $148,900 in markets where there was no change in the number of stations, and $37,880 in markets where one station went off the air. The means differed at a 0.01 level of significance.

Analyses (2) and (3) show similar results for expected revenue per new station, and for the average revenue–cost ratio. Analysis (4) presents a similar result for the number of television homes per new station. In every case the means differ at a 0.01 level.

For purposes of comparison with an earlier study, analysis (5) shows an analysis of variance of the number of television homes per existing station on the air. It shows that the average number of television homes per station was 283,140 in the 18 markets where one station entered. This suggests that a market with three stations would need 849,420 television homes before another station would enter, while a market with four stations would need 1,132,560 television homes before another station would enter the market. For the 76 markets with no exit or entry the average number of television homes per station was 160,660. This implies that a three-station market with 481,980 television homes would have no entry, and a four-station market with 642,640 television homes would have no entry.[3] Finally, the markets in which a station exited averaged

[2] The data used in this study are total market data for television markets in the 48 contiguous states which had 3 or more commercial stations on the air, since those are the only markets for which the FCC publishes complete data. The data used here were obtained from *TV Factbook* and from the FCC publication 'TV Broadcast Financial Data' for various years, and from John A. Dimling, Jr., Ronald W. McCabe and Wayne E. Schmiedeknecht, *Identification and Analysis for Achieving Greater Television Diversity in the United States* (Lexington, Kentucky: Spindletop Research, July 26th, 1968).

[3] In a letter to the author, Edward Greenberg has pointed out that these numbers are not entirely consistent. For example, they show that a market with 3 stations would need 849,420 television homes before a fourth station would enter, while a market with 4 stations and no exit or entry only had on average 642,640 television homes. However, this

82,650 television homes per station, which implies that a three-station market with 247,950 television homes, and a four-station market with 330,600 television homes might be so unprofitable that a station would go out of business.

These results may be compared with a recent study by Edward Greenberg. He estimated that in 1960 or 1962 in a 3-station market the stations would break even with an audience size of 186,000 to 217,000 (depending on the time period and method used), and in a 4 or more station market the stations would break even with from 1,332,000 to 1,641,000 television homes.[4]

TABLE III

ANALYSIS OF VARIANCE FOR ENTRY IN MARKETS WITH 3 OR MORE COMMERCIAL TELEVISION STATIONS, 1964 TO 1966, AND 1962 TO 1964

		1964 Mean values			*1962 Mean values*		
Analysis	*Variable*	n = 0 *for 1964–66* ($n = 85$)	n $\geqslant$ 0 *for 1964–66* ($n = 11$)	F	n = 0 *for 1962–64* ($n = 80$)	n $\geqslant$ 0 *for 1962–64* ($n = 5$)	F
(1)	y	154.3 (493.4)	1495.2 (1516.4)	41.98**	196.0 (617.3)	1099.1 (1003.7)	9.33**
(2)	$\frac{R}{n+1}$	1464 (1162)	5608 (4561)	48.91**	1542 (1733)	5113 (3492)	17.42**
(3)	$\frac{R}{C}$	1.366 (0.247)	1.583 (0.247)	7.57**	1.300 (0.380)	1.525 (0.278)	1.76
(4)	$\frac{T}{n+1}$	124.7 (84.1)	332.1 (232.6)	34.48**	140.2 (119.6)	326.9 (175.3)	10.85**

** indicates that the means are significantly different at the 0.01 level. The numbers in parentheses are the standard deviations of the means.

n = change in the number of stations on the air in the two-year period.
n = number of commercial stations on the air.
R = market revenue of commercial stations in \$ thousands.
C = market expenses of commercial stations in \$ thousands.
T = television homes in thousands.
$y = \frac{R}{n+1} - \frac{C}{n}$.

The results of the present study show considerably lower levels of television homes necessary for entry in markets with 3 stations than the Greenberg study implies are necessary for 4 or more stations to break even. It is not clear what this difference implies. Because Greenberg's data apply to four *or more* station markets, they may overstate the breakeven level necessary for four-station markets alone. It seems unlikely although not impossible, that a fourth

result may make sense since a fourth station might be unwilling to enter a 3 station market unless the market already had a larger potential audience size than the average 4 station market.

[4] Edward Greenberg, 'Television Station Profitability and FCC Regulatory Policy', *Journal of Industrial Economics*, XVII (July 1969), pp. 218–21, 235.

station would enter a market where on average four stations would not be expected to break even.

Table III presents the results of another analysis for entry in the periods 1962–64, and 1964–66. In these two time periods the data were only separated into two groups (either entry or non-entry markets) because there were not enough observations available to break them down into four groups as was done in Table II. Nevertheless, the results are quite striking and highly significant in most cases. In both time periods, the means differ significantly in analyses (1), (2), and (4). They show that television homes per station, income per station and revenue per station were far higher in those markets where entry took place than in markets where no entry took place. On the other hand, analysis (3) is significant only in the later period. However, even in the 1962–64 period the revenue–cost ratio is higher in markets where entry took place than it is in markets where entry did not take place, even though the differences are not statistically significant. Thus, these results tend to reinforce those found in the previous table.

One problem should be noted concerning the interpretation of both Tables II and III. Although the means are significantly differ- in nearly every case, and even though the mean values tend to be considerably higher in markets where entry took place than in markets where no entry or even exit took place, the standard deviations of the means are quite large in many cases. In other words, certain markets had values far higher or lower than the mean of their group. Thus, for example, analysis (1) in Table III shows that there were 85 markets with no change in the number of stations from 1964 to 1966 whose mean income per station was $154,300 in 1964. In fact, however, the standard deviation of the mean was $439,400. Included in that group of markets with no entry or exit was Cleveland with a mean income per station of $3,892,000 at one extreme and Fargo Valley, North Dakota with a mean income of –$47,000 at the other extreme. This shows the large variation in average income per station which exists within one group of markets. It also suggests the difficulty with using these mean values to predict whether or not entry will take place in any particular market.

In a sense these results may seem obvious. Why are they of any real significance? As was mentioned earlier, the FCC has followed a policy since 1945 of determining in advance the maximum number of television stations which may be built in each city or metropolitan area in the United States. In FCC language, it allocates television channel assignments in advance of demand, rather than waiting for demand to develop in specific markets.

One goal of the FCC has been to encourage the building of television stations in as many separate small communities as possible.[5] At the same time, it has limited entry in many of the more profitable markets which are usually in the major metropolitan areas. This policy of limiting entry allows those stations which do obtain licenses to earn higher than normal profits.[6]

TABLE IV

NUMBER OF TELEVISION CHANNEL ALLOCATIONS AND STATIONS BROADCASTING, VARIOUS YEARS

	1952 channel allocations	*1966 channel allocations*	*Stations broadcasting Feb. 1st. 1972*
Commercial stations	1,769	1,141	699
Educational stations	233	615	210
Totals	2,002	1,756	909

Source: U.S. Congress, Senate, Committee on Interstate and Foreign Commerce, *Hearings on the Allocations of TV Channels*, Report of the Ad Hoc Advisory Committee on Allocations, 85th Cong., 2nd Sess., 1958, p. 21; *Broadcasting*, 70 (February 14th, 1966), p. 68; and *Broadcasting*, 82 (February 28th, 1972), p. 72.

Although the FCC allocation plan is partially based on audience size,[7] the FCC still seems unaware of just how important is the effect of audience size on the number of stations on the air in any particular market. There have been a number of earlier studies which show that station revenue and income are highly correlated with audience size.[8] Since commercial stations receive nearly all their revenue from the sale of time to advertisers, and since advertising rates depend

[5] Federal Communications Commission, *Sixth Report and Order* in Dockets 8736, 8795, 8796, and 9175, released April 14th, 1952, Pike and Fisher, *Radio Regulation*, I, sec. 91.501, para. 13–17, 63–8.

[6] Ronald H. Coase, 'Evaluation of Public Policy Relating to Radio and Television Broadcasting: Social and Economic Issues', *Land Economics*, XLI (May 1965), pp. 161–7; Harvey J. Levin, 'Economic Effects of Broadcast Licensing', *Journal of Political Economy*, LXXII (April 1964), pp. 151–62; Harvey J. Levin, 'Federal Control of Entry in the Broadcast Industry', *Journal of Law and Economics*, V (October 1962), pp. 49–67; Ronald H. Coase, 'The Federal Communications Commission', *Journal of Law and Economics*, II (October 1959), pp. 1–40.

[7] Federal Communications Commission, *Fifth Report and Memorandum Opinion and Order* in Docket 14229, released February 11th, 1966, *Federal Register* XXXI, p. 2932ff., para. 65.

[8] Greenberg, *op. cit.*, pp. 210–38; Harvey J. Levin, 'Special Analysis of TV Station Sale Prices, Appendix H of United Research Incorporated, *The Implications of Limiting Multiple Ownership of Television Stations* (Cambridge, Mass: September 29th, 1966); Peter O. Steiner and Harold J. Barnett, with the assistance of Edward Greenberg and Michael Sovereign, 'Comments of Economic Consultants', submitted to the Federal Communications Commission in Dockets 14229 and 15201, April 3rd, 1964; pp. 37–56, 152–8, and appendix B; (Alexander, S. S.), 'CBS Says U.S. TV Limit is 600 Healthy Stations', *Broadcasting-Telecasting*, XLIV (October 17th, 1955), pp. 27–31; Peter R. Levin, 'How Many TV Outlets can the U.S. Support?' *Broadcasting-Telecasting*, XLIV (April 27th, 1953), pp. 102–4 ff.

primarily on the size of the audience viewing a particular program, it is not surprising that revenue and audience size are closely correlated.

One measure of the effectiveness of the FCC allocation plan is the extent to which the FCC has revised its own allocation table over time. Table IV shows the number of channels allocated in the allocation plan of 1952 and in the revised allocation plan of 1966, as well as the number of stations actually on the air on February 1st, 1972. The table indicates that in the 1966 plan the number of commercial allocations was decreased to 628 fewer than there were in 1952, even though the number of educational allocations was increased by 382.

Table V

COMMERCIAL TELEVISION ALLOCATIONS IN THE MARKETS 1–10, AND 90–100, 1970

Market rank[a]	Market name	*Number of channels allocated*	*Number of TV homes in ADI*[b] (000)	*Number of TV homes per channel* (000)
1.	New York	9	5913	657
2.	Los Angeles	14	3409	244
3.	Chicago	13	2508	193
4.	Philadelphia	8	2133	267
5.	Boston	7	1447	207
6.	Detroit	7	1409	201
7.	San Francisco	9	1478	164
8.	Cleveland	6	1215	203
9.	Washington	7	1077	154
10.	Pittsburgh	6	972	162
90.	Fresno	6	253	42
91.	Chattanooga	4	214	54
92.	Evansville	4	167	42
93.	Sioux Falls	4	173	43
94.	South Bend	4	162	41
95.	West Palm Beach	4	158	40
96.	Ft. Wayne	4	165	41
97.	Rockeford, Ill.	4	—	—
98.	Peoria, Ill.	4	158	40
99.	Augusta	4	150	38
100.	Terre Haute	3	127	42

Source: Federal Communications Commission, 'The Economics of the TV-CATV Interface', Staff Report Prepared by the Research Branch, Broadcast Bureau, July 15th, 1970, Table 1, pp. 7–9; and *Television Factbook*, No. 41, 1971–72 edition, pp. 56a–59a.

[a] Markets are ranked according to 1967 net weekly circulation as tabulated by the American Research Bureau.

[b] ADI is the Area of Dominant Influence as defined by the American Research Bureau.

In addition, in the 1966 plan practically no channel assignments were made in cities with a population of under 25,000 although such assignments had been made in the 1952 table.[9] This suggests that by 1966 the FCC had come to realize that its 1952 allocation plan was far too optimistic with respect to commercial station allocations. It may also be seen from Table IV that in February 1972 less than two-thirds of the commercial allocations and about one-third of the educational allocations were in use. The number of commercial stations have only increased by an average of 16 per year in the last ten years (although in one particular year they did increase by 33). The number of educational stations have only increased by an average of 15 per year in the last ten years (although they did increase by 30 in one particular year). This suggests that it will be many years before the remaining allocation are used up.[10]

However, it is not true that the FCC has been overoptimistic in its allocation table in all cases. As Table V shows, the number of television homes per allocated station is quite high in the largest cities (657,000 in New York City) and much lower in smaller cities. It is the largest cities which generally also have the highest income per station, and therefore are the places where additional stations would most likely be profitable, if the FCC would allow them to be built.

CONCLUSION

The main conclusion to be drawn from the results presented here is that entry of television stations is strongly affected by certain economic variables, particularly expected audience viewing size and therefore expected profits. Any attempt by the FCC to limit entry in some large markets in the hope that more entry will take place in other small markets is bound to fail unless the small markets are large enough to support additional stations. FCC station allocations which do not consider the necessity of large enough audience size will never be used in the future.

With the growth of cable television and the possibility of subscription television, the reasons for limiting entry in some markets and preserving unused allocations in other markets become less convincing. The growth of cable television and subscription television offer the possibility of increased quality, diversity, and local programming. As a consequence, they decrease the need to regulate

[9] Federal Communications Commission, *Fifth Report and Memorandum Opinion and Order* in Docket 14229, para. 1, 65.

[10] On this point, see: Douglas W. Webbink, 'The Impact of UHF Promotion: The All Channel Television Receiver Law', *Law and Contemporary Problems*, XXXIV (Summer 1969) pp. 535–561; and Douglas W. Webbink, 'The All-Channel Television Receiver Law and the Future of Ultra-High Frequency Television', Unpublished Ph.D. dissertation, Duke University, 1968, pp. 112–54.

television station entry in order to obtain those goals (assuming that regulation ever actually had those results at all).

Limiting entry in the large profitable markets obviously hurts the viewers in those markets, since they have a smaller number of program choices than might otherwise have been available. On the other hand, reserving channels in small unprofitably markets does not help viewers in those markets if no stations are built, while it may be taking channels away from the viewers in large markets.

In addition, since the largest markets are not only the places where television stations are currently making large 'monopoly' profits, but also the places where cable television might be most profitable, it is rather surprising that the FCC continues to limit the entry of new stations into these markets on the one hand, and places restriction on the growth of cable television in these markets, on the other hand. One can only hope that the newest FCC rules[11] on CATV will begin to reverse that trend.

WASHINGTON, D.C.

[11] FCC, *Cable Television Report and Order* in Dockets 18397, 18397-A, 18373. 18416, 18892, 18894, February 2nd, 1972, 37 Fed. Reg. 3252 (February 12th, 1972).

A NOTE ON VARIABLE PATENT LIFE*

by Fred D. Arditti and Richard L. Sandor

INTRODUCTION

The U.S. patent system seeks to stimulate inventive effort by offering the inventor the incentive of a seventeen-year right to exclusive use and by requiring public disclosure of the invention so that new knowledge is made available to other potential inventors. One distinct fact emerges from a study of this patent system: the seventeen-year life is not based on present-day economic phenomena but is somewhat of a historical accident.[1] This particular duration of exclusive use may not give the firm a large enough fraction of the social benefits associated with the invention to induce it to undertake a major R & D project involving a large investment. In this instance, society would forgo the benefits of the new product or process. On the other hand, a seventeen-year monopoly right might grant the firm a larger fraction of the ensuing social benefits than would be necessary to induce it to undertake a low cost R & D project. In this case, society would bear the social cost associated with an excessive patent life—a deadweight consumption loss.[2]

This reasoning leads one to suspect that there is no single patent life which might be deemed best. In spite of numerous examples in the literature which indicate the shortcomings of a fixed patent life in general, and a seventeen-year patent life in particular, there have been few real attempts to propose and analyze a system which would yield different patent lives for different inventions. It would seem that a system which advocates a variable patent life policy is one which should attempt to consider the alternatives of additional incentive versus the social cost of monopoly. It is the broad purpose of this paper to develop a system which does consider the preceding and to treat some of the difficulties associated with trying to determine patent life.

* We wish to thank Richard R. Nelson for his helpful suggestions and the Institute of Business and Economic Research of the University of California, Berkeley for their financial support.

[1] For a complete discussion, see C. Michael White, 'Why a Seventeen Year Patent', *Journal of the Patent Office Society*, December 1956, pp. 839–60.

[2] Evidence has been presented to show that this consumption loss is not the only social cost of a monopoly. A monopoly position may also result in very little research being done. See R. R. Nelson, M. J. Peck, and E. D. Kalachek, *Technological Advance, Economic Growth and Public Policy*, Washington, D. C., The Brookings Institution, 1967. For a more detailed discussion of the different dimensions of social costs see Alfred Kahn, 'Role of Patents' in John P. Miller, Ed., *Competition, Cartels and Their Regulation*, Amsterdam, North Holland Publishing Co., 1962.

THE CALCULATION OF THE PATENT LIFE UNDER CERTAINTY

A patent system which considers the alternatives of additional incentive versus the social cost of monopoly could be one in which patent life is determined so as to insure that the inventor recovers all of his costs plus a 'fair' return on his investment. Alternatively, the system might be designed so that the inventor can recover the social value of the invention, or at least some part of it. The purpose of this section is to demonstrate how patent life is determined in these instances as well as to show how different factors would affect it. The limitations of this type of variable patent life will also be discussed.

In order to make the exposition as simple as possible, it is useful to initially deal with the case of certainty. In this world of certainty, it is assumed that before the introduction of a patentable invention the marketplace is competitive. Now, the key to the estimation of the patent life is the specification of a necessary rate of return. If a firm is earning a competitive rate of r per cent on its investments, then it must also earn a rate of at least r on any R & D undertaking. If the firm cannot earn this return of r on its R & D projects, then it will be discouraged from pursuing its interests in the R & D field. The specification of the necessary return coupled with the knowledge of past expenditures and future income yields the patent life.

If R_t^p, S_T, C, and T denote net cash flows under patent protection in year t, the value of the invention after the patent expires (the salvage value), the total cost of bringing the product to market, and life of the patent, respectively, then the patent life is determined by searching for that particular patent life which permits the invention to have an internal rate of return equal to r. Consequently, the following equation must be solved for T.

$$C = \sum_{t=0}^{T} \frac{R_t^p}{(1+r)^t} + \frac{S_T}{(1+r)^T} . \qquad (1)$$

The solution of the above equation is found by an iterative technique. A value of T is chosen, and to that value correspond T number of R_t^p's and a certain S_T. The values of these parameters are substituted into the equation to see if they satisfy the equation. If not, another value of T is chosen and one sees if the corresponding values of the parameters satisfy the equation and so on until the solution is reached.[3]

The patent life obtained in this manner depends on a number of factors. Some are obvious, others are not. The obvious ones are the cost, C, the required return, r, and monopoly net cash flows, R_t^p. The patent life varies directly with C and inversely with R_t^p. The higher the cost of development the greater the length of time one must be allowed in order to earn a return of r. The higher the monopoly net cash flows, R_t^p, the shorter the length of time one needs patent protection to recoup his investment, C, at a return of r.

A key factor which affects the determination of patent life and is not readily discernible is the percentage of the total cost, C, that R & D costs comprise. This can be seen if we divide both sides of equation (1) by C and multiply both sides by $(1+r)$. Then (1) becomes

$$(2) \qquad (1+r) = \frac{1}{C}\sum_{t=0}^{T}\frac{R_t^p}{(1+r)^{t-1}} + \frac{S_T}{C(1+r)^{T-1}}.$$

Now, rewrite S_T, which is the present value at time T of all future cash flows, as

$$(3) \qquad S_T = \sum_{t=T+1}^{\infty}\frac{R_t^c}{(1+r)^{t-T}}$$

where R_t^c is the net cash flow under conditions of competition. Then (2) becomes,

[3] If S_T and $R_t^p > 0$ for all $t > 0$, then the right hand side of equation (1) is a monotonically increasing function of T. In this case, a unique solution of T is obtained:

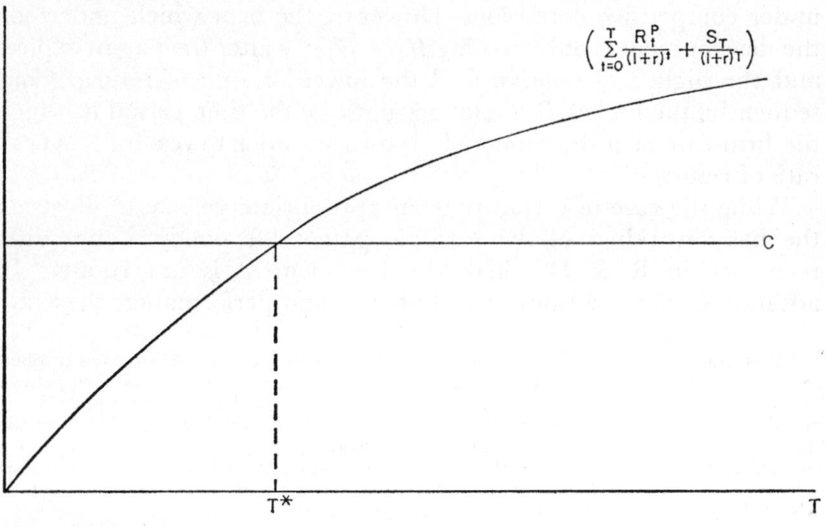

$$(4) \qquad (1+r) = \sum_{t=0}^{T} \frac{R_t^p/C}{(1+r)^{t-1}} + \frac{1}{(1+r)^{T-1}} \sum_{t=T+1}^{\infty} \frac{R_t^c/C}{(1+r)^{t-T}}$$

$$= \sum_{t=0}^{T} \frac{R_t^p/C}{(1+r)^{t-1}} + \sum_{t=T+1}^{\infty} \frac{R_t^c/C}{(1+r)^{t-1}}$$

From (4) one can see that the return r is a weighted sum of the returns under patent protection, R_t^p/C, and the returns under competition, R_t^c/C—the weights being $1/(1+r)^{t-1}$. Now let

$$(5) \qquad C \equiv I+D$$

where:

I = Investment in plant and equipment
D = the cost of R & D

Then (4) can be rewritten as

$$(6) \qquad (1+r) = \sum_{t=0}^{T} \frac{R_t^p/I \cdot \overline{\frac{I}{I+D}}}{(1+r)^{t-1}} + \sum_{t=T+1}^{\infty} \frac{R_t^c/I \cdot \overline{\frac{I}{I+D}}}{(1+r)^{t-1}}$$

If we initially assume that I is the investment in plant and equipment that all other firms make, then R_t^c/I is the return that all other firms in the same cost class will earn after the patent expires. At the end of T years, any firm can have the necessary production information at zero cost. The only cost the new entrants incur is the price of new plant and equipment, I. Their net cash flows are R_t^c. Thus, their return is R_t^c/I which is equal to r, the rate under competitive conditions. However, the firm which undertook the development is only earning $I/(I+D)$ of r after the patent expires and the higher D relative to I the lower its rate of return. Consequently, the higher D the longer must be the time period in which the firm can earn the monopoly return in order to reach an overall rate of return of r.[4]

While the case of certainty is an appropriate vehicle to illustrate the basic workings of the variable patent life policy, it has little relevance in R & D where the key element is uncertainty. In addition to uncertainties regarding cost and performance, there are

[4] It is much more realistic to assume that the amount the patentee invested in plant and equipment, I', was much greater that the amount that its eventual competitors invested in plant and equipment, for the patentee controlled the entire market for T years. Now if each new entrant earns a return of r on his investment, I, and there are decreasing returns to scale, then the return earned by the patentee on his investment in plant and equipment, I', is less than r. It follows that for the patentee to earn an overall return of r, the higher I' relative to I, the longer must be the patent life—the time in which the patentee is able to earn a return higher than r.

usually very great uncertainties regarding the value of the final product. Therefore, the basic technique for the calculation of the variable patent life must be altered in order for it to be more relevant for the real world.

THE CALCULATION OF THE PATENT LIFE UNDER UNCERTAINTY

In turning from the certain world to one of uncertainty, equation (1) must be modified; future net cash flows can no longer be regarded as given but must be recognized as random variables. Nor can the formula be adjusted to take account of uncertainty by replacing the random variables with their expected values because the dispersion of returns cannot be ignored. However, in line with our reasoning in the world of certainty, the following method might be suitable. This method which is dubbed the certainty equivalent approach requires the investor to calculate his expected utility of net cash flows in each future period, under patent protection take its cash equivalent—the cash amount that equates the utility function to the value of expected utility—and discount these cash equivalents at the rate applied to certain income streams. We shall now use R_t^p to denote the cash equivalent of expected utility in year t. Discounting these cash equivalents at the certainty rate is permissible because the cash equivalent is, in effect, the amount the investor is willing to accept for the sale of his income rights and the risks accompanying these rights. In other words, it is the certain stream that he is willing to accept for the uncertain stream generated by his investment.

Consequently, we are once again analyzing the same problem as that presented in the certain world example. We must find that length of time during which the firm is allowed to earn monopoly profits which will guarantee it the rate of return that it could earn in alternative investments. The solution to the variable patent life is again given by equation (1), only R^p now denotes the amount the investor or patentee is willing to accept for relinquishing full rights to his invention in year t—in effect, R_t^p is a complete and compulsory licensing fee, and S_T denotes the price the investor is willing to accept for the sale of the invention after the patent expires. It should be noted that since R_t^p is a function of entrepreneurs' preferences for risk, patent life will also be a function of preferences for risk. The greater the risk aversion, the lower the certainty equivalent and consequently the longer the patent life.[5]

[5] Suppose that some firm or government agency was prepared to offer insurance against large losses during any year and that the premium charged for this insurance is greater

Any possible practical application of this patent policy, of course, requires knowledge of each parameter in equation (1). The appropriate discount rate may be taken as the risk-free rate of return prevailing in the market. The total cost of bringing the product to market, C, is also available since the patent life, T, is not calculated until all costs are in, thus insuring the complete recoupment of all development costs.[6] Measures of the invention's R_t^p's are found by asking the firm to estimate a complete licensing fee for each year. The new licensing fee would be equal to the price at which the firm is indifferent between producing its own product or having some other firm undertake production. The firm must also submit a cash equivalent figure for S_T, the salvage value in year T. This number must represent the amount the firm would accept for its plant and equipment after the patent expires.

To those who believe that firms will always set exorbitant license fees, remember that equation (1) shows that the patent life, T, varies inversely with this parameter. Furthermore, there is no guarantee that a competitor or the government will ever purchase the patent rights. Similarly, the firm that decides to out-think the U.S. Patent Office by submitting low license fees in the hope of obtaining a longer patent life must remember that these are the fees that competitors will pay in any year for the transfer of all rights. The license fee that is set too low may only benefit the competitor. However, the firm may still submit a too-low salvage value equivalent in the hope of obtaining a longer patent life. To prevent this, the government must have the option of buying at the end of T years the firm's plant and equipment at a price equal to the firm's initial estimate of the salvage value. In summary, the submission of high or low R_t^p's and a low S_T in the hope of reaping high license fees or a long patent life may very well be self-defeating.

SOME CONCLUDING REMARKS ON THE LIMITATIONS OF THIS PATENT

In the proposed system inventions with differing social benefits but identical cost will be rewarded in the same manner. This could result in the absence of incentives to produce inventions with greater social benefits. In order to eliminate this shortcoming it might be

than the expected value of the loss but less than the individual's cash equivalent of these losses, i.e. the maximum he would be willing to pay for insurance against such losses. Then, the individual's cash equivalent of the invention's return in any particular year will be increased. Therefore, the calculated patent life will be decreased.

[6] This assumption is a tenuous one. Rarely are all costs involved in the development of a product and the tooling necessary to manufacture known when the first item comes off the production line. Later improvements will increase C. It should also be indicated that empirically it may be difficult to obtain all these costs.

possible to modify equation (1) by using a measure of the social worth of the invention or some fraction of this worth instead of costs. Unfortunately, it is not possible to have this in the variable patent life system. The value to society of the invention is determined by the conditions under which the new product or process is marketed, the maximum social benefit occurring under perfect competition. Therefore, the social value of the invention will depend on the length of the monopoly granted by the patent. But the social value of the invention is needed to determine the length of patent life. Thus, in these circumstances, the social value or any fraction of it and the patent life are indeterminate.[7]

It is apparent that an ideal patent system has not been the product of this paper. Then what can be claimed for this study? A variable patent life policy is not a new concept. It has been discussed—though rather vaguely—in numerous papers. The claim for this study is that it represents an attempt to systematically analyze a particular type of variable patent life system under different conditions. The analysis hopefully provides an interesting framework for discussing the advantages and disadvantages of our present system as well as the nature of the difficulties and complexities encountered in alternative systems.

UNIVERSITY OF CALIFORNIA, BERKELEY

[7] It should be noted that a panel of experts could establish different amounts which would be added to the left side of equation (1). Different amounts would correspond to different degrees of value and, therefore, a system of rewards or incentive is incorporated in the variable patent system. This procedure does allow a variable patent life to be computed. However, it is important to indicate that this does not alter the indeterminancy. It simply has been disguised. Further, the availability of a measure of social value would enable us to resolve a problem encountered earlier but not noted. Recall that in the case of certainty and perfect competition the proposed method of calculating the patent life always guarantees a return of r per cent on any R & D investment; thereby making it impossible to differentiate between investment. However, the inclusion of a measure of social value on the left-hand side of equation (1) and the resulting patent life would imply a rate of return on investment cost different from r and thus enables one to differentiate between projects.

SEASONAL FLUCTUATIONS IN THE MOTOR VEHICLE INDUSTRY: A COMMENT

by P. SMITH

SEASONAL fluctuations in unemployment are generally considered to arise, in the main part, from variations in weather conditions and from movements in demand. A comparison of pre- and post-war patterns of seasonal variations in the motor industry reveals an interesting example of the influence of changes in production practices, allied to changes in the seasonal pattern of demand, both elements reflecting in part the lessening impact of the annual Motor Show.

The statistics used in this discussion relate to unemployment in the city of Coventry, in which the prime influence upon trends in employment (and unemployment) is the motor industry. In 1967, for instance, the motor vehicle industry, defined by minimum list heading 381 of the Standard Industrial Classification (C.S.O., 1958) accounted for more than 40 per cent of manufacturing employment in the area. In the pre-war period, the percentage figure was considerably higher than this. It has been shown that movements in total unemployment in Coventry very closely reflect variations in the level of activity in the motor industry (see Smith, 1971), and it is these figures which are used in the following discussion.

Figures 1 and 2 illustrate the seasonal pattern of unemployment in Coventry for the years 1927–38 and 1951–69, respectively. The difference between the two diagrams is dramatic, displaying almost opposite trends. During the pre-war period, the seasonal 'peak' in unemployment tended to come in the summer months; in particular from June to August. This sort of pattern was likely to have been associated with the practice which car manufacturers made of spending the summer months in 'research and development', intent upon being able to produce new models in time for the Motor Show, which customarily took place in the autumn (see Turner, 1963). During the 1930s, the car firms were numerous, but generally relatively small. This meant that resources were limited, so that 'research and development' and production could not be carried on simultaneously.

However, in the years since the war, this situation has ceased to dominate. The car producers have grown in the scale of their activity, through mergers and in response to the large-scale expansion of demand. It is now possible, therefore, to carry out research and

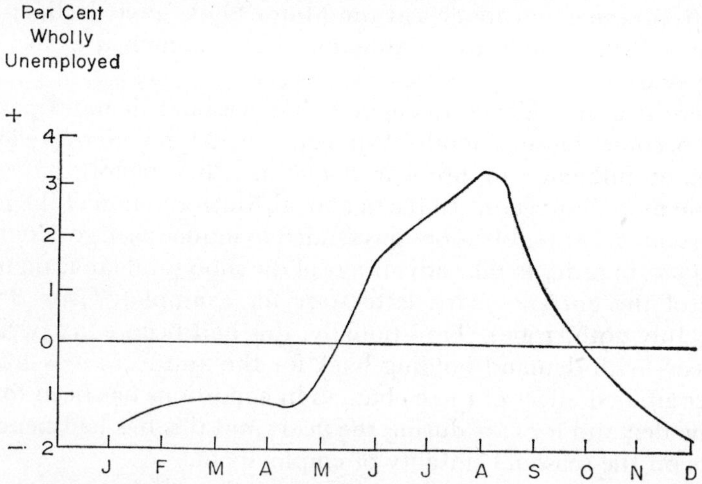

FIGURE 1. Seasonal variations in unemployment in Coventry 1927–1938
Source: Ministry of Town and Country Planning, *West Midlands Plan* (Interim), July 1948.

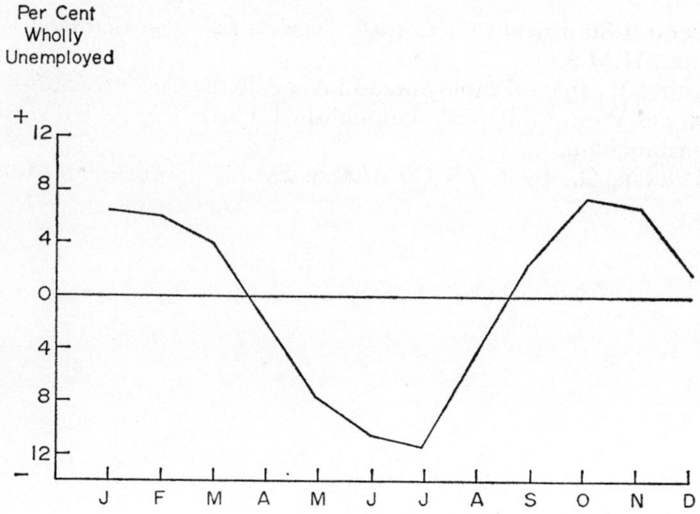

FIGURE 2. Seasonal variations in unemployment in Coventry, 1951–69
Source: Department of Employment, Coventry.

development as a continuous process, without the necessity for interrupting the flow of production. In addition, in recent years the pressures to produce new models at the Motor Show have declined, and new models are liable to be announced and launched at any time of the year.

There is also evidence to suggest that seasonal demand patterns have become more smooth. Whereas the Motor Show was the dominant influence in pre-war demand, other factors have now become more important. In particular, the introduction of the lettering system on car registrations has tended to induce a surge of demand in August, in order to take advantage of the snob (and later, material) value of the current year's letter (see for example, *Times Business News*, July 29th, 1969). Traditionally, this had been a lax period of the year, with demand holding back for the autumn's new models. The combined effect of these changes in conditions has been to level out the demand for cars during the year, and this has had beneficial results on the seasonal stability of employment.

UNIVERSITY COLLEGE
LONDON

REFERENCES

[1] Central Statistical Office, 1958, *Standard Industrial Classification*, 2nd edn., H.M.S.O.

[2] Smith, P., 1971. 'Employment Linkages in the Coventry Sub-Region of the West Midlands', Unpublished Ph.D Thesis, University of Birmingham.

[3] Turner, G., 1963, *The Car Makers*, Eyre & Spottiswoode, London.

ILLUSIONS IN TESTING FOR ADMINISTERED PRICES*

by HOWARD N. ROSS

PROFESSOR PHLIPS in this Journal (Vol. XVIII, November 1969) has mounted what may be the latest foray against administered prices. Applying some routine statistical tests on data for Belgium, the Netherlands and France between 1958–65, Phlips concludes: 'Concentrated industries appear to behave in the same way as unconcentrated industries as far as upward flexibility is concerned. Prices tend to follow increases in unit costs, while market structure does not appear to have any particular influence' (p. 14). These remarks can be placed in a historical context: if 'downward flexibility' is substituted for 'upward flexibility' they would summarize what A. Neal found 30 years ago in his study of prices during the Great Depression in the United States.[1] Apparently, contemporary economics has rejected the hypothesis originated by Gardiner Means relating market power to relative prices for all time and place—the pre- and post-war generations and the U.S. and E.E.C. countries being a statistically huge sample. And yet, of late, the nemesis of stabilization policy in the U.S. and elsewhere has been the persistence of what was thought to be the incompatible evils of inflation and recession. Their protracted occurrence in the U.S. forced a reluctant government to embrace the last resort of wage and price controls, and of lesser impact, prompted critics to speculate on a permanent shift of the Phillips curve. What seemed to underlay the remarkable reversal of policy was the concession that the causes of inflation were resistant to conventional macroeconomic policies even at a social cost of over 6 per cent unemployment. Would such a concession have been as necessary if factor and product markets were broadly and reasonably competitive? The question invites an appraisal of Phlips' essay.

It can be shown that Phlips' conclusions are biased in at least three distinct ways: a failure to consider relevant evidence and argument bearing on the nature of the hypothesis; a specification error in the tested equations; and an econometric procedure that

* The author is grateful to John M. Blair, Joel Dirlam and Damodar Gujarati for their various help.

[1] 'Neither price change nor production change, however, is to be explained by concentration. Rather, differential price changes are explicable by differential unit direct cost changes, and differential production changes are to be explained in terms of demand shifts which are a consequence of the nature of the demands concerned.' Alfred C. Neal, *Industrial Concentration and Price Flexibility* (American Council on Public Affairs, Washington, D.C., 1942), p. 165.

produces questionable regression coefficients and distorts the true relationship between concentration and price change.

THE ANTECEDENTS

From the outset, Phlips appears to regard the administered price hypothesis not only as null, but void as well. In his introduction, he calls the case for administered prices 'rather weak', and then proceeds to invoke the authority of G. J. Stigler, who is universally known to consider the case nonexistent.[2] Only two empirical investigations are mentioned, one by H. DePodwin and R. Selden, another by L. Weiss.[3] The latter guides Phlips in the construction of his behavioral equations: linear regressions of prices on labor cost and raw material cost per unit of output and concentration, and in the process, the errors inherent in the former studies become assimilated. I will recur to this point further on. The acceptance by the author of this small body of opinion, uniformly negative in its findings on administered prices, is matched by the exclusion of a much larger and growing body of research with dissident conclusions. No reference is made to the work of John Blair, most pointedly in the present context, his rejoinder to Stigler;[4] nor to the theoretical implications of full cost pricing and its variant, target return pricing, for price ratchets in oligopolies;[5] nor to the sizable empirical evi-

[2] Phlips sets the tone in the third paragraph (p. 1):

> It would indeed be difficult to defend the hypothesis on theoretical grounds. As G. J. Stigler puts it: 'The traditional economic theory argues that oligopoly and monopoly prices have no special relevance to inflation. A monopolist (to take the simpler case) sets a profit-maximizing price for given demand-and-cost conditions. If inflation leads to a rise in either demand or costs, a new and usually higher price will be set. The price will usually be above the competition level at any given time, but its pattern over time will not be other than passively responsive to monetary conditions.'

G. J. Stigler, 'Administered Prices and Oligopolistic Inflation,' *Journal of Business*, XXXV, No. 2, January 1962, p. 8. One could argue that for 'traditional economic theory' one should read 'neoclassical economic theory', and that the 'simpler case' of the monopolist is the 'unique case' under proper elasticity qualifications. The pattern of relative prices over time is a central concern of oligopoly theory. Apart from the rigid price theories of P. Sweezy and K. Rothschild, there is a larger class of theories in which price is insensitive to short run changes in demand, i.e., full cost theory and its variants.

[3] Horace DePodwin and Richard Selden, 'Business Pricing Policies and Inflation', *Journal of Political Economy*, LXXI, No. 2, April 1963, pp. 116–27. Leonard Weiss, 'Business Pricing Policies and Inflation Reconsidered', *Journal of Political Economy*, LXXIV, No. 2, April 1966, pp. 177–87.

[4] 'Administered Prices and Oligopolistic Inflation: A Reply', *Journal of Business*, XXXVII, No. 1, January 1964, pp. 68–81, also J. M. Blair, 'Administered Prices: A Phenomenon in Search of a Theory', *Papers and Proceedings of the American Economic Association*, XLIX, No. 2, May 1959, pp. 419–50.

[5] Gardner Ackley, 'Administered Prices and the Inflationary Process', *Papers and Proceedings of the American Economic Association*, XLIX, No. 2, May 1959. Charles L. Schultze, 'Recent Inflation in the United States', Study Paper No. 1, *Employment, Growth and Price Levels* (United States Congress, Joint Economic Committee, Washington, D.C., 1959). R. L. Hall and C. J. Hitch, 'Price Theory and Business Behavior', *Oxford Economic*

dence on the positive relationships between concentration and margins, and concentration and profit rates, which connote a relationship between concentration and the pattern of price change.[6]

The recent empirical work on margins—overhead costs plus profits—can be employed to demonstrate propositions of full cost theory, which uniquely regards margins as a decision variable and, therefore, a determinant of absolute and relative prices. To date there have been no systematic applications, but an intriguing contribution by W. J. Yordan, Jr. is illustrative of the kind of material available to Phlips but overlooked.[7] Yordan constructed monthly indexes of price and direct costs from published data for the U.S., weighted by information from the Leontief input-output table for 14 industries evenly divided between concentrated and unconcentrated. A distributed lag technique gave estimates of lags between price and component costs and between price and demand; the price-cost lag was extremely short, about one month, and similar for the two groups of industries. Prices were utterly unresponsive to demand in the concentrated group and only marginally responsive in the unconcentrated group. Measuring margins as the ratio of price to labor and raw material costs, Yordan claims that between 1955–58, 'they (margins) suggest that inflationary pressures were more fully translated into price increases in the concentrated group than in the unconcentrated, and they cast considerable doubt on the hypothesis that recent price increases reflect only belated restorations of normal gross margins'.[8] Moreover, Yordan's data reveal that between the third quarter of 1957 and the second quarter of 1958, a period of inflationary recession when the issue of cost push was forcefully revived in government and academic quarters, margins within the concentrated group rose steadily on average by 2.7 per cent while margins within the unconcentrated group fell by 0.5 per cent.[9] My own current work on margins for all the years

Papers, No. 2, May 1939. P. W. S. Andrews, *Manufacturing Business* (Macmillan, London, 1955). A. D. H. Kaplan, J. Dirlam and R. F. Lanzillotti, *Pricing in Big Business* (The Brookings Institution, Washington, D.C., 1958). R. R. Neild, *Pricing and Employment in the Trade Cycle* (National Institute of Economic and Social Research, Cambridge University Press, Cambridge, 1963).

[6] A summary of previous studies of profit rates and concentration in addition to their own research on profit rates and margins appears in Norman R. Collins and Lee E. Preston, *Concentration and Price-Cost Margins in Manufacturing Industries* (University of California Press, Berkeley and Los Angeles, 1968). Also see their joint article, 'Price-Cost Margins and Industry Structure', *The Review of Economics and Statistics*, LI, No. 3, August 1969, pp. 271–86.

[7] W. J. Yordan, Jr., 'Industrial Concentration and Price Flexibility', *The Review of Economics and Statistics*, XLIII, No. 3, August 1961, pp. 287–94.

[8] W. J. Yordan, Jr., 'A Model of Price Flexibility: Comment', *American Economics Review*, LI, No. 3, June 1961, pp. 391–2.

[9] *Ibid.*, p. 392. The inflation of the 1957–58 recession was partly due to a fortuitous increase in the wholesale prices of farm products of 4 per cent which drove up the prices

between 1952–67 confirms a similar pattern during recessions and a reverse pattern during the inflation beginning in 1966.

THE SPECIFICATION ERROR

Administered price inflation, according to Phlips, 'might be defined as saying that price increases are higher in more concentrated industries, given *positive* changes in demand and costs. Empirically speaking, it implies that, for a cross-section of industries, wholesale-price changes are a positive function of concentration ratios, for given *increases* in demand and unit costs' (p. 1, italics mine). By what is commonly understood to be the behavior of administered prices, this definition must be viewed as aberrant. The hypothetical movement of administered prices is alleged to be perverse with the cycle—rigid, or worse, rising in downswings, and during upswings, increasing more gently than competitive prices. For reinforcement, one need not search any further than G. J. Stigler:

> The main thrust of the doctrine of administered prices is that contractions in business lead to no systematic reduction of industrial prices, and, much more equivocally, expansions in business may only tardily lead to price increases. Whether because of a simple desire for stability, or more subtly because perhaps profits are better protected by stable prices, it has been argued that prices have at best only one-way flexibility, and that upward.[10]

In a reference cited by Phlips, Means himself clearly indicates the expected movement of administered prices as a consequence of their insensitivity to cyclical shifts in demand.[11] Although Stigler's version of administered prices follows closely the lines laid down by

of processed foods and feeds by 5 per cent. Nonetheless, dismay prevailed when the prices of finished steel products rose 3.7 per cent while production decreased 25 per cent, and when increases in automobiles prices of 2.9 per cent accompanied a fall in output of 31.6 per cent. Prices are Bureau of Labor Statistics wholesale prices and production figures are from the Federal Reserve Board index of industrial production; all figures are annual changes.

[10] George J. Stigler and James K. Kindahl, *The Behavior of Industrial Prices* (National Bureau of Economic Research, New York, 1970), pp. 7–9.

[11] But with the discretion implicit in administered prices, it would be possible to have a rise in prices without a prior increase in the public demand for goods. We have already seen that, by keeping their prices on the low side of the area of discretion, business can retard an inflation arising from too much buying power, as happened in the case of administered prices immediately after the war

Conversely, if there were no excess in buying power, business enterprises could decide to raise their prices within the area of discretion so as to increase their unit profit margins.

Administered Prices, Hearings before the Subcommittee on Antitrust and Monopoly of the Committee on the Judiciary, U.S. Senate, Part I, 1957, p. 84.

Means, it ignores a parallel development beginning with the writings on full cost theory that is rich in analytical and empirical substance for price flexibility. Whereas Means' administered prices have depended for their existence on simple correlations of relative price change and concentration, full cost theory offers unique relationships between changes in price and its cost components—direct costs and margins—restricting concentration to the partial determinant it should be. The essence of full cost-administered prices is that they, unlike competitive prices, are cost determined in the short run (the Marshallian short run), where direct costs and margins are estimated at some 'normal' or average output. During recessions, such prices can rise if realized margins fall below estimated margins; competitive markets have no such option. During expansions, which are of a much longer duration than recessions, such prices may rise more slowly than competitive prices if realized margins exceed estimated margins. These propositions are far from well established, but they do provide a coherent foundation for accepting or rejecting the full-cost-administered price hypothesis.

Phlips' error lies in his unawareness that he is dealing with a manifestly cyclical argument. His terminal years are dictated by the availability of data, rather than by turning points or phases of the cycle. The seven year span of the study is long enough to embrace a complete cycle or several cycles, but perhaps too short to reveal secular evidence of administered prices for any one or many institutional and policy reasons that might have existed in the separate countries of his sample. The weak correlation he found between concentration and price change should neither surprise nor disappoint, since there are no unambiguous expectations about what the relationship should be in the long run. The same specification error afflicts the studies by H. De Podwin and R. Selden, and by L. Weiss; the former examined the period 1953–59, the latter 1953–59 and 1959–63. Both studies were inspired by G. Means' testimony before the U.S. Senate Subcommittee on Antitrust and Monopoly, which undertook to explain the price increases between 1953–57.[12] The omission of these works to deal explicitly with the cyclical nature of administered prices generates lower estimates of the relationship between concentration and price change than would be anticipated in an appropriate test.

[12] *Administered Prices, Hearings before the Subcommittee on Antitrust and Monopoly of the Committee on the Judiciary* U.S. Senate, Part IX, 1959, pp. 4746–58; Part X, 1959, pp. 4897–910. In a recent conversation with Dr. John Blair, the then Senior Economist of Subcommittee, he informed me that Gardiner Means was directed by the Subcommittee to comment on the years 1953–57.

THE ECONOMETRIC PROCEDURE

Phlips' basic equation, applied to industry data, is an *ad hoc* relationship in linear form:

$$(1)\quad \frac{P_t}{P_0} = a + bC + c\frac{W_t}{W_o} + d\frac{MC_t}{MC_o} + u$$

P = price level
C = four firm concentration ratio
W = wages per unit of output, alternatively substituted by
SW = salaries and wages per unit of output
MC = net cost of raw materials and fuel per unit of output
u = error term[13]

Consider now the identity, Price ≡ Direct Costs + Margins as

$$(2)\qquad P \equiv R + M$$

where $R = (W + MC)$ in the nomenclature of equation (1); this summing only simplifies the algebra. The coefficient of determination between P and R is:

$$(3)\qquad r^2_{PR} = \frac{(\text{cov}\, P:R)^2}{\sigma^2_P\, \sigma^2_R}$$

$$(4)\qquad \text{cov}\; P:R = \frac{\Sigma[(R'+M')\cdot(R')]}{N} = \frac{\Sigma(R')^2 + \Sigma R'M'}{N}$$

where $$R' = \left(R - \frac{R}{N}\right);\; M' = \left(M - \frac{M}{N}\right)$$

By assumption of no intercorrelation between R and M, $\Sigma R'M' = 0$, therefore[14]

$$(5)\qquad \text{cov}\; P:R = \frac{\Sigma(R')^2}{N} = \sigma^2_R$$

Let σ^2_P be the sum of variances of uncorrelated variables, then equation (3) can be written as

$$(6)\qquad r^2_{PR} = \frac{(\sigma^2_R)^2}{(\sigma^2_R + \sigma^2_M)\,(\sigma^2_R)} = \frac{\sigma^2_R}{\sigma^2_R + \sigma^2_M} \text{ or}$$

$$(7)\qquad r^2_{PR} = \frac{\sigma^2_R}{\sigma^2_P}$$

[13] My symbols in (1) differ from Phlips' only in that he designates W, SW and MC as totals which are divided by the appropriate output O to get unit values.

[14] In principle, there are no plausible reasons for believing that R and M are correlated. Their relationship is a resolution of many forces: the production function, price policies, input prices and demand, suggesting no clear systematic relationship. A correlation would exist in a world where all prices were full cost prices and M was a fixed percentage markup on R, but that world is inconceivable.

In (6) we are reminded that if σ_R is large relative to σ_P, then *a priori*, r^2_{PR} will be large irrespective of the hypothesis. That the correlation of common elements can lead to nonsense estimates is a familiar pitfall.[15]

Phlips is not regressing absolute values but relatives in which case the identity in (2) is transformed into an equation of relatives with an implicit set of weights in parentheses.

$$(8) \qquad \frac{P_t}{P_0} \equiv \left(\frac{R_0}{P_0}\right)\frac{R_t}{R_0} + \left(\frac{M_0}{P_0}\right)\frac{M_t}{M_0}$$

Let $P'' = P_t/P_0$, $R'' = R_t/R_0$ and $M'' = M_t/M_0$, then by similar reasoning as above, assuming no intercorrelation between R'' and M'', we have

$$(9) \qquad r^2_{P''R''} = \left(\frac{R_0}{P_0}\right)^2 \frac{\sigma^2_{R''}}{\sigma^2_{P''}}$$

R_0/P_0 can be estimated as an average across industries. I have tabulated the proportion of aggregate direct costs in value of shipments and the proportion of aggregate direct costs and salaries in value of shipments for large samples of four digit industries in the U.S. The samples were drawn for a study on margin behavior. For any given year, of course, the proportions will represent the fraction of unit direct costs and unit direct costs and salaries in price: an average census value or price for all goods produced in the industry.

If we assume $\sigma_{P''}^2 = \sigma_{R''}^2$, a not unreasonable assumption in view of the large fraction of unit direct costs in price,[16] and accept an average DC/VS of 68 per cent from Table I, then from (9) we get $r^2 = 0.46$. If salaries are added to direct costs, the *a priori* r^2 might even be higher. If the E.E.C. industries are more labor intensive than those of the U.S., the correlation and regression coefficients will be higher still.

Phlips offers such tautological results without comment.[17] Although concentration is significant in some of these regressions, Phlips presents them as intermediate findings and goes on to refine them. Referring to equation (1) (pp. 4–6):

[15] Jacob Marshak, 'Economic Interdependence and Statistical Analysis', *Studies in Mathematical Economics and Econometrics*, eds. Lange, McIntyre, Yntema (University of Chicago Press, Chicago, 1942), pp. 147–8.

[16] I measured these variances for a study of prices in the Great Depression in the U.S. For changes between 1929–31 among 43 four digit industries, $\sigma^2_{P''} = 92$ and $\sigma^2_{R''} = 110$. The reader should be reminded here that $\sigma^2_{P''} < \sigma^2_{R''}$ is possible within the context of equation (8) in the text. By the same token, it is necessary that $\sigma^2_{P''} > \left(\frac{R_0}{P_0}\right)^2 \sigma^2_{R''}$.

[17] Equations III.1, III.2 (p. 9), IV.1 (p. 10), V.1 (p. 13).

The foregoing approach gives equal weight to increases in unit labor or materials cost, irrespective of the importance of these elements in total average cost. It is clear, however, that capital-intensive industries should worry less about a given percentage change in unit labor cost than labor-intensive industries, and that producers of margarine should pay more attention to a given percentage change in unit materials cost than producers of bricks. A natural procedure is then to multiply the cost variables by percentages of wages and material expenses in the value of shipment.

TABLE I

Year	*DC/VS* (%)	*DC+Salaries/VS* (%)	*N*
1952	70.3	77.2	87
1956	69.1	76.6	117
1960	67.1	75.3	113
1964	66.0	73.5	113
1966	66.3	73.6	113

Source: Annual Survey of Manufacturers, U.S. Department of Commerce, Bureau of the Census.

The weights of the cost components are not equal; the implicit weights are merely less obvious. Nor is it so clear that capital-intensive industries 'should worry less' about changes in unit labor cost than labor-intensive industries. The extent to which an increase in unit labor costs is passed on to price—surely that is the issue—would depend not only on the production function but on price policies and conditions of demand as well. Will a given increase in unit labor costs lead to a larger relative increase in the product prices of labor intensive industries than in the product prices of capital intensive industries? The answer is: not necessarily. The variables employed by Phlips in a single equation system—demand is excluded and the concentration ratio presumably serves as a proxy for price policies—can scarcely be expected to provide the answer. Moreover, since concentrated industries are more capital intensive than unconcentrated industries,[18] the weights that appear in the regressions, weights designed to reflect labor and materials intensity, would be *negatively* correlated with concentration. The actual effects of the weights are to elevate r^2, the regression coefficients of unit

[18] Norman R. Collins and Lee E. Preston, 'Price–Cost Margins and Industry Structure', *op. cit.*, p. 272.

costs, and reduce, not surprisingly, concentration to insignificance.[19] Phlips submits these results as the best evidence for rejecting the existence of administered prices. On more objective grounds, they must be deemed specious.

The task of testing the administered price hypothesis is more subtle than Professor Phlips allows. He has told us once again that prices move closely with costs. There should be, if there isn't already, global agreement on that fact. About administered prices, unfortunately, Professor Phlips has told us nothing.

THE CITY UNIVERSITY OF NEW YORK and
THE UNIVERSITY OF SOUTH FLORIDA

[19] Equations III.3, III.5, (p. 9), IV.2 (p. 10), V.2 (p. 13).

ILLUSIONS IN TESTING FOR ADMINISTERED PRICES: A REPLY*

by Louis Phlips

Professor Ross blames me for not having written a paper on the subject he is interested in (and working on). Faced with such a charge, the offender has an easy defence: it suffices generally to answer that one was doing what one was doing. However, Ross raises so many questions (some of which are interesting while others are wrong and/or unfair), that it is worth while to try to answer the more interesting ones. Furthermore, the problem Ross is interested in *is* important and worth investigating. In the second part of this reply I shall give a sketch of the paper I wish Ross had written to make his point.

I. ANSWERING A FEW QUESTIONS

I readily admit that my paper 'ignores a parallel development beginning with the writings on full cost theory that is rich in analytical and empirical substance for price flexibility'. In particular, I did not test the hypothesis that 'inflationary pressures were more fully translated into price increases in the concentrated group than in the unconcentrated', e.g. 'the extent to which an increase in unit labour costs is passed on to price', which in Ross's own words is 'surely' the issue. Why wasn't this the issue *I* was concerned with? Because it did not appear as a problem in Europe at the time the paper was written—admittedly it was a problem in the U.S. during the periods of recession with inflation to which Ross refers.

The period analysed (1958–65) was indeed a long period of *expansion* with rising prices in the countries analysed. (It was chosen for that reason and not for lack of better data. The unavailability of other data prevented me from analysing *other* periods of expansion with rising prices). During such a period, attention is not focussed on the behaviour of a particular group of industries. It is when prices rise while the economy is stagnating that people start wondering whether the group of concentrated industries does not bear a particular responsibility. This sort of 'stagflation' is a recent phenomenon in Europe and makes Ross's topic worth considering in a European context. That is why I want to do the homework[1] on which I report in section II.

* Thanks are due to Luc Mallié for programming assistance and to Paul Peeters for a stimulating discussion of the topic.

[1] The data utilized in my 1969 paper can be found in the Appendix to Chapter 2 of my

In my 1969 paper, the testing relates to the administration inflation hypothesis as I defined it. This definition corresponds to the testimony given by Means before the Kefauver Committee in 1957, which goes in the opposite direction of his pre-war ideas. The De-Podwin-Selden-Weiss approach is appropriate to test both versions and shows that the recent one is wrong. It would be unfair to qualify my definition as aberrant on the ground that common beliefs continue to stick to the pre-war version.

Given this, the attention has to centre on the coefficient of the concentration ratio (C). Demand and unit costs are introduced as additional variables to 'clean up' that coefficient, in order to satisfy the implicit *ceteris paribus* assumption. The same is true for the weighting of the cost variabies, whose purpose is to improve the significance of the concentration coefficient, *not* to test to what extent an increase in costs is passed on to price.

The result is not to reduce the concentration coefficient to insignificance, but to transform unreasonable results into reasonable ones. Who could accept a negative coefficient for C at the cost of admitting that wage increases do not affect prices?

The unweighted 'combined' regression for Benelux is the only exception reasonably pointing towards a stabilizing influence of concentration (as was stated in the text). But as I was testing the opposite, honest research strategy implied giving C the greatest chance of showing up with a positive coefficient. Hence *my* footnote 18 that the weights are negatively correlated with concentration.

The contention that labour-intensiveness is already taken into account in the unweighted cost variables is interesting and possibly correct. If so, one could only conclude that it is the pre-war administrative inflation hypothesis that is not rejected by the (Benelux) data. The hypothesis I was testing comes out even worse.

I do not understand Professor Ross's comment on 'The Econometric Procedure'. Everybody knows a phenomenon called 'spurious correlation'. It is also well known that the non-spurious character of regression results rests on the strength of the underlying theory and not on the difference between R^2 and one: R^2 may be high because some variables are components of other variables without the estimates being 'nonsense', if economic theory implies that these variables have to be components of other variables. The conclusion drawn by Ross from his equations (1) to (9) goes too far.

book *Effects of Industrial Concentration: A Cross-section Analysis for the Common Market*, Contributions to Economic Analysis No. 74, North-Holland Publishing Company, Amsterdam-London, 1971.

II. THE TRANSMISSION OF INFLATIONARY PRESSURES INTO PRICE

I am grateful to Professor Ross for drawing my attention to a vast body of literature on the problem of the transmission of inflationary pressures, when wages and prices are administered. The references to Yordon's work are particularly interesting in the context of the present discussion. To do them full justice, it would be necessary to set up a time series analysis. For lack of time, I would like to limit myself to the set of data utilized in my 1969 paper and try to see what can be done with it to compare the extent to which an increase in unit labour costs is passed on to price in the concentrated and the unconcentrated group. Covariance analysis is again an helpful tool.

The attention now goes to the coefficient of the labour cost variable, the other variables being introduced to insure its relevance to the problem at hand. I am therefore going to leave these other variables in the equation and use unweighted unit labour costs (wages and salaries). For reasons given in my 1969 paper, the variable Q64/Q58 will be deleted, though.

TABLE I

'UNCONCENTRATED' GROUP

	C	$\frac{SW64}{SW58}\Big/\frac{Q64}{Q58}$	$\frac{MC64}{MC58}\Big/\frac{Q64}{Q58}$	R^2	D.F.	F-ratio
Belgium (< 50)	−0.321 (0.250)	0.004 (0.609)	0.842 (0.415)	0.84	3, 4	7.21
Netherlands (< 50)	−0.246 (0.126)	0.209 (0.089)	0.457 (0.109)	0.57	3, 23	10.37
France (< 40)	0.012 (0.200)	0.143 (0.109)	0.727 (0.122)	0.73	3, 21	19.24
Combined	−0.216 (0.098)	0.186 (0.069)	0.590 (0.075)		3, 48	36.12

The choice of a threshold above which industries are 'concentrated' is to some extent arbitrary. I shall adopt $C=50$ as the critical level for Belgium and the Netherlands. Given this choice, I have to take a lower figure for France, knowing that larger countries have smaller concentration ratios.[2] A critical level of 40 was thought appropriate.

Table I reports the regression results obtained for the 'unconcentrated' group in Belgium, the Netherlands and France respectively,[3] and also for the three countries combined. Whereas the national coefficients are not too illuminating, the combined regression reveals a relatively small translation of wage increases into price

[2] See *Effects of Industrial Concentration* . . ., Chapter 6.
[3] The estimated intercepts are not reported.

increases (and a relatively large transmission of increases in unit materials costs). Concentration appears as having a stabilizing influence.

TABLE II

'CONCENTRATED' GROUP

	C	$\frac{SW64}{SW58} / \frac{Q64}{Q58}$	$\frac{MC64}{MC58} / \frac{Q64}{Q58}$	R^2	D.F.	F-ratio
Belgium (> 50)	−0.397	1.439	0.356	0.86	3, 4	8.02
	(0.144)	(0.883)	(0.161)			
Netherlands (> 50)	−0.140	0.117	0.522	0.70	3, 12	9.55
	(0.167)	(0.184)	(0.137)			
France (> 40)	−0.098	0.228	0.306	0.71	3, 11	9.07
	(0.170)	(0.144)	(0.063)			
Combined	−0.191	0.264	0.374		3, 27	22.24
	(0.091)	(0.098)	(0.058)			

The comparison of Table I with Table II, which gives the corresponding results for the 'concentrated' group, is what really matters here. Again, the results for individual countries are not too exciting. But the combined regression is rewarding[4] and tends to support Professor Ross's contention. Indeed, a unit increase in wage costs leads to a price increase that is higher in the concentrated group than in the unconcentrated group—although the difference is not too large and perhaps not significant. *C* is once more gratified with a significant negative coefficient, while pressures on the side of materials costs are less fully transmitted.

All in all, these results should encourage research along the lines suggested by my critic. I look forward to see his time series analysis, and hope that a similar dynamic research will soon be undertaken in a European context.

UNIVERSITÉ CATHOLIQUE DE LOUVAIN

[4] Both groups of industries appear as homogeneous according to an *F*-test on the differences of national slope coefficients.

ON THE SALES MAXIMIZATION HYPOTHESIS: A COMMENT

by J. R. Davies

C. J. Hawkins in a recent article 'On the Sales Maximization Hypothesis'[1] accepts the analysis of sales revenue maximizing behaviour in oligopolistic markets first suggested by W. G. Shepherd.[2] Shepherd and Hawkins argue that in an oligopolistic market, characterized by strong inter-dependence among firms, sales revenue maximizing firms and profit maximizing firms will have the same price-output equilibrium position when price is the only variable in the firms' competitive strategy. It is suggested below that this analysis depends on an implicit assumption regarding the price-elasticity of demand which may not be generally acceptable.

Shepherd has employed the kinked demand curve model to analyse sales revenue maximizing behaviour in oligopolistic markets. He has contended, and this has been accepted without qualification by Hawkins, that 'if the kink is very definite—and it will be seen to be under conditions of strong interdependence—the range of discontinuity in the marginal revenue curve will extend below the x-axis, and the total revenue curve will reach its peak at the level of output where the kink occurs'.[3] But even with the highest degree of interdependence, and with the marked kink in the demand curve that this can entail, the discontinuity in the marginal revenue curve does not necessarily cut the x-axis. Whether or not the discontinuity in the marginal revenue cuts the x-axis will depend on the elasticity of the relevant demand curve. In terms of the kinked demand curve model the highest degree of inter-dependence implies that a price cut by one firm will be followed immediately by similar price reduction by all other firms. In this situation each firm will perceive as the lower arm of its demand curve its share-of-the-market demand curve. Consequently, whether or not the discontinuity in the marginal revenue curve cuts the x-axis depends on the price elasticity of market demand at the prevailing price. As is generally accepted, the kinked demand curve model does not provide an explanation of the price setting process or price level but purports to explain the stability of the existing price. It provides no basis for expecting the price elasticity of demand for a product to fall

[1] C. J. Hawkins, 'On the Sales Revenue Maximization Hypothesis', *Journal of Industrial Economics*, April, 1970, p. 132.

[2] W. G. Shepherd, 'On Sales Maximising and Oligopoly Behaviour', *Economica*, November, 1962.

[3] *Ibid.*, p. 422.

as the interdependence among firms producing the product increases. Indeed, it could be argued that the fewer the firms, and the stronger the interdependence, the greater the probability of finding price along an elastic range of the demand curve. Whether or not the price of a product falls along an inelastic range of the demand curve will depend on various factors such as the nature of the overall demand for the product, the position of the cost curves in relation to the demand curve, and, a closely related factor, the nature and extent of barriers to entry.

Hawkins, concerned with the identification of the goals of the businessman, argues that 'if Shepherd is right in believing that markedly kinked demand curves are typical of oligopoly, a serious problem emerges for the empirical testing of whether revenue maximization is a dominant motive of some firms . . . for both sales revenue maximizer and profit maximizer will operate where mc = mr on their chosen cost and revenue schedules'.[4]

Although high interdependence among firms and markedly kinked demand curves do not necessarily produce a discontinuity in the marginal revenue curve cutting the x-axis Hawkins may be quite right in suggesting that it may be impossible to infer from the price-output equilibrium position the factor motivating businessmen. The situation envisaged by Shepherd emerges, independently of the degree of interdependence and the extent of the kink in the demand curve, if but one firm in the industry is a sales revenue maximizer while all other firms endeavour to maximize profits. A sales maximizing firm will reduce price whenever the elasticity of demand is greater than unity and profits are greater than the minimum required. If the expectations on which the kinked demand curve is based are fulfilled all price reductions by the sales revenue maximizer will generate competitive price reductions by the profit maximizers. Price will continue to fall until the profit constraint becomes effective or revenue is maximized when the price elasticity of market demand becomes equal to unity. In either case the price-output equilibrium position of sales revenue maximizer is the same as that of the profit maximizer.

The notion of the firm employed in the theory of price determination is assumed to be sufficiently representative of firms in the market to allow departures from the predominant form of behaviour to be safely ignored. This analysis suggests it is possible that the behaviour of a single non-conformist firm in an industry is sufficient to make it impossible to identify the primary motivating force of firms in an industry on the basis of the final equilibrium position of price and

[4] Hawkins, *op. cit.*, p. 135.

output. It is interesting to note that in this model with sales revenue maximizers and profit maximizers operating in the same industry the final price and output position for the industry is dictated by the sales maximizing firm.

UNIVERSITY OF STIRLING

CONCENTRATION, BARRIERS TO ENTRY, AND RATES OF RETURN REVISITED: A REPLY

by H. MICHAEL MANN*

RHOADES continues to emphasize one point in response[1] to my comment[2] on his earlier piece.[3] It is that barriers to entry have no significant impact on profitability independent of concentration. He now reports the regression, covering 23 of my original sample of 30 observations, on which he relies for this conclusion.[4] It is:

$$(1) \qquad Y = 6.455 + 1.963 d_H + 0.077 X$$
$$\qquad (1.503) \quad (3.230) \quad t\text{-ratios.}$$

Where Y = the rate of return, X is concentration, and d_H is a dummy variable representing high barriers to entry. The dummy variable is not significant by the conventional 0.05 rule. I have two remarks.

First, equation (1) is sensitive to the use of 23 observations. If Rhoades had used 28 observations, adding 5 for which he did assign concentration ratios,[5] the following equation results:

$$(2) \qquad Y = 6.11 + 3.843 d_H + 0.0811 X$$
$$\qquad (3.17) \quad (3.437) \quad t\text{-ratios.}$$

The high barrier-to-entry dummy is statistically significant, which Rhoades failed to observe when he used 28 observations because he illegitimately combined the high and substantial barrier groups.[6]

Second, high barriers to entry, even though insignificant in equation (1), do interact with concentration, significantly reinforcing its influence.[7] This may suggest that future research should test for interaction as well as independence in order to see what effect seems to better describe the role of high barriers to entry.

* Professor of Economics, Boston College, on leave as the Director, Bureau of Economics, Federal Trade Commission. The views expressed herein are not necessarily those of the Commission.

[1] Stephen A. Rhoades, 'Concentration, Barriers to Entry, and Rates of Return Revisited', *Journal of Industrial Economics* (April 1972), pp. 193–5.

[2] H. Michael Mann, 'The Interaction of Barriers and Concentration: A Reply', *Journal of Industrial Economics* (July 1971), pp. 291–3.

[3] S. A. Rhoades, 'Concentration, Barriers and Rates of Return: A Note', *Journal of Industrial Economics* (Nov. 1970), pp. 82–8.

[4] Rhoades alludes to the equation in his Note (Nov. 1970), fn. 10, p. 84, but did not present it.

[5] These are sulphur, nickel, ethical drugs, bituminous coal, and textile mill products. See his Note (Nov. 1970), fn. 9, p. 84.

[6] See his Note (Nov. 1970), fn. 13, p. 85. In fact, every equation in Rhoades' first piece is misspecified. The Chow test unequivocally rejects Rhoades' pooling of observations from the high and substantial barrier classes, a finding Rhoades does not contest in his reply. To have drawn a correct conclusion for 23 of my observations from a faulty statistical analysis is hardly a comforting outcome.

[7] Mann, *op. cit.*, p. 292.

One matter remains. Rhoades interprets my silence on his finding that the continuous relationship between concentration and profitability was stronger than a relationship depicting a discontinuity as agreement. Curiously, his original article nowhere compares R^2 and t-ratios as his reply to my comment asserts. A recent study indicates that comparisons of R^2s and t-ratios are not, in themselves, appropriate tests of whether the relationship between concentration and profitability is continuous or discontinuous.[8] In any event, my silence only signifies the fact that Rhoades presented no analysis on this issue.

FEDERAL TRADE COMMISSION

[8] James W. Meehan, Jr. and Thomas D. Duchesneau, 'The Critical Level of Concentration: An Empirical Analysis', forthcoming, *Journal of Industrial Economics*.

PUBLICATIONS RECEIVED

Australia's Mineral Wealth, by Ian Coghill. Published by Longman, 1972, £4.00. A beautifully produced and illustrated book, detailing the major deposits and how they were discovered, the opening up of the new wealth, the transport and processing of these ores, and their final marketing, often overseas.

Automation in Developing Countries. Published by the International Labour Office, Geneva, 1972.

Basic Road Statistics 1972. Published by the British Road Federation, 1972, 50p.

Bibliography of Theses and Dissertations Relevant to Pharmacy Administration: Section 7. Published by the American Association of Colleges of Pharmacy Conference of Teachers, 1972.

British Waterways Board: Reorganisation of Water and Sewage Services. British Waterways Board, 1972.

Budapest: An Industrial–Geographical Approach, by Imre Bencze and Erzsebet V. Tajti. Akademiai Kiado, Budapest, 1972.

Business Taxation, by J. M. Cope. Published by Nelson, 1972, £3.95. This volume is not merely business tax law nor simplistic tax theory but more a work of applied economics considering the operation of the U.K. company with reference to an important aspect of its environment. The analysis is also unusual in being both sophisticated and readable.

Cost Benefit Analysis, edited by Richard Layard. Published in Penguin Modern Economics Readings, 1973, £1.00.

Economics and Insurance, by R. L. Carter. Published by PH Press Ltd, 1972, £3.00.

Economic Survey of Denmark 1972. Published by the Royal Danish Ministry of Foreign Affairs, 1972.

Federal Funds for Academic Science: Fiscal Year 1970. Published by the National Science Foundation, 1971, $0.70.

Growth in Selected Indian Industries, by Kesab Lal Nandi. Published by The World Press Private Ltd., 1972, £2.00.

Guidelines for a New Strategy. Published by The National Planning Department, Bogota, 1972.

The IMF: The Second Coming? by Alexandre Kafka. Published by the International Finance Section, Princeton, 1972.

Industrial Organisation: An Empirical Approach, by Stanley E. Boyle. Published by Holt Rinehart & Winston, 1972.

Instability in the International Steel Market, by Lennart Fridén. Published by J. Beckman Pub. Co., 1972, $15.00.

International Trade and its Social and Economic Effects: Supplement to the Final Report. Published by OECD.

An Introduction to Financial Economics, by E. L. Furness. Published in The Heinemann Accountancy and Administration Series, 1972.

Key Issues in Applied Economics 1947–1997. Published by Longman, 1972, £2.95.

Management Kinetics, by Carl Duerr. Published in the Pan Management Series, 1971, 50p.

Marketing in the Common Market, by Henry Deschampsneufs. Published in the Pan Management Series, 1973, 50p.

The Modern Business Enterprise, edited by Michael Gilbert. Published by Penguin, 1972, £1.25.

Nationalised Industries. Published by The Open University, 1972.

The Penguin Dictionary of Economics, by Graham Bannock, R. E. Baxter and Ray Rees. Published by Penguin, 1972, 50p.

Planning of Industrial Complexes by Means of Geometric Programming, by P. Nijkamp. Published by the Rotterdam University Press, 1972.

Problems and Prospects in the Coking Industry in the OECD Countries. Published by OECD, Paris, 1972.

Problems in Adult Training, by Eunice Belbin and R. Meredith Belbin. Published by Heinemann, 1972, £2.80.

Realities of Profitability, by Ralph Horwitz. Published in the Pan Management Series, 1973, 45p.

Recent Trends in Collective Bargaining: International Management Seminar. Published by OECD, Paris, 1972.

Research and Development in Industry 1970. Published by the National Science Foundation, 1972.

The Rise and Decline of Small Firms, by Jonathan Boswell. Published by George Allen & Unwin, 1972, £4.00.

Roads and Industry. Published by the British Road Federation/British Industry Roads Campaign Report, 1972.

Social Responsibility Audit: A Management Tool for Survival, by John Humble. Published by the Foundation for Business Responsibilities, 1973, £1.25.

Taxation Policy edited by Bernard Crick and William A. Robson. Published by Penguin, 1973, 40p

Toward a New Basis for International Monetary Policy. Published by the International Finance Section, Princeton University, 1972.

The World Monetary System: A Minimal Reform Program, by Michael V. Posner. International Finance Section, Dept. of Economics, Princeton, N.J. (Essays in International Finance No. 96, October 1972.)

Yield Tables for Bonds and Bonds Redeemed by Annual Drawings, by Giorgio Questa. Published by Instituto Mobiliare Italiani: Servizio Studi, 1972.

THE JOURNAL OF INDUSTRIAL ECONOMICS

Published first in October 1952, this Journal was founded to develop the analysis of the problems facing modern industry. It is concerned with the individual business and its relation to the economy—e.g. with outputs and prices and their behaviour in the market, and with the business decisions which affect these. It therefore aims to contribute both to economic theory and to practical public and private policies in the industrial field. The journal is naturally meant to interest business men as well as economists.

The Editors welcome contributions covering the fundamental categories in economics (such as prices, costs, investment, finance, location, wages and productivity) as well as the broader 'background' circumstances (such as the changing structure of industry, management policy and public monopoly policy). Preference is given to MSS. bearing on these subjects from the standpoint of individual firms or industries. The Journal's authors have helped to maintain the policy that articles should be found readable by those interested in its field. Theoretical discussion is welcome. Abstract theory is not barred, but authors in this case should provide an introduction and summary, so that non-specialist readers may see what the article is about. Alongside articles of more normal length the Editors are willing to publish shorter notes, especially when these give interim results of important research studies.

The Editors will be glad to receive offers of suitable articles. MSS. from the United States should be sent to Professor Menge, Department of Economics, Dartmouth College, Hanover, New Hampshire 03755, U.S.A; and from other countries to the General Editor, care of Basil Blackwell, Publishers, 49 Broad Street, Oxford, England. All other communications should be addressed to the Publisher.

The annual subscription (three numbers) is £2.25 ($6.75) post free; the price of a single issue is £1.00 ($3.00) post free. Remittances should be sent to Messrs Basil Blackwell.

The contents of Volume XXI, No. 1, November 1972, were:

Company Pricing Policy, by A. M. Alfred, Director of the British Printing Corporation Ltd.

Changes in the Top 100 Quoted Manufacturing Companies in the United Kingdom 1948 to 1968, by G. Whittington, Professor of Accountancy and Finance at Edinburgh University.

Structure and Behavior in British Industries, with U.S. Comparisons, by William G. Shepherd, Professor of Economics at the University of Michigan.

Nonprice Competition in Jet Aircraft Capacity, by Joseph V. Yance, Adjunct Associate Professor of Economics at Boston University.

Some Preliminary Evidence of Imperfections in Markets, by Richard W. Furst and Robert E. Markland, Associate Professor of Finance at the University of South Carolina, and Associate Professor of Management Science at the University of Missouri.

More on the Output Elasticity of Energy Consumption, by L. G. Brookes, a senior member of the Economics and Programming Branch of the United Kingdom Atomic Energy Authority.

REPRINT

A photographic reprint is now available of Vols. 1–13, 1952–1965 bound in cloth or paper, single volumes in paper only.

Send orders to Blackwell's, Broad Street, Oxford, England.

STUDENT SUBSCRIPTION

Bona fide students can obtain the Journal at a greatly reduced subscription rate. Send to publisher for a form.

Printed in Great Britain by Alden & Mowbray Ltd
at the Alden Press, Oxford

THE JOURNAL OF INDUSTRIAL ECONOMICS

Volume XXI JULY 1973 No. 3

HENRY G. GRABOWSKI and NEVINS D. BAXTER
Rivalry in Industrial Research and Development: an Empirical Study.

M. HOWE
A Study of Trade Association Price Fixing.

TREVOR D. HEAVER
The Structure of Liner Conference Rates.

G. HEITMANN
United States Oil Import Quotas and the Price of Foreign Oil.

JOHN P. FORMBY
On Revenue Maximizing Duopoly.

LIONEL KALISH III and R. ALTON GILBERT
An Analysis of Efficiency of Scale and Organizational Form in Commercial Banking.

R. W. SHAW
Investment and Competition from Boom to Recession: a Case Study in the Processes of Competition—the Dry Cleaning Industry.

BASIL BLACKWELL OXFORD ENGLAND

Price — £1.00 net or ($3.00). Annual subscription: £2.25 or ($6.75).

CONTRIBUTORS TO THIS NUMBER

HENRY G. GRABOWSKI: Associate Professor of Economics, Duke University, and Research Associate, National Bureau of Economic Research.

NEVINS D. BAXTER: President, Baxter and Company, Washington, D.C.

M. HOWE: Senior Lecturer in the Division of Economic Studies of the University of Sheffield, with special interests in Managerial and Industrial Economics.

TREVOR D. HEAVER: Associate Professor and Chairman, Division of Transportation, Faculty of Commerce and Business Administration, University of British Columbia.

G. HEITMANN: Associate Professor of Management Science at The Pennsylvania State University.

JOHN P. FORMBY: Associate Professor of Economics and Acting Chairman of the Department of Economics at The University of North Carolina—Greensboro.

LIONEL KALISH III: Assistant Professor at California State University of Fullerton.

R. ALTON GILBERT: Economist at the Federal Reserve Bank of St. Louis.

R. W. SHAW: Lecturer in Economics, University of Stirling.

EDITORIAL NOTE

THE development of the Journal has been such that the Editors have now decided to change the format of the Journal and enlarge its scope. As from the next volume of the Journal, therefore, Volume XXII, 1973–4, it will become a quarterly, appearing in September, December, March and June. Each issue will normally be of 80 pages in an enlarged page-size (technically English standard R8). This should make it possible to present material, especially tabular material, more attractively, and to accommodate the increasing flow of good articles.

These changes must, of course, be accompanied by a change of price. The annual subscription will in future be £3.50 (single copies £1.00).

We shall continue to try, however, to give value for money. Our readers can help by telling us what articles they have found most useful, by offering us good contributions and by talking or writing to any of our editors, new or old, in North America, England or the Continent.

P. W. S. ANDREWS MEMORIAL PRIZE

THE P. W. S. Andrews memorial prize is awarded annually for an essay by a young scholar (under the age of 30 or within 8 years of taking his first degree) in the general field of Industrial Economics and The Theory of the Firm, broadly interpreted. The prize is £100, and the winning essay will normally be published in *The Journal of Industrial Economics*. An essay submitted should be a work of original research by the candidate only, not previously published and not previously awarded any other prize. It should not exceed 15,000 words in length.

The next closing date for entries is December 31st, 1973. Intending candidates for the prize should obtain details of the conditions of entry from the Academic Registrar, University of Lancaster, Bailrigg, Lancaster.

RIVALRY IN INDUSTRIAL RESEARCH AND DEVELOPMENT

AN EMPIRICAL STUDY*

by Henry G. Grabowski and Nevins D. Baxter

Economic theory provides a myriad of possible behavioral models under oligopolistic market conditions. Indeed, empirical studies of price competition under oligopoly have observed a wide spectrum of situations ranging from open price warfare to the stalemated behavioral response pattern of the 'kinked' demand curve model. Perhaps the most prevalent mode of behavior observed is some form of price leadership. [8][11][22]. At the same time, many of these studies have noted the preference of oligopolists to compete not by price changes, but rather by various forms of product differentiation.

Expenditures on research and development constitute the most important form of non-price competition for an important set of technologically progressive industries. Recent empirical studies of the R and D decision have contributed significantly to our knowledge, but large gaps remain. In particular, these studies have not directly considered the effect of competitive interactions on R and D expenditures. It remains an open question, for example, whether there exist counterparts, in R and D competitive behavior, to the price leadership phenomena frequently observed in many oligopolistic industries. It is the main purpose of this paper to investigate this type of question so that the results may be compared and integrated with previous studies of the determinants of R and D and of price competition. Consequently, we employ statistical analyses of time series and cross-sectional data to investigate the effects of competitive interactions along with other factors influencing the level of company-financed R and D.

I. A BRIEF REVIEW OF PAST THEORETICAL AND EMPIRICAL STUDIES OF R AND D ACTIVITY

Research and development expenditures constitute an investment decision to an industrial firm. Thus, the maximizing firm should undertake outlays on R and D up to the point where the marginal

* An earlier draft of this paper was presented to a conference of the Institute of Management Sciences. The authors are indebted to B. G. Malkiel and D. C. Mueller for helpful comments and to F. M. Scherer for the use of his assembled data on professional R and D employees. They also wish to thank the officials of several large chemical companies for their cooperation during informative personal interviews. A grant from the National Science Foundation aided in the completion of this study.

rate of return from R and D is simultaneously equal to that from other kinds of investment outlays as well as to the marginal cost of expending additional investment funds. While most past studies have stopped short of considering the determinants of R and D expenditures in this full simultaneous context,[1] most of the significant determinant factors can be viewed as variables related either to the return from R and D or to the cost of expending additional investment funds. For example, Mansfield [9] has suggested a stock adjustment model in which expected return, sales, profits, general expenditures of the industry, and adjustment costs all play a role. Mueller [14] and Hamberg [6], in separate studies, have used many of these variables and, in addition, have emphasized the role of liquidity variables and interactions with other investment expenditures. In a recent study of the chemical, drug, and petroleum industries, Grabowski [3] found that interfirm differences in R and D intensity are significantly related to a firm's past research productivity, diversification of product line, and the relative size of its internal cash flow.

Taken as a group, these studies of the determinants of R and D provide some direct and indirect links between R and D inputs and the expected return and costs of undertaking this type of investment activity. Competitive interactions are absent from the list of determinant factors explicitly considered in these studies primarily because of data limitations. All of the above-mentioned studies are mainly cross-sectional—covering a group of firms in several industries for a single year or, at best, for a few different years. Such samples allow for investigation of certain questions very well but do not provide an adequate basis for studying others. For example, competitive interactions which occur with lagged responses in time, and variables which are common to all firms at a point in time but vary from year to year, can be considered only with time series of sufficient length. However, consistent data on R and D expenditures which span a number of years have been a very scarce commodity, and this has severely constrained studies of rivalry in R and D expenditures.

Over and above problems of data availability, there have been no well-defined theoretical guidelines for undertaking a study of competitive interactions. Because one is typically dealing with oli-

[1] One of the authors is currently engaged in a joint study involving consideration of R and D in a simultaneous equation context with capital investment and dividend payouts as a possible substitute and complementary use of capital funds. One of the main objectives of this study is to gain some insights into the objectives of the firm (i.e. stockholder welfare or managerial maximization) by investigating investment and dividend behavior under various circumstances. See [3] for the first set of results from this study.

gopolistic firms, all of the analytical ambiguities associated with this type of market structure prevail in such a study of R and D rivalry. In particular, whether a firm's expected profitability is maximized by responding positively, negatively, or not at all to a change in its rival's R and D expenditures will depend crucially on the conjectural variation assumptions employed by the decision makers as well as the structural conditions of the particular situation. The power of economic theory to predict even the direction of competitive responses is therefore somewhat limited for studies of competitive rivalry.

Nevertheless, some recent theoretical work studying competitive interactions by R and D expenditures has emphasized the likelihood of positive responses to rival increases under typical conditions. Scherer [21] studies the timing of R and D expenditures, assuming a convex tradeoff between development cost and development time. He examined a number of solution concepts, including the Cournot model in some detail, and concluded that the acceleration of a competitor's R and D efforts will generally have an invigorating effect on a firm's own R and D outlays. In another study, Grabowski [2] examined equilibrium growth paths in demand shifting investment activity for a pair of duopolistic firms using both a Cournot assumption and a commonly suggested rule-of-thumb decision procedure. He suggested reasons why the equilibrium level of expenditures, but not the equilibrium growth rate, is likely to escalate upward as a result of competitive action reaction sequence over time. In sum, these recent studies provide some theoretical basis for expecting a positive reaction to rivals' expenditures on R and D rather than a negative one.

The theoretical studies discussed above assume that the firm's objective function is to maximize discounted present value of its future earnings. If one assumes a managerial objective function, in which managers are interested in size and growth, *per se*, the case for a positive reaction coefficient would appear even stronger. That is, in industries where R and D is a crucial source of growth, a firm can be expected to respond positively to significant advances in competitors' R and D in order to maintain its relative market position and growth rate.

There are also a few studies of R and D determinants using interview and case study techniques [17] [18] which support this hypothesis of a positive reaction coefficient. They indicate that R and D decisions are typically made in an environment involving considerable marketing and technological uncertainties, and in which considerable time lags may have to be incurred before project completion. Where R and D is also an important means of competing for and maintaining a firm's market share, firms naturally will place a high premium on the avoidance of a laggard or short position in developing new products via R and D. It is therefore not surprising that these studies have suggested that firms are highly sensitive to the behavior of competitors and are ready to respond aggressively to significant changes in the R and D expenditures of rivals. This is not to deny the fact that firms may sometimes adopt a submissive strategy *vis-à-vis* a rival and thus decelerate expenditures in response to a rival's acceleration, but rather suggests that the opposite response is much more likely, given the structural and psychological climate in which most R and D activity is undertaken.

Therefore, while there will always be some *a priori* analytical ambiguity in studying competitive interactions under oligopoly, we shall take as our operating hypothesis in this study that a positive response to competitors' R and D increases is to be expected on the basis of the above considerations. This type of assumption is also in accordance with the phenomenal growth pattern which has been observed in R and D expenditures for virtually all the major firms over the spectrum of technologically progressive industries during the post-war period.

II. TIME SERIES ANALYSIS OF THE CHEMICAL INDUSTRY

A. *Nature of the Sample*

The U.S. chemical industry ranks among the top few industries in intensity of privately financed R and D. The chemical industry also ranks high in innovative output from R and D, e.g. in new product introductions and in number of patent awards. Furthermore, the chemical industry is one of the few that shows a consistent tendency for large firms to spend proportionately more on R and D than smaller ones, and correspondingly to receive proportionately more patents than smaller ones [9] [20]. These findings suggest, but do not confirm, the possibilities of economies to scale in R and D in the chemical industry. This would provide special incentive for firms above some threshold to maintain or enhance their competitive advantage in R and D.

The long history of vigorous competition through innovation in the chemical industry and the particular structure (i.e. several large firms with extensive research programs) make it a singularly attractive industry for a study of rivalry in R and D. It appears to be the only industry for which R and D series extending back to the early post-war period are available for a significant number of competing firms. Accordingly, time series data on total R and D expenditures were solicited from the sixteen largest chemical firms, as ranked by sales averaged over the post-war period. Consistent R and D data series were obtained on a confidential basis for eight of these firms for the twenty-year period 1947–66.[2] Mergers, major accounting changes, and company reorganizations over this twenty-year period made the data of many of the other firms useless for our current purposes. While a larger sample of firms would be desirable, the eight firms for which data were obtained do constitute a substantial portion of the total expenditures in the most research-oriented industry in the U.S. economy. It is therefore a reasonable sample for studying the sort of issues in which we are interested.

In order to gain some insights into the question of competitive rivalry patterns in R and D, we interviewed research directors and financial officials of a sample of firms in the industry.[3] The general impression conveyed to us was that competitors' outlays are a very significant determinant of a firm's expenditures. With regard to specific patterns of rivalry, some firms explicitly mentioned keying off the expenditure pattern of the industry's 'technological leader' in determining their own outlays. Others cited the use of an average of rival activity or overall industry average when formulating their R and D budgets. Although patterns of competitive interactions may take on many forms and can occur with different time lags, we shall investigate some of the more prevalent manifestations in our empirical evidence. The interviews offered some minimal guidelines in constructing the patterns of rivalry that will be discussed below.

B. THE TIME PATTERN OF R AND D EXPENDITURES: SOME PRELIMINARY OBSERVATIONS

The time series data on total research and development expenditures by chemical firms readily indicate the substantial rate of growth in this activity over the post-war period. Table I presents the results

[2] The companies were asked to provide data on total R and D expenditures, as defined by the N.S.F. in their annual surveys begun in 1957. N.S.F. R and D classifications are based on the extent to which expenditures are related to a specific commercial application. In basic research, no final objective has been identified, although the area under investigation may be of potential interest to the firm; at the applied stage, the discovery of new scientific knowledge is tied to some specific product or process. Development entails making scientific knowledge commercially cooperative. In 1966 N.S.F. data show that for the chemical industry, 14 per cent was spent on basic research, 34 per cent on applied research and 52 per cent on development. For all industries the corresponding figures were 4 per cent, 18 per cent, and 78 per cent respectively. For more detailed information see National Science Foundation [16].

[3] Certainly, conclusions drawn from the interviews must be interpreted with caution. However, since the interviews were held in confidence and the individual respondents were assured of anonymity, the results should provide important insights into the decision-making process for R and D and fixed investment. Moreover, the interviews are not used as evidence for any particular position, but rather as an aid in the formulation of the hypotheses tested in the following section.

of a log linear regression of each firm's expenditures on time, as given in equation (1) below:

$$\text{Log}_e R_{it} = a_i + b_i t \quad (1)$$

where R_{it} is total R and D expenditures of the ith firm in period t.
t is time measured in years.
a_i and b_i are the regression estimates for the ith firm.

TABLE I

THE GROWTH IN R AND D EXPENDITURES OVER THE POST-WAR PERIOD FOR EIGHT CHEMICAL FIRMS

$\log_e R_{it} = a_i + b_i t$

Firm (i)	a_i	b_i	*Correlation coefficient*
1	3.53	0.074 (13.74)	0.96
2	2.84	0.106 (11.31)	0.94
3	2.39	0.075 (17.87)	0.97
4	2.10	0.071 (18.81)	0.98
5	1.19	0.096 (29.98)	0.99
6	−0.68	0.170 (14.12)	0.96
7	−0.65	0.151 (14.89)	0.96
8	−0.43	0.125 (18.90)	0.94

Note: Figures in parentheses are t values.
All estimates are significant at the 1 per cent confidence interval.

The estimates of the b coefficients indicate growth rates in the range of 7 to 17 per cent, and on average are considerably higher than the rate of growth in the overall economy during this same period.

The high multiple correlation coefficients associated with the log linear regressions of Table I indicate that a strong time trend is present in the R and D data. Therefore, any attempts to detect the presence of competitive interactions and other influences using the data in this form will tend to be masked by the common trend element which these series share with each other and with many other time dependent variables. For this reason, we shall focus our attention in the empirical work on the yearly changes in R and D expenditures and other variables instead of the absolute level of annual outlays. The differenced series are relatively free from any time trend, and this procedure reduces the problem of multicollinearity and serially correlated residuals which plague time series regressions analysis using absolute values.

A preliminary examination of the differenced data on R and D expenditures for each firm indicates some interesting characteristics relevant to a competitive reaction hypothesis. First of all, the time series for the firm which several others designated as the technological leader of the industry is characterized by some sharp discrete upward changes over this period. In particular, the firm experienced

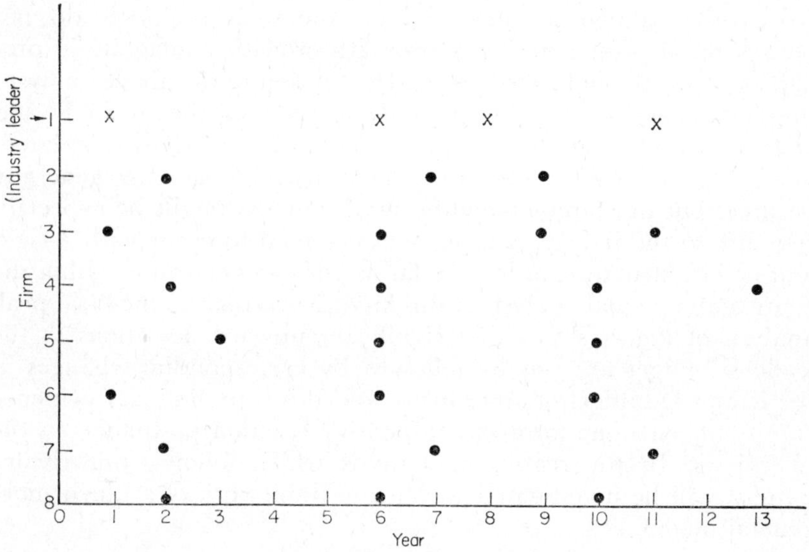

FIGURE 1.

exactly four local peaks during this time period, each of which involved percentage increases over twice the firm's average rate of growth.[4] If response to the industry leader's expenditures is a prevalent force in the determination of the R and D budget, then sharp increases by the leader should lead to similar changes on the part of other firms, albeit with some time lag. Fig. 1 shows the timing of the local peaks for all the firms studied here. Defining year 1 as that year in which the industry leader achieved its first

[4] A local peak is defined as a year in which the annual percentage growth rate in a firm's R and D expenditures exceeds that for the previous and succeeding year. In addition, in the above analysis, peaks were included only where the growth rate of R and D expenditures for that year was at least twice as great as the average rate experienced by the firm over the entire post-war period. This was done in order to focus on years of dramatic change in R and D outlays.

local peak in R and D, the industry leader exhibited local peaks in years 1, 6, 8, and 11. The pattern of local peaks for the other firms is perfectly consistent with the hypothesis of a competitive response to the industry leader. For example, all of the firms experienced local peaks corresponding to the leader's first local peak in year 1 in that same year (two firms) with a one-year lag (four firms), or with a two-year lag (one firm). Similarly, with very few exceptions, each of the other three peaks is followed by corresponding ones in the series of the other firms, most often with a time lag of a year or two.

If the local peaks shown in Fig. 1 are in part manifestations of competitive responses, these series show such responses do not always occur with a uniform time lag or with a magnitude proportionate to the industry leaders. In addition to the above analysis, simple correlations between each firm's annual change in R and D expenditures and those of the industry leader were calculated, using lags of various length. These correlations are generally positive, but not large or highly significant. As might be expected, response to the industry leader does not tend to occur with a rigid and precise structure, at least so far as one can determine within the context of a partial analysis of this kind. Nevertheless, the local peak analysis of Fig. 1 shows that significant upward deviations in the leader's budget are usually followed by corresponding changes in the R and D budget of other firms, and this is preliminary evidence consistent with one form of competitive reaction postulated in the interviews. In the regression analysis which follows, this rivalry pattern will be investigated within the framework of a much more general model.

C. THE DETERMINANTS OF R AND D EXPENDITURES: A GENERAL MODEL

As discussed in Section II, R and D expenditures constitute an investment decision for the firm. Hence, the optimal level of R and D expenditures will be determined according to the marginal conditions[5]

$$mrr_{it} = mcf_{it} \tag{2}$$

where mrr_{it} = the marginal rate of return to firm i for undertaking additional R and D during period t.

mcf_{it} = the marginal cost of funds to firm i in period t.

[5] Whether a firm is maximizing stockholder or managerial welfare, it will follow marginal conditions of the general kind outlined here. Moreover, the directional effect on R and D (but not the magnitude) of most demand and cost variables considered here will be the same on the two theories. In this paper, we make no attempt to distinguish between these two rival motivational theories. The observed relations appear compatible with either notion. For a treatment of this larger issue which attempts such an empirical discrimination, see [3].

Moreover, for the present case of R and D investment, we have

(3) $$mrr_{it} = f(R_{it}, X_{it})$$

and

(4) $$mcf_{it} = g(Z_{it})$$

where R_{it} = the firm's total level of R and D expenditures in period t.
X_{it} = the set of variables influencing its return from R and D over time.
Z_{it} = the set of variables affecting its cost of capital over time.

The assumption of diminishing returns to increased R and D outlays, at least beyond some threshold level, implies that

(3a) $$\partial f / \partial R_{it} < 0$$

In accordance with our discussion of Section II, we include the lagged R and D expenditures of the firm's rival as one of the main variables affecting the firm's *mrr* schedule over time. Moreover, the basic hypothesis we have made is that

(3b) $$\partial f / \partial R_{j,\,t-1} > 0$$

where $R_{j,\,t-1}$ = the lagged R and D expenditures of rival firm(s).

This hypothesis implies the firm's decision-makers will normally decide, on expected profitability grounds, to respond in like fashion to a competitor's change in R and D rather than conversely or not at all. At the same time, this hypothesis says nothing about the joint profitability of the competing firms changing their levels of R and D expenditures as a result of an action reaction sequence. Rather, it says only that, once a change is initiated by one firm, its rival will normally respond in the same manner on the basis of its own marginal profitability calculations.

Ideally, one would like to include among the set of shift variables for the *mrr* equation some variables reflecting the technological and entrepreneurial factors affecting a firm's expectations from R and D. Unfortunately, no satisfactory way exists to measure these factors directly.[6] In his research on investment in plant and equipment,

[6] We experimented with some variables which could be hypothesized to be systematically related to the return from R and D expenditures, but our attempts in this regard were largely unsuccessful. Among the variables tried here and reported on in an earlier draft was the supply of new technical personnel (advanced degree graduates in chemistry

Grunfeld has suggested a proxy measure based on investors' expectations of a firm's prospects [4]. Specifically, Grunfeld uses the market valuation of a firm's assets as an index of the discounted present value of its future earnings. In a research intensive industry like chemicals, a firm's future earnings will depend significantly on its ongoing research activities. Therefore, one might plausibly use the fluctuations in market valuation of chemical firms to measure changes in expectations of the profitability of their R and D programs. However, at best, market valuation is an uncertain measure in this regard as it is influenced by several factors unrelated to R and D, especially financial considerations. Despite this limitation, we include market valuation as a provisional variable in some of the relationships estimated below. At the very least, it is interesting to test whether market valuation is systematically related to R and D investment outlays, given its significant relation to plant and equipment investments observed in previous studies.

In symbolic terms, the hypothesis on market valuation may be represented as

(3b) $$\partial f / \partial V_{it} > 0$$

where V_{it} is the firm's market valuation in period t.

Turning to the cost of capital side, we have already noted above that several previous cross-sectional studies have established the relevance of liquidity and cash flow considerations for R and D outlays[7] [1] [6] [14]. Accordingly, we include a measure of cash flow as one of the determinants of *mcf* and postulate that

(4a) $$\partial g / \partial CF_{it} < 0.$$

The marginal opportunity cost of undertaking additional R and D outlays will also be a function of the profitability of other investment activities, particularly the installation of new plant and equipment. The latter is quantitatively, the main alternative use of funds

and chemical engineering). This was intended to be a measure of the tightness of the labor market for R and D personnel. This is important because industrial R and D expenditures are in large part salaries for highly skilled manpower. Unfortunately, this supply side measure of new graduates did not seem to be an adequate index of the tightness of the labor market (because of other demand sources), and furthermore, there is not an unambiguous expected relation between the tightness of the labor market and the effect on company expenditures. Hence, the lackluster results for this variable (i.e. no statistical significance and no consistent sign pattern) is probably not surprising.

[7] The rationale for this relation is that many firms appear to be reluctant to borrow or issue new stock and they consider their supply of funds curve to exhibit a kink at the point where their internally-generated funds are exhausted. In other words, the cost of capital on borrowed funds or externally-raised equity is considered to be much higher than the required rate of return on internal funds. This issue has been discussed at length in economic literature dealing with the investment decision (see, esp. [12]) which will not be reviewed here.

in the chemical industry. Economic research on firm investment in plant and equipment suggests several relevant determinant variables—predominantly centering around demand pull considerations and the degree of capacity utilization. In principle, one should study R and D and fixed capital investment in a simultaneous equation framework and include all of these factors in the analysis [3] [14]. However, with the limited number of observations available here for each firm, this is not possible. Instead, we attempt to isolate the profitability effect of alternative investments on R and D only in a very discrete manner.

Specifically, we include an intercept dummy variable in the *mcf* equations for those periods when the substitution effect from capital investment to R and D is likely to be maximal. In accordance with the findings of previous investment studies, we postulate that over the cycle the expected return on new plant and equipment will tend to be lowest in years immediately following sales and earnings decreases.[8] Not only will such declines tend to produce excess capacity in existing facilities, but also expectations are strongly influenced by a firm's most recent performance. These factors can be expected to have a much greater impact on investment in plant and equipment than on R and D. Expectations of the latter, with its longer term focus on the generation and improvement of products and processes, are necessarily much less influenced by current levels of performance. Therefore, as the expected profitability on new plant and equipment investment declines in such periods, the marginal opportunity cost of undertaking investment in R and D is less and some substitution of resources from the former to the latter should occur. If this does happen, it will cushion somewhat the otherwise negative effect on R and D arising from the depressed levels of cash flow in these periods. As a result, one would expect R and D outlays to be less cyclical in character than other investment activities.[9]

Collecting together all of the above discussed variables, the full specification of the model becomes

$$mrr_{it} = f(R_{it}, R_{j,\,t-1}, V_t) \qquad (3')$$

$$mcf_{it} = g(CF_{it}, D_{it}) \qquad (4')$$

[8] The specific criterion for the dummy requiring declines in both a firm's sales and earnings was designated to select only these years when substantial changes in performance occur and when the effect is likely to be maximal, from both a capacity utilization or expectation standpoint.

[9] In the interviews, some research managers also stressed the importance from a morale standpoint of avoiding significant cutbacks in professional personnel in cyclical downturns. One device apparently utilized to prevent this is to cut back on work on contract 'out of house' before that involving in house personnel.

subject to inequalities 3(a)–3(c) and (4a) where all variables conform to previous definitions and D_{it} is a cyclical dummy taking on the value 1 in years following those where both sales and earnings decline, and 0 otherwise.

If, for purposes of econometric estimation, we assume a linear structure between the *mrr* and *mcf* functions and the variables discussed above, we then have the following pair of relationships:

$$(5) \qquad mrr_{it} = k_1 + a_0 R_{it} + a_1 R_{j,\ t-1} + a_2 V_{it} + \mu_{it}$$

with $a_0 < 0$, $a_1 > 0$, and $a_2 > 0$

$$(6) \qquad mcf_{it} = k_2 + a_1' D_{it} + a_2' CF_{it} + \mu'_{it}$$

with $a_1' < 0$ and $a_2' < 0$, where k_1 and k_2 are positive intercept terms and μ_{it} and μ_{it} are statistical disturbance terms.

Equating these two functions and rearranging terms, we obtain the firm's optimal or desired level of R and D expenditures, R^*_{it}, as a function of the other variables in equations (5) and (6). Specifically, we obtain the following reduced form structure:

$$(7) \qquad R^*_{it} = k_3 + b_1 D_{it} + b_2 R_{j,\ t-1} + b_3 CF_{it} + b_4 V_{it} + \mu''_{it}$$

where $b_1 = a'_1/a_0 > 0$
$b_2 = -a_1/a_0 > 0$
$b_3 = a'_2/a_0 > 0$
$b_4 = -a_2/a_0 > 0$.

Equation (7) gives the value of R and D expenditures which equates *mrr* and *mcf* or the firm's *desired* level of R and D expenditures in time period t. However, it will usually not be possible for the firm to adjust completely to this optimal level, and its *actual* expenditures, R_{it}, will differ somewhat from R^*_{it}. Accordingly a dynamic adjustment mechanism must be specified to complete our model of the time path of R and D expenditures. Following several other studies of investment behavior, we shall assume an adjustment process such that in each period

$$(8) \qquad R_{it} - R_{i,t-1} = \theta[R^*_{it} - R_{it-1}]. \quad 0 \leq \theta \leq 1.$$

Equation (8) implies that the change in a firm's expenditures between any period and the previous period will be some constant fraction, θ, of the difference between the desired level and last period's actual expenditures.

Rearranging terms and substituting the relationship for R_{it} given by equation (7) into equation (8), we now show a relation between the firm's actual level of R and D expenditures, R_{it}, and the other variables in the model. This results in the relation

(9) $R_{it} = k_3+c_1D_{it}+c_2R_{j,t-1}+c_3CF_{it}+c_4V_{it}+c_5R_{it-1}+\mu_{it}'''$
where $c_k = \theta b_k$ for $k = 0,4$ and $c_5 = (1-\theta)$.

Because the coefficient θ is hypothesized always to be positive (and also to be between 0 and 1), all of the predictions regarding the signs of the b coefficients hold identically for the c coefficients. It should also be noted the coefficient on the firm's own lagged R and D expenditures, c_5, being equal to $1-\theta$, provides us with a way of estimating the adjustment coefficient, θ. Furthermore, in the limiting case where the firm adjusts completely to the desired level of expenditures within the time period covered by each observation, this term drops out of the hypothesized structure given above.

For statistical purposes, we shall use first differenced rather than absolute values of each variable in estimating equation (9) for each of the chemical firms in our sample. This helps eliminate the trend component from each of the variables and reduces the likelihood of auto-correlation in the residuals. Of course, this is a purely statistical transformation and in no way changes the predictions of the coefficients in equation (9). In differenced form, the full model becomes

(10) $\Delta R_{it} = c_1\Delta D_{it}+c_2\Delta R_{j,t-1}+c_3\Delta CF_{it}+c_4\Delta V_{it}+c_5\Delta R_{i,t-1}+v_{it}$

where v_{it} is the statistical error term for the differenced form of the model.

The specification given by equation (10) is the focus of our empirical work. It may be noted that one may alternatively formulate the *mrr*, *mcf* and adjustment process equations utilizing multiplicative formulas (i.e. linear in logarithms) and arrive at a parallel formulation for the equation (10) involving the first differences of the logarithms of these variables (with the exception of the dummy variable). Such a procedure yields results which differ in individual cases, but which overall are quite comparable to those discussed below for the linear case.

D. THE EMPIRICAL RESULTS

Before discussing the coefficient estimates for equation (10), we may note briefly the source and exact formulation of each of the variables. R and D expenditures were obtained on a confidential basis from the firms themselves and conform in general to the NSF definitions.

All of the financial variables were obtained directly from the Standard and Poor's Compustat Tape. A firm's level of cash flow in any period t was taken to be the sum of its profits after tax, depreciation and depletion allowances for the immediately preceding period; a year lag in this variable is assumed to allow for information and organization decision lags. Market valuation in year t is the sum in dollar terms of the firm's common stock, preferred stock and outstanding debt. The value of each firm's common stock was calculated at its mid-point price in each year. This was done to average out, as much as possible, transitory fluctuations in market price. On the other hand, preferred stock and debt were recorded at book value because many of these issues trade infrequently and market price data for them were not readily available. Because these latter components constitute a relatively small portion of market value fluctuations, this approximation should not introduce any serious error.

The choice of the appropriate rival firm, or groups of firms, to be used in estimating equation (10) is not an easy task. In the absence of inside knowledge, any procedure that one employs is bound to be *ad hoc* in nature. Fortunately, the firm that leads the industry in R and D expenditures and which was designated by some of the others as the technological leader (Section II), is among the firms in our sample. Following up on our local peak analysis, one natural set of competitive interactions to investigate is the pattern in which each firm reacts to the lagged expenditures of the technical leader. The R and D expenditures of the industry leader are then in turn related, with a lag, to those of the second largest firm. The latter is a firm with a large and diversified R and D program and appears to constitute a natural competitive rival to the industry leader.

A second procedure for determining potential rivals consisted of ranking the firms on the basis of their share of total industry R and D. We then selected the immediately preceding firm in this ranking as the firm's competitor.[10] This technique was selected because there is considerable evidence in the industrial organization literature that market share considerations are quite important from a motivational standpoint to oligopolistic firms.

With both procedures for determining rivals, we used a one-year response lag for competitive reactions in our empirical estimations. While the local peak analysis suggests that the length of the lag

[10] The ranking in terms of research share is highly correlated but not identical with that based on market share. We feel ranking based on research share is conceptually better because a firm is likely to be more responsive in its R and D decisions to a rival with a high R and D-low current market share than one with a low R and D-high current market share.

may vary considerably, a one-year lag offers the best approximation to the normal response interval.

In the first round of empirical estimation, we omitted market valuation from the analysis because of the weaker theoretical basis of this variable. Thus we estimated the structure

$$(11)\qquad \Delta R_{it} = c_1\Delta D_{it}+c_2\Delta R_{jt-1}+c_3\Delta CF_{it}+c_5\Delta R_{it-1}+v_{it}$$

where the *j*th firm in each case is selected from the two procedures described above as the one giving the best overall fit. The firms are listed in order of their R and D rank in Table II and the rank

TABLE II

THE DETERMINANTS OF ANNUAL CHANGES IN R AND D EXPENDITURES FOR EIGHT CHEMICAL FIRMS OVER THE PERIOD 1948–67

$$\Delta R_{it} = c_1\Delta D_{it}+c_2\Delta R_{j,t-1}+c_3\Delta CF_{it}+c_5\Delta R_{i,t-1}+v_{it}$$

R and D Rank Firm/Rival	ΔD_{it}	$\Delta R_{j,t-1}$	ΔCF_{it}	$\Delta R_{i,t-1}$	R^2
1/2	−1.68	.62*	.02	.24	.43
	(.61)	(3.00)	(.81)	(1.16)	
2/1	2.37	.40**	.10**	.27	.42
	(1.26)	(2.11)	(2.57)	(1.46)	
3/1	1.64**	.04	.16*	.35**	.28
	(2.54)	(.64)	(4.04)	(1.89)	
4/3	.29	.35	.12*	−.16	.35
	(.38)	(1.27)	(2.76)	(.54)	
5/4	.70**	.51*	.19*	−.42**	.62
	(2.11)	(3.66)	(4.51)	(1.85)	
6/1	.14	.03	.15*	.06	.73
	(.48)	(1.75)	(6.93)	(.40)	
7/1	.25**	.03**	.11*	.22	.36
	(1.87)	(1.85)	(3.38)	(1.31)	
8/1	.07	−.01	.17**	.95*	.22
	(.25)	(.90)	(1.77)	(3.34)	

* Statistically significant at 1 per cent level.
** Statistically significant at 5 per cent level.

of the rival firm used for estimating each equation is given in column 1. Not surprisingly, the model of followers responding to the industry leader outperformed the alternative model of competition between firms with similar shares of the total industry R and D. The latter is statistically superior in only two cases.

The regression estimates of Table II indicate that almost all of the coefficients are of the postulated sign and many are statistically significant. Considering the two non-R and D variables first, we find the estimate of the cash flow coefficient performs extremely well. It is positive in every case and statistically significant at the five per cent level or better for 6 of the 8 firms. The estimate for the dummy variable takes on the predicted positive sign in all but one instance, and is statistically significant in 3 instances. This latter set of results may be viewed as moderate support for the hypothesis of a substitution effect toward R and D and away from fixed capital investment in periods following declines in a firm's sales and earnings as discussed above. Since this phenomenon is captured only in a very approximate way through the dummy variable technique, this remains a very interesting question to investigate on more extensive data samples. Other work in progress by one of the authors reinforces the notion of substitutive interactions between R and D and other investment expenditures in concurrent periods, along with complementary relations over lagged intervals [3] [13].

The estimates of the c_5 coefficients, associated with the firm's own lagged R and D expenditure, are positive in 6 of the 8 cases. However, the firm's own firm expenditures generally have much less explanatory power than the lagged expenditures of its rival. Remembering that the c_5 coefficients are equal to $1-\theta$, the dynamic adjustment coefficient, we see that the size of these coefficients suggests a fairly rapid adjustment process. Most of the adjustment coefficients are in the region from 0.6 to 0.8 and a few are close to 1.0 in value.[11] Given the character of R and D expenditures, this rapid adjustment is a somewhat surprising finding. However, the lagged formulation of several of the variables means that the response to several of the variables does, in fact, take several time periods to be substantially completed.

The estimates of the competitive reaction terms provide some very interesting results. The coefficients for this variable are positive in every case but one and statistically significant in half the equations. Of particular interest is the observed relation between the firms ranked first and second in R and D expenditures. The estimates on the rival R and D coefficients for these variables imply an actual reaction coefficient, b_2, for the leader firm to the second firm's lagged expenditures of 0.80, while the estimated reaction coefficient for the second firm to the leader's expenditures is somewhat lower, 0.55.[12] Thus, these two firms which appear on *a priori* grounds to be

[11] The negative value for firms 4 and 5 imply an investment coefficient greater than 1.0. Because this is not consistent with the basic notion of our hypothesized adjustment mechanism, it either implies a different adjustment process or some econometric problems occurring that obscure matters. Rather than re-estimating the adjustment structure for these firms, we take the estimate to be 1.0 for the purpose of the above analysis.

[12] These are computed by taking the estimate of θ for each firm, as obtained from the relation, $c_5 = 1-\theta$, and then using this estimate to compute b_2 from the relation $b_2 = c_2/\theta$. Both relations follow directly from equations (8) and (9) as presented in Section II-C.

natural rivals, do indeed exhibit a vigorous competitive interaction pattern.

In four of the other six cases, the reaction terms offered a statistically superior fit for the model of each firm reacting to the industry leader than for the model of each firm reacting to the one closest to it in share of industry R and D. The reaction coefficients for these four are considerably smaller than that observed in the case of the top 2 firms. However, since the bottom 3 firms in particular have considerably smaller market shares and R and D programs, the response coefficients are considerably higher when viewed in percentage terms. In particular, the elasticity of R and D expenditures with respect to competitive outlays calculated at the mean is close to 1.0 for both firms 6 and 7. This suggests a fairly vigorous response for these two smaller firms.

The reaction coefficients for firms 4 and 5, for which the rivalry pattern based on R and D ranking offered the better fit, are somewhat smaller in value but are nevertheless substantial in magnitude. Moreover, the observed coefficients undoubtedly capture only a part of the total competitive reaction for these firms, in that they probably respond to competitors other than the firms to which they are paired.

The competitive reaction hypothesis exhibited its worst performance for firms 3 and 8 where the t values were both less than 1.0 in value. Here one may only conjecture that these firms may have other patterns of rivalry than the two considered here, or respond to rivals not present in the current sample. Alternatively, the optimal or desired level of expenditures may respond with a greater lag to competitors' actions. We could experiment with various other combinations of rivalry patterns and lag structures within the current sample, but without an *a priori* justification for selecting other alternatives, this does not appear to be a very fruitful course of action.

A response lag of one year, assumed in estimating the reaction coefficients in Table II, is somewhat arbitrary, but it captures the essential point: it will usually be impossible for firms to react to competitors in the same time period as the initial action. In the case of R and D, information lags alone can result in a significant reaction time. Moreover, decisions on the total level of R and D expenditures are usually made at a very high level of management, thus requiring additional organizational response time. Hence, if the estimates on the c_2 coefficients are really due to competitive interactions and not merely a common response to other factors, the size and significance of these coefficient estimates should decline when a rival's R and D expenditures are related with an unlagged time structure. To see if this is the case, equation (11) is re-estimated in the following form for all firms:

$$\Delta R_{it} = c_1 \Delta D_{it} + c_2 \Delta R_{jt} + c_3 \Delta CF_{it} + c_4 \Delta R_{it-1} + v_{it} \tag{12}$$

and the results presented in Table III.

TABLE III

RE-ESTIMATION OF TABLE 2 USING AN UNLAGGED COMPETITIVE RESPONSE TERM
$\Delta R_{it} = c_1 \Delta D_{it} + c_2 \Delta R_{jt} + c_3 \Delta CF_{it} + c_5 \Delta R_{i,t-1} + v_{it}$

R and D Rank Firm/Rival	ΔD_{it}	ΔR_{jt}	ΔCF_{it}	$\Delta R_{i,t-1}$	R^2
1/2	−5.46**	.31	.02	.44	.13
	(1.77)	(1.22)	(.76)	(1.71)	
2/1	2.97	.04	.12**	.45	.22
	(1.31)	(.11)	(2.43)	(1.32)	
3/1	1.75**	−.03	.17*	.44**	.26
	(2.62)	(.34)	(4.14)	(2.23)	
4/3	.56	.22	.11**	.004	.33
	(.74)	(1.04)	(2.34)	(.02)	
5/4	.56	.18	.17**	.18	.34
	(1.25)	(1.45)	(2.64)	(.99)	
6/1	−5.89	.00	.15*	.19	.68
	(.19)	(.04)	(6.03)	(1.15)	
7/1	.35**	.01	.35**	.27	.24
	(2.51)	(.99)	(2.51)	(1.41)	
8/1	−1.49	.00	.16	.84**	.18
	(.05)	(.13)	(1.58)	(2.55)	

* Statistically significant at 1 per cent level.
** Statistically significant at 5 per cent level.

The estimates of the c_2 coefficients show that when the expenditures of rivals are included in unlagged fashion, they all decline in magnitude and none are statistically significant. This suggests that the estimates presented in Table II cannot easily be interpreted as a common response to other forces, such as the tightness of the labor market for scientists and engineers, where a large part of the response is likely to be concurrent in nature. Nevertheless, most firms follow the expenditure of the industry leader, so one might interpret the results of Tables II and III as support for the hypothesis that the leading firm is reacting to common opportunities and developments with a shorter lag than other firms. While there may be some truth to this notion, the fact that a closed loop pattern of rivalry was observed with firm 1 itself strongly reacting to firm 2's R and D outlays, makes this less plausible than the competitive reaction hypothesis.

Until now, we have not considered the market valuation variable which has been omitted from all the estimated equations. Our results concerning this variable are essentially negative. It is generally statistically insignificant when added to the previous regression equation. The results are presented in Table IV (equation (a)). Only one firm has a statistically significant coefficient and 6 of the 8

TABLE IV

ESTIMATION OF THE DETERMINANT EQUATIONS

$$\text{(a) } \Delta R_{it} = c_1\Delta D_{it}+c_2\Delta R_{j,t-1}+c_3\Delta CF_{it}+c_4\Delta V_{it}+c_5\Delta R_{i,t-1}+v_{it}$$
$$\text{(b) } \Delta R_{it} = c_0+c_1\Delta D_{it}+c_2\Delta R_{j,t-1}+c_3\Delta CF_{it}+c_4\Delta V_{it}+c_5\Delta R_{i,t-1}+v_{it}$$

Firm	c_0	ΔV_{it}	ΔD_{it}	$\Delta R_{j,t-1}$	ΔCF_{it}	$\Delta R_{i,t-1}$	R^2
1/2 (a)	—	.05	−1.18	.63*	.02	.25	.43
		(.52)	(.40)	(2.95)	(.94)	(1.15)	
(b)	1.45	.05	−1.18	.57**	.01	.13	.47
	(.81)	(.50)	(.39)	(2.45)	(.62)	(.51)	
2/1 (a)	—	.19	2.48	.39**	.10**	.27	.45
		(.76)	(1.30)	(2.02)	(2.35)	(1.39)	
(b)	−4.46	.35	3.55**	.65*	.17*	.57**	.57
	(1.79)	(1.46)	(1.91)	(2.84)	(3.05)	(2.29)	
3/1 (a)	—	.06	1.69**	.05	.17*	.34	.28
		(.20)	(2.34)	(.64)	(3.11)	(1.76)	
(b)	.96	−.18	1.49**	.01	.13**	.13	.32
	(.78)	(.51)	(1.91)	(.10)	(1.92)	(.39)	
4/3 (a)	—	.44	−.25	.24	.09**	−.05	.42
		(1.22)	(.29)	(.88)	(1.82)	(.15)	
(b)	−.15	.47	−.23	.27	.09	−.03	.42
	(.18)	(1.17)	(.25)	(.83)	(1.66)	(.11)	
5/4 (a)	—	.16	.70**	.48*	.19*	−.42**	.64
		(.81)	(2.06)	(3.28)	(4.23)	(1.82)	
(b)	.24	.11	.62	.46*	.16*	−.48**	.66
	(.83)	(.53)	(1.78)	(3.11)	(3.16)	(1.96)	
6/1 (a)	—	−.08	.24	.03**	.15*	.02	.75
		(.65)	(.72)	(1.83)	(6.51)	(.15)	
(b)	−.04	−.08	.24	.35	.15*	.04	.75
	(.21)	(.53)	(.69)	(1.49)	(5.49)	(.21)	
7/1 (a)	—	.41**	.21	.03**	.08**	.20	.50
		(1.88)	(1.57)	(2.31)	(2.39)	(1.25)	
(b)	−.09	.50	.22	.03**	.09**	.30	.52
	(.50)	(1.71)	(1.61)	(2.08)	(2.32)	(1.16)	
8/1 (a)	—	.28	.04	−.01	.17	.91*	.24
		(.43)	(.15)	(.84)	(1.65)	(2.95)	
(b)	.25	.23	.08	−.02	.10	.66**	.31
	(1.75)	(.04)	(.30)	(1.67)	(.92)	(2.03)	

coefficients have t values less than 1.0. In fact, general economy-wide trends dominate the yearly fluctuations in the market valuation variable, and the results of Table 4 suggest these have little direct influence on R and D behavior. We confirmed its relationship to aggregate factors by correlating the individual firm series for these eight chemical firms with an aggregate stock index (the Standard and Poor industrials). We obtained a correlation above 0.9 in every case. In future research, one might still consider utilizing this variable as a proxy for R and D expectations when a cross-sectional analysis is employed and these aggregative influences are held constant over the sample.[13] In the present time series analysis, however, they are clearly dominating other components.

In Table IV we have also presented estimates with an intercept term added to the model in differenced form. In undifferenced form, this intercept term corresponds to the linear time trend. The addition of an intercept is thus equivalent to the inclusion of this time trend element among the original set of variables influencing the *mrr* or *mcf* equations. The results in Table IV (equation set (b)) indicate that the intercept is never statistically significant and has little effect on other coefficients present in these equations. Thus, when the behavioral model is fully specified, the time trend has no explanatory power. Given the strong structural relationships previously observed between R and D and time (Table I) it is reassuring that it is the trend elements and not the determinant variables which become statistically insignificant.

We now can briefly summarize our main results in this section. The estimates of the reaction coefficients for eight chemical firms provide some direct evidence that firms increase R and D expenditures in response to rivals' outlays and that the top two firms in the industry are particularly responsive to each other. Cash flow also seems to be a major determinant of change in a firm's R and D outlays over time. In the next section we consider further the role of these factors, using a cross-sectional sample of firms ranging over several industries, including many which have not historically been very technologically progressive.

III. CROSS-SECTIONAL ANALYSIS

It would be desirable to do time series analysis like that undertaken above for the chemical industry across a wide spectrum of different industry samples. One could then relate inter-industry differences in R and D allocative practices, in particular parameters associated with the degree of competitive interaction, to various industrial structural characteristics such as degree of concentration, indices of technological base, etc. Unfortunately, time series data do not exist in nearly sufficient quantity to undertake such an analysis at the present time. However, for select years, information does exist on one important input measure of R and D activity, the size of a firm's professional R and D staff, across a wide sample of U.S.

[13] Even in cross-sectional work, fluctuations in market valuation may reflect developments in existing products much more strongly than those in the R and D stage.

manufacturing firms. We shall use these data to consider, in a very preliminary way, a first level hypothesis regarding inter-industry differences in the degree of R and D competitive interactions.

The basic issue which we would like to investigate with this cross-sectional data sample is the relationship that exists between competitive reaction coefficients and the degree of industrial concentration in an industry. As concentration increases, the sensitivity of firms to the inter-dependence of their decisions with other firms should also increase. Moreover, the incentives to compete through activities differentiating and improving product lines, like R and D, rather than by price changes should also be stronger in more oligopolistic industries. Thus there are grounds for expecting the degree of competitive interaction to increase as the degree of concentration increases.

However, with only one-year cross-sectional slices of data available at infrequent intervals, we have no means of directly estimating the size of the reaction coefficients in different industries. Nevertheless, as the strength of the reaction coefficients becomes larger in an industry, one would expect a greater conformity in the level of R and D inputs across firms in that industry. To test a hypothesis of the type given above, therefore, we may use the degree of conformity in R and D inputs relative to the industry mean at a given moment of time as an indication of the average size of the reaction coefficients.[14]

Of course, the cross-sectional mean and variance in R and D can be expected to depend on other factors in addition to the competitive reaction coefficients. In particular, it will depend on the mean firm size and variations around the mean size that exists in an industry. That is, the average scale of operations in an industry will directly influence the absolute level of dollars spent on R and D. Hence if one is meaningfully to test the above hypothesis, one must standardize in some way for such scale effects before doing an inter-industry analysis.

Following the practice employed in other studies, we shall focus on variations in *research intensity* rather than the absolute amounts of R and D undertaken by firms in order to keep scale effects from dominating the inter-industry comparisons. Thus we are suggesting that, other things equal, greater concentration will be associated with greater conformity in firm research intensity. The specific

[14] The mean level of industry R and D inputs may increase or decrease with increases in the size of the reaction coefficients. This ambiguity arises from the fact that as reaction coefficients become large, they may inhibit initiation of increases of R and D. On the other hand, in an environment when firms are not stalemated in this fashion, higher reaction coefficients can be expected to lead to higher mean levels of R and D.

measure of research intensity that will be employed here is the R and D to sales ratio.[15] An industry will be taken to exhibit a greater degree of conformity in its pattern of R and D allocations if the variation in research intensity is low relative to the mean research intensity for that industry. Thus our basic measure indexing the extent of competitive interactions in an industry is the *coefficient of variation in research intensity* in that industry.

The hypothesis presented above now translates into the empirically testable proposition:

Other things being equal, as the concentration ratios increase across industries, the coefficient of variation in firm research intensities will decrease.

Because we have no basis for predicting the specific type of relationship which may exist between these variables, we will use rank correlations to relate these variables. This procedure allows one to observe directional effects that might be obscured if a specific relationship were imposed arbitrarily. This type of analysis is also appropriate here because only very general tendencies can be reasonably investigated where so many other potential determinant factors have been excluded from the current analysis.

In order to test the above hypothesis, we constructed industry samples which best approximate the SIC three-digit grouping for the manufacturing sector of the U.S. economy.[16] If data samples permitted, more disaggregate industry groupings would be desirable, because competitive interactions are likely to be obscured when observing firms with heterogeneous product lines. Any evidence using three-digit SIC classification therefore is likely to underestimate the degree of competitive interactions.

For each industry sample, the R and D employment to sales ratios[17] were computed for each firm among the eight largest, ranked by sales, that supplied data to the 1955 survey of research

[15] While the results in the previous section might suggest the use of cash flow as a deflator, sales has a few characteristics which make it more desirable in the current situation. In particular it is a less volatile measure of the firm's resource base than cash flow. In any given year, the latter may give an inaccurate picture of a firm's capacity to do R and D and indeed may even be negative. There is also some rationale for using sales based on behavioral hypotheses advanced in the interview studies [17] [18].

[16] The choice of the three-digit SIC category corresponded to those employed by Stigler [23], so that the industry concentration ratios compiled by him could be employed directly in the present study. The classification of firms into industries was based on information derived from the Standard and Poor's Compustat tape, the *Newsfront Industrial Directory*, and Moody's *Industrial Manual*. The specific firms included in each industry group are enumerated in the Appendix to this paper.

[17] The use of R and D professional employers rather than R and D expenditures probably has no great effect on the subsequent results. Intra-industry and inter-industry correlations between R and D professional employers and total R and D expenditures are generally above 0.9. See, for example, [13].

laboratories of the National Research Council.[18] All industries in which five or more of the top eight firms failed to respond to the survey were discarded from the analysis. An appendix, available from the authors on request, lists all the firms used in this part of the analysis and the basis on which some industries were excluded from the analysis. It should be noted that a few industries where defense contracting plays a large role (e.g. aerospace and electronics) were purposely excluded. One would not expect the above hypothesis to hold if research were performed in large part on a cost-plus fee and the final decision to engage in research were made by the government. The 29 industries which had a sufficient response rate and met other criteria form the basis for the present investigation.

In Table V, the 29 industries are listed in decreasing order of research intensity as measured by the mean value of the R and D to sales ratio. The industries span the entire spectrum with respect to the importance of innovative effort. In the second column of Table IV, the coefficient of variation in the R and D to sales ratio is given for each industry. In the last column of Table V, the concentration ratio which existed in each industry for 1954 is presented.

If the above hypothesis holds, the coefficient of variation should be inversely related to the degree of concentration. Accordingly, the rank correlation coefficient was computed between these concentration ratios and the coefficient of variation in the R and D to sales ratio. This correlation has the expected negative sign and is equal to -0.33 which is statistically significant at the five per cent level (with a normal value of 2.15). Interestingly, the rank correlation between the concentration ratio and the mean research intensity of an industry is positive but not statistically significant (with a normal value less than 1.00).[19] Furthermore, when the partial Kendall rank correlation between the coefficient of variation and concentration ratio variables is computed holding mean research intensity constant, this coefficient actually increases slightly over the simple rank correlation coefficient. Thus there is evidence that greater conformity in research intensity exists for firms in more concentrated industries, whatever the degree of industry research intensity. The possible interpretation of the above relation therefore narrows considerably.[20]

[18] The choice of the year 1955 was based on the fact that this was the only year for which *both* concentration ratio data and R and D data were available. Moreover, collection of comparable data for the few other years in which R and D employers data are available would have required substantial additional effort. There is no reason to believe, however, that the results obtained for 1955 are atypical.

[19] The relationship of concentration to research intensity has been investigated elsewhere with mixed results. For a good summary discussion, see [22], pp. 372–6.

[20] For example, one might interpret the degree of research intensity as a good index

Extending the above analysis somewhat further, we note that if we hold the level of concentration constant, and compute the partial correlation between mean industry research intensity and the coefficient of variation in research intensity, there is significant negative rank correlation coefficient between these variables ($r = -.35$ with

TABLE V

INTER-INDUSTRY DIFFERENCES FOR THE EIGHT LARGEST FIRMS IN THE RATIO OF R AND D PROFESSIONAL EMPLOYEES TO TOTAL SALES*

Industry	*Number of Firms*	*Mean (Employees Per Million Dollars of Sales)*	*Coefficient of Variation*	*Concentration Ratio***
Drugs	8	2.15	0.52	30.5
Industrial chemicals	6	1.51	0.33	55.1
Fertilizers	6	1.36	0.40	30.9
Paints and varnishes	6	1.27	0.25	36.4
Soaps and detergents	8	0.93	0.47	65.1
Metalworking machinery	4	0.81	0.27	17.0
Electric appliances	6	0.72	0.50	50.0
Perfumes and cosmetics	4	0.63	0.56	25.0
Gypsum, asbestos, and miscellaneous stone products	8	0.57	0.52	48.4
Motor vehicles	5	0.56	0.40	88.1
Metal cans	4	0.51	0.43	80.0
Petroleum refining	8	0.49	0.54	33.0
Flat glass and containers	7	0.45	0.28	68.9
General industry machinery	7	0.42	0.41	35.7
Coating, engraving and miscellaneous metal products	6	0.41	0.51	26.2
Distilled liquors	4	0.33	0.46	64.0
Canning and preserving	6	0.27	0.30	32.3
Sugar	4	0.27	0.45	65.0
Cotton goods	6	0.27	1.07	18.0
Construction and farm equipment	6	0.26	0.53	24.7
Confectionery	4	0.26	0.72	36.4
Grain mill products	6	0.25	0.70	32.7
Pulp, paper, and products	8	0.23	0.82	23.8
Cigarettes	5	0.19	0.44	79.4
Smelting—copper, lead, and zinc	6	0.18	0.63	72.2
Steel	8	0.13	0.38	56.0
Meat packing	7	0.13	0.48	32.7
Dairy products	6	0.10	0.73	37.6
Bakery products	5	0.09	0.70	30.5

* Mean and Coefficients of Variations (standard deviation÷mean) computed for R and D to sales ratios. Sales are for 1955. R and D employment figures are from National Research Council, *Industrial Research Laboratories of United States*, Tenth Edition, 1956. Sales data are from *Moody's*, 1956.

** Concentration ratios are for 1954. See George J. Stigler, *Capital and Rates of Return in Manufacturing Industries* (Princeton, National Bureau of Economic Research, 1963), p. 214.

of 'technological opportunity' existing in an industry. If concentration ratios and research intensity were then significantly related and the above relation between concentration and R and D conformity failed to hold when standardizing for research intensity, one might then conclude the above relation was spurious and reflected factors tied to technological opportunities rather than industry concentration.

a normal value of 2.60). While there are a variety of factors which can affect mean research intensity, the above correlation suggests that as the decision-making environment shifts to one in which R and D becomes more important as a competitive weapon, the pressures and incentives for firms to react strongly to competitors' actions correspondingly increase.[21] Hence, the smaller observed coefficients of variations in more research intensive industries.[22] Because we have no meaningful way at the present time of disentangling the separate forces underlying an industry's research intensity, and because there is undoubtedly a simultaneity between R and D and various industrial structural characteristics, we shall not try to go beyond the general tendencies indicated by the results of these rank correlations here.

In summary, the basic finding emerging from the present cross-sectional analysis is that the degree of competitive reactions in R and D varies in a plausible way with the degree of industrial concentration. We are able to conclude this only by somewhat indirect means, and the finding is preliminary, of course. Eventually, enough data should be available to relate estimates of reaction coefficients for different industries directly to various industrial structural characteristics in the context of a general model. Studies of a time series nature like that of Section II then can be used in an interdependent fashion with cross-sectional analyses to gain fuller insights into the competitive process for R and D activity.

IV. SUMMARY AND CONCLUSIONS

This study has considered the determination of expenditures on research and development in the context of the investment policy of the firm. Results from the analysis of time series and cross-section data suggest that, in research intensive industries, each firm's R and D expenditures are sensitive to what competitors allocate to this activity. For the chemical industry a phenomenon akin to price leadership was observed with several firms apparently responding to the R and D policies of the industry R and D leader. For the two firms at the top of the industry, a very strong action-reaction pattern of rivalry was indicated by our regression results. While the rivalry pattern was less clearcut and discernible for the other six firms, a

[21] Some support for this type of relationship has been suggested by Scherer based on a study using *patent* data as the index of innovational activity. See [22, p. 376].

[22] If one restricts consideration to the largest four firms in each industry (ranked by sales) the relationship becomes even stronger. The coefficient of variation now ranges as low as .07 (for industrial chemicals) and are smaller for almost all the research intensive industries. This is consistent with one of our basic findings in the time series analysis, namely, that competitive responsiveness is likely to be more pronounced among the top few firms in each industry.

pattern of responsiveness to the R and D outlays of the industry leader also seems to be characteristic of their R and D budgeting practices. In the cross-section analysis, our rank correlations suggest that the R and D allocation outlays of the largest firms (ranked by size) conform more to each other in industries where concentration levels are higher and where mean research intensity is larger.

In view of the interdependent, uncertain environment in which R and D decisions usually are made, competitive response patterns of the type observed here may be perfectly consistent with the maximization of an individual firm's expected profits or other objectives (excluding overt collusion as an alternative). One might classify it as an example of an 'adaptively rational' decision-making approach. However, the social desirability and welfare implications of such competitive action-reaction patterns are not easy to assess. If as some research studies suggest [9] [10], the rate of return to R and D over this period has been significantly above other types of investment activity, then the presence of strong rivalry interactions probably has been quite beneficial.

DUKE UNIVERSITY AND NATIONAL BUREAU OF ECONOMIC RESEARCH
BAXTER AND COMPANY

REFERENCES

[1] GRABOWSKI, H. G., 'Determinants of Industrial Research and Development', *Journal of Political Economy*, April, 1968.

[2] GRABOWSKI, H. G., 'Demand Shifting, Optimal Firm Growth, and Rule-of-Thumb Decision Making', *Quarterly Journal of Economics*, May, 1970.

[3] GRABOWSKI, H. G. and D. M. MUELLER, 'Managerial and Stockholder Welfare Models of Firm Expenditures', *Review of Economics and Statistics*, February, 1972.

[4] GRUNFELD, Y., 'The Determinants of Corporate Investment', in A. C. Harberger, ed., *The Demand For Durable Goods* (University of Chicago, 1960).

[5] HALL, MARSHALL, 'The Determinants of Investment Variation in Research and Development', *IEEE Transactions in Engineering Management*, Vol. EM-11, March, 1964.

[6] HAMBERG, D., *R & D: Essays on the Economics of Research and Development* (Random House, 1966).

[7] JORGENSON, D. W. and C. D. SIEBERT, 'A Comparison of Alternative Theories of Corporate Investment', *American Economic Review*, September, 1968.

[8] LANZILLOTTI, R. F., 'Pricing Objectives in Large Companies', *American Economic Review*, December, 1958.

[9] MANSFIELD, E., *Industrial Research and Technological Innovation: An Econometric Analysis* (W. W. Norton, 1968).

[10] MANSFIELD, E. and R. BRANDENBURG, 'The Allocation, Characteristics and Outcome of the Firm's Research and Development Portfolio', *Journal of Business*, October, 1966.

[11] MARKHAM, J., 'The Nature and Significance of Price Leadership', *American Economic Review*, December, 1951.

[12] MEYER, J. R. and H. KUH, *The Investment Decision: An Empirical Inquiry* (Harvard University Press, 1957).

[13] MUELLER, D., 'Patents, Research and Development and the Measurement of Inventive Activity', *Journal of Industrial Economics*, Nov. 1966.

[14] MUELLER, D., 'The Firm Decision Process: An Econometric Investigation', *Quarterly Journal of Economics*, February, 1967.

[15] National Research Council, *Industrial Research Laboratories of the U.S.* (Washington, D.C., 1956).

[16] National Science Foundation, *Research and Development in Industry*, 1967.

[17] National Science Foundation, 'Decision Making on Research and Development in the Business Firm', *Review of Data on R and D*, February, 1964.

[18] National Science Foundation, *Science and Engineering in American Industry*, 1956.

[19] PULLARA, F. J. and L. R. WALKER, 'The Evaluation of Capital Expenditure Proposals: A Survey of Firms in the Chemical Industry', *Journal of Business*, October, 1965.

[20] SCHERER, F. M., 'Firm Size, Market Structure, Opportunity and the Output of Patented Inventions', *American Economic Review*, December, 1954.

[21] SCHERER, F. M., 'Research and Development Resource Allocation Under Rivalry', *Quarterly Journal of Economics*, August, 1967.

[22] SCHERER, F. M., *Industrial Market Structure and Economic Performance* (Rand McNally, 1970).

[23] STIGLER, G. J., *Capital and Rates of Return in Manufacturing Industries* (National Bureau of Economic Research, 1963).

A STUDY OF TRADE ASSOCIATION PRICE FIXING

by M. Howe

Since the passing of the Monopolies and Restrictive Practices (Inquiry and Control) Act in 1948 and, particularly, the Restrictive Trade Practices Act in 1956, considerable information has become available upon the activities of industrial trade associations and the effects of those activities upon the competitive process. Of greatest interest to economists is collective price fixing. Yet there have been few studies in the literature of economics of trade association pricing methods,[1] perhaps reflecting the economist's traditional unconcern with the decision-making process *per se*, and also few attempts to analyse the economic effects of particular pricing methods.[2] An opportunity to study trade association pricing methods arose for the present writer in 1963/4 when he acted on behalf of the trade associations in the wire rope industry in the preparation and hearing of a case under the 1956 Act. It is not the purpose of this paper to present a comprehensive survey of what was a very long and complex restrictive practices case or to evaluate the arguments of the two sides and the judgment of the Court in the light of subsequent events.[3] The intention is rather to examine and analyse the pricing methods themselves. These should be of interest in their own right to any student of the behaviour of business organizations. History they may now be, but they are nonetheless revealing and suggestive of the behaviour of large tracts of British manufacturing industry in the heydey of collective agreements.

THE INDUSTRY AND ITS ASSOCIATIONS

The wire rope industry is mainly concerned with the production of rope from steel wire. The wire for most steel rope is 'patented steel wire' i.e. wire which has undergone the heat treatment process known as patenting, but a small quantity of rope is made from mild steel or stainless steel wire. The core of the rope is generally made of jute, sisal or manila. Wire rope products are conveniently if broadly divided into two groups according to methods of manufacture, locked coil ropes and stranded ropes. Locked coil ropes have

[1] One of the few articles is B. Fog, 'How are Cartel Prices Determined?' *Journal of Industrial Economics*, Vol. 5, 1956/57, pp. 16–23.
[2] The many papers analysing particular Restrictive Practices Court judgments have had a wider purpose and may have touched upon pricing methods indirectly.
[3] The wire rope industry is currently the subject of a reference to the Monopolies Commission.

a limited number of specialized uses as winding ropes in mining shafts, in aerial ropeways and in suspension bridges while stranded ropes serve a wider variety of uses in the mining, engineering and marine industries. Locked coil ropes require more specialized equipment and production skills than stranded rope.

Since 1946, output of locked coil rope had expanded at an average rate of 6 per cent p.a., though only at about two-thirds of that rate in the period after 1959. Output of all stranded rope fell marginally over the period 1959–63 but deliveries of rope to the mining industry fell sharply, by as much as one third. Deliveries of rope for marine purposes remained more-or-less constant while the engineering industries' rope consumption expanded modestly at just under 1 per cent p.a. However, output of engineering ropes grew more steadily over the period 1959–63 than output of locked coil, the other expanding section of the wire rope industry.

After the passing of the 1956 Act, three trade associations operated in the industry, the Locked Coil Ropemakers' Association (L.C.R.A.), the Mining Ropes Association (M.R.A.) and the Wire Rope Manufacturers' Association (W.R.M.A.). In 1963 there were seven manufacturers of locked coil ropes and of these two were members of the British Ropes group, the dominant firm in the industry, accounting for more than 50 per cent of the output of all wire rope and a similar proportion of locked coil. Two other producers were interconnected, one a subsidiary of the other. There were no producers outside the association. The five independent manufacturers of locked coil rope formed a tight-knit oligopoly, the three largest firms producing more than 80 per cent of the industry's output. The main agreement in the L.C.R.A. was to fix the actual prices at which members sold locked coil rope to home users, principally the National Coal Board (N.C.B.),[4] in conjunction with an agreed schedule of extras and agreed terms of sale.

Whereas locked coil rope constitutes a distinctive product type involving distinctive production methods, the distinction between 'mining ropes' covered by the M.R.A. and the stranded ropes covered by the W.R.M.A. is more artificial. The W.R.M.A. was responsible for pricing 'engineering ropes' and special ropes sold to the Admiralty but not 'marine ropes', collective price fixing of which had been abandoned by the time of the case.[5] The creation of the two separate Associations was explicitly designed to improve the industry's

[4] The N.C.B. accounted for over 90 per cent of home deliveries of locked coil rope.

[5] In fact, in 1960, in response to the abandonment of common pricing of fibre rope, The Marine Wire Rope Society was formed to collect and distribute information to its members including information on current prices. British Ropes Ltd., in fact, emerged as price leader on marine ropes.

chances of fighting a successful case under the 1956 Act by means of the argument that an agreement on the price of mining ropes was a necessary defence against the preponderant buying power of the N.C.B. This aspect of the case has been discussed by the writer elsewhere.[6] All that needs to be said here is that membership of the two associations covering stranded ropes was identical and numbered 32 firms. In 1963 there were, however, only 20 active manufacturers in the M.R.A. Six of these companies were in the British Ropes group, including British Ropes Ltd. itself, and there were two other pairs of connected companies. Active producers in the W.R.M.A. in 1963 numbered 25, counting interconnected firms separately. The British Ropes group dominated stranded rope production in 1963, a position built up partly by internal expansion at the expense of smaller producers and partly by an active acquisitions policy in the years after the Second World War. The largest three producers of stranded rope accounted for almost 70 per cent of the associations' output. There was a small number of producers outside the stranded rope associations but they were of negligible importance.

The N.C.B. and the Admiralty were major purchasers of stranded rope, both mainly in specifications designed for their particular needs, but stranded ropes were also used by countless other customers, especially in the engineering trades. The basic agreement within the M.R.A. was on common prices of 'mining ropes' to all home users, principally the N.C.B., and within the W.R.M.A. on common prices of other stranded rope. Ancillary agreements covered extras and discounts, etc. The prices were to be those set out in the relevant association's price list or those calculated according to the associations' agreed procedure. This latter provision is a reminder of the great variety of wire rope specifications that may be demanded and which could not be included in a single price list. Even so, the published price lists of the associations were of almost bewildering complexity. After many pages of detailed instructions on how the price list was to be used, the W.R.M.A. list, for example, included prices for almost 40,000 different sizes, constructions, tensiles and/or qualities of rope.[7] Of course, a manufacturer would not be called upon to produce more than a proportion of these in any period. But a medium-sized maker might easily produce 1000 different sizes and constructions in reasonable quantities in one year.

[6] M. Howe, 'The Restrictive Practices Court and the Definition of the Market', *Manchester School*, Vol. 34, 1966, pp. 41–61.

[7] The price list itself extended over 134 foolscap-size pages. The lists of the other two associations were less voluminous.

TRADE ASSOCIATION PRICING IN WIRE ROPE

As in many industries, trade association price fixing in the wire rope industry dated from the 1930s. Between 1940 and 1953 maximum prices were fixed by the Government, and the industry agreed to regard them also as minimum prices. After decontrol in 1953, the trade associations (at that time the L.C.R.A. and the Federation of Wire Rope Manufacturers) took complete responsibility for price fixing and by the end of the 1950s the price fixing methods that were the subject of the restrictive practices case had evolved. By this time the M.R.A. and the W.R.M.A. had been constituted to take over price fixing from the Federation. The Federation continued in being and circulated various information among its members relating to the trade as a whole and of considerable relevance to its members in their reaction to the operations of the price-fixing associations. Thus the Federation provided information on market shares on a quarterly basis and also on the profitability of a sample[8] of producers also on a quarterly basis. It also dealt with labour relations and wage negotiations on behalf of all manufacturers.

There seem to be three main methods of trade association price fixing. First, there is the method of charging the prices that ruled in some base year adjusted in some fashion to take account of subsequent changes in costs;[9] then the method of negotiation around the table, perhaps with complicated rules on the voting power of members; and finally the fixing of prices in relation to the costs of production of members. The third method is usually used by larger and more formally organized associations. The wire rope associations had by 1963 developed a method of the last type although, as with any trade association pricing, it always included an element of both the other methods.[10] The methods of the three associations were broadly similar and are outlined in the next sections of the paper. The discussion begins with the methods of the W.R.M.A. and there follows a briefer discussion of separate features of the methods of the M.R.A. and the L.C.R.A. The fixing of extras, discounts and other ancillary dimensions of price is not discussed. This is not because these are unimportant. On the contrary, in an industry with wide product variety such as wire rope and in any industry which endeavours to impose a common price on members, these are indeed vital aspects of the price decision. But considerations

[8] The cross sections, see below, p. 240.

[9] The writer knows of a trade association using this method in 1965 where the base year price list dated from the middle of the nineteenth century.

[10] As we shall see, in the wire rope industry there was negotiation with major customers as well as among association members.

of space restrict us to a discussion of what we may term the basic price, unadorned by the extras, allowances and discounts that may ultimately affect the transactions price. Prices were in all cases delivered prices. The associations provided for the exchange of information on such matters as orders received month by month, deliveries and orders on hand. These arrangements are not discussed in this paper.

PRICE FIXING METHODS OF THE WIRE ROPE MANUFACTURERS' ASSOCIATION

The basis of the W.R.M.A. basic price list at the time of the case was costs of selected products collected from a cross-section of 12 member firms. Although only about one-half the total number of active producers, the cross-section represented about 75 per cent of the trade by tonnage in those ropes. Obviously, therefore, the cross-section included most of the larger producers though it did also contain some small manufacturers. There was no explicit criterion for membership of the cross-section. In fact the make-up of the cross-section was largely a legacy of Government price control. There had been some changes of membership since decontrol, some firms being added if they could be expected to have the required cost data or if they wished to participate in the circulation of cost figures among the cross-section, but these changes had been minor and unsystematic. Prices of Admiralty specifications were based on costs submitted by all producers, about half a dozen in all.

In the early years after control costs were collected and prices reconsidered irregularly by the wire rope associations as pressure developed from members for a pricing review. Later a somewhat more formal procedure developed in each association with costs to be submitted to the Secretariate[11] for a price review every six months. For various reasons the six months' rule was not always followed exactly. The labour of collecting costs sometimes meant longer intervals between cost reviews and in the meantime percentage across-the-board adjustments to ruling prices might be made. Indeed changes in costs could, and did, occur after the collection of costs and before the pricing committee's final decisions, a period usually of several weeks. Again across-the-board adjustments were then typically incorporated in the price review to take account of these subsequent cost changes.

The costs collected were average total costs. They were extracted from the cost-accounting systems of members of the cross-section.

[11] A leading firm of chartered accountants. At one time a single office of this firm was acting as Secretary to some 30 common price agreements.

Some submitted historical costs which therefore reflected past conditions on factors such as the rate of output, the number of shifts, rope lengths, resource prices, etc. whereas others submitted standard costs reflecting (those firms') normal operating conditions. In addition the costs submitted reflected the accounting methods and conventions adopted by the individual firms, e.g. on depreciation and overhead allocation. These differences could be expected to produce significant differences in relative product costs submitted by different members of the cross-section. Although the introduction of a uniform costing system had never been seriously considered and would have presented formidable difficulties in an industry with such wide product variety, some more modest steps to increase uniformity were taken over the years. These were largely restricted to standardization of the classification of particular items of expense to the broad cost headings used by the associations.

A feature of the pricing methods of the association was the right of members of the cross-section to submit notional costs if they had produced no output of a particular product in the relevant period. This possibility arose because of the wide product variety and the flexibility of plant and equipment in the production of stranded ropes. The right to submit notional costs was discretionary. No instructions were given on how notional costs should be calculated. Unless a firm had a standard costing system, when standard costs might be submitted, the notional costs would be devised from the costs of similar ropes produced in the period or from costs of the product when last produced.

It should be clear that costs were not collected for every product. Nor could they be. Costs were available for only a tiny proportion of the number of wire rope products known as 'key items'. For the most part these were the bulk produced ropes. There were 40 engineering and 48 special Admiralty key items in all at the time of the case. The costs of these ropes formed the basis of the whole pricing exercise. Product costs for these items were submitted by the cross-section, coded and assembled by the Secretariate under the following headings: material, direct labour, oncosts, carriage, selling expenses (which included administrative expenses) and total cost. Before 1958 the arithmetic average of the (average) total costs submitted was the basic information used in any pricing review although any extremely high costs would sometimes but arbitrarily have been excluded before the average was struck. More recently (from about 1957) a system had been adopted whereby only the six lowest costs received for each key item were averaged. Moreover, if any of the six lowest costs that were averaged turned out to be 10 per cent or more above that average then they also were excluded and the average recomputed. It was this average which formed the basis of most of the W.R.M.A.'s major price reviews in the 1960s until the unfavourable judgment in the restrictive practices case at the end of 1964.

Costs of key items were used as the basis of calculation of costs of other sizes of ropes of the same specification by graphical means. Costs of other types of rope were calculated by adding or subtracting material cost differences or by applying a system of more-or-less historical additions and subtractions to the costs of other rope constructions. In all cases the procedure was arbitrary and was only occasionally checked by cost investigations. Again the variety of products produced made frequent checking impracticable.

Given these costs, the final stage was to apply a target profit margin. In 1963 the target margin on engineering ropes was $16\frac{2}{3}$ per cent on sales or 20 per cent on costs. The magnitude of the target margin was, of course, decided by members by discussion and negotiation in the light of their experience of market conditions facing the industry as well as their individual profit objectives. It is interesting (as a reflection of association thinking) that the margin had been changed from 15 per cent in October 1962 when the members agreed to offer a discount to large buyers which the Secretariate estimated would cost $1\frac{2}{3}$ per cent as an average of all sales.[12]

By these methods a price list was arrived at covering all ropes in regular demand. If a rope was demanded which was not listed it would usually be priced by the Secretariate. The price quoted would be based on the price of the rope of the most similar specification to that demanded, but reflecting any difference in wire costs[13] and including a premium to contribute towards the likely high production costs of a non-standard item. Often the Secretariate would consult with members as to the appropriateness of a price arrived at this way, but in the nature of things no special costing of the specific item was conducted.

THE MINING ROPE ASSOCIATION

Not surprisingly in view of the identical membership and Secretariate and the similarity of the products of the M.R.A. and the W.R.M.A., the M.R.A. used the same basic pricing method. But a special feature of M.R.A. pricing until 1962 had been consultation

[12] The discounts offered were $2\frac{1}{2}$ per cent or 5 per cent depending upon the annual amount of a buyer's *total* purchases of wire rope. Special discounts were granted to the Admiralty.

[13] Wire prices were also fixed by a trade association at this time.

with the N.C.B., a major purchaser of wire ropes and a preponderant buyer of those specifications of stranded rope covered by the M.R.A. and styled 'mining ropes' by the association.[14] Arising from these consultations the industry had agreed to give the N.C.B. (whenever possible) advance warning of price changes, to base its prices and price changes on costs of key items agreed with the N.C.B. and also to be submitted to the N.C.B., and to apply target margins (6½ per cent, 9 per cent and 12½ per cent on sales according to the product) agreed by the N.C.B. It was indeed from these discussions between the National Coal Board and the Federation in the years after decontrol that the 'key item' system emerged for all stranded rope. As with the W.R.M.A., by 1963 the cost base of the pricing procedure had become the average of the six lowest (non-standardized) average costs submitted by members of the (same) cross-section, sometimes including notional costs from non-producers, but excluding any costs which turned out to be 10 per cent or more above the average. Prices of non-costed products were derived from the prices of the key items in similar fashion to the W.R.M.A.

THE LOCKED COIL ROPEMAKERS' ASSOCIATION

The pricing procedure used by this association was similar to that of the M.R.A. and had also involved considerable discussion with the N.C.B., the major user of locked coil rope in the home market. The main difference arose from the small number of producers of locked coil rope. Thus, there was no cross-section. All producers were entitled to submit costs of key items although rarely were as many as six costs received.[15] The lowest six costs received including again any notional costs were averaged but in this association using a weighted average, the weights being members' production of the product in the previous quarter. The other associations used simple averages largely, they asserted, because of the clerical difficulty in collecting production figures for individual stranded ropes. Calculations by the writer showed that the choice of a particular average did not have a systematic effect on prices one way or the other. As in the M.R.A., the target margins had been agreed with the N.C.B. during the consultations that had been a feature of the industry between decontrol in 1953 and 1962. By the time of the case the margin on all locked coil ropes had become 12½ per cent on sales.

[14] After 1962 the N.C.B. discontinued these consultations and proposed to institute a system of centralized competitive tendering for its wire rope needs.

[15] Costs were submitted by individual members whether or not they were members of a group or otherwise inter-connected. The amount of competition allowed between members of the same group is an interesting aspect usually neglected—as it is here!

APPRAISAL OF THE PRICE FIXING METHODS

The Restrictive Practices Court has held that the pricing methods of an association are less important than the results those methods produce: 'we must draw a clear and important distinction between the reasonableness of the prices actually charged by the association and the validity of the methods used to arrive at those prices'.[16] Many economists would agree. But even with all the evidence available in a restrictive practices case, it is extremely difficult to judge how reasonable has been the performance of an industry in terms of the level and flexibility of prices, the level and variability of the costs of the producers, technical progressiveness and the level of profit—and, therefore, upon the presumption of the Act that agreements work against the public interest. The difficulties are not only the absence of ready-made competitive standards against which to judge these various dimensions of performance but even, for some aspects, the lack of an adequate theory, for example on the relation between competition and technical progressiveness. Inevitably, therefore, the price-fixing methods of associations *are* examined, usually microscopically, in restrictive practices cases and inferences about the industry drawn. In the wire rope cases, the associations and the Registrar, and their respective counsel, certainly undertook such an examination. Unusually, however, the Court felt able to reach its final judgment without commenting upon either the pricing methods or the performance of the firms operating them. This was because the industry mainly relied upon the arguments that the agreements were necessary to protect the industry from a preponderant buyer (the N.C.B.) or, for the W.R.M.A., that they contributed substantially to British exports. When these arguments failed so did the case, and the pricing methods became irrelevant to the Court.

Yet the wire rope associations had evolved a pricing system which they considered not only satisfactory to themselves but also fair to consumers. Industry is always strongly of the opinion that, to be fair, prices should be related to producers' costs.[17] This opinion was certainly held by the wire rope associations who argued that their own cost-based procedure was particularly satisfactory with the emphasis it gave in its system of averaging either to the six

[16] *Re Permanent Magnet Association's Agreement*, L.R., 3, R.P., pp. 173–4.

[17] An opinion which the Restrictive Practices Court, the Monopolies Commission, the National Board for Prices and Incomes, various Government Departments in their purchasing and contracting policies, have all from time to time endorsed. Like most associations, the wire rope associations set much store on the fact that the Government had encouraged trade associations in the 1930s and had itself operated a cost-based common pricing system during the war and in the immediate post-war period.

lowest costs received (in the stranded rope associations) or to the costs submitted by the larger producers (in the L.C.R.A.).

Yet in application the methods had obvious weaknesses. One was the small proportion of the total number of products in regular demand that were designated key items and regularly costed for pricing purposes. Another was the lack of standardization of costs. Evidence was produced of correspondence between members of the cross-section and the Secretariate which revealed striking differences in the basis of members' costings. Not only would these differences be reflected in prices but they would also make less meaningful the comparisons of members' costs of the key items which the associations so stressed as a useful by-product of the main price-fixing agreement. Another criticism was of the submission of notional costs by non-producers. Evidence was brought of the lowest cost producer accounting for 100 per cent of output of some ropes and the notional costs pulling up the average used in pricing. The practice of the W.R.M.A. and the M.R.A. of averaging the six lowest costs received would also have been a much more satisfactory feature had steps been taken to control the selection of the cross-section to give some assurance that the cross-section included the more efficient firms. Certainly evidence was brought of various inadequacies (even clerical errors) in the pricing procedure and a number of anomolies in the price structure were identified.

The associations argued that these objections were trivial in relation to the complexity of the price-fixing operation. In one sense the argument had weight, for the huge product variety of the industry made highly detailed and completely accurate product costing an unattainable ideal. Just as in the case of an individual firm facing a highly diverse demand, a trade association must use short cuts and simplifications in its costing and pricing.[18] However, anomalies in the price structure have more effect when that structure is applied collectively and can be altered only formally (assuming members abide by the agreement) and at prescribed intervals. The pricing system is necessarily more rigid than independent price fixing and any resultant distortions in that sense are more important.

With this last point on the greater rigidity of trade association pricing our comment on the application of the price-fixing *methods* is shading into a discussion of the way in which the methods *worked*. As mentioned, it is not our intention here to provide a comprehensive study of the effect of the agreements upon the performance of the wire rope industry but some analysis of the more salient effects is

[18] For some discussion of these issues see M. Howe, 'Competition and the Multiplication of Products', *Yorkshire Bulletin of Economic and Social Research*, Vol. 12, 1960, pp. 57–72.

offered for, as Professor T. Wilson has observed, 'we know little about the extent to which competitive pressure remains effective within a cartel. We have certainly no right to assume that its more efficient and ambitious members will be content with policies designed to leave their less efficient members safe and secure'.[19] This is surely the crucial question about trade association pricing and one upon which the evidence heard in restrictive practices cases can be made to throw some light. In attempting an answer for the wire rope industry, it will be useful, following Jack Downie,[20] to keep in mind two sources of pressure, one short-term pressure arising from the transfer of business from the currently less efficient to the currently more efficient in an industry, the other longer-term pressure arising from differences between firms in the pace of application of innovations. Trade association pricing may affect these two sources of pressure differently.

Any trade association is likely to claim that its pricing methods do not 'featherbed' the less efficient members, even though associations are invariably defensive in origin and outlook and cannot expect to retain members who feel that their interests would be better served outside the agreement.[21] The wire rope associations were no exception. We have commented upon the pricing methods and the way they used the average of the six lowest costs received. In order to appraise this method we need to examine first the variability of the costs of members. Cost variation between the firms in an industry is inevitable for a host of obvious reasons, but, with given technology, the less the variability at any time the more efficient an industry's performance would generally be considered to be. Competition is generally thought likely to reduce the variability in firms' costs. With changing technology, more variability is to be expected. If changes in technology are relatively infrequent, and knowledge of new techniques easily transmitted, we might expect cost variability from technical change to be slight and to diminish over a long enough period. If, on the other hand, technological change is rapid and stochastic considerable variability may be expected and may persist.[22] The effect of competition where cost variation is due to changing technology is less clear. The main source of technical change is organized research and development. Effective research and development activity is a long-run activity and may

[19] T. Wilson, 'A Review of Policies on Monopolies, Mergers and Restrictive Practices' in J. B. Heath (ed.), *International Conference on Monopolies, Mergers and Restrictive Practices* (H.M.S.O., 1969), p. 69.

[20] J. Downie, *The Competitive Process* (Duckworth, 1958).

[21] The arrangements of most associations, including the wire rope associations, were such that it was no easy matter for a dissatisfied member to quit.

[22] Though the identity of the lowest cost firms need not remain the same.

be inhibited by the high risks associated with the more intense forms of short-run competition, particularly in oligopolies.

Ad-hoc evidence in the wire rope case showed considerable variation in costs between different members and products. But the only systematic evidence was provided in a costing exercise as of 30 September 1961 and the basis of one of the six-monthly price reviews.[23] A problem in referring to these data, summarized in Table I, even for a snap-shot picture at that point in time is the lack of standardization of costs in the multi-product context already mentioned. However, assuming that the data are reasonably reliable, we see that on 40 of the 58 engineering ropes listed the highest cost

TABLE I

HIGHEST COST SUBMITTED AS PERCENTAGE OF LOWEST COST SUBMITTED

Percentage	*Engineering Ropes*	*Mining Ropes*	*Locked Coil Ropes*
	No. of items	*No. of items*	*No. of items*
100–109.9	10	1	3
110–119.9	30	15	8
120–129.9	10	3	5
130–139.9	3	11	2
140–149.9	1	4	—
150–and above	4	2	1

submitted was less than 120 per cent of the lowest cost received; in mining this was so on 16 out of 36 ropes and in locked coil on 11 out of 19. The variability was less than found, but condemned, by the Monopolies Commission in a number of its investigations (e.g. fibre cordage, electric cables, linoleum, rubber footwear and electrical machinery). But three points need to be added. First it is possible that the (stranded rope) producers not in the cross-section included the highest cost producers. Second, the observed variability of average costs must be interpreted with the fact in mind that raw material costs, about two-thirds of the total, were virtually uniform between producers, patented wire prices also being fixed by an association (of which several vertically integrated wire rope producers were also members). These two points suggest Table I may give an unduly favourable impression. But there is the third point. With

[23] An attempt was made to reconstruct this exercise after the event as evidence for the Court. Differences between the figures made available to the Court and those said to be used in the pricing committees caused much confusion during the hearing and led to some critical comment by the Court in its final judgment.

the diverse nature of demand for, and hence of output of, wire rope, there is a premium in the industry on flexibility. Some of the industry's plant is specialized in the production of a particular construction of rope especially locked coil and other heavy ropes. But most is flexible; though most efficient in the production of a particular construction, it can be used in the manufacture of a variety of constructions. However, as Stigler pointed out long ago,[24] the price of flexibility is some loss of efficiency, here in the production of constructions other than those for which a firm's plant is best suited.

It is, of course, difficult to assess the effect of the agreements on this observed cost variability. Technical change was not a significant factor, however, certainly for the products included in Table I. The technology of the wire rope industry is traditional, not science based. Innovations have been relatively minor and have been fairly rapidly transmitted among the various producers. An exception was in the production of a particular type of engineering rope, small cords. Here British Ropes Ltd. had effected a major reduction in costs and at September 30th 1961 their costs were between one-half and one-third of the costs of the highest cost producer depending upon the size and construction. The association argued that, over time, this variability would be reduced as other producers were forced to adopt similar cost-reducing methods. This argument depends upon the effects of the agreements upon profitability. Consideration of this aspect of performance will enable us to assess whether or not the agreements protected high-cost producers and discouraged innovation.

We shall look first at individual product profit margins. As with the great majority of individual firms with pricing discretion, we have seen that the wire rope associations arrived at their desired selling prices by applying target profit margins to the average cost. There is nothing objectionable in the procedure. Obviously, however, whatever an association's costing procedures, it can always seek to protect inefficient firms by the addition of a generous profit margin[25] which exploits the association's monopoly power. How effective the protection is will depend on the variability of members' costs and the level of demand forthcoming at the target prices. The target margin of 16⅔ per cent on sales used by the W.R.M.A. certainly appears generous in an industry where something like two-thirds of total cost could be accounted for by raw materials,

[24] G. Stigler, 'Production and Distribution in the Short Run', *Journal of Political Economy*, Vol. 47, 1939, pp. 305–27.
[25] Or by the use of generous extras added to the basic price.

and also in relation to the margins accepted in the other two associations where a major customer's view had to be considered.[26] The association's main justification was the relatively low sales to capital ratio with engineering ropes which are generally made on relatively slow machines and the diversity of demand and the resultant relatively high cost of producing small orders and of stockholding, which were not fully reflected in costs. This latter argument is not wholly convincing. While it is true that the full cost of stockholding is rarely included in cost accounts (which are not kept on an opportunity cost basis), it would be *relative* product costs that would not accurately take account of the cost of producing small orders. It was not the case that *all* engineering ropes were produced in smaller quantities and on slower machines than *all* mining ropes in firms producing both (though this was a general tendency) yet the higher margin applied to all ropes. In fact, since an extra could be charged for small orders of many ropes the association did appear to have been seeking a double compensation for these costs. Certainly the argument pointed to the need to standardize costing methods in the matter of the batch and order sizes to be used in the costs submitted to the Secretariate.

Three target margins were used by the M.R.A. The different margins were designed to take account of differences in handling and distribution costs and of technical services for the customer which, it was argued, were also not accurately reflected in product costs but (like the costs of small orders in the W.R.M.A.), spread over all production. This argument is also itself a criticism of the industry's costing systems though again the wide product variety inevitably restricts the detailed product costing that is possible. A second reason given for differences in the target margins was differences in the rate of turnover of capital. Certain mining ropes are made on faster machines and in larger quantities than the bulk of engineering ropes. But whether the lower target margins of $6\frac{1}{2}$ per cent and 9 per cent on the mining ropes of similar constructions to the W.R.M.A.'s ropes can be wholly explained this way is doubtful. Undoubtedly the lower margins in the M.R.A. were in part the result of N.C.B. pressure and in part the result of the declining demand for ropes from the mining industry.

The target margins of the L.C.R.A. were similar to those on the most comparable ropes of the M.R.A. Again there had been consultation with the N.C.B. on their size and with locked coil ropes the

[26] On more than one occasion the Admiralty had objected to the W.R.M.A. prices of Admiralty specification ropes and had attempted its own investigations of members' costs. These investigations were not very successful, however, and at the end of the day the Admiralty acquiesced in the Association's prices.

margins applied most certainly took account of the very significant buying power of the N.C.B.

Despite the influence of market and buyer pressures upon the choice of target margins, their magnitude was inevitably arbitrary and relatively insensitive to differences in the demand conditions facing individual constructions of rope and in demand conditions at different stages in the business cycle. It is here, once again, that trade association pricing methods begin to diverge from the methods of individual firms with pricing discretion; the one case is a more rigid application than the other. Trade association prices tend to be less flexible in the face of market changes than an individual firm's prices. This is a more severe weakness, the more volatile are those changes. As it happens, demand fluctuations and market changes are of relatively minor significance in the wire rope industry, but nevertheless the associations' methods did prevent any member taking a more flexible approach to the stimulation or exploitation of changes in the pattern of demand. For example, it is doubtful whether pressures upon customers to standardize their orders can be as great under association as under individual firm pricing.[27]

Returning to the protection of the inefficient firms afforded by the price fixing methods, we can refer to the costing exercise already mentioned and used as evidence in the case. Using this exercise, it was possible to calculate the margins that would have been earned on the various costed products before and after the price changes introduced after that review respectively for the lowest cost producer, for the highest cost producer (both among those submitting costs) and for a producer whose costs equalled the average of the costs submitted (not on this occasion the particular average cost used in the pricing exercise, e.g. the average of the six lowest costs). Table II shows the margins implied for such producers by the new selling prices on a selection of the costed ropes.

It can be seen that for each of the product groups the profit margins implied by the new prices for the average cost producer centred around the target margins though the range of implied margins was quite wide. For each group a negative margin was implied for the average cost producer on at least one of the products costed. More significant are the margins for the highest cost producer. On substantial proportions of the costed products the new prices still implied a negative margin for the highest cost producer. For mining (coal cutter) ropes, this was so for 75 per cent of the products. Now we have already stated that with the wide product variety of wire rope producers and the lack of standardization of

[27] See Howe, *Yorkshire Bulletin*, *op. cit.*

costing methods, there was inevitably arbitrariness in the submitted relative product costs. But even accepting some limitations in the costs, it is quite clear that the common prices determined in this 1961 price review did not entirely insulate the less efficient firms from competitive pressures. Yet, despite Professor Wilson's comment that we have 'no right' to assume that cartel arrangements leave the 'less efficient members safe and secure',[28] this assumption is in fact commonly held among economists. The evidence in this case showed that the agreements left marginal producers under considerable pressure to reduce their costs or, in the long run, see their business transferred to their more efficient competitors. Certainly, the price level was insufficiently high to give them any scope for expansion.

TABLE II

PROFIT MARGINS IMPLIED BY NEW PRICES OF SELECTED ROPES

(a) Engineering Ropes (target margin 15%)
(b) Mining Ropes (coal cutter ropes, target margin 9%
(c) Locked Coil Ropes (winding ropes, target margin 12½%)

Size of margin (% of selling price)	*Number of Cases* *Ave. Cost* *a.*	*b.*	*c.*	*Highest Cost* *a.*	*b.*	*c.*	*Lowest Cost* *a.*	*b.*	*c.*
less than 0	2	1	1	14	9	3	—	—	—
0–4.9	1	5	1	6	3	—	—	—	—
5–9.9	8	4	1	24	—	3	—	—	—
10–14.9	34	2	2	11	—	1	1	4	—
15–19.9	11	—	2	2	—	—	33	6	1
20–24.9	1	—	—	—	—	—	17	2	2
25 and above	—	—	—	—	—	—	6	—	4

Of course we must ask whether the pressure would not have been greater without the agreement. This depends upon what would have happened to prices and that depends upon a complex of factors including the reaction of the low cost firms.[29] The consensus that emerged during the case on this question was that, first, locked coil prices were in general unlikely to be lower without the agreement. This view was based upon the tightly oligopolistic structure of the selling side of the market and the predominance of the N.C.B. on the buying side, a balance strengthened by the modest long-term growth of demand for locked coil ropes. On stranded ropes the view was less clear cut. There were significantly more producers of stranded than locked coil rope although British Ropes Ltd. accounted

[28] Wilson, *op. cit.*

[29] And also including the reaction of major buyers. The National Coal Board proposed to substitute centralized competitive tendering for its current policy of Divisional and Area buying. The likely effects of this change were a major issue in the case but it is not discussed in this paper.

for more than half the output and, it was generally accepted, would operate as price leader if there were no agreements. But, of course, there is a variety of styles of leadership. It did not seem likely that British Ropes would immediately adopt a highly aggressive role. Markham's observation that the origins of the leadership role 'must be found in the historical background of an industry and the institutional and other features that have helped to shape its development'[30] seemed apt, for this industry was most unlikely immediately to throw off the effects of its long history of co-operation. The consensus was that prices of engineering ropes would probably not in general be less, bearing in mind again the modest upward trend in demand for these ropes. Consequently, on these two classes of rope the evidence seemed to suggest that the transfer of business and resources from the less efficient to the more efficient producers would not be much different without as with the agreements since it seemed unlikely that the price leader or any other low-cost firm would want to see prices fall below the level that had prevailed with the agreement. Of course there probably would be some price differences in an industry with such product variety and scope for price discrimination. But the general level was not expected to be very different.

The sector where this view was not held was mining ropes. Demand for mining ropes had been and was declining. Evidence was brought of substantial and persistent excess capacity in the industry, by no means evenly distributed over the various producers and concentrated particularly among those firms concentrating on these types of rope and particularly among the smaller producers. There seems no doubt that the agreement served to keep prices of these ropes above the level that would have prevailed under competition even with short-run competition to some extent restricted by the emergence of a price leader. It follows that the elimination of excess capacity by the absorption of the less efficient by the more efficient producers was here probably slowed down. True, wire rope plant is specialized and long-lived and it is unlikely that the adjustment of capacity to declining demand would have been accomplished rapidly had the agreements not existed. It is also the case that several firms, particularly British Ropes Ltd., had initiated rationalization programmes and closed some surplus capacity with the agreements in force. But that the process would have been faster without the agreements is suggested by the more rapid rate of rationalization since their abrogation.

[30] J. W. Markham, 'The Nature and Significance of Price Leadership', *American Economic Review*, Vol. 41, 1951, p. 896.

Information provided in the case on the overall profitability of wire rope producers also suggests a state of disequilibrium in (at least sections of) the industry. As in most monopoly investigations, very considerable effort and argument was expended by both sides in the case over estimates of the profits earned by the wire rope makers and comparisons with industry generally.[31] Table III gives a summary of the data used in the case, profitability being measured as the return on balance sheet capital employed. Unfortunately data could not be produced for the products of the three separate associations. The industry argued effectively that the average profitability of the industry did not differ significantly from the average of manufacturing industry, and also that the trend of profitability had been downwards over the recession years 1960–62 but we have

TABLE III

PROFIT ON CAPITAL EMPLOYED OF A CROSS-SECTION OF WIRE ROPE MAKERS, 1956–62

	Lowest	*Average*	*Highest*
1956	n.a.	15.17	n a
1957	n.a.	13.46	n.a.
1958	n.a.	10.89	n.a.
1959	n.a.	10.05	n.a.
1960	5.47	16.72	43.80
1961	1.57	14.56	45.62
1962	−8.30	9.69	34.02

Note: Pre- and post-1960 figures not exactly comparable.

already mentioned that the Court did not feel obliged to comment upon this argument. The notable feature of Table III, however, is the wide range of profitability. There can be no doubt that even had the agreements been allowed to continue some high cost, low profitability producers would have been eliminated in the relative short term.

Their rapidly deteriorating profitability over the years 1960–62 is striking. Without the agreements, this process of adjustment would probably have been significantly faster only in the case of ropes for mining purposes. In this section it seems likely that there would

[31] In the wire rope case, as no doubt in others, both sides appointed professional accountants to collect the necessary information in an agreed form from members of the association. For an interesting discussion of the problems, see C. K. Rowley, 'The Monopolies Commission and the Rate of Return on Capital', *Economic Journal*, Vol. 79, 1969, pp. 42–65, a critique by A. Sutherland, *Economic Journal*, Vol. 81, 1971, pp. 264–72 and Rowley's reply, *Ibid.*, pp. 602–8, and a further interchange, *Economic Journal*, Vol. 82, 1972, pp. 702–5.

have been a more rapid movement to a more concentrated structure and less variation in both the costs and profitability of remaining producers.

Finally, we must refer to the high rate of profit earned by the most profitable firms in the cross-section providing the data for Table III and the high profit margins in Table II earned by the lowest cost producers at the common selling prices fixed in the 1961 pricing exercise. We have already mentioned that the wire rope industry was not, and is not, an industry of rapid or spectacular technical change. It could be argued that these comfortable profits made under the agreement would reduce the incentive for the more efficient firms to reduce their costs still further, a possibility reinforced by the price fixing method which would deny any low cost firm which further reduced its costs the full advantage in the price of that cost reduction. On this argument a price fixing agreement reduces the pace of innovation and blunts this important source of long-run competitive pressure. On the other hand, it can be argued that the prevention of short-run price competition with its attendant risks provides a superior climate for organized research and development and further that common prices divert the energies of the more efficient firms into methods of reducing costs as the main way open to them for increasing their profits and providing the wherewithal for further expansion. It can also be added that a pricing agreement based on six-monthly costing reviews gives other firms time themselves to adopt any innovation, a possibility increased by any arrangements to share technical information among members of the association. A verdict on these conflicting arguments is difficult. On balance it seems detrimental that any innovator should be denied by a price agreement the opportunity to exploit his innovation how he chooses, including by a price reduction of any amount he favours. In the wire rope case, however, these arguments did not become crucial, and the evidence suggested that the agreements had had little detrimental effect upon innovation and long-run competition and that termination of the agreements was unlikely to generate competitive conditions prejudicial to effective technical development. The associations indeed argued that the effects of the agreements were positively beneficial by dint of the exchange of cost and technical information and the encouragement of visits among members' factories. But these arguments were hardly convincing.

CONCLUSION

We have listed a significant number of criticisms of the pricing methods of the wire rope associations. Several of these criticisms must be muted, however. It is surely unfair to criticize a trade association for procedures which are commonly employed by individual firms with pricing discretion. In industries producing a wide variety of products some arbitrariness in product costing and in the choice of target profit margins is inevitable. It is simply impossible to cost and price every item uniquely. Trade associations should not be judged against the standard of pricing methods which no real-world business could operate. Attacks on associations in the Restrictive Practices Court have sometimes been unjustified on this point, especially in industries with a complex product structure like wire rope. However, when an association attempts to fix a price in advance for as many as 40,000 products, many of which are manufactured in common production facilities, and when the cost data it uses are far from standardized, there is bound to be additional arbitrariness to that which any individual wire rope producer would perforce have to accept. Moreover, the system of price fixing, six-monthly cost reviews, cost averaging, comparison by a pricing committee of actual and target margins and adjustment where indicated, was inevitably time-consuming. A major objection to the associations' pricing agreement was therefore not that the prices were based on costs of key items only, or that notional costs could be submitted, or what not, but that the system was excessively rigid. Arbitrariness and anomalies tended to be perpetuated by the overly mechanical cost-based plus extras procedure. An individual firm would no doubt build up its prices from costs: almost all do. And an individual firm would hope to be able to fix a price in relation to costs which it could expect to maintain over the long run irrespective of minor changes in market or cost conditions: again almost every firm takes a long-run view in price fixing. But the individual firm's prices would certainly be more flexible in the face of major technical and market changes than the prices fixed by a trade association, first with respect to changes in extras and allowances applied to the basic prices and second, if and when necessary, with respect to changes in the basic prices themselves.

We have also referred to some of the evidence produced in the case on such aspects of the industry's performance as variability of producers' costs, profit margins and overall profitability. Bearing in mind that the wire rope industry is not one where technical change is particularly rapid or spectacular, we have seen that the agreements did not appear to have unduly protected less efficient members except perhaps in the mining rope section where most of the persistent excess capacity was concentrated. In the other sections it seemed unlikely that abrogation of the agreements would have made much difference to the working of short-run competition because of the oligopolistic structure of the industry. On the working of long-run competition the verdict is less clear. It certainly seems that, contrary to the associations' arguments, innovation was not encouraged by the agreements. Whether they discouraged the more innovative members or merely were neutral in effect is more debateable.

We mentioned that in this case the Restrictive Practices Court did not have to pass a judgement on the pricing methods themselves. During the hearing the methods themselves came in for much criticism. But if we follow the dictum of the Court quoted in the article and consider the reasonableness of the results rather than the methods themselves, our conclusion is that the detriments arising from the wire rope industry's arrangements were of a minor character. What cannot be said, however, is that the arrangements bestowed substantial benefits upon the consumers of wire rope. And that, of course, is the rub of the 1956 Restrictive Trade Practices Act.

UNIVERSITY OF SHEFFIELD

THE STRUCTURE OF LINER CONFERENCE RATES

by Trevor D. Heaver

INTRODUCTION

This paper describes the findings of research* into the structure of shipping conference tariffs, that is, the general factors which account for the differences between rates on commodities in a tariff. The results support the contention that the actions of shipper organizations can be important determinants of the structure. This is to be expected because of the imperfect nature of the liner market and the influence which may be exerted by 'purchasers associations'.[1]

The practices of the conferences have been described frequently, but the bases on which the conferences have set rates have remained obscure.[2] The lack of determinatiness about the bases for rates is surprising. Certainly, very many factors may affect the level of individual rates, but it is likely that only a limited number of these factors are generally important. If this is the case it seems reasonable to expect that these general factors would be evident in the relationship between the rates in a tariff. This expectation is enhanced by the centralized nature of the rate making process.

On most trade routes conferences have dealt with shippers who have been unorganized. It is only relatively recently that shippers have been organized into associations or shippers' councils.[3] Consequently, the structure of conference tariffs has been determined essentially by the conferences acting as discriminatory monopolists. Today, commodity based associations exert some influence on individual rates and it is evident that strong shippers' councils can have a short run influence, at least, on the general level of rates.[4] However, on most trade routes the shipping conferences have

* The research has been carried out with the assistance of a grant from The Transportation Centre, University of British Columbia.

[1] A. C. Pigou, *The Economics of Welfare*, London: Macmillan, 4th ed. 1962, Chapter XIX, pp. 319–28.

[2] D. Marx, *International Shipping Cartels, A Study of Industrial Self-Regulation by Shipping Conferences*. Princeton, N. J. Princeton Univ. Press. 1958, p. 23; S. G. Sturmey 'Economics and International Liner Services', *Journal of Transport Economics and Policy*, Vol. 1, No. 2 (May, 1967), p. 193; *Committee of Inquiry into Shipping*, Report presented to Parliament by the President of the Board of Trade, London, H.M.S.O., 1970, p. 119.

[3] See especially, United Nations Conference on Trade and Development, *Consultation in Shipping*, mimeographed, TD/B/C.4/78, Dec. 1970.

[4] Recent years have seen several conferences increase rates by less than the amounts originally proposed after significant struggles with shipper organizations. See, for example, 'Dispute over Tariff Rate Increase Finally Settled', *Zosen* (Jan. 1971), p. 6.

been the dominant organization able to determine the discriminatory structure of the tariff.

RATE MAKING FACTORS

The tariffs which have been selected for analysis are those on the routes between the Pacific Coast of North America and Japan and Australia. These countries were selected because they dominate the liner routes between the Pacific Coast of North America and the Far East and Australasia.[5] Consequently, the trade conditions on the routes are clearly reflected in the published national trade statistics. The rates on these routes are related by linear multiple regression analysis to four independent variables; they are, the stowage factor, the value per ton, the total quantity shipped a year and, in the case of the Australian trade, the requirement of refrigerated stowage. The form of the regression model is as follows:

$$X_1 = b_1X_2 + b_2X_3 + b_3X_4 + b_4X_5 + b_5X_6$$

where X_1 is the freight rate per ton of each commodity on a leg of a route in dollars.
X_2 is the stowage factor for each commodity expressed in cubic feet per long ton.
X_3 is the f.o.b. value per long ton in dollars for each commodity.
X_4 is the total f.o.b. trade value in dollars for each commodity in one direction on a route.
X_5 is the requirement of a commodity for refrigerated space (dummy variable).
X_6 is the constant.

For each leg of the routes a sample was obtained from the conference tariffs of items for which the trade is specified in the U.S. Department of Commerce Waterborne Trade Statistics, 1968. The rates recorded were the contract rates and these, like the other data, were converted where necessary to a long-ton basis. The value per ton and the total value traded were obtained from the trade statistics. This implies that the value per ton recorded for U.S. trade is similar to that for the west coast and the quantity traded nationally is pertinent to rate making for the continent's west coast trade. The stowage factor of cargo was estimated with the assistance of shipping agents. The system required matching items described in the tariff with those described in the trade statistics, hardly the best way to obtain a random sample. However,

[5] T. D. Heaver, 'Trans-Pacific Trade, Liner Shipping and Conference Rates', *Logistics and Transportation Review*, Spring, 1972.

a wide cross-section of items actually traded was obtained for each route. The commodity characteristics selected are generally recognized as being significant in rate making.

RESEARCH RESULTS

The regression results are shown in Tables I and II.

TABLE I

MULTIPLE REGRESSION EQUATION FOR TRANS-PACIFIC CONFERENCE RATES

Route	Samp. Size	Constant $ per Long Ton	Coefficients of Variables per Long Ton: $ per cu. ft. a Ton	$ per $100 value a Ton	$ per million $ Trade	R^2
Japan to Pac. coast	39	−9.14 *(1.4)	1.04 (13.4)	0.86 (10.7)	−0.19 (3.0)	0.92
Pac. coast to Japan	36	17.66 (2.1)	1.00 (7.8)	0.51 (5.5)	−0.93 (2.5)	0.83
Pac. coast to Aust.	34	4.81 (0.43)	1.21 (9.3)	1.34 (3.7)	—	0.75

* Figures in parentheses are *t*-statistics.

TABLE II

PARTIAL CORRELATION COEFFICIENTS OF THE INDEPENDENT VARIABLES IN TABLE I

Route	Stowage Factor	Value per Long Ton	Value of Total Trade
Japan to Pac. coast	0.91	0.87	0.46
Pac. coast to Japan	0.82	0.72	0.39
Pac. coast to Australia	0.86	0.56	—

Between 75 and 92 per cent of the variation between the rates has been explained. From Table I it is difficult to compare the relative importance of the independent variables; Table II gives the partial correlation coefficients to provide a comparative basis. The most important single factor in explaining the rates is the stowage factor. The single demand orientated factor, value per ton, is very important, but it is not dominant. In both the eastbound and westbound tariffs with Japan the total value of the trade is significant, suggesting that bargaining is important. Eastbound the bargaining position of large shippers is no doubt enhanced by the presence of tramps sailing east in ballast. Westbound large shippers may be aided by the shortage of general cargoes; the shortage is such that liners often take on open rated low value cargoes. On the Australian route it is not surprising that total value traded is not significant as tramp competition is not common, the liner trade is closely balanced and few items in the sample traded in a very large volume.

These results are generally consistent with the evidence available from other studies. A study of the structure of freight rates outbound from Latin American countries found considerable variation between tariff structures, but found that 'in the majority of cases the stowage factor accounts for most of the differences'.[6] A comparable study carried out into the ocean freight rates of south-east Asia came to a

TABLE III

REGRESSION RESULTS, AUSTRALIA TO THE PACIFIC COAST OF NORTH AMERICA*

Sample Size	Constant $ per Long Ton	Coefficients of Variables per Long Ton: $ per cu. ft. a Ton	$ per $100 Value a Ton	$ per Million $ Trade	Refrigeration	R^2
28	9.26	0.95	0.71	—	32.83	0.77
	†(1.1)	(7.6)	(1.6)		(2.0)	
		Partial Correlation Coefficients				
		0.84	0.30		0.40	

* The significance of this analysis is less clear than for the other trans-Pacific tariffs; the coefficient for value is not significant at the 10 per cent level; significant inter-correlation (0.58) between total trade value and refrigeration makes the coefficients obtained for refrigeration of uncertain validity.

† Figures in parentheses are *t*-statistics.

similar conclusion.[7] Both studies examined the export rates from several countries. These countries were often a small part of a trade route so that it is particularly difficult to interpret the results which do not follow the general pattern. The peculiarities may be associated with some special features of the route segment which are not identifiable or, as always, they may be due to some chance feature of the data.

However, two routes on which the rate structure appears to differ are particularly interesting. The first is Australia northbound to the Pacific Coast of North America. The regression result for this route is shown in Table III.

The main factors explaining rates are the stowage factor and

[6] Economic Commission for Latin America, *Maritime Freight Rates in the Foreign Trade of Latin America*, E/CN.12/812, October, 1969, p. 117.

[7] Arthur D. Little Inc., 'A Study of Ocean Freight Rates', Technical Appendix in *Southeast Asian Regional Transport Survey*, undated, pp. 30–35.

the refrigerated stowage requirement of perishable cargoes; the latter is a special phenomenon. The route, therefore, is peculiar because of the unique dependence which is placed on the stowage factor.[8] The explanation for this appears to lie in the effective action of Australian shippers 'to pare freight charges to a minimum'.[9] The general strength of the Australian shippers is derived from their basis in commodity boards, the effective backing of the Government and the existence of an Australian shipping line. Australia is one of the few countries that has successfully negotiated freight rates on a cost-plus basis.[10] The countervailing power of the shippers appears to have influenced not only the level of rates but also the basis for differential pricing. While the numeric relationship of costs and rates is not known to the writer, it is apparent that indirect costs and profit are covered in a 'mark-up' beyond, but largely proportional with direct cost and hence related to the stowage factor. Whether this is the best way to practice discriminatory pricing is debatable.[11]

The second route worthy of special attention is the north-bound route between Morocco and France studied by the United Nations Conference on Trade & Development (UNCTAD).[12] On this route the Moroccan Office de Commercialisation et d'Exportation (O.C.E.) sets freight rates on fruit and vegetables after discussions with individual shipping companies. The companies which serve this trade make considerable use of ships chartered seasonally and the lines include the Compagnie Morocaine de Navigation, which is controlled by the Moroccan State. The conference, Comité de Liaison France/Maroc, sets freight rates on other commodities, but it is a weak conference, apparently because of competition from tramps and outside lines.

[8] The equation is changed little by the elimination of the refrigerated items; the regression equation is then:

$$\underset{}{\$8.51} + \underset{(7.4)}{0.96c} + \underset{(1.5)}{0.70v}$$
$$R^2 = 0.75$$

Where c is the stowage factor in cubic feet per long ton, v is the value per long ton in hundreds of dollars.

[9] P. E. Stonham, 'The Demand for Overseas Shipping in the Australian Export Trade', *Journal of Transport Economics and Policy*, Vol. 3, No. 3 (Sept. 1969), p. 345.

[10] D. Marx, 'Regulation of International Liner Shipping and Freedom of the Seas', *Journal of Industrial Economics*, Vol. XVI, No. 1 (November, 1967), p. 47.

[11] For a discussion of discrimination in ocean freight rates see United Nations Conference on Trade and Development, *Level and Structure of Freight Rates, Conference Practices and the Adequacy of Shipping Services*. New York: United Nations, 1969, Chapter X, pp. 87–95.

[12] United Nations Conference on Trade and Development, *Level and Structure of Freight Rates, Route Study: The Liner Trades between France and Morocco*. TD/B/C.4/61, January, 1970, mimeographed.

The statistical analysis by UNCTAD did not attempt multiple regression analysis nor was any allowance made for the presence of refrigerated items. Since rates on the latter exceed normally stowed items by a considerable amount it is not surprising that no meaningful results were obtained. Re-examination of the UNCTAD data by multiple regression analysis and allowing for the refrigeration factor as a dummy variable yields the following result.

REGRESSION EQUATION FOR MOROCCO TO FRANCE*

Sample Size	*Constant French Francs per Metric Ton*	*Refrigerated Stowage French Francs per Metric Ton*	*Value per Ton French Francs per 100 Francs Value per Metric Ton*	R^2
28	87.00 †(11.1)	85.12 (6.3)	1.02 (2.8)	0.64

* The sample used here includes only items on which OCE sets the rates, but excludes the products for which only the average of normal and refrigerated stowage rates were used in the UNCTAD publication.

† Figures in parentheses are *t*-statistics.

The level of explanation of the rates is significant but not high, especially since the major variation between rates is accounted for by the requirement of refrigerated stowage; the effect is obvious without statistical analysis. The value per ton is also significant although its impact on rate levels is small; excluding the refrigerated items the equation is 86.56 Fr. francs plus 1.05 francs per 100 francs value per metric ton, R^2, 0.22. The stowage factor is not statistically significant and has a negative coefficient which is contrary to expectation. The low level of explanation excluding the refrigerated items may well arise from the relatively narrow range of rates. However, the conclusion of the UNCTAD research, and supported by these regression results, is that the OCE relies heavily on an average total cost per ton in setting rates. It appears that the value of the items is of some significance, but most of the variation between rates is unaccounted for.

Thus on both routes on which shipper organization is strong it appears that cost factors are particularly significant in explaining rates. However, while on the Australian route rates appear to be largely proportional with direct costs, as measured by the stowage factor, on the Moroccan route rates appear to be based on an average cost per ton. Whether these structures are in the interest of shippers and shipping lines depends on the relationship between the rates and direct and indirect costs. These relationships are not known to the writer.

CONCLUSIONS AND RESEARCH IMPLICATIONS

The most significant conclusions arising from the research into conference tariffs are that a systematic structure does generally underlie the rates in a tariff and that within this structure the stowage factor is the most important element. The importance of the stowage factor is attributable to its positive relationship with cargo loading and discharging costs and its importance to the utilization of vessel weight and cubic capacities. Conference rates, therefore, rather than being set on the basis of 'what the traffic will bear', accident and chance, are set in a system in which a cost factor is a fundamental part of the rationale.

The value of cargo is also significant in the rate structure which presumably does reflect the importance of charging 'what the traffic will bear'. Charging on such a basis may be both a profitable and economically efficient way for the conference line to cover their indirect costs and earn a profit. The significance of the bargaining position of some shippers is also substantiated in the trade route with Japan although it has not been statistically evident in the other routes. This may be the result of the imbalanced cargo characteristics on the Japanese route, the characteristics of the sample, or other factors.

Knowledge that a fundamental structure does underlie conference tariffs leads to a number of questions. Firstly, is there any consistent pattern between the structure of the rates and the conditions on the trade routes. For example, on routes with an imbalance of general cargo, is the stowage factor of less importance on the low cargo leg because the opportunity cost of ship space is less? To be able to answer such questions requires the examination of rate structures in relation to trade conditions for more routes than has been possible in this research.

Secondly, if rate making policies are discernible how can these be fitted into a general theory of liner shipping economics. Sturmey was unsuccessful in explaining liner practices in terms of a profit maximizing theory,[13] a result consistent with the low return on investment for which liner companies are noted! An alternate hypothesis is that the liner firms conform to Baumol's maximum sales model,[14] a hypothesis which would explain the low profits in an industry without substantial economies of scale but practicing price discrimination. This hypothesis would also be consistent with the

[13] Sturmey, *op. cit.*
[14] W. J. Baumol, *Business Behaviour, Value and Growth.* New York: Harcourt, Brace and World, Revised Edition, 1967.

frequently stated objective of conferences to 'promote' commerce and to be 'fair' to both shippers and shipping lines.

A third issue which arises from the recognition of a rational pattern within existing tariffs is whether it is in the interest of the shipping lines to preserve this structure. The rapid changes in vessel and cargo handling technology as well as the various increases in ship operating and capital costs require changes in conference rates. But what should these changes be and how should they be introduced? The most common means of change is a percentage increase with variations from the general pattern for a limited number of commodities which can resist the upward pressure effectively. In spite, then, of discussions of FAK rates (Freight All Kind) and other radical departures, the new rates are simply projections forward in time and upward in level of a rate structure which is decades old. With limited exceptions, the rates now charged for cargo carried through container systems by new high cubic container vessels reflect cargo handling and space cost factors of an earlier technology. It seems logical to conclude, therefore, that the shipping lines and conferences must review the basis of their rate structure.

Pressure for a rationalization of the rate structure also comes from a number of government and shipper organizations. The claims of unjust discrimination in liner freight rates may or may not be justified, but they should result in a closer examination of the bases on which rates are set. It appears appropriate for shipping lines concerned with the profitability of rates and routes, and those concerned with the equity of rates, to give more attention to the bases on which rates are set than to the comparison of rates on heterogeneous commodities transported under quite different route conditions. Some evidence has been presented in this paper that where shipper organizations are strong cost considerations appear to be particularly significant in rate making. If shipper organizations are to exert an increasing influence on the development of the rate structure, what policy should they espouse. No pricing policy is likely to be perceived as fair by all shippers, but a structure with cost as an explicit base and allowing some value of service pricing is likely to be both the most efficient and acceptable to shippers and carriers. Such an explicit system could benefit shipping lines by preventing rates on some items being set below costs either unwittingly or because of political pressures.

Rate making could not be reduced to a precise science because so many factors, many of them immeasurable, do affect the rates to be charged. However, tariffs currently evidence a basic rationale and more attention to the cost structure of liner operations might lead to more profitable liner operations and fewer charges of unreasonableness.

UNIVERSITY OF BRITISH COLUMBIA

UNITED STATES OIL IMPORT QUOTAS AND THE PRICE OF FOREIGN OIL

by G. HEITMANN

IN 1969, an economic analysis of the oil import program was commissioned by the Energy Policy Staff of the Executive Office of the President. The report, prepared by Charles River Associates (CRA) of Cambridge, Massachusetts, was subsequently submitted to the Cabinet Task Force on Oil Import Control and, upon its release, generated a storm of controversy. More recently, the two principal authors of the CRA study, James C. Burrows and Thomas A. Domencich, have published a book, *An Analysis of the United States Oil Import Quota*,[1] based on the earlier report. The authors reaffirm the 'remarkable conclusion that a group of oil producing countries would bring about a cut in world crude prices if U.S. import controls were ended'.[2] This conclusion has been emotionally challenged, but not analytically refuted. Because the report was highly influential in the Cabinet Task Force's reevaluation of national oil policies, a critical examination of the CRA analysis is of interest and importance.

In Part I, the argument offered by Burrows and Domencich is briefly summarized. Part II demonstrates that the authors' technical discussion of demand elasticities, upon which their price conclusions are based, is of doubtful validity.

I

The analysis underlying the conclusion that it would be advantageous for the OPEC nations[3] to lower crude oil prices has been conveniently summarized as follows:

> (1) The demand curve facing a dominant group of producers following a coordinated policy slopes downward: at a lower price more oil will be purchased from the group of producers. If such a demand curve shifts to the right (*i.e., more is demanded at any given price*), and if the marginal costs of production are constant, then the group of producers will find it profitable to

[1] James C. Burrows and Thomas A. Domencich, *An Analysis of the United States Oil Import Quota*, Lexington, Massachusetts: D. C. Heath and Company, 1970.

[2] The statement is attributed to Standard Oil of New Jersey. See 'Industry Blasts Charles River Report', *Oil and Gas Journal*, August 25th, 1969, p. 59.

[3] The Organization of the Petroleum Exporting Countries (OPEC) consists of the major oil exporting nations, viz., Abu Dhabi, Algeria, Indonesia, Iran, Iraq, Kuwait, Libyan Arab Republic, Nigeria, Qatar, Saudi Arabia, and Venezuela. Production in the member nations accounts for over 85 per cent of the world's oil exports.

raise the price only if, at the original price, the new demand curve is less elastic than the original demand curve.

(2) In the case of OPEC, the elasticity of the new demand curve at the original price would be a weighted average of the U.S. demand elasticity for imports and the rest-of-the-world demand elasticity for oil (for simplicity, 'rest-of-world' is shortened to 'European' in the following).

(3) Except under unreasonable assumptions, the U.S. elasticity of demand for imports is greater than the European demand elasticity. Therefore, by step (2) the new demand curve that would face OPEC is more elastic than the old (European) demand elasticity. It then follows from step (1) that OPEC would not find it profitable to raise taxes (and price) (emphasis added).[4]

World demand for foreign oil, Q, is given as the sum of U.S. and European demands, q_1 and q_2, respectively. The U.S. demand component, a demand for imports, is defined residually as the difference between domestic oil consumption, Q_D, and domestic supply, Q_s. The elasticity of demand for foreign oil, E, is taken as a weighted average of the U.S. demand elasticity for imports, E_1, and the elasticity of European demand, E_2. Specifically, we have

$$E = \frac{q_1}{Q}E_1 + \frac{q_2}{Q}E_2 = \frac{q_1}{Q}\left(\frac{Q_D}{q_1}E_D - \frac{Q_s}{q_1}E_s\right) + \frac{q_2}{Q}E_2$$

where E_D and E_s are the (total) U.S. demand and supply elasticities, respectively.

The elasticity of supply, E_s, and the elasticity coefficients, Q_D/q_1 and Q_s/q_1, are all positive, and thus we can conclude that E_1, the elasticity of demand for imports, is 'greater' (i.e., more negative) than E_D, the elasticity of total domestic demand. Employing 1967 import statistics, and accepting the predictive speculation that foreign oil, in the absence of import restrictions, would capture about 50 per cent of the domestic market, it can be conservatively concluded that E_1 will have a value from 2 to 5 times greater than E_D.

U.S. and European demand elasticities, E_D and E_2, respectively, are weighted averages of individual component product demand elasticities. The patterns of petroleum end uses in the United States and Europe differ substantially, and, in particular, the relative demand for highly inelastic fuels (gasoline and jet fuels) is much greater in the U.S. market. Thus E_D with its more highly weighted

[4] Burrows and Domencich, *op. cit.*, p. 100.

lower elasticity items should be exceeded by E_2. However, as Burrows and Domencich state:

> It can be shown . . . *that if the elasticity of demand for each individual product is the same in the United States and Europe at the current world market price*, even under the most extreme assumptions, the European demand elasticity can be no more than 60 percent larger than the U.S. consumption demand elasticity (emphasis added).[5]

That is, $E_2/E_D \leqslant 1.6$. Add to this the finding that E_1 exceeds E_D by 2 to 5 times, and we must conclude that E_2 cannot be larger than E_1. But this implies, assuming that a rational policy can and will be implemented, that the appropriate OPEC response to a relaxation of U.S. import restrictions would be to lower world oil prices.

II

The above stated conclusion depends firstly on the empirical finding that $E_2/E_D \leq 1.6$. We shall show that this numerical result is based on some doubtful analytical assumptions. Secondly, and more fundamentally, the analysis depends on the appropriateness of the authors' elasticity argument. We shall show that the analysis, while formally correct, is empirically improbable.

Having concluded that $E_2/E_D \leqslant 1.6$, the authors admit that

> . . . it might be argued that the elasticity of demand for each individual product is greater in Europe than in the United States. *However, there is no empirical evidence to support this view and there are no obvious qualitative reasons why this should be so* (emphasis added).[6]

The assumption of equal product elasticities in both markets would appear neutral and intuitively reasonable. However, there are good theoretical reasons for rejecting this seemingly innocuous assumption.

Consider a demand schedule given by

$$x = f(p,y)$$

where x is the quantity demanded, p is price and y is some parameter, say, income. In Figure 1, we have shown a typical demand schedule d_0 associated with the income level y_0. At any price, say p_0, the elasticity of demand is given by the ratio Op_0/p_0A. A parameter change can be expected to result in a positional shift of the demand schedule. Thus, for example, the schedule d_1 might be associated with the

[5] Burrows and Domencich, *op. cit.*, p. 106.
[6] *Ibid.*, p. 100.

income level $y_1 > y_0$. At price p_0, the elasticity of demand on schedule d_1 is given by Op_0/p_0B. Clearly, the elasticities of demand at the same price p_0 are different on schedules d_0 and d_1.

Unless all relevant parameters, such as income levels, are the same in the American and European markets, the assumption of equal elasticities in both markets is inappropriate. In fact, only considering the income parameter, there are valid reasons for assuming that the U.S. demand schedule would be more inelastic at any price than its European counterpart. (Note, the elasticity of demand at p_0 is greater on d_0 than on d_1.) If the demand parameters in the United States market are such that the domestic demand schedule is everywhere to the right of the European demand schedule for oil, then it is likely[7] that demand is more inelastic in the domestic market. The

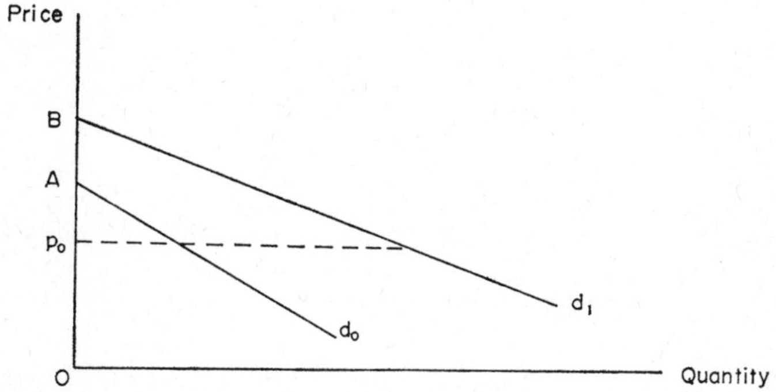

FIGURE 1

equal elasticities assumption of Burrows and Domencich is not, therefore, neutral. It would seem more likely to suppose that demand elasticities differ in such a way as to weaken the conclusion that $E_2/E_D \leqslant 1.6$. Obviously, the question can only be finally resolved by empirical investigation. In the absence of factual data, however, the assumption of equal product elasticities in both markets would be contrary to theoretical expectations.

A more fundamental weakness in the analysis is revealed by an examination of Figure 2. We have constructed two parallel, linear demand schedules, d_0 and d_1. Suppose we assume that marginal cost is constantly zero (this assumption in no way affects the generality of the argument and is employed only for expositional convenience). The prices at which profits are maximized are p_0 and p_1,

[7] Given linear demand schedules the conclusion must follow. It is possible, however, to construct demand schedules that do not have the indicated properties. Such schedules would be unlikely to arise in a situation where demand is everywhere greater than previously.

respectively. These prices, as is well known, are associated with demand elasticities of -1, a value found at the midpoint of the relevant demand schedules. Now, if the demand schedule shifts from d_1 to d_0, the elasticity of demand on curve d_0 at price p_1 is greater (more negative) than the elasticity on curve d_1 at the (original equilibrium) price p_1. And, as we see, a new equilibrium price will be established at a lower price, viz., p_0. Conversely, if the demand schedule shifts from d_0 to d_1, the reduced elasticity of demand on d_1 at p_0 is associated with the establishment of a new higher equilibrium price. This relationship between price and elasticity is, of course, associative and not causative. At times, it might be observed, the analysis of Burrows and Domencich only narrowly escapes confusing association with causation. The formal relationship between elasticity and price which underlies the authors' analysis is, however, correctly stated.

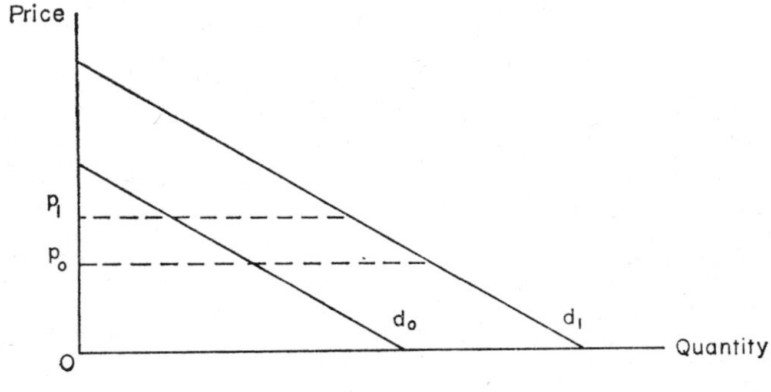

FIGURE 2

Opening the domestic market to foreign competition would presumably lead to a rightward shift of the demand schedule for OPEC oil. Assuming linear demand schedules (an assumption which is sufficient but not necessary for the conclusions), an increased demand must lead to an increase in the price of foreign oil if the new demand schedule is everywhere to the right of the new schedule. We note that Burrows and Domencich specifically assume a situation in which 'more is demanded at any given price'.[8] Such a situation is represented in Figure 2 by a shift of the demand schedule from d_0 to d_1. At all comparable prices, demand is more inelastic on d_1 than on d_0. Any equilibrium price established with respect to d_0 must be less than the equilibrium price associated with d_1. Given constant marginal cost and monopolistic behavior, an increase in

[8] See footnote 4.

demand will lead to an increase in price. This is the conclusion we sought to demonstrate.

The elasticity conditions necessary for a price reduction to be rationally dictated are as Burrows and Domencich indicate. These conditions will not, however, be realized when demand increases. Rather, eliminating import restrictions would lead a monopolist to raise prices. Whether the producing nations can exert such influence upon prices is, of course, a different question. Recent experience does, however, suggest a possibly affirmative answer to this related issue. We might further observe that the conclusion reached above was based on an assumption of marginal cost invariancy with respect to output. The analysis holds, *a fortiori*, if marginal costs are positively correlated with production levels.

THE PENNSYLVANIA STATE UNIVERSITY

ON REVENUE MAXIMIZING DUOPLY*

by JOHN P. FORMBY

PROFESSOR BAUMOL's constrained revenue maximizing model was advanced to explain the behavior of oligopolists.[1] W. G. Shepherd has pointed out, however, that the model does not allow for mutually interdependent reactions and responses of rival firms.[2] Since mutual interdependence is the fundamental ingredient of the oligopoly problem, Baumol's model is essentially an analysis of monopoly. To make the model a part of oligopoly theory proper requires an analysis of mutually interdependent constrained revenue maximizing firms. Shepherd used kinked demand curve analysis to show that the prices, output, and profits of mutually interdependent revenue maximizers would differ little if any from that of profit maximizers.

C. J. Hawkins has argued that Shepherd's conclusions are valid for a single product firm only if advertising expenditures are totally ineffective or impossible.[3] Hawkins went on to argue that under conditions of free entry, revenue maximizers would become multi-product firms with long-run results identical to profit maximization under competitive conditions. Hawkins failed to make the obvious point, however, that in the long run, free entry generates atomistic results. This is the case irrespective of the number of products sold or the motivations of firms. Under conditions of free entry, firms must maximize profits in order to survive. Hawkins' multi-product analysis, unlike Shepherd's, does not place the revenue maximizing firm within the context of the oligopoly problem.

Shepherd's kinked demand analysis is only one of many possible ways to analyze mutually interdependent firms. It is not at all clear that it is the best way. As is well known, the kinked analysis rests squarely upon the assumption of excess capacity[4] and suffers from the defect of being unable to explain how the kink happens to occur at a particular price-output point. In this paper Chamberlin and Cournot type duopolists are investigated. Constrained revenue maximizing rather than profit maximizing behavior is assumed. Adding mutual interdependence to revenue maximizing behavior

* The author wishes to thank M. Z. Kafoglis, Paul G. Althaus, and an unnamed reviewer for their helpful suggestions and comments on an earlier draft of this paper.

[1] W. J. Baumol, 'On the Theory of Oligopoly', *Economica*, Vol. XXV (958).

[2] W. G. Shepherd, 'On Sales Maximizing and Oligopoly Behavior', *Economica*, Vol. XXIX (1962).

[3] C. J. Hawkins, 'On the Sales Revenue Maximization Hypothesis', *Journal of Industrial Economics*, Vol. XVIII (1970).

[4] C. F. Efroymson, 'A Note on Kinked Demand Curves', *American Economic Review*, Vol. XXXIII (1943), p. 103.

is shown to leave output unchanged in some circumstances but to modify it in others. Chamberlin type constrained revenue maximizing duopolists are shown to: (1) produce an output greater than Chamberlin profit maximizing duopolists and less than the competitive output; (2) produce the same output as a revenue maximizing monopolist when the price elasticity of demand is less than or equal to unity; and (3) have a unique contract (collusion) point when the price elasticity of demand is greater than unity. In the latter situation, the output of Chamberlin revenue maximizing duopolists may be greater or less than a revenue maximizing monopolist. Cournot type constrained revenue maximizing solutions are shown to be of three types: (1) the first has a determinate and stable solution with an output one-third greater than that of a revenue maximizing monopolist; (2) the second is indeterminate with two or more stable equilibria, all having outputs greater than the profit maximizing Cournot output; and (3) the last is indeterminate with three stable equilibria, one of which is the same as the standard profit maximizing Cournot solution. In contradistinction to Shepherd's conclusion, the revenue maximizing duopolists of this paper, in every case except one, have greater outputs and lower prices and profits than profit maximizing duopolists.

Duopoly is characterized by indeterminacy. Even under profit maximizing assumptions the number of alternative reactions which may exist between sellers is so great that a unique solution is impossible. It has long been recognized that profit maximizing duopoly equilibrium can be made determinate only by restricting the reactions and responses of rivals by assumption.[5] Consequently, existing duopoly theory consists of a number of duopoly models each resting upon a different set of assumed behavioral responses of rival firms. The analysis of nonprofit maximizing duopoly cannot remove the general indeterminacy of the duopoly problem. Changing the behavioral motivations of firms simply creates additional possible solutions and thereby expands the repertory of duopoly theory.

We make a number of simplifying assumptions common to profit maximizing duopoly models. It is assumed that sellers, Alpha and Beta, produce homogeneous products and have identical costs. The market demand function is assumed linear,

$$p = k - nq \tag{1}$$

Total output is the sum of Alpha's and Beta's outputs, $q = q_a + q_b$. The demand function is thus:

[5] K. W. Rothschild, 'Price Theory and Oligopoly', *The Economic Journal*, Vol. LVII (1947), pp. 302–3.

(1′) $$p = k - nq_a - nq_b$$

The cost functions are assumed constant,

(2) $$ac = mc = c$$

The homogeneity assumption deserves comment. It permits abstraction from advertising expenditures. In Professor Baumol's model, the firm uses any profit in excess of the minimum profit constraint to finance advertising expenditures, making revenue a function of advertising outlay.[6] The mutual interdependence of costs and revenue makes the one-firm constrained revenue maximizing model considerably more complex than the typical textbook presentation.[7] The homogeneity assumption removes the rationale of advertising and makes costs and revenues independent. In addition, the assumption abstracts from product differentiation as a variable affecting the reactions and responses of rival firms. In short, the assumption puts the constrained revenue maximizing duopoly problem in its simplest form.

In order to have bench marks to which the constrained revenue maximizing solutions can be compared, it is useful to begin by specifying the Cournot and Chamberlin *profit maximizing solutions* to the duopoly problem. If Alpha assumes q_b is constant, multiplying (1′) through by q_a yields Alpha's total revenue function,

(3) $$TR_a = kq_a - nq_a^2 - nq_bq_a$$

Alpha's marginal revenue function is

(4) $$mr_a = k - 2nq_a - nq_b$$

The profit maximizing reaction function of Alpha is determined by setting $mr_a = mc$ and solving for q_a,

(5) $$q_a = (k - c - nq_b)/2n$$

Similarly, Beta's profit maximizing reaction function is

(5′) $$q_b = (k - c - nq_a)/2n$$

In Figure 1, Alpha's reaction function is shown as AA' and Beta's, as BB'.

[6] W. J. Baumol, 'On the Theory of Oligopoly', *Economica*, Vol. XXV (1958), pp. 192–3.

[7] Compare the analyses of R. Haveman and G. DeBarttolo, 'The Revenue Maximization Oligopoly Model: Comment', *American Economic Review*, Vol. LVIII (1968); M. Z. Kafoglis and R. Bushnell, 'The Revenue Maximization Oligopoly Model: Comment', *American Economic Review*, Vol. LX (1970); C. J. Hawkins, 'The Revenue Maximization Oligopoly Model: Comment', *American Economic Review*, Vol. LX (1970); and R. Haveman and G. DeBarttolo, 'The Revenue Maximization Oligopoly Model: Reply', *American Economic Review*, Vol. LX (1970), to any textbook presentation of the model.

The profit maximizing reaction functions have a fixed and invariant relationship to the duopolist's family of iso-profit curves. Alpha's iso-profit curves are concave with respect to Alpha's output axis. Each point on the reaction function AA' passes through the vertex of one of Alpha's iso-profit curves. Thus the profit maximixing reaction functions are the loci of maxima of the iso-profit curves. Moving along Alpha's profit maximizing reaction function from A to A', the profit level of Alpha declines; that is, one encounters the maxima of successively lower iso-profit curves. Similarly, moving along Beta's profit maximizing reaction function from B to B', successively lower iso-profit curves of Beta are encountered.

The intercepts of the profit maximizing reaction functions occur at the monopoly and competitive outputs. Setting $q_b = 0$ and solving (5) for q_a yields the profit maximizing monopoly output $(k-c)/2n$. The competitive output $(k-c)/n$, is determined by substituting (2) into (1) and solving for q. That the intercepts of the profit maximizing reaction functions occur at the competitive output is seen by setting $q_a = 0$ and solving (5) for q_b. The distances OA and OB in Figure 1 are thus equal to the monopoly output, and distances OA' and OB' are equal to the competitive output. The line $A'B'$ is the locus of competitive solutions to the duopoly problem with each point on the line representing a different division of the competitive output between the duopolists. The line AB in Figure 1 is the locus of profit maximizing monopoly solutions to the duopoly problem,

$$q_a = (k-c-q_b)/2n \tag{6}$$

It is well known that the monopoly solution locus is the profit maximizing duopolists contract or conflict curve.[8] The area bounded by the monopoly and competitive solution loci, $AA'B'B$ in Figure 1, includes all standard solutions to the duopoly problem. Whether the duopolists pursue maximum profit or maximum utility with a profit constraint, and regardless of the reactions and responses of the firms, the solution necessarily occurs in the area $AA'B'B$.

If the duopolists are profit maximizers and behave *à la* Cournot, the solution is given by the simultaneous solution of (5) and (5'), $q = 2(k-c)/3n$. In Figure 1 this solution is shown at point C, the intersection of the profit maximizing reaction functions. The equal cost assumption insures the profit maximizing Cournot solution occurs along the 45° ray through the origin. As is well known, the total Cournot output is two-thirds of the competitive output with

[8] R. L. Bishop, 'Duopoly: Collusion or Warfare', *American Economic Review*, Vol. L (1960), pp. 935–6.

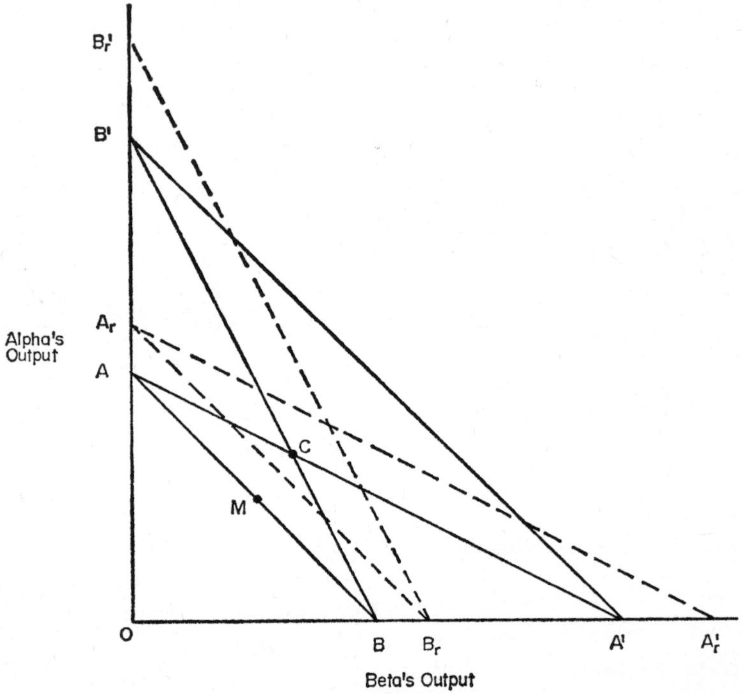

FIGURE 1

Alpha and Beta producing equal amounts. The profit maximizing Chamberlin solution is determined by setting $q_a = q_b$ and solving (6),

$$q = (k-c)/2n \tag{7}$$

This solution is shown at point M in Figure 1, the midpoint of the profit maximizing duopoly collusion locus.

We use the *unconstrained* revenue maximizing reaction functions as the starting point for our analysis of revenue maximizing duopoly. Alpha's function is determined by setting $mr_a = 0$ and solving (4) for q_a,

$$q_a = (k-nq_b)/2n \tag{8}$$

Similarly, Beta's *unconstrained* revenue maximizing reaction function is

$$q_b = (k-nq_a)/2n \tag{8'}$$

The *unconstrained* revenue maximizing reaction functions show the output the duopolists would choose if they assumed *à la* Cournot that their rivals' output was constant and if they could pursue maximum revenue unhindered by any sort of profit constraint. If costs were zero, equations (5) and (7) would be identical and the profit and *unconstrained* revenue maximizing reaction functions would be the same. However, with positive and constant costs the *unconstrained* revenue maximizing reaction functions are parallel and to the right of the profit maximizing reaction functions. The distance between them depends upon the magnitude of costs. The *unconstrained* revenue maximizing reaction functions, denoted A_rA_r' and B_rB_r', are shown as dashed lines in Figure 1.[9]

The *unconstrained* revenue maximizing reaction functions of duopolists are related to the family of iso-revenue curves in the same manner as the profit maximizing reaction functions are related to the iso-profit curves. To clarify, Alpha's *unconstrained* function is the loci of the maxima of iso-revenue curves. Moving from A_r to A_r' in Figure 1, encounters the vertexes of successively lower iso-revenue curves. Similarly, the *unconstrained* revenue maximizing monopoly collusion locus is related to the iso-revenue curves and *unconstrained* revenue maximizing reaction functions as the ordinary monopoly collusion locus, AB, is related to the iso-profit curves and profit maximizing reaction functions. In Figure 1, the dashed line A_rB_r is the *unconstrained* revenue maximizing collusion (conflict) locus. Total output along A_rB_r is equal to what an *unconstrained* revenue maximizing monopolist would produce. Setting $q_b = 0$ and solving (7) for q_a, the output along the *unconstrained* collusion locus is

$$q = k/2n \tag{9}$$

The collusion locus itself is given by $q_a = k/2n - q_b$.

We assume the duopolists have the same minimum profit constraint π_j. Alpha's profit constraint is the iso-profit function π_{ja} and Beta's is π_{jb}. Alpha's objective function can be represented as $\pi_{ja} \geq nq_a - cq_a$. Substituting the demand function (1′) for p, the constraint becomes:

$$q_a \leq \pi_{ja}/k - nq_a - nq_b - c \tag{1}$$

The boundary of the constraint is $q_a = \pi_{ja}/k - nq_a - nq_b - c$. Solving for q_a the boundary of Alpha's constraint becomes:

$$q_a = -(c + nq_b - k) \pm \sqrt{(c + nq_b - k)^2 - 4n\pi_{ja}/2n} \tag{10}$$

[9] In Figure 1, portions of the unconstrained revenue maximizing reaction functions are below the competitive solution locus. The costs could be so high that A_rA_r', B_rB_r', and A_rB_r are outside $B'A'$.

Similarly, Beta's constraint boundary is

$$(10') \qquad q_b = -(c+nq_a-k) \pm \sqrt{(c+nq_a-k)^2 - 4n\pi_{jb}/2n}$$

The profit constraint boundaries given by (10) and (10′) are simply iso-profit curves of the magnitude π_{ja} and π_{jb}. In Figure 2, Alpha's minimum constraint is shown by the iso-profit curve aa_1a_2 and Beta's is shown by bb_1b_2. The portion of Alpha's constraint boundary above the profit maximizing reaction function, AA', is termed the 'upper boundary' and the portion below AA' is the lower boundary. In Figure 2 Alpha's upper boundary is aa_1 and Beta's is bb_1. The lower boundaries are a_1a_2 and b_1b_2.[10]

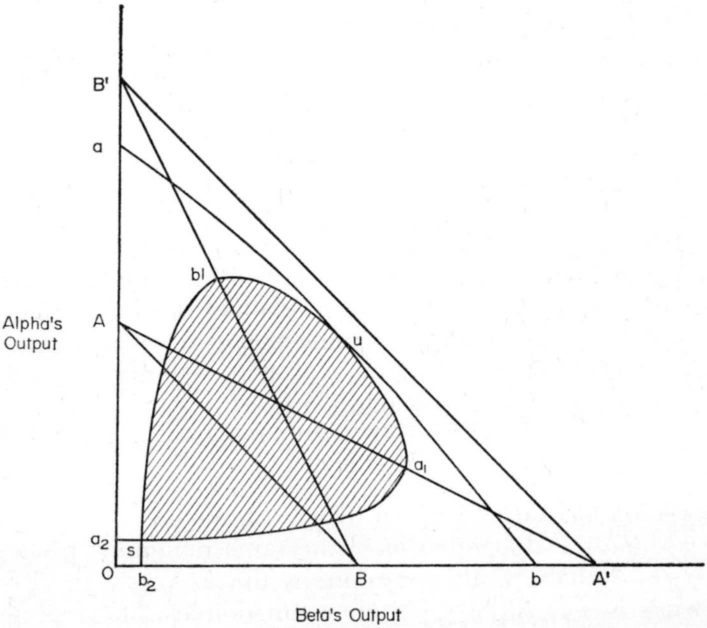

FIGURE 2

The profit constraint boundaries are of considerable importance in analyzing constrained duopoly behavior. However, the profit constraints (as distinct from the boundaries) are inequalities. This means any output within the upper and lower boundaries is feasible,

[10] For any given output, q_b, the positive root of the second term of (10) shows the maximum quantity Alpha can produce and end up with a profit of π_{Ja}, while the negative root shows the minimum quantity which yields the profit π_{Ja}. When the term under the radical in (10) is zero, the iso-profit curve π_{Ja} intersects Alpha's profit maximizing reaction function; that is, π_{Ja} is at its vertex with respect to Alpha's output axis. Hence, the positive root determines the upper boundary and the negative root determines the lower boundary.

having profits greater than the minimum acceptable level of π_j. The boundary simply separates the feasible outputs of a duopolist from the nonfeasible ones. In Figure 2 the cross-hatched area sb_1ua_1 shows the overlap of Alpha and Beta's profit constraints. Taking the profit constraints as exogenous, the area of the overlap is the feasible region of the constrained duopoly problem. It shows the possible solutions to the duopoly problem which are within the profit constraint boundaries of both duopolists.[11] The lower the minimum profit constraints, the larger the feasible region and the greater the minimum profit constraints, the smaller the feasible region.[12]

CONSTRAINED CHAMBERLIN SOLUTIONS

Constrained revenue maximizing Chamberlin type duopolists, like profit maximizing Chamberlin duopolists, strike an implicit bargain which results in equal divisions of the monopoly output, profits, and revenue. However, unlike the profit maximizing Chamberlin solution, the constrained revenue maximizing Chamberlin type solution depends upon the elasticity of demand. A linear demand function as assumed here has elasticity coefficients varying between zero and infinity. The magnitude of costs and the size of the minimum profit constraints determine the range of elasticity coefficients which are possible. Two general cases can be distinguished. The costs and profit constraints may be sufficiently low so that the constrained Chamberlin duopoly solution occurs in the range of outputs at which the coefficient of price elasticity (η) is less than or equal to one. This case is denoted as $\eta \leq 1$. It is characterized by a solution at the point of unitary elasticity which maximizes the joint total revenue of the duopolists. The costs and minimum profit constraints may be sufficiently high so that the constrained Chamberlin solution is restricted to the range of output at which the price elasticity coefficient is greater than one. This situation is denoted as $\eta > 1$. It is characterized by quantity maximization subject to the minimum profit constraint and a failure to maximize joint total revenue.

The price elasticity of demand of the demand function (1) is unitary at the output $k/2n$. As demonstrated above, output along the *unconstrained* revenue maximizing collusion locus is also $k/2n$. Consequently, outputs which fall below the *unconstrained* collusion locus

[11] It is shown below that constrained revenue maximizing Cournot type solutions may occur outside the feasible region. However, any solution outside the feasible region requires that one or both duopolists abandon their minimum profit constraint and become profit maximizers.

[12] For a discussion of the effects of minimum profit constraints which are so great that constraint boundaries do not intersect, see footnotes 15 and 20 below.

in Figure 2 have elasticity coefficients which are greater than one and outputs above the *unconstrained* collusion locus have elasticiy coefficients less than one. Elasticity is unitary along the *unconstrained* collusion locus. When the costs and minimum profit constraints are such that the *unconstrained* collusion locus is outside the feasible duopoly region, output is restricted to the range of outputs at which demand is elastic and what we have termed the case of $\eta > 1$ occurs. When the costs and minimum profits are so low that a segment of the *unconstrained* revenue maximizing collusion is within the feasible region, the case of $\eta \leq 1$ occurs.

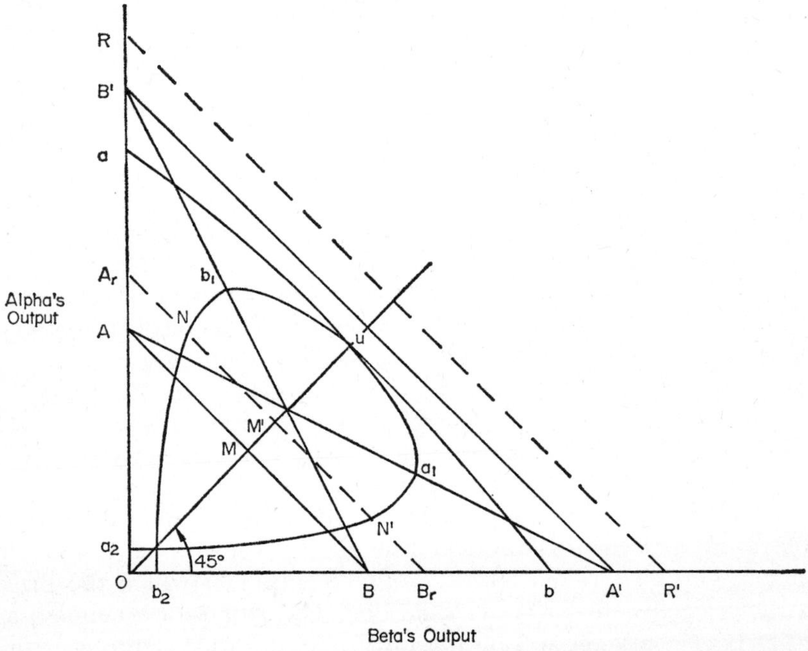

FIGURE 3

In Figure 3 a segment, NN', of the *unconstrained* revenue maximizing collusion locus is inside the feasible duopoly region. This is the necessary and sufficient condition for what has been termed the case of $\eta \leq 1$. At each point along NN', the duopolists receive profits greater than or equal to their minimum constraints and the combined output and revenue is the same as that of a constrained revenue maximizing monopolist. Thus, in the case of $\eta \leq 1$, NN' is the *constrained* revenue maximizing collusion (conflict) locus. The Chamberlin type solution in Figure 3 occurs at point M' and reflects an equal division of market shares (output, revenue, and profits). By equation (9) total output at M' is $k/2n$, with q_a and q_b equal to $k/4n$. Subtracting equation (7) from (9) shows that in the case of $\eta \leq 1$, the constrained revenue maximizing Chamberlin output is greater than the profit maximizing Chamberlin output at point M by the magnitude $c/2n$.

The constrained Chamberlin revenue maximizing solution in Figure 3, like the Chamberlin profit maximizing solution, offers each duopolist an incentive to break the implicit joint monopoly agreement and pursue an independent policy. At M' both duopolists earn profits in excess of their minimum profit constraints and thus have an incentive to expand output. However, such independent action is attractive to Alpha only if Beta refrains from such action. If both duopolists pursue independent policies and expand output, they move off the collusion locus and revenue, as well as profits, decline. The fall in revenue makes both duopolists worse off. Thus, the danger of declining revenue brought on by independent revenue maximizing behavior may lead the duopolists to a relatively permanent and, hence, stable joint monopoly agreement. Stable in the present context means that mutual fear of the consequences of independent maximizing behavior may lead each duopolist to adhere to the joint monopoly solution. Under present assumptions, there is no a priori reason to expect the Chamberlin constrained revenue maximizing solution in the case of $\eta \leq 1$ to be any more or less stable than the conventional profit maximizing Chamberlin solution.

If RR' in Figure 3 rather than A_rB_r is the *unconstrained* revenue maximizing collusion locus, the case of $\eta > 1$ occurs. Line RR' is everywhere outside the feasible duopoly region indicating that the costs and minimum profit constraints are such that any solution satisfying the minimum profit constraints of both duopolists has output less than $k/2n$ and, hence, has an elasticity coefficient greater than one. In this situation the constrained revenue maximizing Chamberlin solution occurs at point U, the intersection of the upper constraint boundaries. At point U the duopolists maximize revenue by maximizing quantity. Total output at point U is given by the larger of the two simultaneous solutions of equations (10) and (10'). The exact output will, of course, depend upon the magnitude of π_{ja} and π_{jb}. It is clear that output will be less than $k/2n$, the output along the unconstrained collusion locus, and greater than $(k-c)/2n$, the output along the profit maximizing collusion locus.

The output of revenue maximizing Chamberlin duopolists in the case of $\eta > 1$ will be the same as a revenue maximizing monopolist *if and only if* the combined minimum profit constraints of the duopolists are exactly equivalent to the minimum profit constraint of the monopolist. If the combined minimum profit constraints are greater than those of a monopolist, the output of the duopolists will be less than that of the monopolist. Combined minimum profit constraints less than those of a monopolist would result in an equilibrium duopoly output greater than the monopoly output. Unfortunately, the magnitude of the minimum profit constraint, even for a monopolist, is not known with certainty. Originally, Professor Baumol defined the minimum profit constraint as '. . . that stream of profits which allows for the financing of maximum long-run sales'.[13] This was described as profits high enough to provide for dividends sufficient to make future equity issues attractive and provide retained earnings to finance current expansion. Later, it was decided that the profit level was not a constraint at all in the long run but, rather, a growth optimizing magnitude. In the short run, however, the minimum profit level remains an exogenous constraint which must '. . . provide a rate of return sufficient to make certain that the company's securities remain attractive to the capital market'.[14] In terms of either notion of the profit constraint, it seems there is not an *a priori* reason to expect the combined minimum profit constraints of duopolists to be exactly equal to that of a monopolist. It might appear that the assumption of identical cost and profit constraints for the duopolists insures the combined profit constraint is the same as that of a monopolist, but such is not the case. Securities can be attractive in capital markets with different rates of return. Indeed, the competitive rate of return and competitive profit level represent a floor below which minimum profit levels cannot go. The combined profit constraints may be lesser or greater than those of a monopolist. Consequently, Chamberlin duopoly output in the case of $\eta > 1$ may be either above or below that of a constrained revenue maximizing monopolist.

In the case of $\eta > 1$, there is no constrained duopoly collusion locus comparable to NN' in the case of $\eta \leq 1$. With the unconstrained collusion locus RR', point U has greater revenue than any other point within the feasible duopoly region. Consequently, for $\eta > 1$ point U is the unique contract point for constrained revenue maximizing Chamberlin duopolists. Once point U is attained, the incentive to pursue independent maximizing policies is extremely weak. Any movement away from point U, other than to a point like

[13] W. J. Baumol, 'On the Theory of Oligopoly', *Economica*, Vol. XXV (1958), p. 188.

[14] W. J. Baumol, *Business Behavior Value and Growth*, rev. ed. (New York, 1967), pp. 50 and 100.

b_1 would harm both firms and would not be undertaken. Alpha, of course, would prefer to move to point b_1 but such a movement would require that Beta voluntarily agree to produce accordingly and this he would never do. Alpha's gains in going from point U to b_1 would be less than Beta's losses, hence, there is no way that Beta could be bribed to acquiesce in a solution at b_1. Owing to the uniqueness of point U and the very weak incentive for independent action at point U, it appears that the constrained Chamberlin type solution in the case of $\eta > 1$ is more likely to be stable than the profit maximizing and $\eta \leq 1$ Chamberlin solutions.[15]

CONSTRAINED COURNOT SOLUTIONS

If each duopolist assumes that his rival's output is constant and adjusts his own output to the level which maximizes revenue subject to a minimum profit constraint, then Cournot type constrained revenue maximizing solutions can be identified. As with constrained Chamberlin solutions, several types of constrained Cournot solutions may occur. However, constrained Cournot solutions, unlike constrained Chamberlin solutions, cannot be easily categorized with respect to the price elasticity of demand. Cournot duopolists respond to their rival's output by producing along a reaction function. The magnitude of costs and the size of the minimum profit constraint determine the constrained reaction functions. The relation between the constrained reaction functions then determines the nature of the constrained Cournot solutions. Three general types of constrained Cournot solutions may occur: (1) The magnitude of costs and the size of the minimum profit constraints are sufficiently low so that the duopolists maximize revenue without maximizing quantity. (2) The magnitude of costs and the size of minimum profit constraints are sufficiently high so that the constrained duopolists maximize revenue by maximizing quantity. (3) The minimum profit constraints are so high that both duopolists in seeking maximum revenues subject to a profit constraint may be forced into profit maximizing behavior. It will be shown below that the first situation results in a stable and determinate constrained Cournot solution,

[15] A constrained Chamberlin duopoly situation which fits neither $\eta \leq 1$ nor $\eta > 1$ may occur temporarily. The minimum profit constraints of Chamberlin revenue maximizing duopolists could be set so high that a constrained Chamberlin solution is not possible. In equilibrium *profit maximizing* Chamberlin duopolists receive the profit $\pi_m = k^2 - 2ck + c^2/8n$. This equation describes the iso-profit curves tangent at point m in Figure 3. With profit constraints of this magnitude, the feasible region consists of the single tangency point. If minimum profit constraints are set in excess of π_m, there is no feasible region and, consequently, no constrained revenue maximizing Chamberlin solution. Minimum constraints in excess of π_m are mutually inconsistent, and any output must result in one or both duopolists being disappointed. Hence even if profit constraints in excess of π_m were established, the resulting disequilibrium would necessitate modification of the constraints.

while indeterminacy occurs in the other two. In the second there are multiple equilibrium with two or more stable solutions. In the third, there are three stable solutions, one of which is equivalent to the classic Cournot profit maximizing solution.

For any given output of Beta, Alpha's *constrained* revenue maximizing reaction function shows the output of Alpha which maximizes revenue subject to the minimum profit constraint. Alpha's *constrained* revenue maximizing reaction function consists of the segment of the

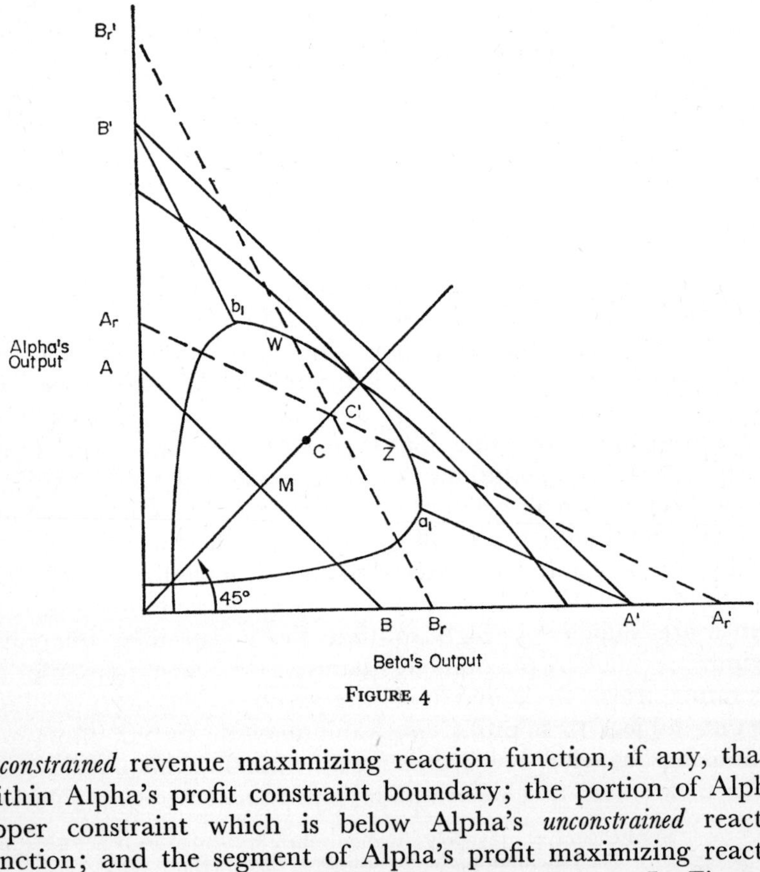

FIGURE 4

unconstrained revenue maximizing reaction function, if any, that is within Alpha's profit constraint boundary; the portion of Alpha's upper constraint which is below Alpha's *unconstrained* reaction function; and the segment of Alpha's profit maximizing reaction function outside Alpha's profit constraint boundary. In Figure 4, Alpha's *constrained* reaction function is $A_r Z a_1 A'$ and Beta's is $B_r W b_1 B'$. These *constrained* reaction functions require some explanation. If Beta's output in Figure 4 is between the quantity indicated at point Z and zero, Alpha will respond by choosing its output along the *unconstrained* revenue maximizing reaction function. In this range of output, Alpha's *unconstrained* reaction function is inside Alpha's profit constraint boundary and, consequently, Alpha is able to maximize revenue without bumping up against his profit constraint, that is, he maximizes revenue in essentially an unconstrained fashion. However, if Beta's output is greater than the quantity at point Z but less than the quantity at point a_1, Alpha produces the output which permits it to earn its profit constraint π_{ja} and which yields the greatest revenue. This requires that Alpha respond to Beta by choosing output along the upper constraint boundary, thus maximizing revenue by maximizing output. That segment Za_1 of the profit constraint boundary is a part of the *unconstrained* reaction function is easily demonstrable. Given Beta's output in the range indicated by point Z and a_1, Alpha has three alternatives: (1) to respond to Beta's output by producing the quantity indicated by the *unconstrained* revenue maximizing reaction function; (2) to respond to Beta by producing the quantity indicated by the profit constraint boundary between points Z and a_1; and (3) by choosing an output smaller than that indicated by the profit constraint boundary. Since in this range of output Alpha's *unconstrained* reaction function is outside the profit constraint boundary, the first alternative is clearly not possible. Choosing it would require Alpha to sacrifice the attainment of the profit constraint in order to maximize revenue. The third alternative would require that Alpha earn a profit in excess of the minimum constraint while failing to maximize revenue. Profits in excess of the minimum constraint are sacrificable. Alpha would produce the largest possible quantity which is just sufficient to attain the minimum profit constraint, that is, he would choose alternative two. This permits Alpha to most closely approach the maximum revenue shown by segment $Z\,A_r'$ of the *unconstrained* revenue maximizing reaction function.

Finally, if Beta's output in Figure 4 is between the quantity indicated at point a_1 and the competitive output at point A', any response by Alpha will yield a profit less than the minimum constraint. In this situation Alpha's constrained revenue maximizing Cournot response is to produce the output which yields the greatest profit. Thus, when Beta's output is so great that Alpha cannot attain the minimum constraint, Alpha reacts along the profit maximizing reaction function, AA'. In this fashion, Alpha makes the best of a bad situation.

In Figure 4 the costs and minimum profit constraints are sufficiently low so that the *constrained* revenue maximizing reaction functions, A_rZa_1A' and B_rWb_1B' intersect only once, insuring a determinate, and as will be seen below, a stable constrained revenue maximizing

Cournot solution at point C'. In the neighborhood of point C' the constrained revenue maximizing reaction functions consist of segments of the *unconstrained* reaction functions. Consequently, total output is given by the simultaneous solution of equations (8) and (8′),

$$q = 2k/3n \tag{11}$$

The Cournot revenue maximizing output of Figure 4 is one-third greater than $k/2n$, the output which a revenue maximizing monopolist would produce. Subtracting the profit maximizing Cournot output, $2(k-c)/3n$, from (11) shows the revenue maximizing Cournot output to be greater than the Cournot profit maximizing output by the magnitude $2c/3n$.

The constrained revenue maximizing Cournot solution of Figure 4 is determinate because the costs and minimum profit constraints are sufficiently low so that the *unconstrained* revenue maximizing reaction functions intersect inside the feasible duopoly region, insuring a unique equilibrium at C'. However, the costs and minimum profit constraints may be sufficiently high so that the *unconstrained* revenue maximizing reaction functions do not intersect in the feasible region. If this occurs, the constrained revenue maximizing Cournot equilibrium is indeterminate. Let us keep the iso-profit levels fixed as in Figure 4. However, we let costs be greater than in Figure 4 so that the *unconstrained* reaction function do not intersect in the feasible region. In Figure 5 the costs are so high that the *unconstrained* reactions functions are completely outside the profit constraint boundaries and the feasible region. In this situation the constrained reaction function of a duopolist consists of the upper constraint boundary and the segment of the duopolist's profit maximizing reaction function outside the constraint boundary. Alpha's *constrained* reaction function is aa_1A' and Beta's is bb_1B'. In Figure 5 the *constrained* reaction functions intersect at points T, U, and V, indicating three possible constrained Cournot solutions.

At point U revenue is maximized by maximizing quantity, and both duopolists receive their minimum profit constraints. At point T Alpha receives the minimum profit constraint, but Beta fails to receive it and is forced into profit maximizing behavior. At point V the situation is reversed, and Beta receives the minimum profit constraint while Alpha fails to receive it.

Given the nature of the output responses of Cournot duopolists, the stability of a Cournot equilibrium point is revealed by the relationship between the reaction functions. With Beta's output on the ordinate and Alpha's on the abscissa, a stable Cournot equilibrium point occurs when Beta's reaction function is *above* Alpha's reaction function to the left of the equilibrium point and *below* Alpha's to the right of the equilibrium point. This relation insures that successive output responses of Cournot duopolists eventually result in a stable equilibrium.[16] Both the profit maximizing Cournot equilibrium and the constrained revenue maximizing equilibrium at point C' in Figure 4 meet this requirement and, hence, have stable equilibrium points. When Beta's reaction function is *below* Alpha's to the left of the equilibrium point and *above* Alpha's to the right of

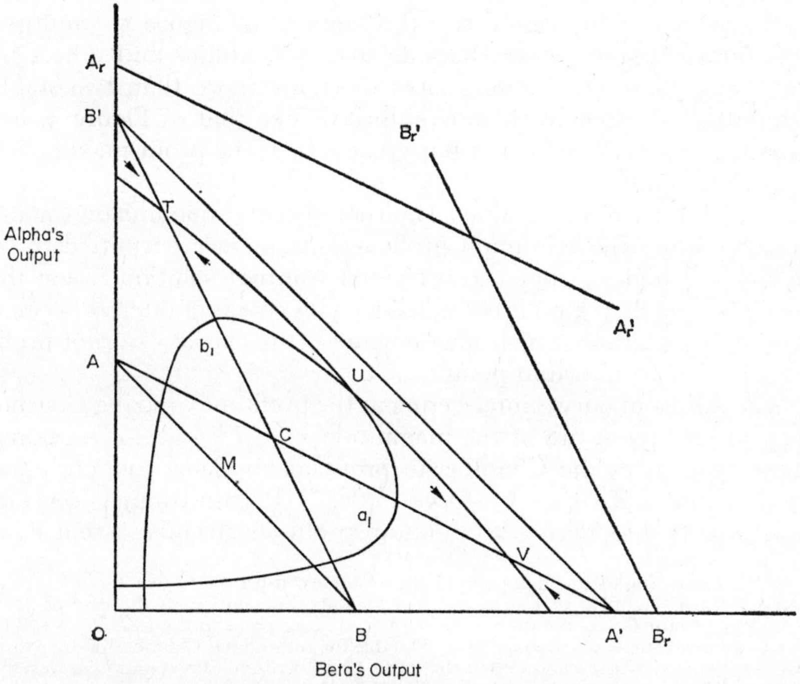

FIGURE 5

the equilibrium point, the output responses of Cournot duopolists result in an unstable equilibrium.

In Figure 5 the arrows indicate the direction of change resulting from the output responses of constrained revenue maximizing Cournot duopolists. Points T and V meet the requirements of stable Cournot equilibrium points. Between points T and U, Beta's constrained reaction function, bb_1B', is below Alpha's reaction function, aa_1A';

[16] T. W. Swan and J. W. Friedman both discuss the stability conditions associated with reaction functions. See J. W. Friedman, 'Reaction Functions and the Theory of Duopoly', *Review of Economic Studies*, Vol. XXXV (1968), pp. 257–72, and T. W. Swan, 'Circular Causation', *Economic Record*, Vol. XXXVIII (1962), pp. 422–3.

and between points U and V, it is above Alpha's. Hence, point U is unstable. A solution at point U would be purely accidental, and any deviation away from point U would result in output responses which establish equilibrium at either points T or V.[17]

By imagining somewhat lower cost than in Figure 5, we would shift the *unconstrained* reaction functions leftward and could have the unconstrained reaction functions intersecting outside the feasible region, yet having segments of the *unconstrained* reaction functions inside the profit constraint boundaries. Several variations on this theme exist but the results are the same as in Figure 5—multiple equilibrium points, some characterized by stability and others by instability. In some circumstances there are more than two stable solutions.[18] Output in these equilibria is like that of Figure 5, less than the competitive output but greater than the profit maximizing Cournot output.

A final type of constrained Cournot revenue maximizing model emerges when the minimum profit constraints are permitted to be sufficiently high so that a constrained Cournot solution inside the feasible duopoly region is not possible. This case is of interest because one of the solutions which may emerge is the classic Cournot profit maximizing equilibrium point.

The iso-profit curves intersecting at the profit maximizing Cournot equilibrium point are of the magnitude $\pi_c = k^2 - 2ck + c^2/12n$, and those tangent at the Chamberlin profit maximizing duopoly point have profits of $\pi_m = k^2 - 2ck + c^2/8n$.[19] If constrained revenue maximizing duopolists set minimum profit constraints so that $\pi_m >$

[17] It is interesting to note that point U, the unstable constrained Cournot solution point of Figure 5, is identical to the constrained Chamberlin solution in the case of $\eta > 1$. Recall that point U was the unique contract (collusion) point in the case of $\eta > 1$. This latter characteristic tends to make point U stable for constrained Chamberlin duopolists. It is somewhat surprising to find that the stable Chamberlin solution point is an unstable Cournot solution point.

[18] Actually when a segment of the *unconstrained* reaction function is inside the profit constraint boundary there are three sub-cases. One yields three revenue maximizing Cournot equilibria and is formally identical to Figure 5. It differs from Figure 5 only in that a segment of the *unconstrained* reaction function is inside the profit constraint boundary. A second case occurs when A_rA_r' is tangent to Beta's profit constraint boundary between points b_1 and U in Figure 5, and B_rB_r' is tangent to Alpha's profit constraint boundary between points a_1 and U. This case yields five equilibria, two stable points like points T and V in Figure 5, one unstable point like point U in Figure 5, and two points which are stable in one direction and unstable in the other. The third case yields seven equilibria and occurs when A_rA_r' twice intersects Beta's iso-profit constraint boundary between points a_1 and U (once from above and once from below) and B_rB_r' twice intersects Alpha's profit constraint boundary between points b_1 and U (once from above and once from below). Four of the seven equilibria are stable and three are unstable. Due to space limitations the diagrams showing these three sub-cases are not reproduced here. However, the author has a supply of mimeographed diagrams and explanations of these three sub-cases, which will be provided to any interested reader upon request.

[19] These equations are determined by substituting each duopolist's equilibrium output into equation (10) and solving for π_{ja}.

$\pi_j > \pi_c$, then the iso-profit curve showing the profit constraint boundary will be between the iso-profit curves attained by profit maximizing Cournot and Chamberlin duopolists. The constrained revenue maximizing Cournot solutions in this situation are shown in Figure 6.

The constrained reaction functions of Figure 6 are the same as those of Figure 5: Alpha's is aa_1A' and Beta's is bb_1B'. However, in Figure 6 the minimum profit constraint is such that the constrained reaction functions intersect five times. None of the five possible constrained equilibria are within or on the boundary of the feasible region,

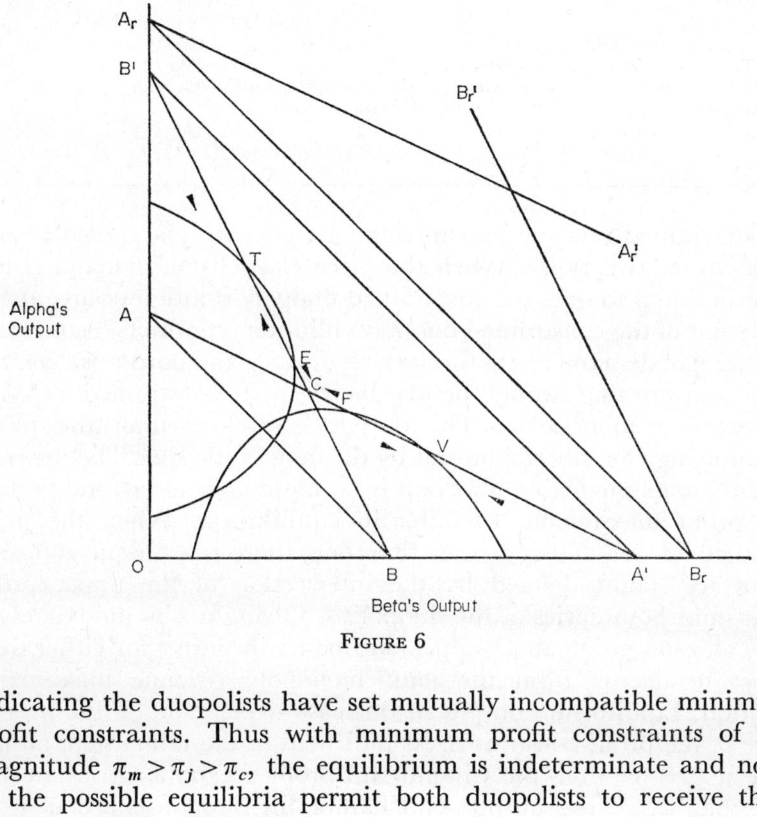

FIGURE 6

indicating the duopolists have set mutually incompatible minimum profit constraints. Thus with minimum profit constraints of the magnitude $\pi_m > \pi_j > \pi_c$, the equilibrium is indeterminate and none of the possible equilibria permit both duopolists to receive their minimum profit constraints.

Three of the possible Cournot equilibrium points are stable and two are unstable. Points *T* and *V*, as in Figure 5, are stable. Point *C*, the classic Cournot profit maximizing point, is also stable. Points *E* and *F* are unstable. Consequently, the equilibrium solution will occur at either point *T*, *V*, or *C*. Total output at point *C* is $2(k-c)/3n$ and at points T and V it is greater than at C, with the exact magnitude dependent upon π_j.[20]

SUMMARY AND CONCLUSIONS

The tabulation below shows the duopoly solutions analyzed in this paper.

	output
Competitive solution	$q = (k-c)/n$
Chamberlin profit maximizing solution	$q = (k-c)/2n$
Cournot profit maximizing solution	$q = 2(k-c)/3n$
Chamberlin constrained revenue maximizing solution	
$\eta \leq 1$	$q = k/2n$
$\eta > 1$	$(k-c)/2n < q < k/2n$
Cournot constrained revenue maximizing solutions	
Type 1—determinant and stable	$q = 2k/3n$
Type 2—indeterminate, two or more stable solutions	$2(k-c)/3n < q < (k-c)/n$
Type 3—indeterminate, three stable solutions—one of which is the profit maximizing Cournot solution	$q = 2(k-c)/3n$ or $2(k-c)/3n < q < (k-c)/n$

Constrained revenue maximizing Chamberlin type duopoly solutions are of two types. When the price elasticity of demand is less than or equal to one, the constrained duopoly solution occurs at the midpoint of the constrained duopoly collusion (contract) locus. Price elasticity of demand along this locus is unitary and output is $k/2n$, the same output that would be produced by a constrained revenue maximizing monopolist. The output is greater than the profit maximizing Chamberlin output by the magnitude $c/2n$. The duopoly revenue maximizing equilibrium is no more and no less stable than the profit maximizing Chamberlin equilibrium. When the price elasticity of demand is greater than one, there is a unique collusion (contract) point defined by the intersection of the upper profit constraint boundaries of the duopolists. Owing to the uniqueness of the collusion point, there appears to be no incentive for either duopolist to depart from the joint monopoly revenue maximizing solution. Equilibrium output in this case depends upon the magnitude of the profit constraints. As indicated in the tabulation, output will be greater than the Chamberlin profit maximizing output and less than $k/2n$, the output of Chamberlin duopolists when $\eta \leq 1$.

[20] In the event that constrained revenue maximizing Cournot duopolists set profit constraints in excess of π_m, a most unlikely situation, a determinate and stable constrained Cournot equilibrium exists at the classic profit maximizing Cournot point. With profit constraints of this magnitude, there is no feasible region and constrained Cournot duopolists, in an attempt to most closely approximate their profit constraints, react along their profit maximizing reaction functions. This behavior is no different from that of profit maximizing Cournot duopolists and the equilibrium established is identical.

Depending upon the magnitude of the combined minimum profit constraints, the output may be of greater or less than the output of a revenue maximizing monopolist. If the combined profit constraints of duopolists are exactly equal to the monopolist's profit constraint, then the outputs will be equal.

Constrained revenue maximizing Cournot solutions are of three types. In the first, there is a determinate, stable solution with output one third greater than that of revenue maximizing monopolists and $2c/3n$ greater than the Cournot profit maximizing output. In the second, multiple equilibria exist. Some of the equilibria are stable while others are unstable. However, output at each equilibrium point is greater than the Cournot profit maximizing output and less than thc competitive output. The size of the output depends upon the magnitude of the minimum profit constraints. One unstable Cournot equilibrium point is equivalent to the unique Chamberlinian collusion point in the case of $\eta > 1$. In the third type of constrained Cournot model, multiple equilibria again exist, with three stable and two unstable solutions. One of the stable solutions has an output exactly equal the profit maximizing Cournot output, while the others have outputs greater than this but less than the competitive output.

The analysis of this paper and the specification of the types of solutions rests squarely upon the assumptions of linear demand functions and constant costs. The history of duopoly theory is, of course, replete with these assumptions. Nevertheless, changing either of these assumptions would modify the analysis and, no doubt, some of the conclusions. For example, suppose the demand function was elastic throughout its range. The reaction functions would be curvilinear, the iso-profit and revenue functions would be considerably more complex, and the models more difficult to specify. While non-linear analysis would be more general, the insights and substantial conclusions flowing from the linear analysis would not likely be modified greatly.

The linear analysis of this paper suggests very strongly that adding mutual interdependence to revenue maximizing behavior does not necessarily generate profit maximizing results as Shepherd contends nor competitive results as Hawkins suggests. The linear analysis shows that Baumol's conclusions are left unscathed in some circumstances and are modified in others. Specifically, if revenue maximizing duopolists behave *à la* Chamberlin and demand elasticity is less than or equal to unity, the duopoly and monopoly results are identical. However, demand elasticity greater than unity may cause Chamberlin type duopolists to deviate away from the revenue maximizing monopoly output. Revenue maximizing duopolists who behave *à la* Cournot may under certain circumstances produce the profit maximizing Cournot output, but in general they produce an output greater than this but less than the competitive output. Nonlinear analysis is not likely to modify these substantive conclusions.

THE UNIVERSITY OF NORTH CAROLINA
AT GREENSBORO

AN ANALYSIS OF EFFICIENCY OF SCALE AND ORGANIZATIONAL FORM IN COMMERCIAL BANKING

by Lionel Kalish III and R. Alton Gilbert*

Cost and output observations for a sample of banks are examined in this article to determine how the efficiency of banks is related to their size and organizational form. Three organizational forms are compared—unit banks, branch banks, and holding company subsidiaries. Knowledge about the ways in which size and organizational form affect bank efficiency is important because one objective of bank regulation is efficient production, and the policies of bank regulators influence the size and organizational form of banks. Regulatory decisions on chartering new banks and allowing bank mergers affect the size of banks through the effects of such decisions on the number of banks in individual bank markets. Regulatory decisions on establishing branch offices and acquiring banks through holding companies influence the organizational form of banks.

The sample of banks used in this study consists of 898 commercial banks that participated in the Federal Reserve's Functional Cost Analysis Program in 1968.[1] The banks in the sample are grouped in Table I by amount of their assets and their organizational form. Banks of all three organizational forms are drawn from a wide range of asset sizes, with concentrations in the range from $10 million to $50 million. Unit banks make up 51 per cent of the sample, 39 per cent of the banks are branch banks, and 10 per cent are holding company subsidiaries.

ESTIMATING COST CURVES FOR BANKS

A bank's average cost reflects the value of resources it uses in production per unit of output. The average cost of each bank can be divided into two components: the minimum average cost at which banks of the same size and organizational form can operate and the

* This paper is taken from a dissertation by Lionel Kalish III, written at Washington University. The dissertation can be obtained from the St. Louis Federal Reserve Bank on request as Working Paper #15. The authors wish to thank Gary Brown for many helpful comments. Statements in this article do not necessarily reflect the views of the Federal Reserve System.

[1] A total of 979 banks participated in the program in 1968. Banks were deleted from the sample used in this article if they were in the following categories:
(a) the bank had not been in operation for three or more years,
(b) the bank was located in Massachusetts or Connecticut, where county borders are not consistent with Standard Metropolitan Statistical Area borders, or
(c) the bank was both a branch bank and a holding company subsidiary.

TABLE I

BANK SAMPLE BY ASSET SIZE

Assets in thousands of dollars	*Unit banks*	*Branch banks*[a]	*Holding company banks*	*Total*
Less than $5000	17	1	4	22
$5000 to $10,000	82	15	6	103
$10,000 to $20,000	126	49	21	196
$20,000 to $50,000	132	120	35	287
$50,000 to $100,000	59	58	10	127
$100,000 to $200,000	26	38	6	70
Greater than $200,000	18	71	4	93
Total	460	352	86	898

[a] Teller windows are not considered branches of a bank.

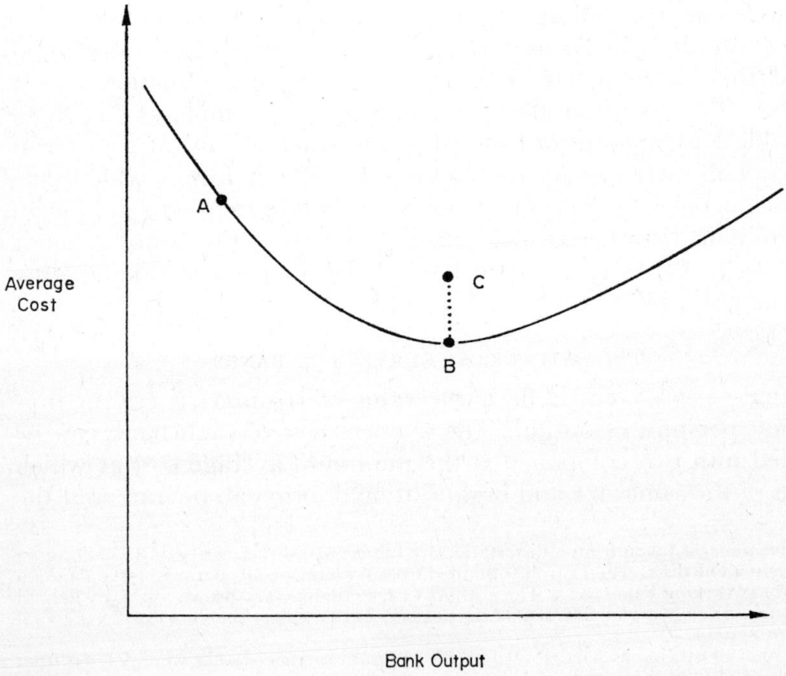

FIGURE 1. Long-run average cost curve

bank's excess cost per unit of output over this minimum average cost. The technical efficiency of a bank equals the first component of its average cost, and a bank's operational efficiency equals the second component.

Technical and operational efficiency of banks are illustrated in Figure 1. The curve labelled *LAC* is a hypothetical long-run average cost curve for banks of a given organizational form. The long-run average cost curve shows the minimum average cost at each level of output at which banks can operate. The banks producing at minimum average cost are run with maximum efficiency and have the plant size and technology best suited for their levels of output.

Banks that produce at combinations of average cost and output on the long-run average cost curve, such as banks *A* and *B* in Figure 1, have maximum operational efficiency. In the range of output in which the long-run average cost curve has a negative slope, larger banks are technically more efficient than smaller banks, and conversely, in the range of output in which the long-run average cost curve has a positive slope, smaller banks are technically more efficient than larger banks. Thus in Figure 1, bank *B* is technically more efficient than bank *A*. Bank *C* is operationally inefficient because it produces the same level of output as bank *B* but at higher cost. However, bank *C* is technically more efficient than bank *A* since bank *C* is capable of producing at lower average cost if operated efficiently.

The Nature of Frontier Cost Curves

Long-run average cost curves are estimated for banks of the three organizational forms using a frontier estimation procedure.[2] Estimation of frontier cost curves is based upon the following line of reasoning. The average cost of banks known to be operationally inefficient should lie above the estimated long-run average cost curve. The total number of banks in the sample that are operated inefficiently can be determined only if the position of the long-run average cost curve is known. Since banks with higher costs than other banks of the same size are known to be operationally inefficient, these banks should not influence the position of the estimated cost curve. Only the banks in the sample with the lowest average cost

[2] The estimation of the cost curves in this study is similar to the frontier technique that has been used to estimate production functions. See M. J. Farrell, 'The Measurement of Productive Efficiency', *Journal of the Royal Statistical Society*, CXX, Part III (1957), pp. 253–81; M. J. Farrell and M. Fieldhouse, 'Estimating Efficient Production Functions under Increasing Returns to Scale', *Journal of the Royal Statistical Society*, Series A (1962), pp. 252–67; W. D. Seitz, 'The Measurement of Efficiency Relative to a Frontier Production Function', *American Journal of Agricultural Economics*, LII (November 1970), pp. 505–11.

at each level of output should influence the position of the estimated cost curve. A line connecting the average cost of the low cost banks, called frontier banks, forms the frontier cost curve.[3] Frontier banks and frontier cost curves have the following characteristics:

(a) frontier banks have the lowest average cost at their output levels of the banks in the sample,
(b) the frontier cost curve, formed by connecting the average cost of adjacent frontier banks with straight lines, must be convex, and[4]
(c) no banks in the sample have average cost that lies below the frontier cost curve.

Uses for Different Cost Curves

Works by David Alhadeff and Lyle Gramley are representative of other bank cost studies in which the estimated cost curves are based upon the average performance of banks at each level of output. Alhadeff estimated a cost curve for unit banks in California by dividing these banks into several size categories and averaging the cost per unit of output of banks in each size category.[5] Cost curves based upon regression analysis also reflect average bank performance. Gramley's study of scale economies of unit banks in the Tenth Federal Reserve District is an example of the bank cost studies that use multiple regression analysis.[6] A major distinction between these two statistical techniques is that the latter allows several influences to be held constant in estimating the relation between cost and output.

Frontier cost curves are better approximations to the long-run average cost curves than either type of estimated cost curve based upon average bank performance. The position and shape of cost curves based upon average bank performance are influenced by the tendencies for banks of different sizes and organizational forms to operate inefficiently, while cost curves estimated by frontier procedures are not sensitive to banks known to be operationally inefficient.

One criticism of frontier cost curves is that they may be biased due to measurement error since these curves are derived from the average cost and output observations of a small number of frontier

[3] See Working Paper #15, St. Louis Federal Reserve Bank, for a discussion of Babb's Algorithm which was used to estimate the cost curves.

[4] Convexity is not a requirement of the frontier procedure but is adopted in this study because cost curves are generally assumed to be convex in economic theory.

[5] David A. Alhadeff, *Monopoly and Competition in Banking* (Berkeley: University of California Press, 1954).

[6] Lyle E. Gramley, *A Study of Scale Economics in Commercial Banking* (Kansas City, Mo: Federal Reserve Bank of Kansas City, 1962).

banks.[7] However, cost curves based upon 'averaging' or regression techniques are also subject to this source of bias.

BANK OUTPUT

The nature of banking creates some difficult problems for measuring bank output. Since banks produce a large number of services, a set of weights must be developed in order to aggregate bank services into a measure of total output of a bank. In this study deposits are treated as inputs of banks, and banks are assumed to produce output by holding interest earning assets. This view of banking has two important implications for the calculation of bank output. First, the revenue banks receive from service charges on demand deposits is not considered a return on output produced, but merely a reduction in the cost of the demand deposit input. Second, the services provided for depositors, such as the number of checks cleared or the number of the accounts which make up a dollar volume of demand deposits, do not affect the measure of a bank's output, but do affect the cost of its inputs.

Both the usual balance sheet and income statement measures of bank output are used in the study. The balance sheet measure of bank output used is loans plus investments. For each bank in the sample, monthly holdings of interest earning assets are averaged for the year 1968. This is similar to the balance sheet measure of output in other studies.[8]

The income statement measure of bank output used in this article is bank revenue adjusted for the market power of banks less revenue from service charges. This output measure, called the adjusted revenue measure of bank output, is similar to measures of bank output developed by Greenbaum and by Schweitzer.[9] The weights used in aggregating a bank's interest earning assets are estimates of the rates of return banks would earn on each asset category if they had no market power. These estimated rates of return are assumed

[7] Measurement error in the Functional Cost data may be smaller than the measurement error in the Call Report data, which is used in most other studies of bank costs. The purpose of the Functional Cost Program is to aid the banks that volunteer to participate in improving the operations, and therefore, the participating banks have an incentive to make accurate reports.

[8] See: Alhadeff, *op. cit.*; Paul M. Horvitz, 'Economies of Scale in Banking in Commission on Money and Credit', *Private Financial Institutions* (Englewood Cliffs, N.J.: Prentice-Hall, Inc., 1963), pp. 1–54; I. Schweiger and J. S. McGee, 'Chicago Banking: The Structure and Performance at Banks and Related Financial Institutions in Chicago and Other Areas', *Journal of Business* (July 1961), pp. 201–366; Gramley, *op. cit.*

[9] Stuart I. Greenbaum, 'Banking Structure and Costs: A Statistical Study of the Costs–Output Relationship in Commercial Banking' (unpublished Ph.D. dissertation, Johns Hopkins University, Baltimore, 1964); Stuart A. Schweitzer, 'Costs and Production in Banking: The Case of Ninth Federal Reserve District' (unpublished dissertation, University of Minnesota, Minneapolis, August 1970).

to reflect the social value banks produce by holding different assets.[10]

The adjusted revenue measure of bank output is calculated with the following equation:

$$(1) \qquad RA_i = \sum_{j=1}^{j=8} b_j A_i^j + NLI_i - SC_i$$

where:

RA_i = the output of bank i

b_j = estimated yield of the j'th loan category specified in the Functional Cost data

A_i^j = the holdings of asset j by bank i

NLI_i = the nonlending income of bank i, composed of revenue from investments, revenue from non-banking services, such as safe deposit boxes and trust accounts, and service charge revenue.

SC_i = the revenue received as service charges on deposits by bank i.

To estimate the b_j's used in calculating adjusted revenue in (1), the revenue a bank receives from each type of asset it holds is assumed to depend upon its holdings of that asset and its market power. Furthermore the relationship between the yield a bank receives on a given financial asset and the market power of the bank is assumed to be linear. The yield on each financial asset can then be written as follows:

$$(2) \qquad \frac{R_i^j}{A_i^j} = B_0 + B_1 X_i$$

where

R_i^j is the revenue bank i receives from asset j

A_i^j is the holdings of asset j by bank i

B_0 is the intercept

X_i is the degree of market power by bank i

Equation (2) is estimated by regression analysis for eight categories of loans specified in the Functional Cost data. Two concentration ratios of local banking business are used as measures of the market power of banks in their market areas. The market area of a bank is specified as its Standard Metropolitan Statistical Area wherever possible, otherwise as the county in which it is located. Local banking business is measured as deposits under \$10,000 of individuals, partnerships, and corporations.[11] The first concentration ratio used is the percentage of local deposits held by the five largest banks in the

[10] For a discussion of different measures of bank output, see George Benston, 'Economies of Scale in Financial Institutions', Working Paper No. 7019A for University of Rochester, College of Business Administration, October 1970.

[11] Information on deposits of less than \$10,000 comes from the Summary of Deposits data provided by the Federal Deposit Insurance Corporation.

market area. The second concentration ratio is computed by squaring the percentage of local deposits held by each bank in a market area and summing these squared shares for all banks in the market area.[12]

The weights b_j are determined by the regression estimates of equation (2) for each category of loans. The concentration ratios approach zero as the number of competing banks in a market increases. The yields that banks with zero market power are estimated to earn on assets in each loan category, therefore, equal the intercepts of the regression equations in the form of equation (2). Two regressions are run for each loan category, one for each concentration ratio. The intercept for each loan category used in calculating adjusted revenue in (1) is taken from the regression equation in which the t value for the concentration ratio is the largest.

No adjustments are made in this study for the biases in the adjusted revenue measure of bank output. Some of these biases are discussed in other studies.[13] A bias not discussed in other bank cost studies results from bank–customer relationships.[14] Some banks accept the compensating balances of firms in place of a higher nominal yield on loans. This loan policy tends to lower the yield on business loans relative to the yields on other loans, thus biasing downward the output associated with holding business loans.

BANK COSTS

The cost observation for each bank in the sample is total annual operating expenses from the Functional Cost data less service charge revenue from the same period. Cost and output observations are made on an annual basis for each bank in the sample. Costs are more likely to have been incurred producing the output of the same period with output and cost observations for a year than if shorter time periods were used.[15]

ESTIMATED FRONTIER

Frontier cost curves for unit, branch, and holding company banks are presented in this section. Frontier cost curves with loans plus investments and adjusted revenue as output measures are illustrated in Figures 2 and 3, respectively. The levels of average cost on the

[12] Eugene Singer, *Anti-Trust Economics: Selected Legal Cases and Economic Models* (Englewood Cliffs, New Jersey: Prentice-Hall, 1968), p. 136.

[13] Stuart Greenbaum, 'A Study of Bank Costs', *The National Banking Review* (June 1967), pp. 420–2.

[14] See Donald Hodgman, *Commercial Bank Loan and Investment Policy* (Champaign, Illinois: Bureau of Economic and Business Research, University of Illinois, 1963).

[15] For a discussion of biases in bank operating cost observations, see Benston, *op. cit.*

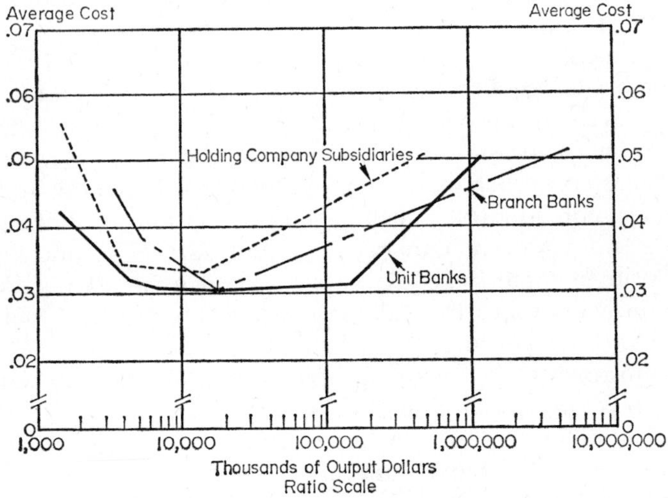

FIGURE 2. Frontier long-run average cost curves with the loans plus investments output measure

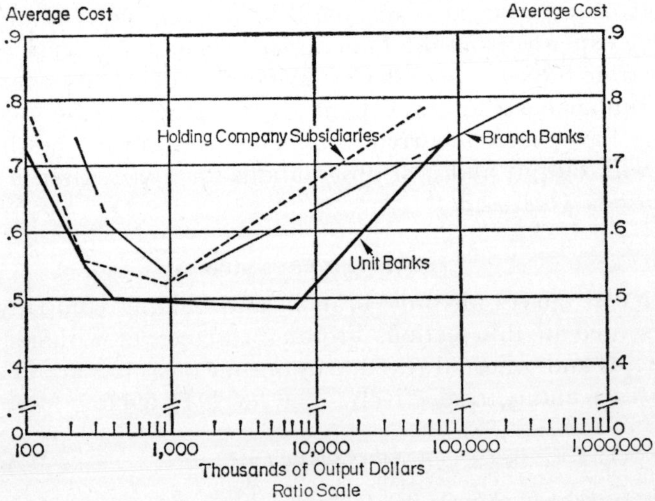

FIGURE 3. Frontier long-run average cost curves with the adjusted revenue output measure

frontier cost curves using loans plus investments and adjusted revenue as measures of output are given in Tables II and III. The first column of these tables refers to the bank's relative size within its own organizational group. For example, in Table II the second unit bank which

TABLE II

FRONTIER COST CURVES WITH LOANS PLUS INVESTMENTS AS OUTPUT

Banks' relative position	*Output* $	*Average cost* $	*Slope*
	UNIT BANKS		
1	1,409,060	0.04221	
			-3.50×10^{-9}
22	4,399,500	0.03174	
			-4.68×10^{-10}
54	6,470,753	0.03077	
			-8.861×10^{-11}
134	10,675,222	0.03040	
			1.34×10^{-11}
428	110,036,062	0.03173	
			1.57×10^{-11}
460	1,284,230,000	0.05020	
	BRANCH BANKS		
Banks' relative position	*Output* $	*Average cost* $	*Slope*
1	3,477,609	0.04595	
			-4.18×10^{-9}
5	5,360,507	0.03807	
			-1.03×10^{-9}
8	6,090,812	0.03732	
			-5.87×10^{-10}
67	17,640,650	0.03054	
			4.29×10^{-12}
353	4,854,586,000	0.05131	
	HOLDING COMPANY SUBSIDIARIES		
Banks' relative position	*Output* $	*Average cost* $	*Slope*
1	1,462,108	0.05556	
			-8.59×10^{-9}
3	3,928,579	0.03437	
			-1.18×10^{-10}
22	14,776,520	0.03309	
			3.85×10^{-11}
86	471,513,000	0.05069	

falls on the estimated curve has larger output measured as loans plus investments than 21 other unit banks in the sample. The second column is bank output, the third column average cost, and the fourth column gives the slope of the frontier cost curve between adjacent frontier banks.

The estimated cost curves for each output measure and for banks of each organizational form are of the same general shape. Relatively large economies of scale exist in the range of small bank output. The economies of scale are less for larger banks, with minimum average cost at a low output level relative to the output levels of the largest banks in the sample. For all six estimated cost curves, the largest of

TABLE III

FRONTIER COST CURVES WITH ADJUSTED REVENUE AS OUTPUT

UNIT BANKS

Banks' relative position	*Output* $	*Average cost* $	*Slopes*
1	82,434	0.721	
			-1.00×10^{-6}
21	255,106	0.547	
			-3.24×10^{-7}
59	397,792	0.501	
			-2.21×10^{-9}
430	7,176,716	0.486	
			3.19×10^{-9}
460	87,014,000	0.741	

BRANCH BANKS

Banks' relative position	*Output* $	*Average cost* $	*Slope*
1	213,845	0.742	
			-8.26×10^{-7}
9	371,335	0.612	
			-1.29×10^{-7}
64	1,017,361	0.529	
			8.56×10^{-10}
353	312,934,437	0.796	

HOLDING COMPANY SUBSIDIARIES

Banks' relative position	*Output* $	*Average cost* $	*Slope*
1	103,682	0.783	
			-1.63×10^{-6}
3	241,392	0.559	
			-5.211×10^{-8}
22	912,722	0.524	
			7.18×10^{-9}
86	31,960,371	0.747	

the banks with minimum average cost is about 1/12 the size of the largest bank in its respective sample. In the range of output larger than the point of minimum average cost, all of the estimated cost curves have small positive slopes. Nevertheless, the levels of bank output being dealt with are large enough that the savings which could be achieved by dividing large banks into optimum size banks would be significant. For example, the annual savings in terms of resources consumed from dividing the largest unit bank (as measured by loans plus investments) into banks of optimal size would be more than $25 million.

Statements about the relative efficiencies of banks with different organizational forms can be made by comparing the relative positions of the frontier cost curves for banks of the three organizational forms at each output level. Figures 2 and 3 show the relative positions of the frontier cost curves for banks of the three organizational forms for both measures of output. Since the relative positions of the curves are the same for both measures of output, their implications for economies of organizational form are discussed simultaneously.

Unit banks appear to have the greatest technical efficiency along almost the whole range of unit bank output in the sample. The one exception is that the cost curves for unit banks lie above the cost curves for branch banks at the output level of the largest unit bank. The result that unit banks have lower operating cost than branch banks at the same level of output is consistent with the findings of past studies.[16]

Holding company subsidiary banks have greater technical efficiency than branch banks up to bank size of about $1,000,000 in adjusted revenue and $10,000,000 in loans plus investments measures of output. This is the first study to compare the operating efficiency of branch banks and holding company subsidiary banks, so this finding in this study cannot be compared with the findings of other studies.

The cost curves for holding company subsidiary banks are above the cost curves for unit banks at every output level in the study. This result is inconsistent with the only other study on the subject.[17]

Comparisons of Cost Studies

The frontier cost curves for unit and branch banks are compared with the bank cost curves in other studies in Tables IV and V.[18] In Table IV the shape of the cost curve for unit banks with loans plus investments as the measure of output is compared with the

[16] See Jack Guttentag and Edward Herman, 'Banking Structure and Performance', New York University Institute of Finance Bulletin, Nos. 41–3 (February 1967).

[17] Schweitzer, *op. cit.*, p. 98.

[18] The source of data in the studies by Alhadeff, Gramley, and Greenbaum is the Call Report data, which gives only mid-year or end of year observations. The information used to estimate bank output in this study is annual averages of monthly figures. Therefore, the information on asset holdings of banks used in estimating the frontier cost curves better approximates the holding of assets over the year than the information in the Call Report data. For a discussion of problems with using the Call Report data, see Greenbaum, p. 420.

shapes of estimated unit bank cost curves in other studies that also used balance sheet definitions of bank output. In Table V the shapes of the frontier cost curves for unit and branch banks with the adjusted revenue measure of output are compared with the shapes of unit and branch bank cost curves in another study that also used an adjusted revenue measure of bank output.

TABLE IV

COMPARISON OF ESTIMATED LONG-RUN AVERAGE COST CURVES OF UNIT BANKS WITH BALANCE SHEET ITEMS At OUTPUT PROXIES

(Dollar denominated numbers are cost per dollar of output; numbers in parentheses are percentages)

Bank size (thousands of dollars)	*Alhadeff*[A]	*Gramley*[B]	*Frontier*
Under $2,000	$0.0438 (100.00)	$0.0278[a] (100.00)	$0.0401 (100.00)
$2,000 to $5,000	$0.0289 (65.98)		$0.0349 (86.92)
$5,000 to $15,000	$0.0256 (58.45)	$0.0239[b] (86.00)	$0.0304 (75.88)
$15,000 to $50,000	$0.0282 (64.38)		$0.0307 (76.46)
$50,000 to $150,000	$0.0255 (58.22)	$0.0200[c] (71.94)	$0.0318 (79.45)
Above $150,000	$0.0199 (45.43)	$0.0196[d] (70.50)	$0.0323 (80.62)
1,000,000[C]			$0.0457 (113.90)

[A] Data from California banks were used in this study. This particular estimate is for 1950. The output measure was loans plus investments, but the size groupings were in terms of deposits.

[B] Banks from the Tenth Federal Reserve District made up the sample used in this study. Total assets were the output measure. Cost and output observations are for the years 1956–59.

[a] at $1,000,000 of assets
[b] at $10,000,000 of assets
[c] at $100,000,000 of assets
[d] at $200,000,000 of assets

[C] Estimates for $1,000,000,000 were only for the curves estimated in our bank sample since the other sample did not include banks of that size.

The estimated cost curves which are compared with the frontier estimate in Table IV are taken from studies by Alhadeff and Gramley. Average cost on each cost curve is given for several ranges of bank output. Below each average cost observation is the percent the average cost figure is of the average cost of banks in the smallest output category on the same cost curve. The percent figures are best for comparing the shapes of cost curves since the average cost observations vary with the balance sheet item used to measure output, the source of data used for calculating cost and output, and the year in which the cost and output observations were measured.

The cost curves estimated by Alhadeff and Gramley show increasing returns to scale throughout the range of bank output in their studies. The frontier cost curve also shows increasing returns to scale throughout the range of output from under $2 million to $15 million, but decreasing returns to scale for banks of larger output. The diseconomies of scale on the frontier cost curve are small in the range of bank output covered by the other two studies relative to the diseconomies of scale for banks in the output range covered only by the frontier cost curve.

TABLE V

COMPARISON OF ESTIMATED LONG-RUN AVERAGE COST CURVES WITH ADJUSTED REVENUE AS THE OUTPUT PROXY

(Dollar denominated numbers are cost per dollar of output; the numbers in parentheses are percentages)

UNIT BANKS			BRANCH BANKS		
Bank size (thousands of dollars)	*Greenbaum*[A]	*Frontier*	*Bank size (thousands of dollars)*	*Greenbaum*[A]	*Frontier*
$100	$0.792 (100.00)	$0.719 (100.00)	$500	$0.766 (100.00)	$0.600 (100.00)
$500	$0.750 (94.70)	$0.501 (69.68)	$1,000	$0.762 (99.48)	$0.531 (88.50)
$1,000	$0.698 (88.13)	$0.500 (69.54)	$5,000	$0.728 (95.04)	$0.531 (88.50)
$2,000	$0.594 (75.00)	$0.498 (69.26)	$10,000	$0.687 (89.69)	$0.537 (89.50)
$3,000	$0.490 (61.87)	$0.495 (68.85)	$15,000	$0.645 (84.20)	$0.541 (90.17)
$4,000	$0.386 (48.74)	$0.493 (68.57)	$20,000	$0.603 (78.72)	$0.545 (90.83)
$10,000		$0.495 (68.85)	$100,000		$0.614 (1.023)

[A] See 'A Study of Bank Costs', *The National Banking Review* (June 1967), pp. 415–34.

The frontier cost curves for unit and branch banks based upon the adjusted revenue output measure are compared with Greenbaum's unit and branch bank cost curves in Table V. The adjusted revenue output measure used in this study is similar to Greenbaum's output measure. As in Table IV, the shapes of the cost curves are compared by using the percentages that the average cost at various output levels is of the average cost of the smallest banks on the cost curves.

Average cost on the unit bank cost curves is calculated at several points in the bank output range from $100,000 to $4 million. Both the frontier cost curve and Greenbaum's cost curve show increasing returns to scale over this output range. The percentage decline in average cost in the $100,000–$4 million output range is greater for Greenbaum's unit bank cost curve than for the frontier cost curve. Decreasing returns to scale on the frontier cost curve for unit banks begins for a bank output size slightly larger than $7 million.

Greenbaum's cost curve for branch banks shows increasing returns to scale throughout the output range of output he examined. The frontier cost curves for branch banks show increasing returns to scale in the output range up to about $1 million, but decreasing returns to scale in the range of bank output larger than $1 million.

CONCLUSIONS

The positions and shapes of the bank cost curves derived in this study have implications for the economies of organizational form and economies of scale in commercial banking. With regard to the economies of organizational form, one finding of this study is that the cost curves for branch banks lie above the cost curves for unit banks. Other studies with cost curves for both branch and unit banks show the same result. A second finding of this study is that holding company subsidiary banks have greater technical efficiency than branch banks at relatively low levels of bank output and are less efficient at high levels of bank output. A third finding is that the cost curves for holding company subsidiary banks lie above the cost curves for unit banks at each level of output, whereas the only other study that compares the efficiency of the two types of banks gives the opposite results.

The shapes of the cost curves estimated in this study have important implications for bank regulation. A controversy in bank regulation has centred around the existence of a trade-off between the goals of bank production at least cost and competitive pricing of bank output. Most past estimates of long-run average cost curves for banks show no range of output in which the cost curves have positive slopes. For this reason, the trade-off is often referred to in the extreme—contrasting the benefits society could gain from the existence of one huge bank, which could take full advantage of economies of scale, and the danger to society inherent in the monopoly power which one large bank would possess.[19]

The findings in this study suggest that the dimension of the trade-off between economies of scale and competitive pricing of output in commercial banking is actually more restricted than previously believed. The frontier estimated cost curves show decreasing returns

[19] Donald P. Jacobs, 'The Framework of Commercial Bank Regulation: An Appraisal', *The National Banking Review*, I (March 1964), p. 344.

to scale beginning at relatively low levels of bank output. According to this finding, the full advantages of economies of scale can be achieved in banking without having one monopoly bank. Efficient production and competition among banks may be consistent in bank markets large enough to support several banks of optimal size.

CALIFORNIA STATE UNIVERSITY AT FULLERTON
FEDERAL RESERVE BANK OF ST. LOUIS

INVESTMENT AND COMPETITION FROM BOOM TO RECESSION: A CASE STUDY IN THE PROCESSES OF COMPETITION—THE DRY CLEANING INDUSTRY.[1]

by R. W. Shaw

INTRODUCTION

The purpose of this paper is to analyse the relationship between investment and the competitive process in response to an innovatory disturbance in the Dry Cleaning Industry. Relatively high profits combined with the recognition of the ease of entry led to massive new entry, expansion and retaliatory investment culminating in excess capacity, price wars and a struggle for survival. The major disturbance initiating this process was the advent of small on-the-premises cleaning unit shops providing a rapid and personal service and replacing the relatively slow factory based operations which serviced large numbers of cleaning reception centres (receiving offices). The paper reports on the processes of adjustment as the industry responded to the prolonged disequilibrium situation.[2] The analysis relates largely to the theoretical contributions of Professors E. T. Penrose,[3] J. Robinson,[4] and F. M. Scherer[5] concerning respectively: the inducements, resources and direction of expansion of firms; the impossibility of competition in a free entry industry; and the relative speed of innovative reactions of firms dominating a market compared with others.

The market structure is described in Section 1. It is followed by a discussion of investment and diversification policy. Finally, the consequences of excessive industrial expansion are analysed in a section on investment and competition.

The analysis is based partly on interview data obtained from 39

[1] I would like to acknowledge the many helpful comments and criticisms of A. D. Bain, J. R. Davies, B. J. Loasby, E. A. Lowe, G. R. Rainnie, S. A. Shaw and C. J. Sutton.

[2] The problem of public policy in relation to excessive and ill-advised entry is examined in 'Innovation, Freedom of Entry and Excess Capacity in the Dry Cleaning Industry', University of Stirling, Discussion Papers in Economics, Finance and Investment, No. 11, 1972.

[3] E. T. Penrose, *The Theory of the Growth of the Firm*, Basil Blackwell, Oxford, 1959, particularly Chapter 5.

[4] J. Robinson, 'The Impossibility of Competition', in *Monopoly and Competition and their Regulation*; Ed. E. H. Chamberlin, Macmillan, London, 1954.

[5] F. M. Scherer, *Industrial Market Structure and Economic Performance*, Rand McNally and Co., Chicago, 1970, Chapter 17—particularly pp. 366 ff.; and 'Research and Development Resource Allocation under Rivalry'; *Quarterly Journal of Economics*, August, 1967, Volume LXXXI, No. 3.

companies operating mostly in the West Riding of Yorkshire and the North East dry cleaning, laundry and launderette trades.[6] Other sources include company reports and the trade press.[7] Laundry and launderette firms were included because they typically engage in dry cleaning activities[8] but geographical coverage was restricted to facilitate the examination of the competitive process.

MARKET STRUCTURE AND DEVELOPMENTS

In 1966 there were 1834 firms in the dry cleaning industry in Great Britain.[9] At one end of the scale the industry was dominated by the Johnson Group which had around 1800 shops and a turnover of over £8.6 million, Sketchley Ltd. with over 500 shops and a turnover of over £8 million,[10] and other smaller chain cleaners; at the other extreme there were 1168 small firms each with a turnover of less than £10,000 p.a. operating one, two or three shops. Industry turnover was £56 million.

In the north of England, and particularly in the West Riding, several chain cleaners, as well as launderers with substantial cleaning interests competed with one another and with the small firms. In each small town, city centre, or residential area, however, there was only a small number of shops so that local oligopolistic situations were normal.

Entry conditions were free but not always easy, there being little to prevent an attempted entry but some difficulty in establishing a successful entry. The capital requirements for entry and/or expansion in the early 1960s were low: a small shop taking cleaning over the counter ready to be sent to a central factory for processing could be opened for an investment of £50–£200 and bearing a rent of £2–£3 per week; a unit shop doing cleaning on the premises could be opened with an investment of only £5000 if the shop was leased.[11] Since financing arrangements through the equipment manufacturers enabled a substantial part of this sum to be borrowed the initial

[6] In 1969, the survey companies operated in 37 factories and over a thousand shops.

[7] A classification of the cooperating firms as well as details of other sources is given in Appendix 1. The author thanks the executives of these companies and organizations for their kind cooperation.

[8] A detailed analysis of the costs and prices of the washing activities of launderettes is contained in T. Kempner, 'Costs and Prices in Launderettes', *Journal of Industrial Economics*, Vol. VIII, No. 3, June, 1960. Since self-service coin-op cleaning was only then being introduced Kempner's analysis omits reference to dry cleaning though the general tenor of the analysis is still valid. However, a major structural change in the industry occurred in the 1960s with the entry of several launderette machinery suppliers and hence the effective breakdown of a 'geographical franchise' system.

[9] Report on the Census of Distribution and other services, H.M.S.O. 1966. There were also 1205 laundries and 2554 launderette firms.

[10] Partly derived from its textile interests.

[11] £6000–£8000 was the typical initial investment by new entrants in the survey in the mid-1960s.

commitment could be very small indeed: two firms in the survey opening unit shops managed to borrow over 80 per cent of their original capital expenditure leaving in one case only £600 to be found by the partners. Launderettes offering self-service dry cleaning could be opened for a similarly small investment. Hence expansion by existing cleaning firms and diversification by laundries was inexpensive and even new entrants could manage with only a trivial investment.

A further potential barrier to entry, knowledge of the technology, provided no problem. Entrants found the basic knowledge required to operate a dry cleaning business easy to acquire and no professional qualifications were necessary.

The main barriers to entry and/or expansion were the difficulty of acquiring suitable shop sites, the limited size of local markets and consumer loyalty to existing shops and firms. Thus, although entry to local oligopolies was free, successful entry was by no means assured. The overall competitive situation was overlaid by the rate of growth of the market, by the development of the on-the-premises cleaning unit shop and self-service coin-ops, the trend to washable garments, and the imposition of selective employment tax and withdrawal of investment incentives from the industry.

The dry-cleaning industry whose sales had grown steadily in the 1950s continued to grow at 5 per cent per annum between 1961 and 1966; growth then slowed down and demand even declined slightly in 1968 and 1969 so that a recovery in 1970 only restored turnover to the 1967 level.[12] The sister laundry industry, however, suffered from relative stagnation in the 1950s as the domestic market declined and this led to active diversification by laundries into dry cleaning which continued during the 1960s. The launderette industry grew throughout the period especially during the early and mid-1960s.

The advent and proliferation of the on-the-premises cleaning unit shop represented a major change in the structure of the industry. In the 1950s the industry was dominated by major dry cleaning firms operating from one or more factories which were serviced by vans and vast numbers of receiving offices. By 1970 many of the receiving offices had been closed and others converted to unit shops so that

[12] *Trade and Industry* (formerly the *Board of Trade Journal*). The value of sales index for dry cleaning businesses (1966 = 100) behaved as follows:

1966	100
1967	101
1968	99
1969	97
1970	101

Some part of the stagnation reflected the increased importance of coin-op sales not reflected in the Department of Trade and Industry returns. See below.

the industry was no longer primarily factory based. This change was made possible by two innovations in the British market. The introduction of machines employing non-inflammable cleaning solvents, carbon tetrachloride and trichloroethylene, in the 1930s enabled the beginnings of unit shops. Secondly, the diffusion of the unit shop was facilitated by the development of totally enclosed dry-cleaning machines in the late 1940s, which reduced the health hazard, and the introduction of a range of suitably sized machines (e.g. 20 lb and 40 lb) in the 1950s.[13] The availability of perchlorethylene, a non-inflammable cleaning solvent more suitable for artificial fibres, was also an important enabling factor.

Other significant developments were the rapid expansion in launderettes at the end of the 1950s and in the early 1960s, the subsequent installation of coin-op dry cleaning in them and in coin-op cleaning only shops; and the introduction of more garments requiring washing rather than dry cleaning. Finally the removal of investment incentives from the industry in 1966 coupled with the imposition of selective employment tax and the subsequent increases in 1968 and 1969 significantly raised costs in an industry where labour costs had been approximately 50 per cent of turnover.[14]

As a result of these developments the dry-cleaning industry which had been quite profitable in the 1950s and early 1960s found profits declining rapidly so that in the late 1960s with a stagnant market and rising costs many firms became unprofitable[15] and large numbers of firms went out of business while others drastically reduced the number of their shops.

This history may be summarized as follows: in the late 1950s and early 1960s entry and expansion, particularly of unit shops, led to rapid increases in capacity which exceeded the increases in demand.[16] By the mid-1960s when demand stagnated significant excess capacity existed and the subsequent competitive process involved the elimination of some of this surplus. Indeed the industry displays some of the characteristics described by Professor Joan Robinson in

[13] Foreign enclosed machines had existed well before the Second World War. Some development of unit shops did take place mainly by small firms using these and the small open Burtol machine. However, the war retarded this development.

[14] Even after considerable rationalization the Johnson Group paid £416,000 in S.E.T. in 1969 which amounted to over 4.6 per cent of turnover.

[15] e.g. the Johnson Group which had reported before tax profits averaging 9.2 per cent on capital in 1960—64 could only report profits averaging 5.1 per cent in 1967—69 including the company's first-ever trading loss in 1968. Similarly, Martin's the Cleaners (≏300 shops before its sale in 1968) and Clarks of Retford (≏80 shops) made trading losses between 1967–69. Sketchley Ltd. saw its before-tax profits reduced from 18.0 per cent in 1960—64 to 10.3 per cent in 1967–69.

[16] National Board for Prices and Incomes, *Laundry and Dry Cleaning Charges*, Report No. 20, Cmnd. 3093, 1966, H.M.S.O.

The Impossibility of Competition:[17] entrants rushed into a free-entry boom industry, and existing firms expanded and engaged in retaliatory investment until by 1966 there was clear excess capacity; thereafter the longevity of processing plant ensured a protracted period of downward adjustment in capacity.

INVESTMENT AND DIVERSIFICATION POLICY

In this section the policies of three groups of firms: established dry cleaners, established laundries and joint laundries and dry cleaners, and new entrants are considered in turn. A major feature of this analysis is the widely differing perspective of these groups of firms. Both established cleaners' and launderers' investment policies were constrained by existing assets and trading patterns though this led to divergent policies for the two groups.[18] Completely new firms entering the dry-cleaning industry had no such constraints: they merely saw an opportunity to obtain a share of a growing market by offering an improved cleaning service.

(i) *Established Dry Cleaners*

Although there were exceptions the general policy followed by established dry cleaning firms in the 1960s was to concentrate their investment in unit shops offering quick on-the-premises dry cleaning following a period of experimentation in the late 1950s.[19,20] The development of this policy is important because it significantly affected the course of competitive relationships.

The established cleaners already possessed central factories and large numbers of receiving offices, Table I, and hence were concerned with assimilating any unit shops development into an existing and balanced system.

The massive adjustments to the trading systems of these companies were accomplished by opening new unit shops, converting the larger receiving offices into unit shops, and initially by opening new or purchasing existing receiving offices from other companies to boost turnover at the central factories, and later by large-scale closures of unprofitable receiving offices.

[17] J. Robinson, *The Impossibility of Competition, op. cit.* The effects of varying two structural features compared with Professor Robinson's model are discussed later. These features are the presence of relatively large regional companies, and the versatility of some shop capacity.

[18] See E. T. Penrose, *op. cit.*

[19] S. M. Cleaners who built a new central factory at the beginning of the 1960s for processing dry cleaning intake from surrounding receiving offices clearly attempted a different strategy, though apparently unsuccessfully.

[20] e.g. 'After some years of initial experiment the Group has made a successful entry into this field.' Chairman's Statement 1961, The Johnson Group Cleaners Ltd.

Despite a later enthusiasm for unit shops the established companies were relatively slow off the mark[21] giving the new entrants a competitive advantage. There were four major reasons for this delay. Since the established companies already operated chains of receiving offices which sent garments to be cleaned at a central factory the profitability of investment in unit shops, which might divert trade from existing shops and factories, had to be assessed in the light of this interdependence problem.[22] The creation of additional shop and processing capacity was likely to reduce the contribution to fixed costs and profits of existing facilities so that

TABLE I

SHOPS OF THE TWO MAJOR ESTABLISHED CLEANERS*

Year	*Johnson Group Cleaners Ltd.*			*Sketchley Ltd.*		
	Receiving Offices	*Unit Shops*	*Unit Shops/ Total Shops %*	*Receiving Offices*	*Unit Shops*	*Unit Shops/ Total Shops %*
< 1960		experimentation			experimentation	
1960		first group				
1961	1600	118	7	348	9	3
1963	n a†	n a	n a	379	25	6
1965	1489	275	16	463	76	14
1967	1392	340	20	428	159	27
1970	636	456	42	309	337	52

Source: annual company reports.
Notes:
* Most other companies developed along similar lines, though obviously at different rates.
† Not available.

established companies might expect unit shop investment to earn a lower rate of profit than newly formed companies unencumbered by past investments. The second and third problems: capital cost and managerial capacity are associated with the scale of the receiving shop chains. The Johnson Group reported that its investment in unit shops by 1961 exceeded £570,000[23] and since, at that

[21] Reports in the trade press were already discussing the trend to units in 1956 and 1957. See, for example, *Power Laundry & Cleaning News*, November 30th, 1956, p. 973 and January 11th, 1957, p. 71. Enclosed cleaning machines suitable for shops had existed in the 1930s and were readily available in Britain in the late 1940s and early 1950s.

[22] 'A number of these [receiving offices] are quite large enough to contain a unit cleaning plant and it will be our long-term policy to do this when we can replace the work which they send to Worcester from other sources.' Chairman's Statement, 1963, Quality Cleaners Ltd.

[23] Chairman's Statement, 1961, Johnson Group Cleaners, Ltd.

stage, only about 7 per cent of its shops were units, it is clear that while the cost of individual shop conversions was low the transformation of a factory-based cleaner into a unit shop chain cleaner would require investment on a massive scale.[24] Further, the managerial effort required to convert large numbers of receiving offices and to open new unit shops was obviously considerable and possibly acted as an additional restraining factor. Finally, business prudence and conservatism inhibited the reactions of established firms to the new unit shops.[25] The initial experimentation with unit shops apparently continued until about 1960 for both Johnson's (see note 20 above) and Sketchley's. Meanwhile, Martin's, another chain cleaner, having recognized the potential of unit shops earlier, already had nearly a quarter of its shops as units (60 units, 200 RO's), and new entrants were recognizing and seizing the opportunity. A contributory factor may have been the family control of some established cleaners which may have enabled them to be less responsive to new market developments than managerially controlled firms subject to stock market discipline.[26]

Even in the early 1960s it was abundantly clear that the rapid and personal service offered by unit shops gave them a marked competitive advantage over the relatively impersonal and slow service offered by the combination of receiving office and factory. Further, customers were finding it easier to find unit shops so that the position of the receiving office was progressively deteriorating. Hence the unit shops development programme became an increasingly defensive reaction to the competitive threat.[27] However, the combination of increasing wages, the imposition of Selective Employment Tax, and stagnating trade intensified rivalry and turned a difficult situation into a crisis. The established cleaners were forced into drastic reorganization programmes in which receiving offices and factories were closed and the changeover to unit shop chains

[24] Although the absolute scale of investment required was greatest for the largest companies the problem was just as severe for the smaller privately owned chains with limited financial resources. It should be noted that a complete changeover was hardly contemplated, at least in the early 1960s, particularly since many of the smaller shops were unsuitable for conversion into units.

[25] The substantial property interests of the chain cleaners may also have reduced their concern for new developments in the dry-cleaning industry.

[26] Family control of firms in other industries such as brewing and wool textiles may have had a similar effect in reducing financial discipline. A useful analysis, as well as a literature review, of the extent of stock market discipline is provided by A. Singh in *Take-overs, Their Relevance to the Stock Market and the Theory of the Firm*, University of Cambridge, Department of Applied Economics Monograph, 19, Cambridge University Press, 1971.

[27] e.g. 'We see no alternative to this major transformation of the pattern of our trading if we are to compete successfully in the years ahead with the large number of small local plants which have been and continue to be opened.' Chairman's Review, 1965, Sketchley Ltd.

was accelerated. A significant part of these programmes was the reciprocal agreements between firms to close and to exchange shops in the effort to reduce capacity and destructive competition.[28,29]

The investment policy outlined above seems to conform with the hypothesis that established firms with dominant market positions are unlikely to be active innovators but may well retaliate vigorously should their market share be threatened.[30] These companies held their markets with their rings of receiving offices in and around town centres and the cleaning was done in the factories. With a growing market there was room for balanced expansion. The unit shops threatened this balance and to this extent were an unwelcome intrusion whenever a company held a large share of the market. For new firms, or existing firms with smaller market shares, the unit shops provided a means of breaking into the market and the share of the larger competitors. Given the opportunity, then, for entry and expansion, unit shops were developed and the established firms, even in their strongholds, were forced to retaliate to protect their market position. The vigour of their competitive response is discussed later.

(ii) *Established Laundries and Joint Laundries and Cleaners*[31]

The thirteen survey companies in these categories[32] were founded before 1930. All have entered the dry-cleaning industry at least to the extent of accepting dry cleaning as a service along with laundry on the van rounds. Nearly all entered the dry-cleaning industry to diversify their operations although most delayed any significant dry cleaning effort until the postwar period.

Some companies entered dry cleaning as a 'boom industry' with the view that every laundry customer was a potential dry-cleaning customer. Others were more explicitly defensive: 'most

[28] 'Some progress in the reduction of outlets has already been made by agreements for reciprocal closing but there is still considerable further scope. The trade must surely accept the need for rationalization as an alternative to a long and painful process of attrition.' Chairman's Review, 1968, Sketchley Ltd.

'The Group closed 410 receiving shops and 33 unit shops during the year, some as part of reciprocal arrangements with competitors and some in a rationalization scheme as between Associated Companies within the Group, but in the majority of cases because shops were proving unprofitable in today's conditions.' Chairman's Statement, 1969, Johnson Group Cleaners Ltd.

[29] The position was also eased by the takeover of some cleaning firms by others so permitting rationalization: e.g. Martin's the Cleaners with nearly 300 shops was sold in 1968 to the Johnson Group which subsequently closed the factory and many of the shops.

[30] See F. M. Scherer, *op. cit.*

[31] Joint laundries and cleaners are those companies with one-third or more of their turnover in each section.

[32] Including one diversified laundry company.

laundries at this particular time (1950s) were deciding that if they were going to live they must have dry cleaning' to replace declining domestic laundry turnover and to increase revenue in the face of the growing costs of van rounds.

Generally entry took the form of installing dry-cleaning plant at the central laundry, opening receiving offices, and accepting dry cleaning on the laundry van rounds. Despite the substantial involvement of some launderers in the dry-cleaning industry most failed to open on-the-premises unit dry-cleaning shops or did so only to a minor extent: at the time of the survey (1969–70) the thirteen launderers operated only 21 unit shops compared with 176 receiving offices. For most of these launderers diversification into dry cleaning was seen largely as a means of providing work for the laundry and existing van rounds.

Although the number of laundries has declined throughout the 1960s trading conditions have remained sufficiently difficult for diversification investment to be a major effort. In this capital shortages have played a significant role: the small privately owned laundry has felt unable to enter the linen hire business and so has struggled on with laundry amalgamations and expansion in dry cleaning. The medium sized laundry has similarly felt a squeeze and has had to limit its diversification so that linen hire entry and laundry replacements have precluded significant unit shop dry-cleaning investment. Hence the substantial inroads made by laundries have on the whole been through vulnerable investment in receiving offices and van collections. This development by laundries of linen hire and dry-cleaning activities adjacent to the traditional laundry trade reflected the technical and market expertise of laundry managers and is consistent with Penrose's thesis of the short, sideways diversification step.[33] It also suggests the weakness of the strategy when the move arises from competitive pressure: most laundries were moving in the same directions.

(iii) *New Entrants*

Nineteen companies in the survey were first generation companies founded since the Second World War:[34] fourteen started as dry cleaners, though two have diversified substantially; and five started as launderettes. Most of the proprietors wanted to establish an independent business of their own and the dry cleaning and launderette industries provided the opportunity since only limited

[33] E. T. Penrose, *op. cit.*

[34] Three entrants were founded in the late 1940s, two in the 1950s, and 14 in the 1960s.

capital and either existing or easily acquired technical skills were required.

Ten new entrants have undertaken further investment in shops. Several companies opened satellite receiving offices to increase company turnover partly as security against increased competition and partly to remedy the defects of poor siting of the parent shop. Others have pursued a more determined growth policy in which profits have been ploughed back so that whenever a suitable shop site presented itself the company could expand.[35]

Four points, apart from the existence of an opportunity, are significant in relation to both the entry and timing of entry of these firms. Firstly, entry required knowledge of the opportunity. Two of the largest first-generation companies founded in 1955 and 1958 had close connections with the trade: in the first case the initiative was taken by an employee of a chain-cleaning group which was already exploiting unit shops; in the second the father was already involved in dry-cleaning developments so that the son again had the benefit of an early demonstration of the potential profitability.[36] Secondly, new entrants were not inhibited by any interdependence problem whereby any new investment detracted from the profitability of existing investments. This meant that once knowledge of the opportunity existed investment was likely to seem more profitable to entrants than to established firms. Thirdly, since the capital required for entry was so low there was a vast number of potential entrants who could raise the necessary finance and hence the cumulative impact on the industry of firms operating small single-unit shops was considerable. Further, because of the delays in transmission of knowledge a mass of new entrants appeared just as the established firms began large-scale investment in unit shops. Finally, because of inexperience and a strong desire to own an independent business some entrants did not examine the potential profitability of new shops very carefully.[37] In this respect the bandwagon effect of apparent profitability in a free entry industry almost certainly contributed significantly to the excess capacity characteristic of such industries when demand ceases to grow.

INVESTMENT AND COMPETITION

In this section the interactions of investment and competition are

[35] Hire-purchase financing and shop leasing have played an important role in facilitating this growth.

[36] The three 1940s entrants also had trade connections.

[37] The prospect of high returns for a few may also have outweighed the likelihood of low returns for most.

described. The workings of the market illustrate very clearly the standard economic predictions for free-entry oligopolies. As supply increased relative to demand price competition became more and more severe. Nevertheless, new entrants were tempted into the industry and existing firms continued to expand wherever there appeared to be a gap in supply. High fixed costs combined with the aggressive actions of those seeking to gain a share of the market and the defensive reactions of those defending their share ensured continuing conflicts of interest and hence competition rather than cooperation. Finally this developed into a war of attrition as far as the smaller and weaker firms were concerned and a degree of cooperation among the larger and stronger firms as they sought to rationalize their operations and reduce competitive excess capacity.

The dry-cleaning market is made up of a series of geographically linked local markets. Each shop normally has a monopoly, or something up to twenty competitors at most, of whom only three or four would be thought significant.

Four competitive weapons used are: price, speed of cleaning, quality and location.

The siting of shops to offer a convenient service is a strategic weapon aimed at providing a company with a basic competitive advantage on which it can build the rest of the policy. In the immediate market the shop actually on the customers' route to other shops and having good parking facilities may have an almost insurmountable advantage. Further, in the area market, a group of shops may be used to blanket a town perhaps embarrassing particular rival town centre shops but also providing an advertising service for the whole group.

Although the quality of cleaning is often stressed, its importance within the professional group of cleaners probably declined in the 1960s. Nevertheless, most companies were anxious to avoid consumer experimentation and hence tried to maintain sufficient quality to ensure habitual consumer behaviour. This relatively passive attitude to quality differentials was not extended, however, to the difference between 'professional' cleaning and 'do it yourself' or attendant supervised cleaning at coin-ops. Since the professional cleaner could hardly compete in price with the self-service coin-ops the former's main weapon had to be the emphasis on quality differential.

Despite the strategic importance of a good site and a reputation for quality the main thrust of competition in the 1960s has been on speed of cleaning and price. One-day or even one-hour cleaning as opposed to the two- to seven-day service offered at receiving offices provided a major competitive advantage to the on-the-premises cleaning unit shop.[38] As unit shops became more common the speed of service factor became increasingly important with consumers expecting the same-day service. Consequently the competitive position of the receiving office deteriorated continuously, though the attraction of a low-investment shop counter providing work for the factory remained. The steady decline of the receiving office was, however, turned to rout by rising labour costs including, very importantly, selective employment tax.

Vigorous price competition has been a feature of the industry[39] in the West Riding and North East throughout the period. New entrants with unit shops and hence a rapid and personal cleaning service have either matched or shaded the normal price of the chain cleaners. Partly as a counter measure, partly to gain trade at the expense of other chains, and partly to extend industry demand some of the larger cleaners have regularly used price offers (e.g. 'Two for one') as a normal feature of trade promotion.[40] Not surprisingly competitors have retaliated so that attempts to gain trade may have been frustrated. In large part the problem arose because of the high sensitivity of profits to volume. Given a shop, or factory and shops, a high proportion of costs are fixed so that the marginal costs of extra turnover are often low. Thus with rent, rates, depreciation, basic counter and processing labour costs, and for chain companies head office and area overheads, fixed, there was considerable pressure to spread the fixed burden over as large a volume as possible. The above pressures towards low prices were possibly reinforced by three policy considerations. Firms aiming at

[38] Customers apparently often require only the option of collecting their cleaning when they need it rather than actually using the same-day service. The impersonality of sending clothes away to the factory also caused unfavourable comparisons for the receiving office as opposed to the unit shop.

[39] List prices rose markedly during the 1960s but since cut price offers were extended (see note 40 below) the rise in actual prices was more moderate. Costs also rose substantially. The National Board for Prices and Incomes survey showed prices rose by just over 10 per cent between the beginning of 1963 and the beginning of 1966. However, this excluded any allowance for reduced charges, N.B.P.I. Report No. 20—*Laundry and Dry Cleaning Charges*, September, 1966, Cmnd. 3093. Meanwhile between April 1963 and April 1966 average weekly earnings in the industry for men and women rose by 16.5 per cent and 12.4 per cent respectively. Over the longer period April 1962–November 1970 one medium-sized company increased its prices by about one-third. However, offers clearly modified the extent of price increases, there being marked discrepancies in prices depending on the degree of local competition.

[40] In the West Riding 'Martin's the Cleaners' and after a considerable lag the Johnson Group have been particularly heavy users. Originally price offers were used to boost off-peak winter demand but the periods were gradually extended until offers became a regular feature of trade: 'The rapid extension of the unit dry cleaning shop offering quick services forced the bigger companies to extend cut-prices even into the traditionally peak periods', P. Garner, *Financial Times*, February 18th, 1970. As early as 1962 15 per cent of the orders of one group were reported to be at offer prices. By 1966 a subsequent investigation indicated that the sales revenue for the group was only 75 per cent of the full price equivalent. Trading conditions deteriorated subsequently, see above.

mass as opposed to quality markets considered the aggregate price elasticity of demand to be greater and hence favoured a lower price structure. Since this tended to widen price differentials all firms were affected by this policy. Secondly, it has been suggested that at least one firm partly viewed a low price structure as an entry deterrent. Finally, it was alleged that the owner of one of the chains was seeking a short-term marketing advantage through cut-price offers in order to obtain a larger market share to boost profitability before the sale of the company. Since the company was sold at the beginning of the 1960s this may be true, although it may also be an *ex-post* rationalization.

Whatever the earlier reasons for the low price and offer policies the entry of new competitors creating additional capacity, combined with a slackening growth of demand, exacerbated the fixed cost problem. The new unit shops which damaged the turnover of the existing receiving offices, and hence the throughput of the factories, could be most effectively challenged from other unit shops. Thus the chains were drawn into an extensive programme of converting receiving offices into unit shops and in so doing intensified the excess capacity problem at the central factories. This in turn increased the incentive to cut price.

Although the consequences of retaliatory price competition were clearly recognized there was good reason why it was not abandoned. Firstly, the large number of competitors; the hope of the cut prices going unnoticed; and the profusion of low price coin-ops hitting particular shops[41] ensured that any price truce would be broken. New entrants, a firm facing difficulties, or a particularly aggressive competitor would try to shade and the price competition would re-emerge. Secondly, as the excess capacity problem increased and industry stagnation combined with rapidly rising costs, some firms became more concerned with price competition as a predatory weapon. The low pricing policy adopted was viewed as 'a deliberate action taken by these people to put the small people out of work'. The larger chains with considerable financial resources were prepared to accept low profits and possibly losses as a short-term policy designed to eliminate competitors: one chain cleaner, recognizing the precarious finances of many new entrants, stated 'the small local man is stupid if he tries to open close to us'.[42] Just as the

[41] Although the effect of coin-ops on professional cleaners was disputed some firms claimed that their shops had suffered a 20 per cent cut in turnover due to the opening of coin-ops.

[42] Small family firms did have two advantages: since dry cleaning is a cash trade tax evasion was possible for such firms, and self-employed labour was exempt from selective employment tax.

National Board for Prices and Incomes[43] hoped, price competition was to become a method of eliminating capacity.

Nevertheless, some competitors were trying to re-establish quality differentials as a protective device against new entrants and the price competition of the mass market cleaners. One move was to propose the reactivation of an industry advertising campaign to be promoted by qualified and quality attested cleaners.[44] Another was the use of the trade press and conferences to publicize the need for professional cleaning based on quality at 'reasonable' prices. Although both are well-known techniques for stabilizing the competitive environment there seems little prospect of any significant success along these lines until the excess capacity is virtually eliminated.

The final competitive problem concerns the elimination of firms and capacity. The two aspects are deliberately kept separate since surviving firms drastically reduced capacity, while eliminated firms sometimes sold their plant and shops to others which retained the physical capacity. The time lag problem was caused by the durability of physical assets and their expense being a sunk cost.

Relatively strong firms had three choices regarding competitors: buy them out and close down some of the total group's capacity; agree with competitors to reciprocal closing of shops; and engage in a competitive war of attrition. The chain cleaners used all three methods of eliminating capacity: chains retreated into their own territories by mutual closure of shops so reducing competition between the established companies; some firms were bought and to a considerable extent closed down; and the weakest firms including many new entrants were faced with a war of attrition. Although the chain companies must share the blame for the creation of excess capacity their presence facilitated its subsequent elimination. In an atomistic market, as envisaged by Professor Robinson, the longevity of plant might have extended the attrition element in the rundown whereas the existence of substantial oligopolists permitted both the recognition and ability to arrange for cooperative reduction in capacity. This was aided by the versatility of the shops enabling the large firms to eliminate surplus non-processing capacity relatively quickly (see Table I above) and hence escape from part of the asymmetry caused by rapid gestation and long physical life.[45]

The problem for the firm in danger of elimination was that the

[43] National Board for Prices and Incomes, Report No. 20, *op. cit.*

[44] The Dyers and Cleaners Research Organization announced a quality assessment scheme in 1970. A quality attesting scheme had already been combined with a collective advertising campaign in Eire and was reported to be highly successful.

[45] See J. Robinson, *op. cit.*

sale value of its assets was extremely low: as both cleaners and launderers found their machinery often had only a scrap value and even when factories and shops were closed they might remain empty in the absence of any purchasers or leaseholders.[46] In these circumstances the question of whether the owner's capital could be better employed was meaningless—the assets were hopelessly illiquid even where there was some hope of their future value being significant. Thus low accounting profitability in the short run at least did not necessarily mean exit from the industry: nearly all firms suffered from low profits.[47] The relevant questions were whether a firm could hope to survive until trading conditions improved; whether this seemed possible or not, would another firm be prepared to buy it out to avoid a war of attrition; and what was the labour opportunity cost of continuing in the industry after allowing for the preference for independence. For some firms the hope of outlasting competitors meant a simple policy of hanging on and hoping until the money ran out or trade improved.[48] For others, particularly those with laundries, successive amalgamations to reduce factory capacity combined with shop and trade purchases to boost turnover, and limited diversification, or specialization,[49] provided active means of fighting for survival. The joint managing director of one company that was in the process of a second round of amalgamations indicated that the 'reasons [we] have kept this going is that [we] are not going to be beaten . . . and [we] provide jobs for people and, if [we] last [we] get a better return'. While the economic case for leaving the industry before physical plant failure was often small, the goal of business survival was probably also a factor in delaying the demise of firms.

[46] Since the economy as a whole was suffering from stagnation in the late 1960s firms sometimes found their factory and shop sites difficult to lease or sell at a price acceptable to themselves. Presumably this reflected their view that the ruling market prices were then *temporarily* depressed.

[47] Micro-economic theory predicts that firms earning subnormal profits will leave the industry in the long run. In the short run, while fixed assets do not need replacement, prospects of low accounting profits may be consistent with prospects of acceptable profits on realizable assets and hence continuance in the industry. As the prospective stream of profits declines so does the realizable value of assets thus preserving the rate of profit on capital. Indeed, for firms believing that they could out-survive their competitors there was a possibility that abnormal profits on the current realizable value of assets could be earned by staying in business. Hence in the short run it is arguable that the relevant opportunity cost of staying in business was the outside earning power of proprietor-managers. Since in some cases age, and experience confined to the dry cleaning and laundry trades, combined with economic recession probably reduced the labour opportunity cost exit was made even less likely.

[48] The proprietor of one survey company that finally went out of business in 1970 was taking an income of only £13 per week plus the use of a car. His wife, working part-time was taking £5.25 per week. Three years before over £11,000 had been invested in the business. Another taking less than £500 per annum but with some outside income was hanging on for projected town redevelopment.

[49] Laundries tried to develop large contracts and flatwork (sheets, towels, etc.).

SUMMARY AND CONCLUSIONS

Relatively high profits in the late 1950s and early 1960s along with free entry and expansion combined to give a rapid growth of capacity which outpaced the growth of demand. Established firms contributed to this creation of excess capacity in two ways: firstly, because of their established methods of trading they were slow to recognize the importance of the unit shop and hence they left a profitable opportunity to new entrants; and secondly, in an attempt to meet the new competition in increasingly difficult circumstances they themselves added to the unit shop capacity.

Already vigorous competition turned towards predatory competition in the late 1960s with the emergence of widespread excess capacity. The established companies sought to avoid a war of attrition among themselves by reciprocal closing of capacity and buying out some competitors. But the new entrants were faced with a fight for survival prolonged by the realization that their business had a negligible sales value. Thus, although large numbers of firms left the industry this could often best be described as salvaging the remaining capital rather than consciously reinvesting where there was a prospect of a better return. In a free entry industry high profits in the good years led almost inevitably to low profits, losses and a struggle for survival.

Finally, the time scale of the adjustment process, obscured in a comparative-statics analysis, is illuminated by the study of the competitive moves and counter moves. The competitive disturbances caused by the advent of the on-the-premises cleaning unit shop were first felt on a significant scale in the mid-1950s but were still reverberating in 1971. Firstly, the recognition of the opportunity by both new entrants and established cleaners was slow; secondly, established cleaners were reluctant to divert trade from existing shops and factories; thirdly, the response to the opportunity was limited by the financial investment required and the need to find suitable shop properties; and finally, the defensive reaction of retaliatory investment in unit shops was delayed until their competitive impact was clear. Nevertheless, unit shop capacity was built up before the central factory and receiving shop capacity were cut back, causing the emergence of excess capacity and even keener price competition. Just as unit shop entry and expansion was both initially slow and prolonged, the longevity of physical plant ensured that the reduction in the excess capacity would be delayed until the competitive process completely eliminated the financial capacity of some firms to survive and others accepted that survival required drastic reorganization. Thus, while the wheels of competition grind surely they do it slowly.

UNIVERSITY OF STIRLING

APPENDIX

DATA SOURCES

THE survey of firms was carried out in 1969 and 1970. Just over 100 firms were contacted and of these 43 agreed to co-operate; 2 were already amalgamated or in the process of amalgamating with other firms; and 4 refused. Of the remaining 58 firms, 16 could not be traced by the Post Office and 42 failed to reply. Since between 1967 and 1969 many firms were going out of business, it seems likely that the 42 non-respondents included some firms that had closed or were closing down.

Insufficient information was obtained from 4 companies so that the bulk of the analysis is based on 39 respondents. Table I contains a classification of the co-operating firms.

TABLE I

Turnover 1968–69	Types of Business					
£	*Dry Cleaners*	*Laundries*	*Joint Laundries and Cleaners**	*Diversified Businesses†*	*Self Service Launderettes*	*Total§*
≥500,000	2	2	1	1	—	6
≥100,000—500,000	4‡	3	2‡	1	—	10
≥25,000—100,000	—	3	—	1	2	6
<25,000	11	—	1	—	3	15
Total	17	8	4	3	5	37

Notes: * One third or more of the turnover in each section.

† One third or more of the turnover obtained from interests outside the dry cleaning and laundry trades.

‡ One company was a wholly owned subsidiary of a much larger public company.

§ The total includes three businesses which were sold before the investigation and one which was largely sold or closed down. All three are included in the size group immediately preceding sale or reorganization. Two companies which had ceased trading in 1968 are excluded from the above analysis. The total includes 3 public companies (excluding subsidiaries), 24 private companies, 8 unincorporated businesses and 2 co-operatives.

Other sources of information included: The Association of Launderers and Cleaners Ltd.; the National Association of Launderette Owners; equipment manufacturers; a specialist launderette and dry-cleaning estate agency; The Dyers and Cleaners Research Organization; the trade press; company reports; and the National Board for Prices and Incomes Report No. 20, *Laundry and Dry Cleaning*.

PUBLICATIONS RECEIVED

An Analysis of R & D Funding by Function (National Science Foundation, 1973).

Company Industrial Relations Policies, by N. H. Cuthbert and K. H. Hawkins (Longman, 1973) Price: £6.50.

Developing New Brands, by Stephen King (Pitman Publishing, 1973). Price: £2.80.

The Earnings Conflict, by Wilfred Brown (Penguin, 1973). Price: 35p.

An Economic Analysis of the Pulp and Paper Industry, by John A. Guthrie (Washington State University Press, 1973). Price: $12.00.

Economic Organisation in Medical Equipment and Supply, by R. D. Peterson and C. R. MacPhee (Lexington Books, 1973). Price: $15.00.

Federal Funds for Research & Development and Other Scientific Activities (National Science Foundation, 1973).

Import of Capital and Technology, by K. K. Subrahmanian (People's Publishing House, New Delhi, 1972). Price: Rs 25.00.

Input–Output and Regional Economics, by Harry W. Richardson (Weidenfeld & Nicolson, 1973). Price: £5.50 (hardback), £2.25 (paperback).

Japanese Imperialism Today, by Jon Halliday and Gavan McCormack (Penguin, 1973). Price: 50p.

The New Inflation, by Aubrey Jones (Penguin, 1973). Price: 40p.

Resources for Scientific Activities at Universities and Colleges (National Science Foundation, 1973).

Stemming Inflation, by H. B. Yoshpe *et al.* (Executive Office of the President: Office of Emergency Preparedness, 1972).

Strategies for Agricultural Development, by Vernon W. Ruttan and Yujiro Hayami (Food Research Institute, Stanford University, 1973). Price: $1.25.

Supply Relationships in the Canadian Economy, by Lawrence H. Officer *et al.* (Michigan State University, 1972). Price $8.00.

THE JOURNAL OF INDUSTRIAL ECONOMICS

Published first in October 1952, this Journal was founded to develop the analysis of the problems facing modern industry. It is concerned with the individual business and its relation to the economy—e.g. with outputs and prices and their behaviour in the market, and with the business decisions which affect these. It therefore aims to contribute both to economic theory and to practical public and private policies in the industrial field. The journal is naturally meant to interest business men as well as economists.

The Editors welcome contributions covering the fundamental categories in economics (such as prices, costs, investment, finance, location, wages and productivity) as well as the broader 'background' circumstances (such as the changing structure of industry, management policy and public monopoly policy). Preference is given to MSS. bearing on these subjects from the standpoint of individual firms or industries. The Journal's authors have helped to maintain the policy that articles should be found readable by those interested in its field. Theoretical discussion is welcome. Abstract theory is not barred, but authors in this case should provide an introduction and summary, so that non-specialist readers may see what the article is about. Alongside articles of more normal length the Editors are willing to publish shorter notes, especially when these give interim results of important research studies.

The Editors will be glad to receive offers of suitable articles. MSS. from the United States should be sent to Professor Menge, Department of Economics, Dartmouth College, Hanover, New Hampshire 03755, U.S.A; and from other countries to the General Editor, care of Basil Blackwell, Publishers, 49 Broad Street, Oxford, England. All other communications should be addressed to the Publisher.

The annual subscription (three numbers) is £2.25 ($6.75) post free; the price of a single issue is £1.00 ($3.00) post free. Remittances should be sent to Messrs Basil Blackwell.

The contents of Volume XXI, No. 2, April 1973, were:

Industrial Electricity Consumption—an Example of an Intermediate Good, by A. R. Bell, an economist in the Commercial Department (Economics and Forecasting Section)of the Electricity Council in London. .

U.S. and French Productivity in 19 Manufacturing Industries, by Krishnamurti Chandrasekar, Associate Professor of Economics in the Divisions of Business and Management and Social Sciences, New York Institute of Technology.

In Defence of the Industrial Training Act, by James J. Hughes, Lecturer in Economics, Faculty of Social Sciences, University of Kent at Canterbury.

Capacity-Utilization, Concentration, and Price-Cost Margins, by Pawan K. Sawhney and Bansi L. Sawhnay, respectively Assistant Professor of Economics at Northeastern University and Assistant Professor of Economics at the University of Baltimore.

The Economic Significance of Small Firms, by David Waite, working at the Bank of England.

Regulation, Profits and Entry in the Television Broadcasting Industry, by Douglas W. Webbink, Bureau of Economics, Federal Trade Commission.

A Note on Variable Patent Life, by Fred D. Arditti and Richard L. Sandor, respectively Associate Professor of Finance, Graduate School of Business, University of Florida, and Assistant Professor, School of Business Administration, University of California at Berkeley, and Vice-President, Chief Economist, Chicago Board of Trade.

Seasonal Fluctuations in the Motor Vehicle Industry: a Comment, by P. Smith, Research Assistant, Department of Political Economy, University College, London.

Illusions in Testing for Administered Prices, by Howard N. Ross, Visiting Professor of Economics, University of South Florida, and faculty member of Bernard M. Baruch College, The City University of New York.

Illusions in Testing for Administered Prices: a Reply, by Louis Phlips, Professor of Economics, Université Catholique de Louvain.

On the Sales Maximization Hypothesis—a Comment, by J. R. Davies, Lecturer in Ecomonics at the University of Stirling.

Concentration, Barriers to Entry, and Rates of Return Revisited: a Reply, by H. Michael Mann, Professor of Economics, Boston College, on leave as the Director, Bureau of Economics, Federal Trade Commission.

REPRINT

STUDENT SUBSCRIPTION

Printed in Great Britain by Alden & Mowbray Ltd
at the Alden Press, Oxford